Joyful Stories Press

First Printing, 2009

For additional information, please contact Dasanbooks / Joyful Stories Press. 120 Sylvan Ave. #301, Englewood Cliffs, New Jersey, U.S.A 07632

Printed in Korea

T. S. Lee
The Obama Story: The Boy with the Biggest Dream

ISBN 978-0-9819542-0-2
1. Biography—Juvenile
2. Comic/Graphic—Juvenile

Translated by Janet Jaywan Shin
Edited by J.E Chae / Brittany Pogue-Mohammed

The boy with the biggest dream!

The Obama Story

Written and illustrated by **T. S. Lee**

Translated by **Janet Jaywan Shin**

JSP

Joyful
Stories
Press

Contents

Barack Obama

Barack Obama, the United States of America's first African-American president, is a man upon whom the whole world has focused their attention. His story begins in Honolulu, Hawaii, where he was born in 1961 to Kenyan father Barack Obama, Sr., and American mother Ann Dunham. Obama's name, which he inherited from his father, means "blessed one". When he was six years old, Obama moved to Indonesia with his mother where he experienced discrimination from his classmates and had a lonely childhood. Even when he returned to Hawaii at the age of 10, he faced discrimination from American friends. He spent his teenage years wandering through the confusion of searching for his identity, feeling like he belonged in neither his father's homeland nor his mother's homeland.

When Obama started college, he pledged to himself to begin a new life. As he began to study hard and participate actively in campus life, he began changing into a completely different person. It was then that he decided to visit his father's homeland, Kenya, in search of his roots. Returning from Kenya where he was able to meditate on the value of family and the importance of his father in his life, Obama began studying at Harvard Law School, where only the most highly capable people are said to gather. Upon graduating, Obama began working as a civil rights lawyer, with a desire to help make a world in which everyone could live in happiness and harmony.

When Obama was 35 years old, he decided to enter the world of politics because he felt there was a need for more drastic efforts to help people in need. With his sincere speeches and charismatic presence captivating audiences, the young politician succeeded in becoming the Democratic Party's first African-American presidential candidate. Then, on November 4, 2008, in the midst of the world's attention, he became the first black president of the United States of America.

Having overcome the obstacles before him and written a new page in history, Barack Obama has become the symbol of dreams and hope for many people.

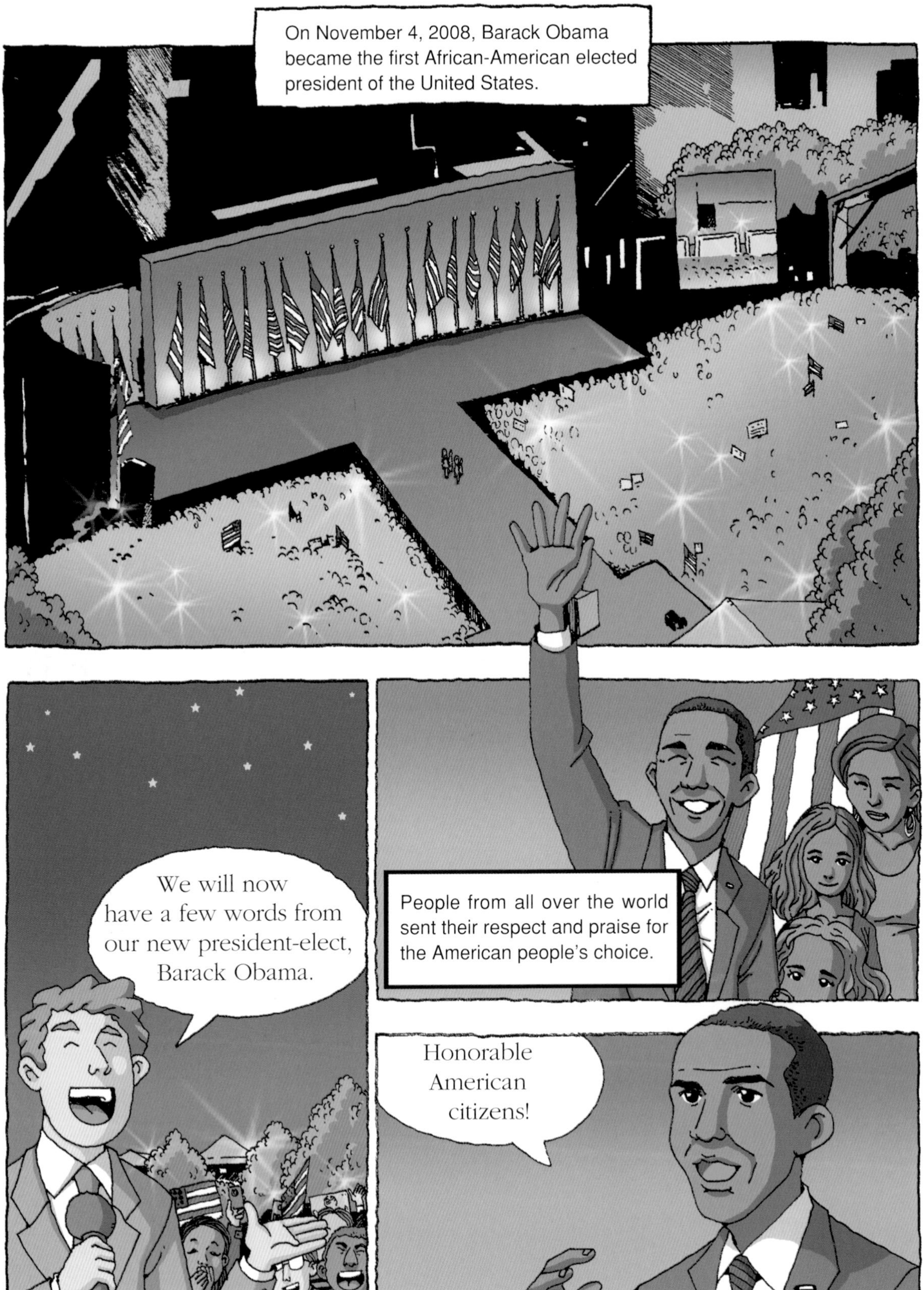

On November 4, 2008, Barack Obama became the first African-American elected president of the United States.
We will now have a few words from our new president-elect, Barack Obama.
People from all over the world sent their respect and praise for the American people's choice.
Honorable American citizens!

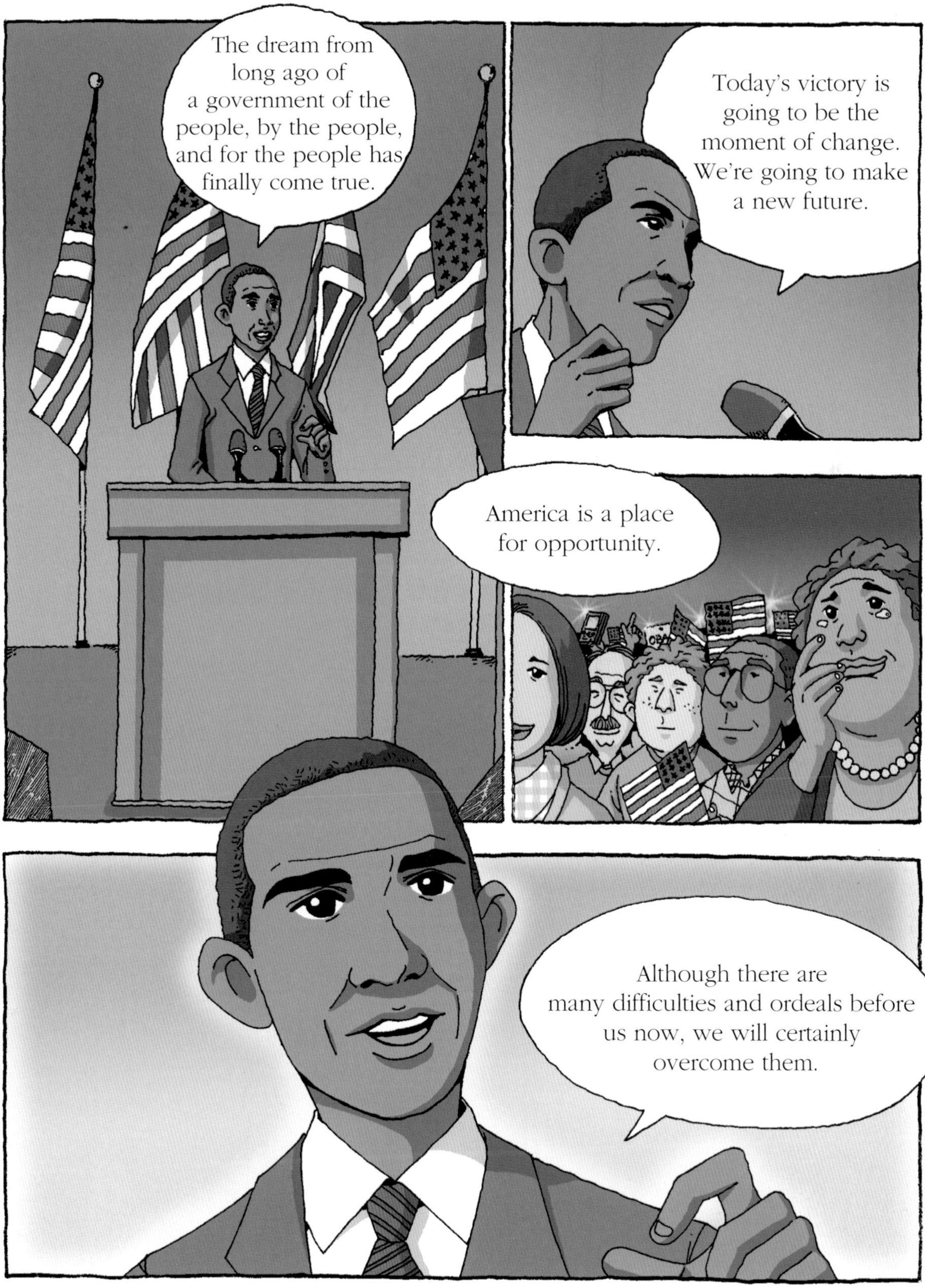
The dream from long ago of a government of the people, by the people, and for the people has finally come true.
Today's victory is going to be the moment of change. We're going to make a new future.
America is a place for opportunity.
Although there are many difficulties and ordeals before us now, we will certainly overcome them.

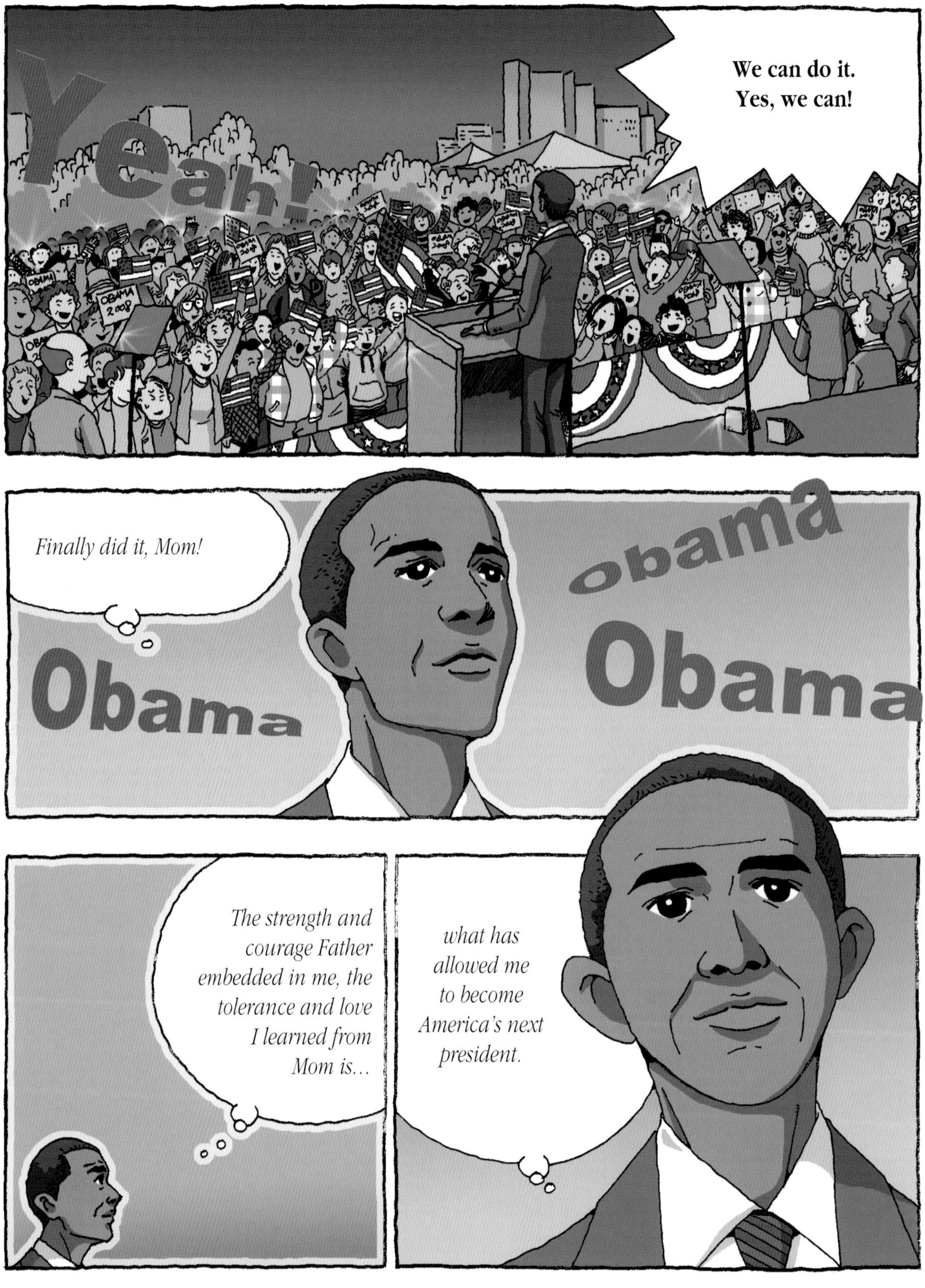
Yeah!
We can do it. Yes, we can!
OBAMA 2008
Finally did it, Mom!
obama
Obama
Obama
Obama
The strength and courage Father embedded in me, the tolerance and love I learned from Mom is…
what has allowed me to become America's next president.

Chapter 1

Barack's Childhood

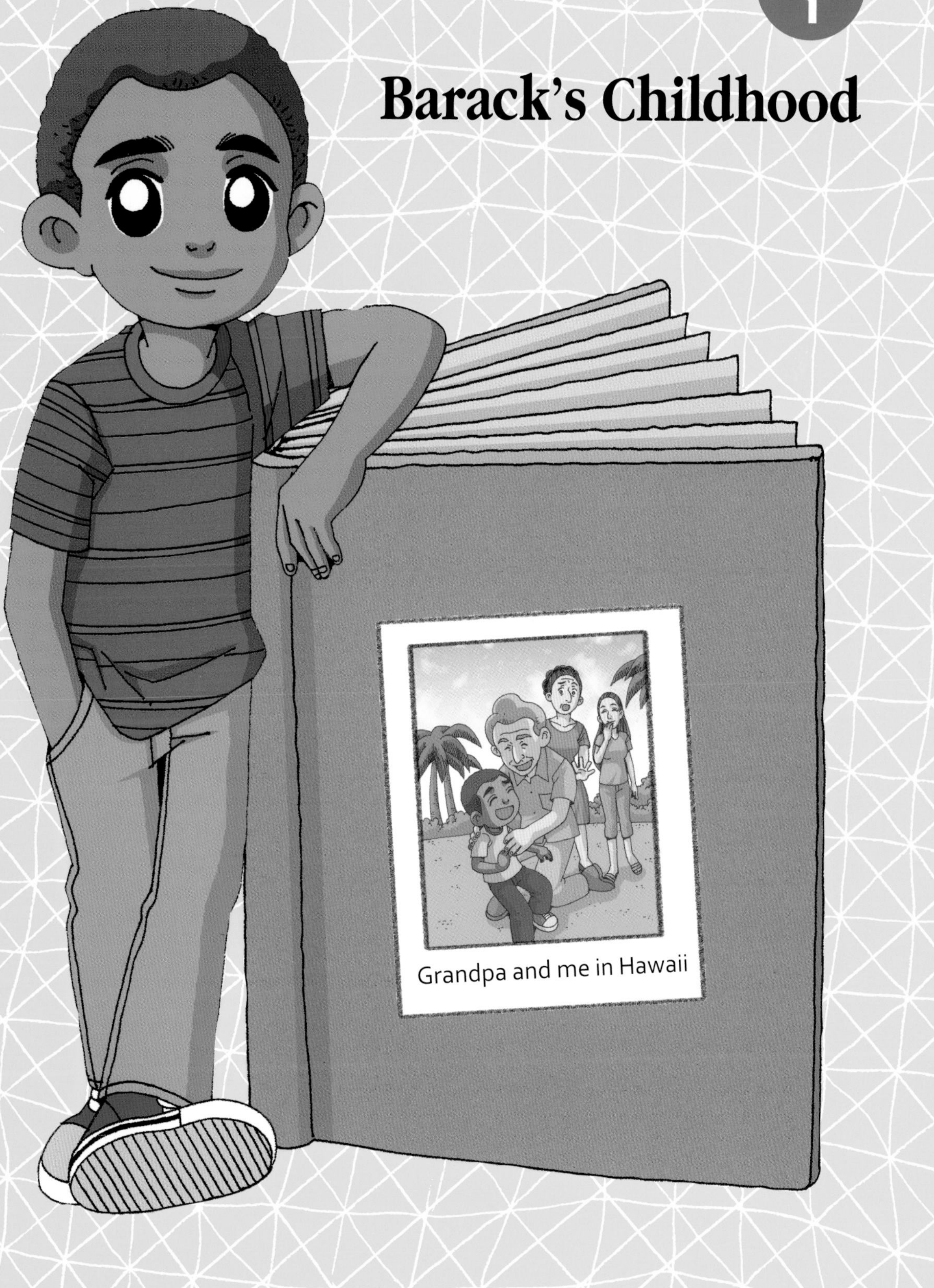
Grandpa and me in Hawaii

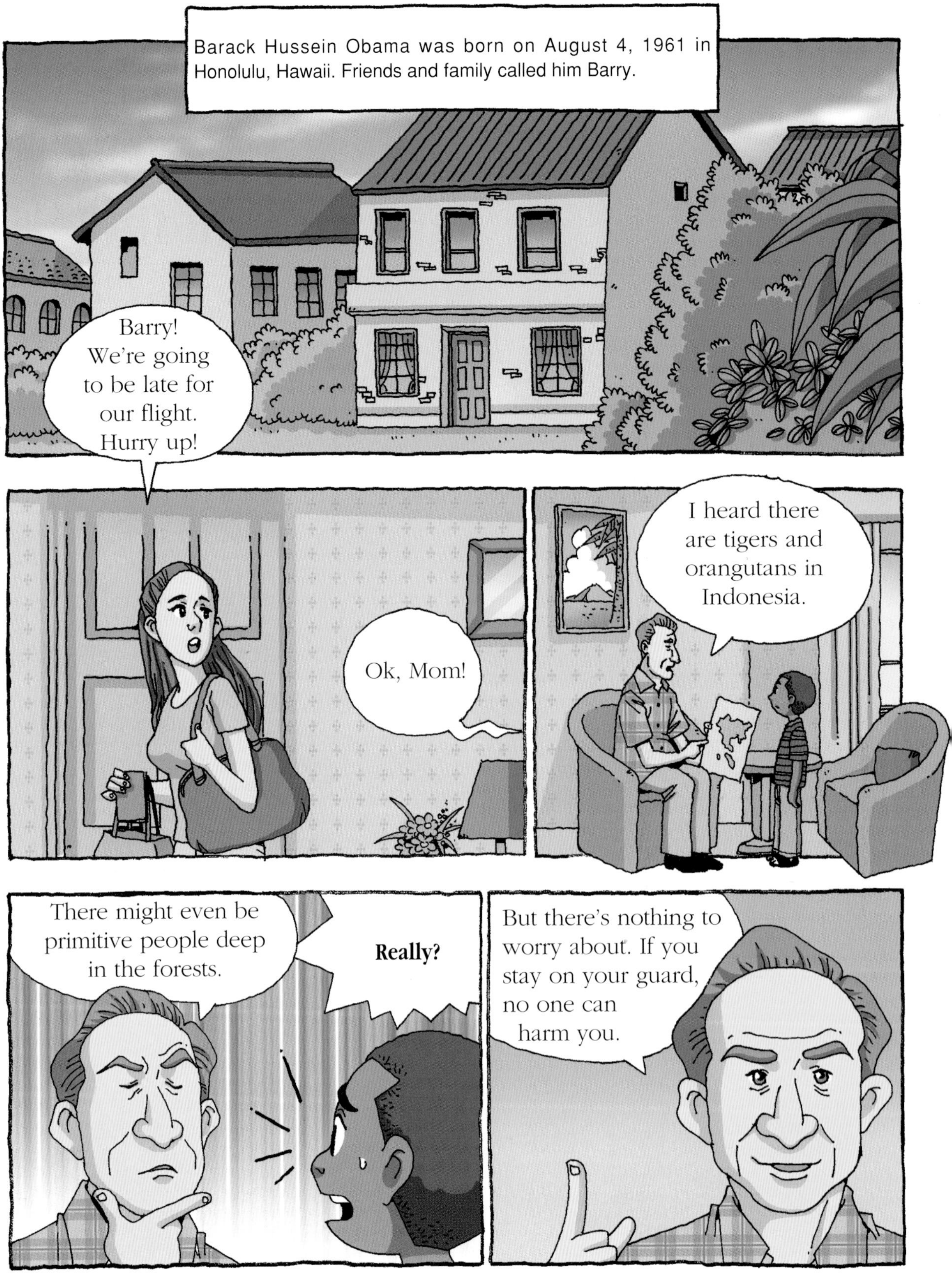

Barack Hussein Obama was born on August 4, 1961 in Honolulu, Hawaii. Friends and family called him Barry.
Barry! We're going to be late for our flight. Hurry up!
Ok, Mom!
I heard there are tigers and orangutans in Indonesia.
There might even be primitive people deep in the forests.
Really?
But there's nothing to worry about. If you stay on your guard, no one can harm you.

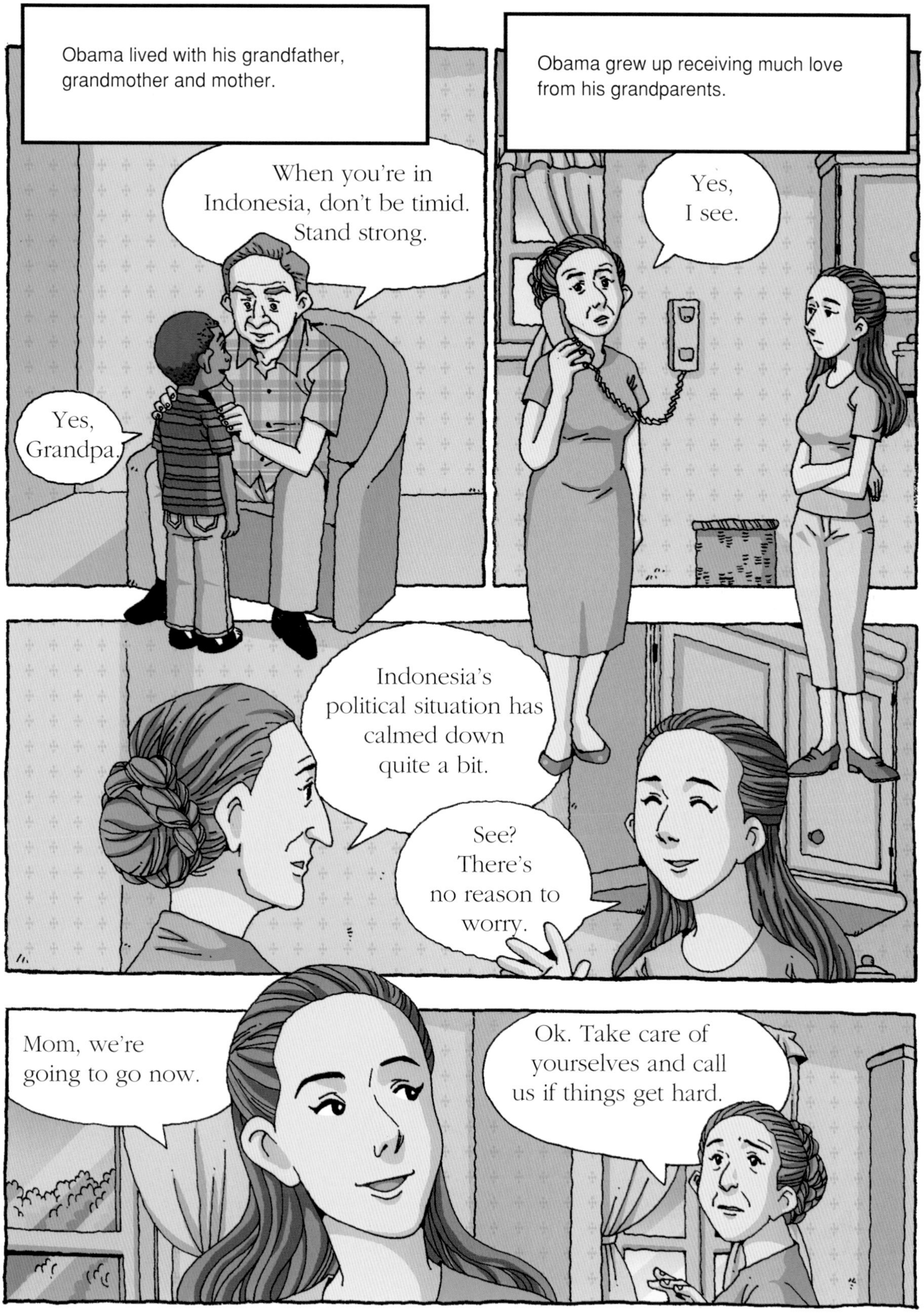
Obama lived with his grandfather, grandmother and mother.
When you're in Indonesia, don't be timid. Stand strong.
Yes, Grandpa.
Obama grew up receiving much love from his grandparents.
Yes, I see.
Indonesia's political situation has calmed down quite a bit.
See? There's no reason to worry.
Mom, we're going to go now.
Ok. Take care of yourselves and call us if things get hard.

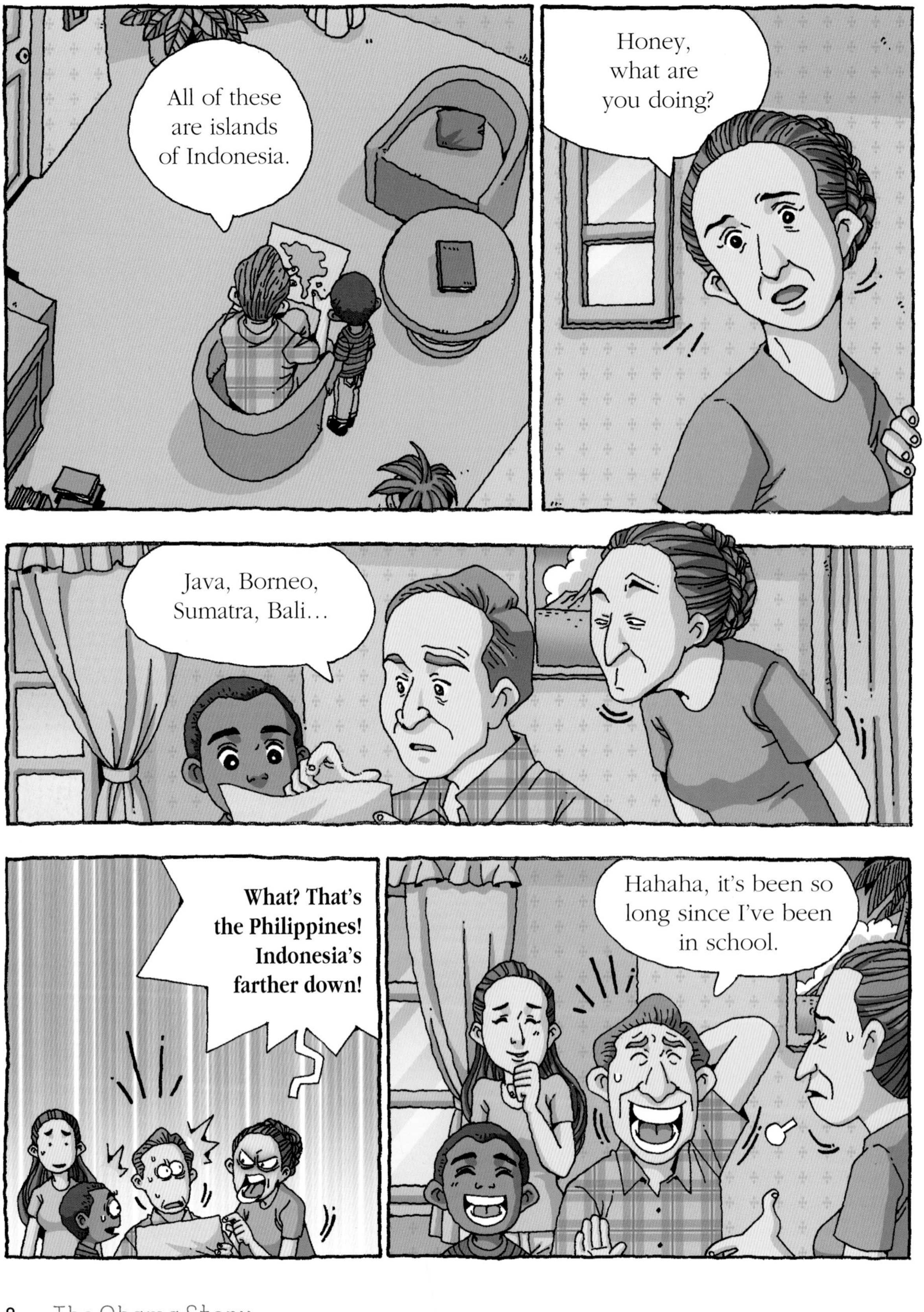
All of these are islands of Indonesia.
Honey, what are you doing?
Java, Borneo, Sumatra, Bali…
What? That's the Philippines! Indonesia's farther down!
Hahaha, it's been so long since I've been in school.

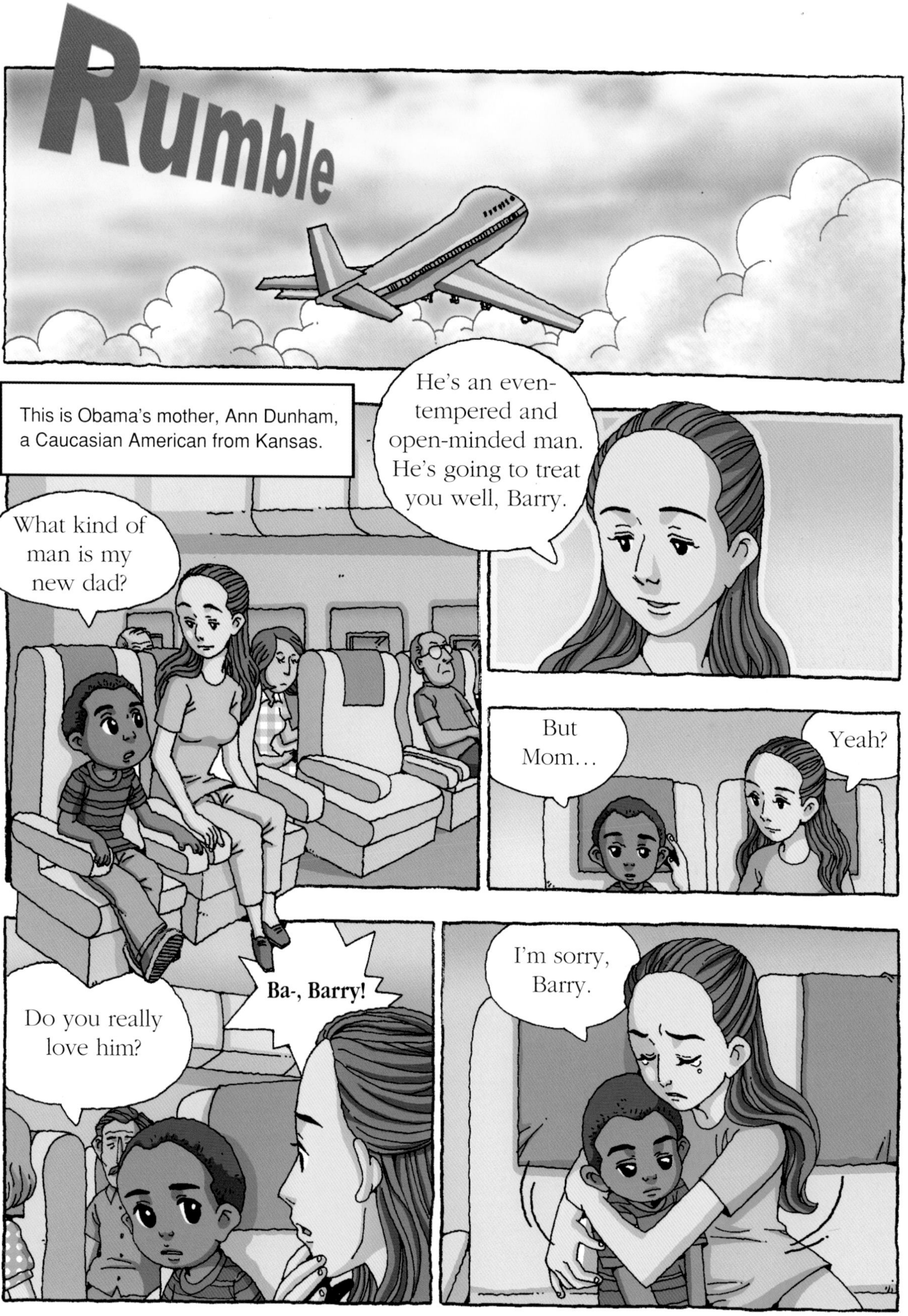
Rumble
This is Obama's mother, Ann Dunham, a Caucasian American from Kansas.
What kind of man is my new dad?
He's an even-tempered and open-minded man. He's going to treat you well, Barry.
But Mom…
Yeah?
Do you really love him?
Ba-, Barry!
I'm sorry, Barry.

*Obama was named after his father, Barack Obama, Sr.

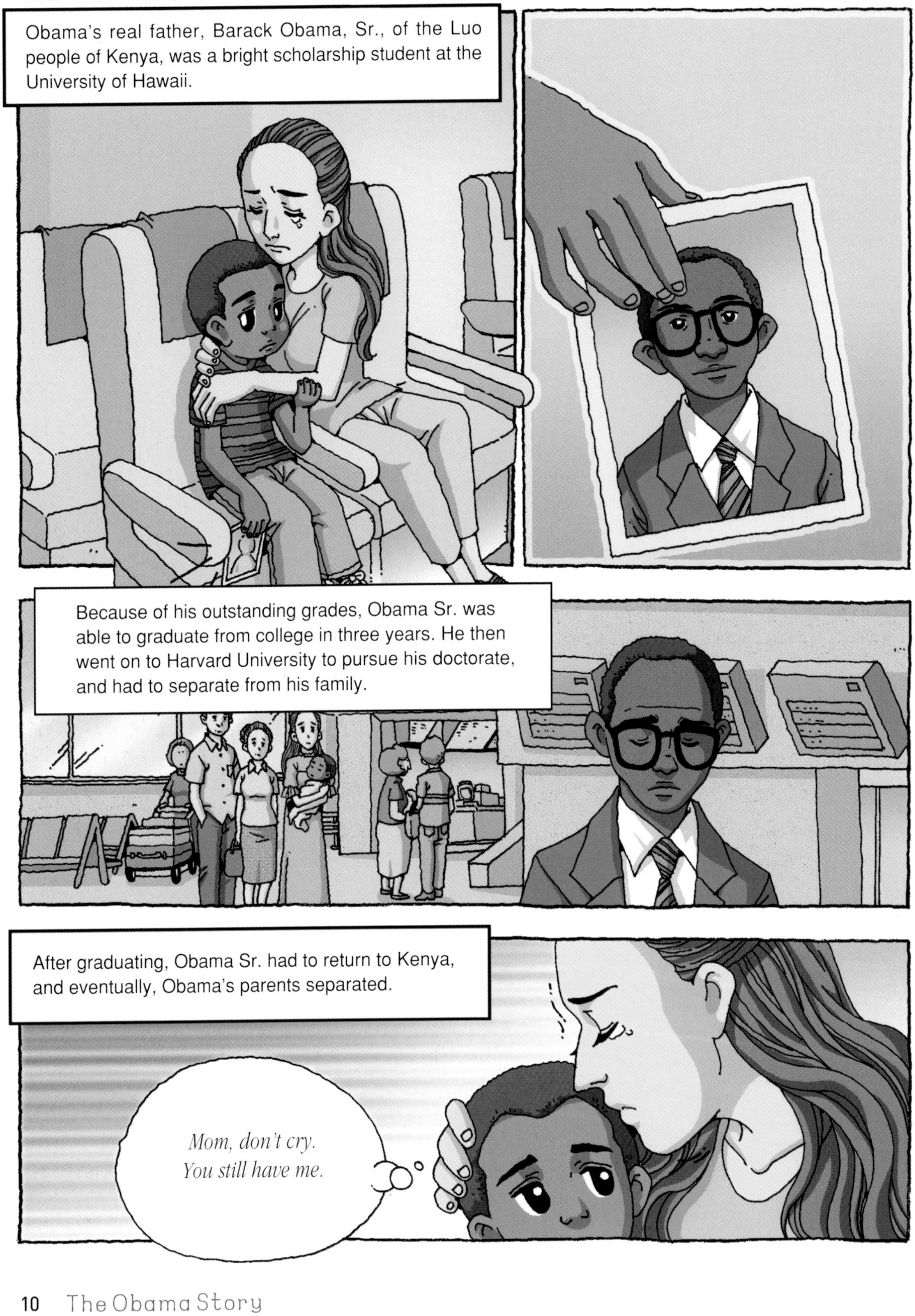
Obama's real father, Barack Obama, Sr., of the Luo people of Kenya, was a bright scholarship student at the University of Hawaii.
Because of his outstanding grades, Obama Sr. was able to graduate from college in three years. He then went on to Harvard University to pursue his doctorate, and had to separate from his family.
After graduating, Obama Sr. had to return to Kenya, and eventually, Obama's parents separated.
Mom, don't cry. You still have me.

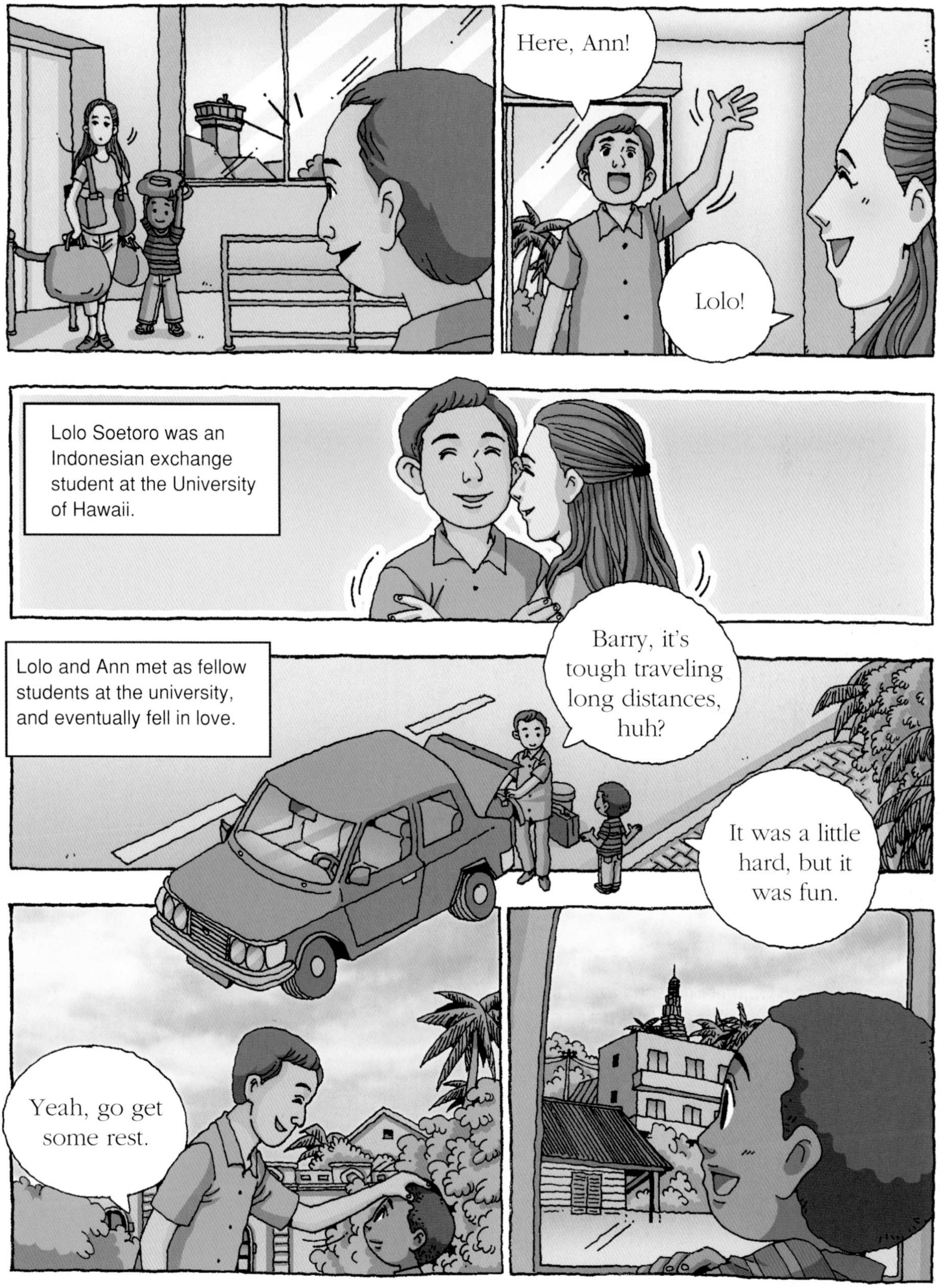
Here, Ann!
Lolo!
Lolo Soetoro was an Indonesian exchange student at the University of Hawaii.
Lolo and Ann met as fellow students at the university, and eventually fell in love.
Barry, it's tough traveling long distances, huh?
It was a little hard, but it was fun.
Yeah, go get some rest.

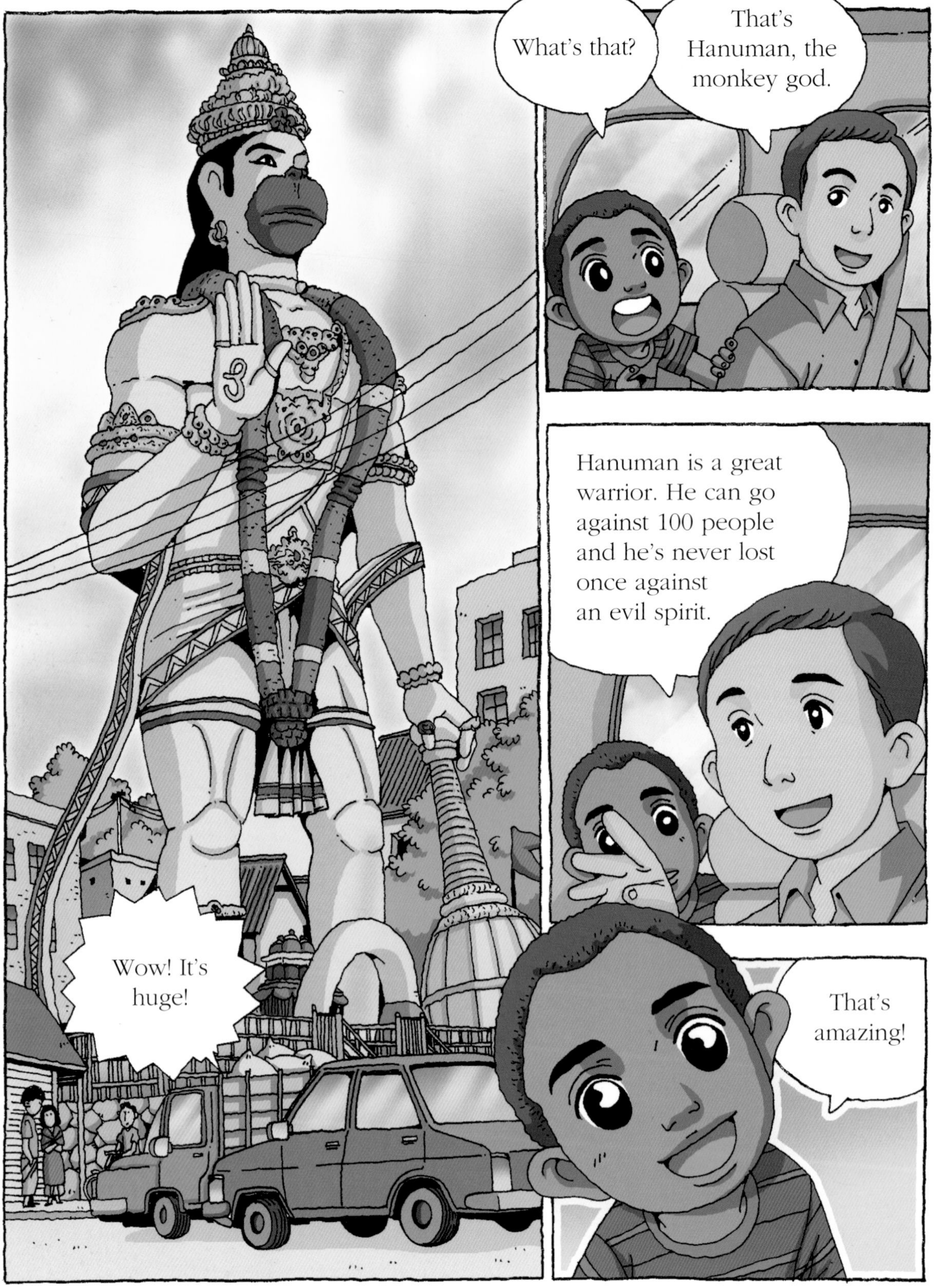
What's that?
That's Hanuman, the monkey god.
Hanuman is a great warrior. He can go against 100 people and he's never lost once against an evil spirit.
Wow! It's huge!
That's amazing!

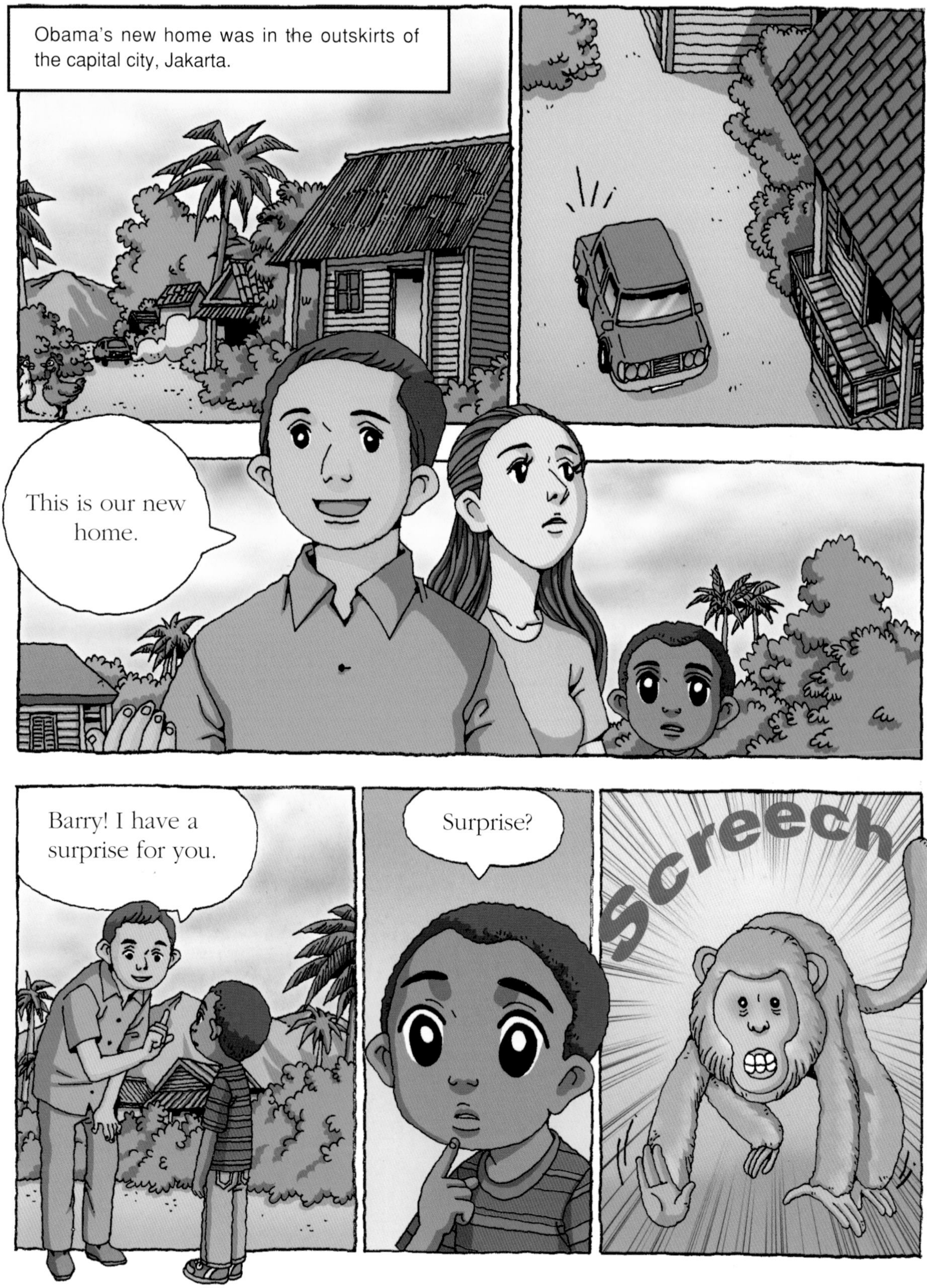
Obama's new home was in the outskirts of the capital city, Jakarta.
This is our new home.
Barry! I have a surprise for you.
Surprise?
Screech

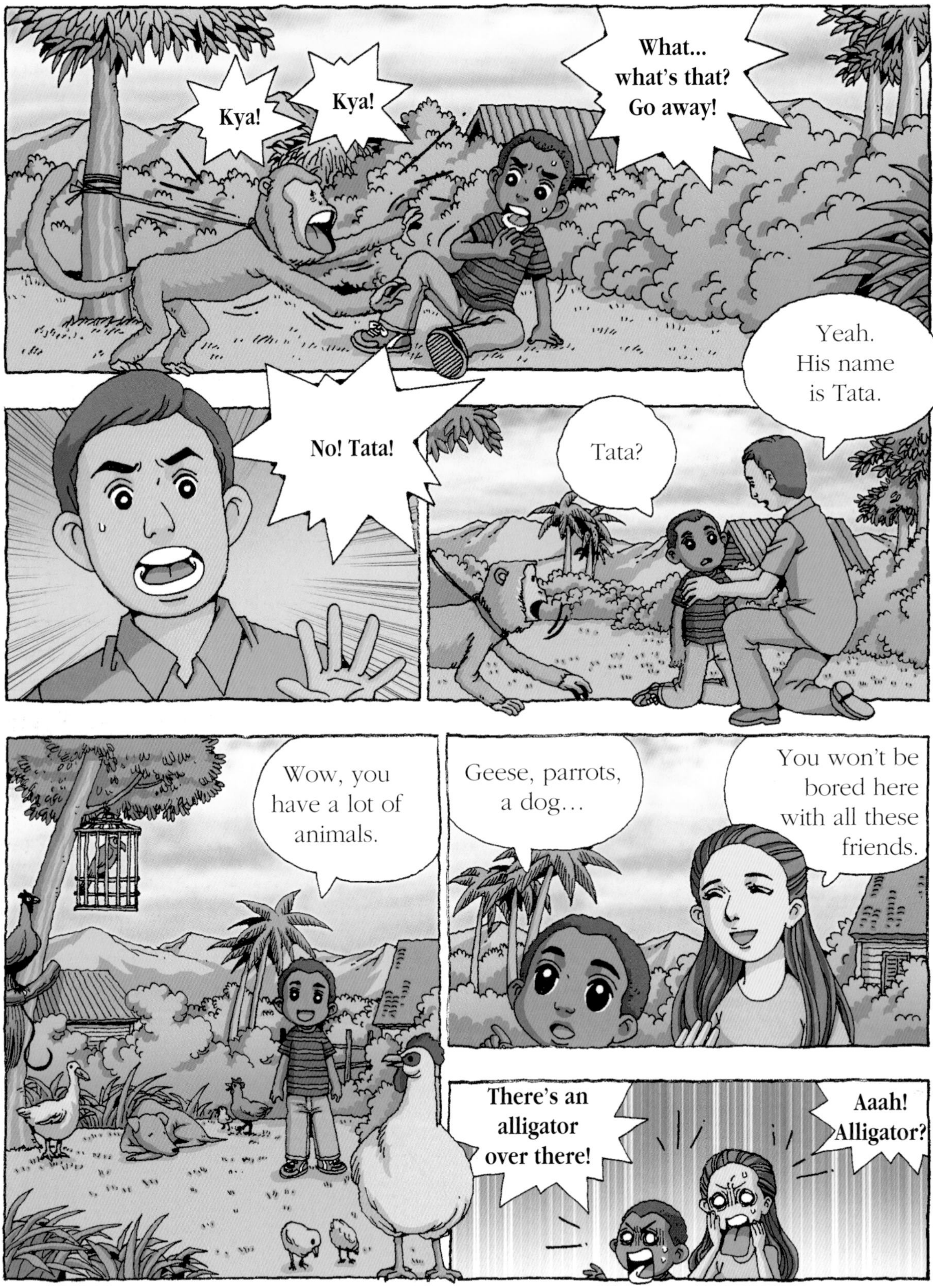

Kya!
Kya!
What... what's that? Go away!
No! Tata!
Tata?
Yeah. His name is Tata.
Wow, you have a lot of animals.
Geese, parrots, a dog…
You won't be bored here with all these friends.
There's an alligator over there!
Aaah! Alligator?

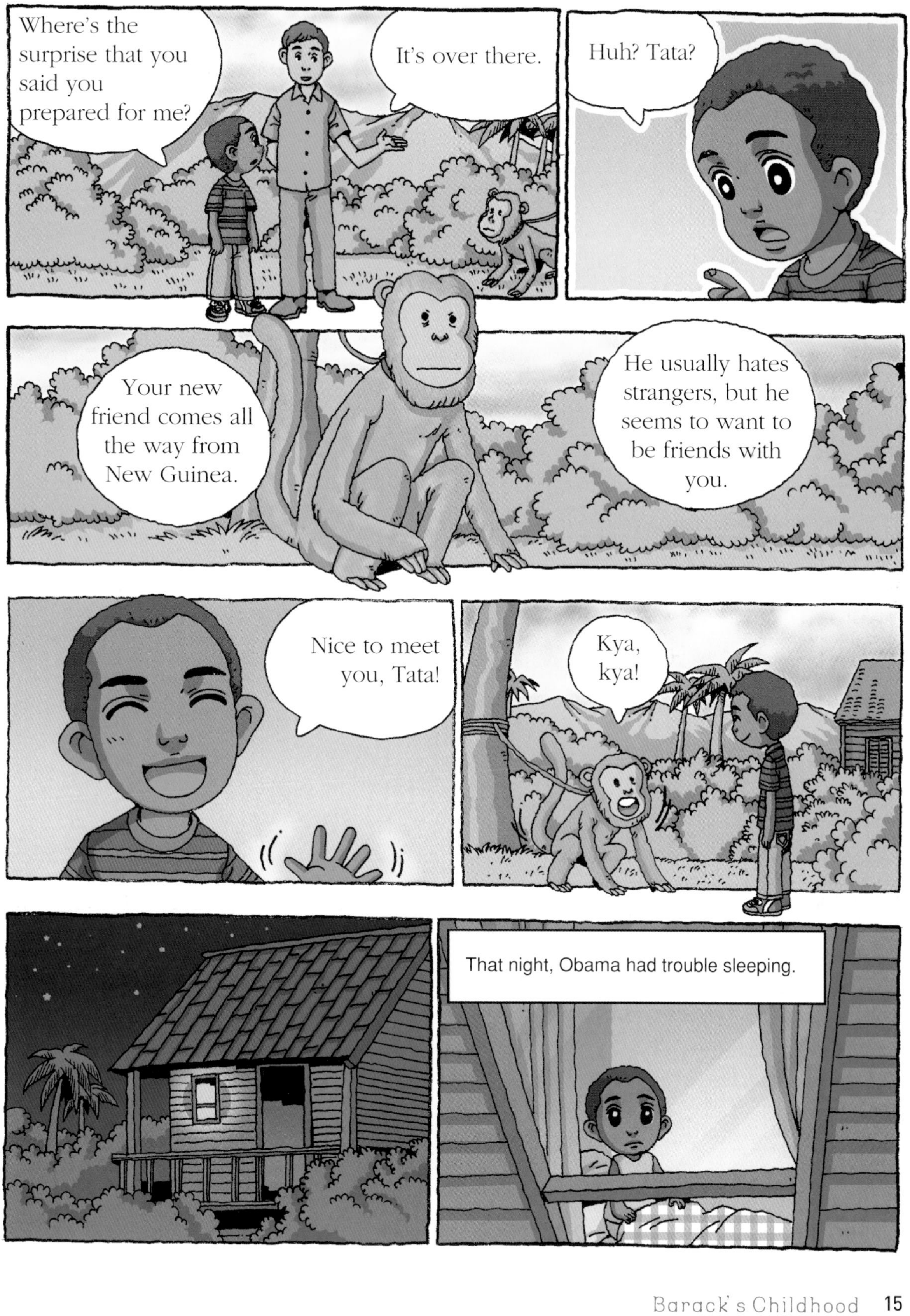
Where's the surprise that you said you prepared for me?
It's over there.
Huh? Tata?
Your new friend comes all the way from New Guinea.
He usually hates strangers, but he seems to want to be friends with you.
Nice to meet you, Tata!
Kya, kya!
That night, Obama had trouble sleeping.

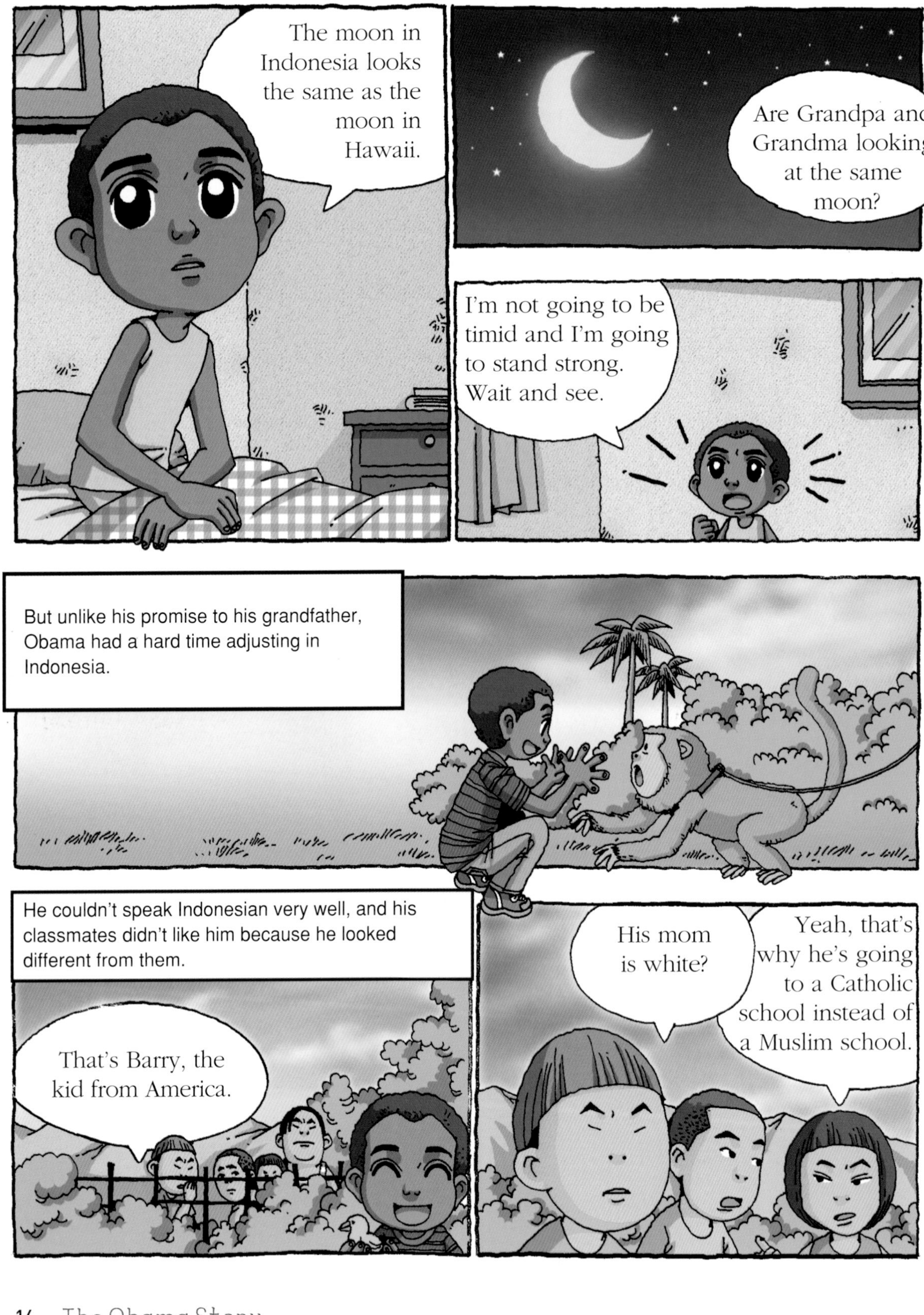
The moon in Indonesia looks the same as the moon in Hawaii.
Are Grandpa and Grandma looking at the same moon?
I'm not going to be timid and I'm going to stand strong. Wait and see.
But unlike his promise to his grandfather, Obama had a hard time adjusting in Indonesia.
He couldn't speak Indonesian very well, and his classmates didn't like him because he looked different from them.
That's Barry, the kid from America.
His mom is white?
Yeah, that's why he's going to a Catholic school instead of a Muslim school.

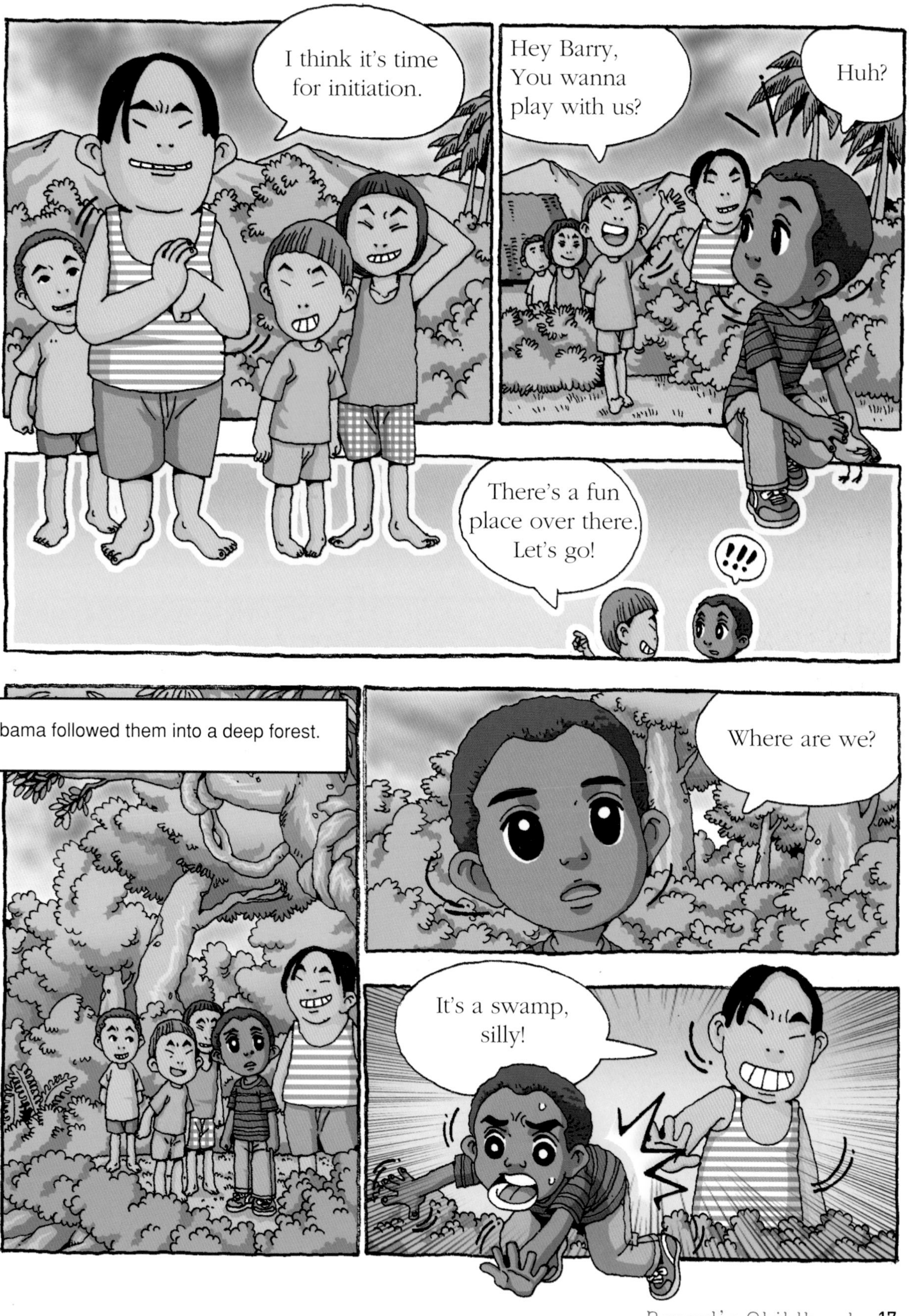
I think it's time for initiation.
Hey Barry, You wanna play with us?
Huh?
There's a fun place over there. Let's go!
!!!
Obama followed them into a deep forest.
Where are we?
It's a swamp, silly!

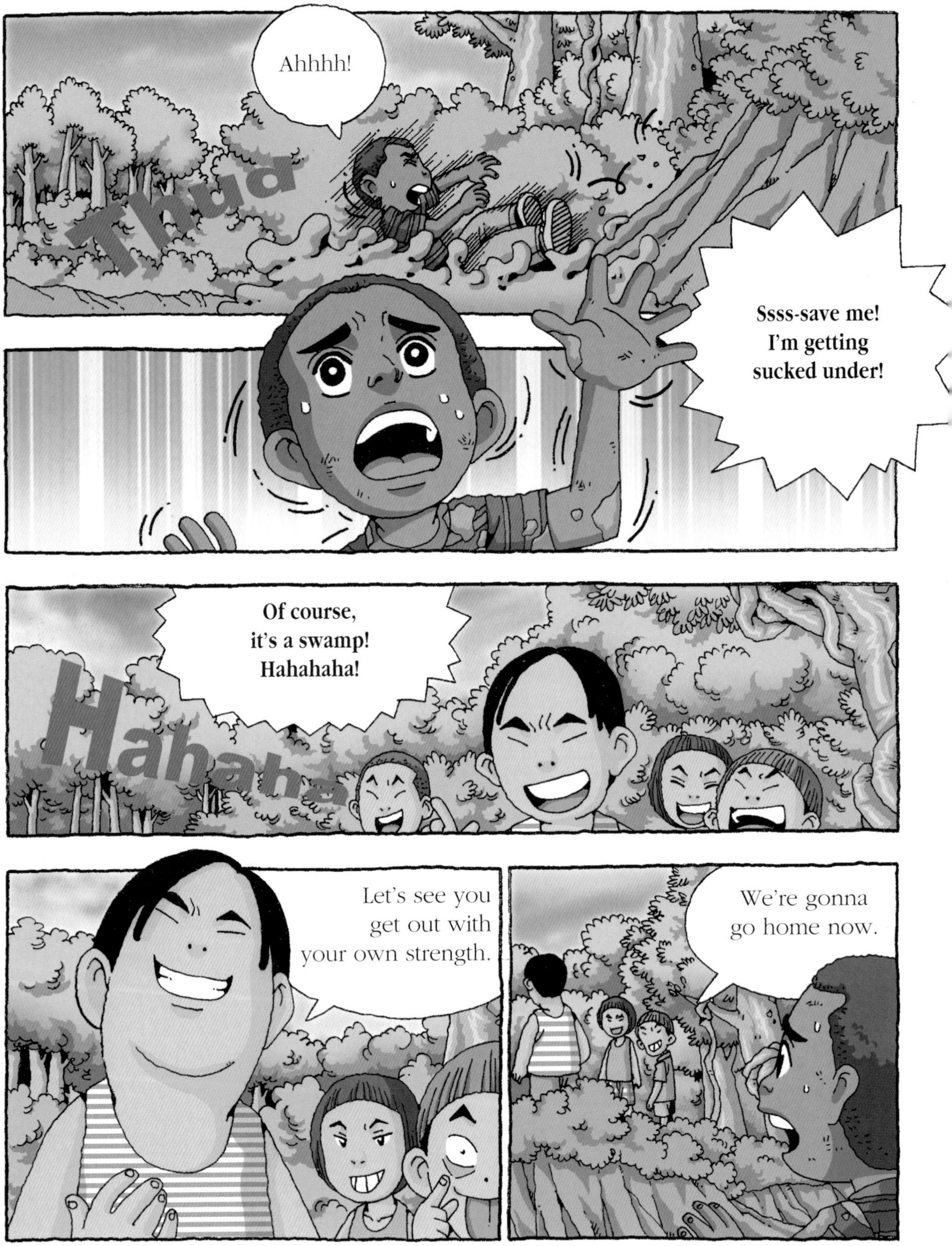
Ahhhh!
Thud
Ssss-save me! I'm getting sucked under!
Of course, it's a swamp! Hahahaha!
Hahaha
Let's see you get out with your own strength.
We're gonna go home now.

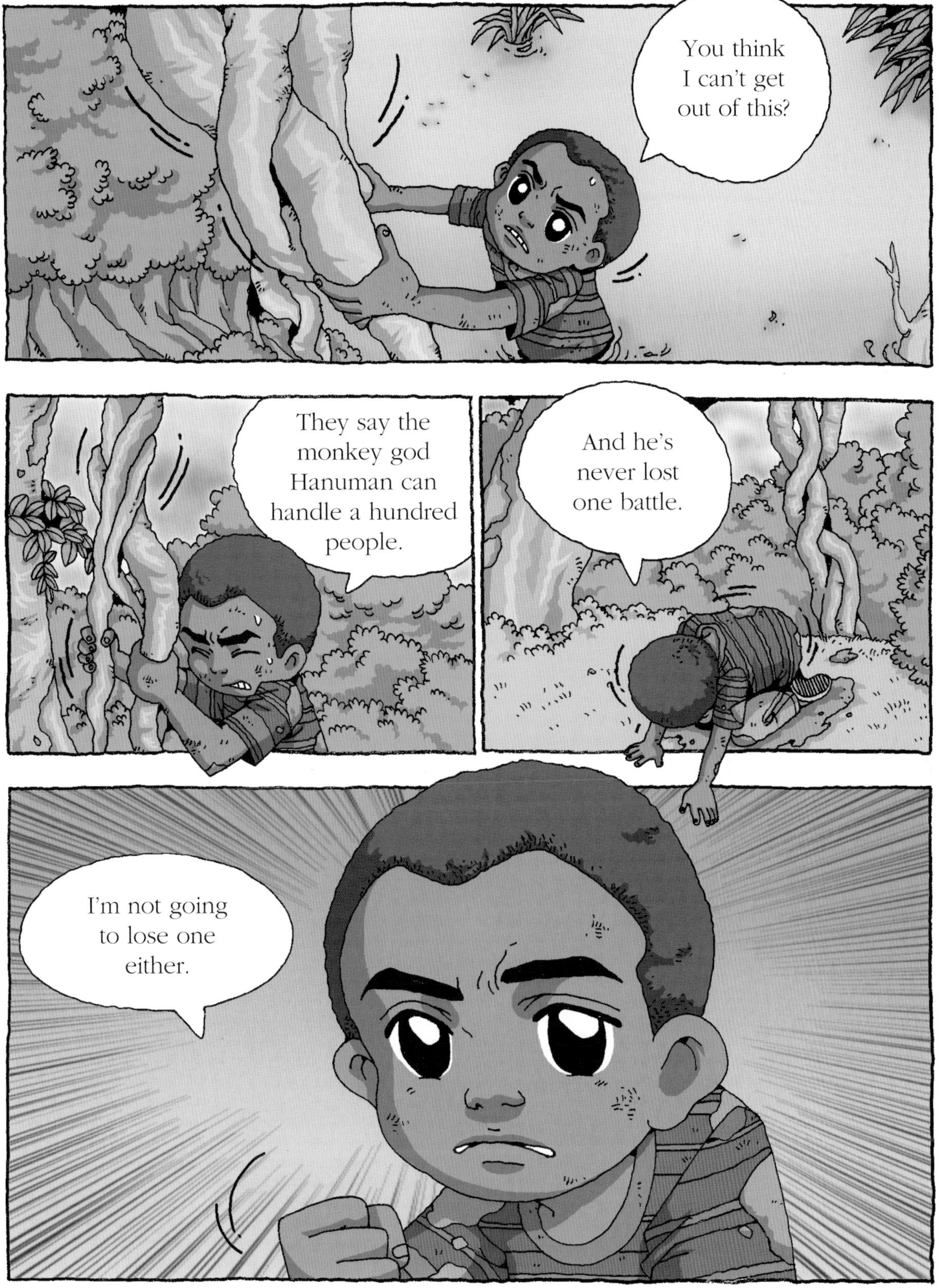
You think I can't get out of this?
They say the monkey god Hanuman can handle a hundred people.
And he's never lost one battle.
I'm not going to lose one either.

People who have influenced Obama 1

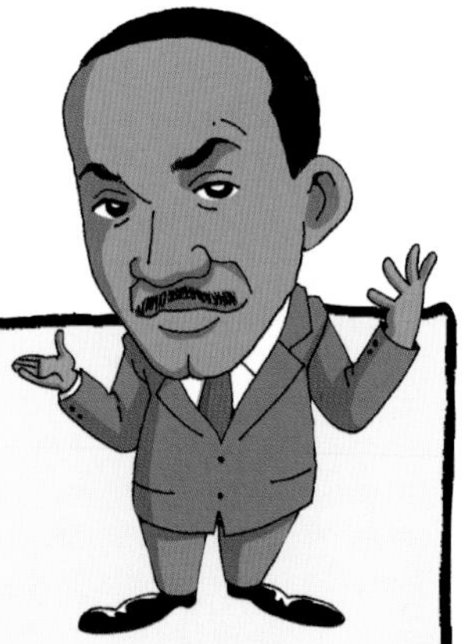

Martin Luther King, Jr.

One of the people that President Obama reveres most is Reverend Martin Luther King, Jr. Rev. Martin Luther King was an African-American civil rights activist who is respected by many people.

He was born in 1929 to Martin Luther King, Sr., the pastor of a Baptist church in Atlanta, Georgia. In 1954, after receiving a doctorate degree at Boston University, Martin Luther King became the pastor of Dexter Avenue Baptist church in Montgomery, Alabama. In December 1955, during his second year as pastor, a black woman who did not yield her seat on a bus to a white man was arrested. In response to this incident, King rallied 50,000 African-Americans to participate in the Montgomery Bus Boycott. One year later in December, 1956, segregation on buses was declared unconstitutional.

Afterwards, Rev. King began to lead human rights movements in every part of the U.S. to combat racial discrimination with non-violent protests. He surrendered himself to the Birmingham city police on April 12, 1963 for protesting at a demonstration, and was detained in a solitary prison cell until April 19th. In that same year, Martin Luther King Jr. gave his famous "I Have a Dream" speech in Washington, D.C., which rang in the hearts of many and raised greater awareness of racial discrimination.

Martin Luther King received the Nobel Peace Prize on October 14, 1964. Then, on April 4, 1968, at the height of the Vietnam War, King was assassinated on a hotel balcony by James Earl Ray, a white man. In memory of Martin Luther King Jr., Americans celebrate his birthday (January 15) on every third Monday of January as "Martin Luther King Jr. Day."

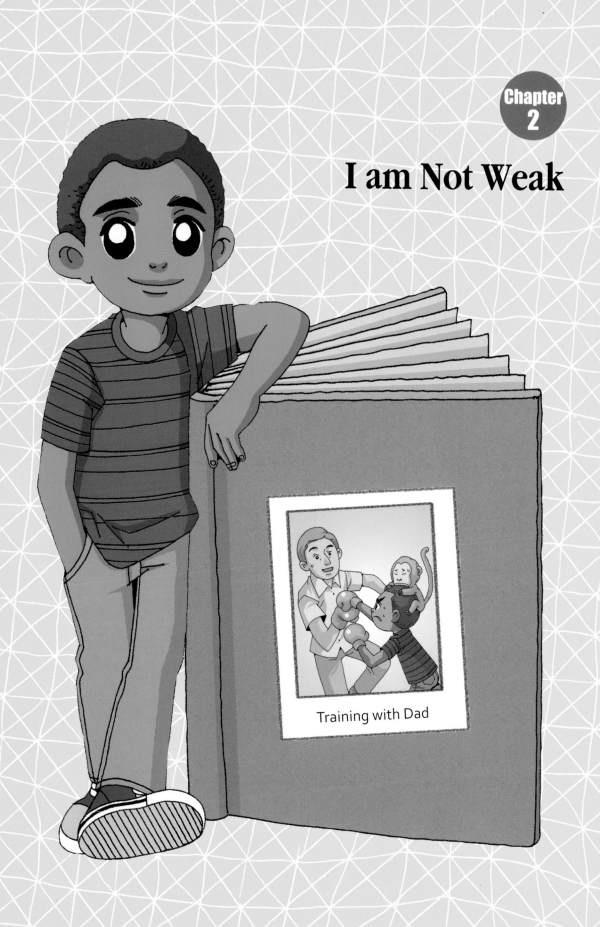

I am Not Weak

Training with Dad

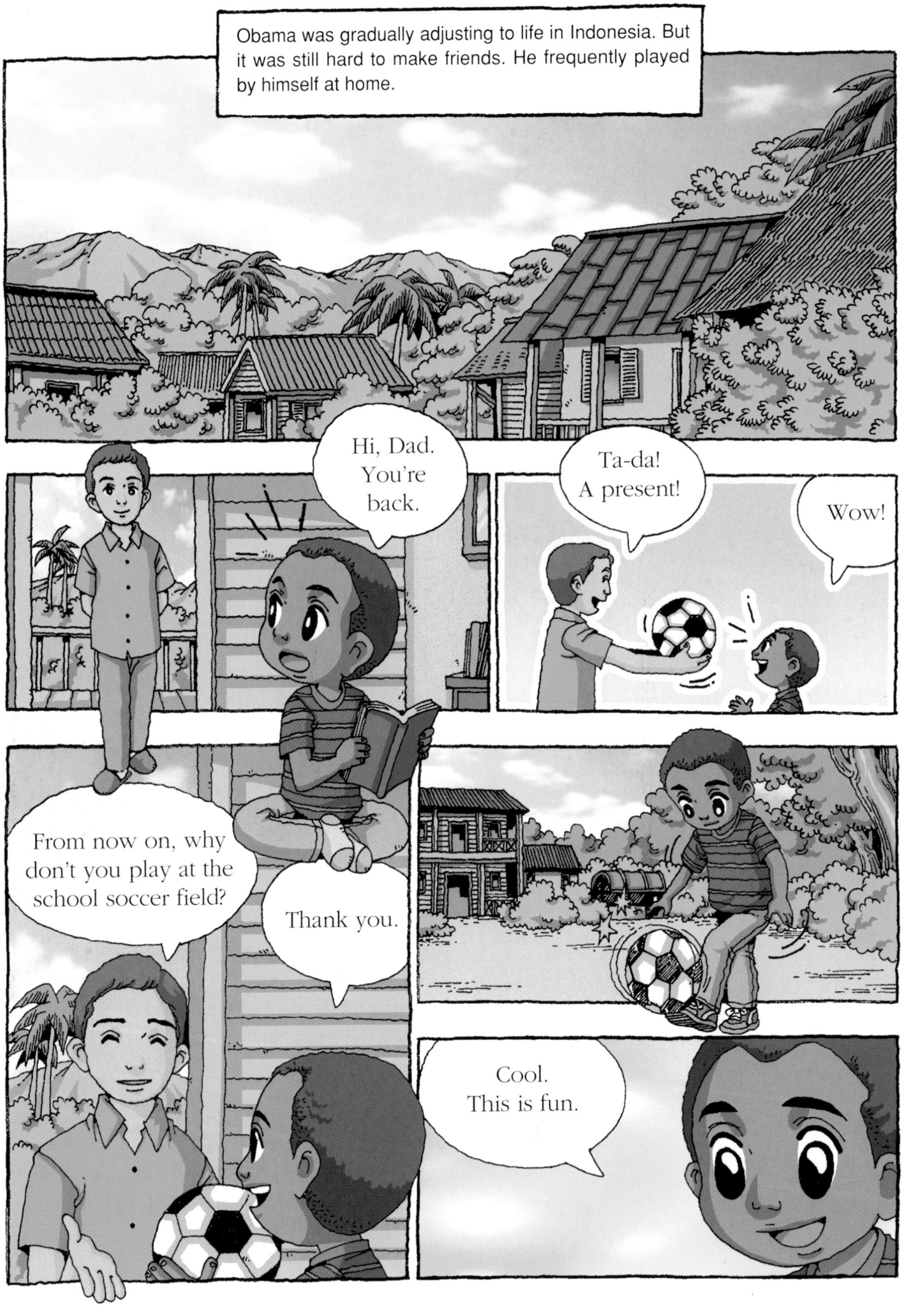
Obama was gradually adjusting to life in Indonesia. But it was still hard to make friends. He frequently played by himself at home.
Hi, Dad. You're back.
Ta-da! A present!
Wow!
From now on, why don't you play at the school soccer field?
Thank you.
Cool. This is fun.

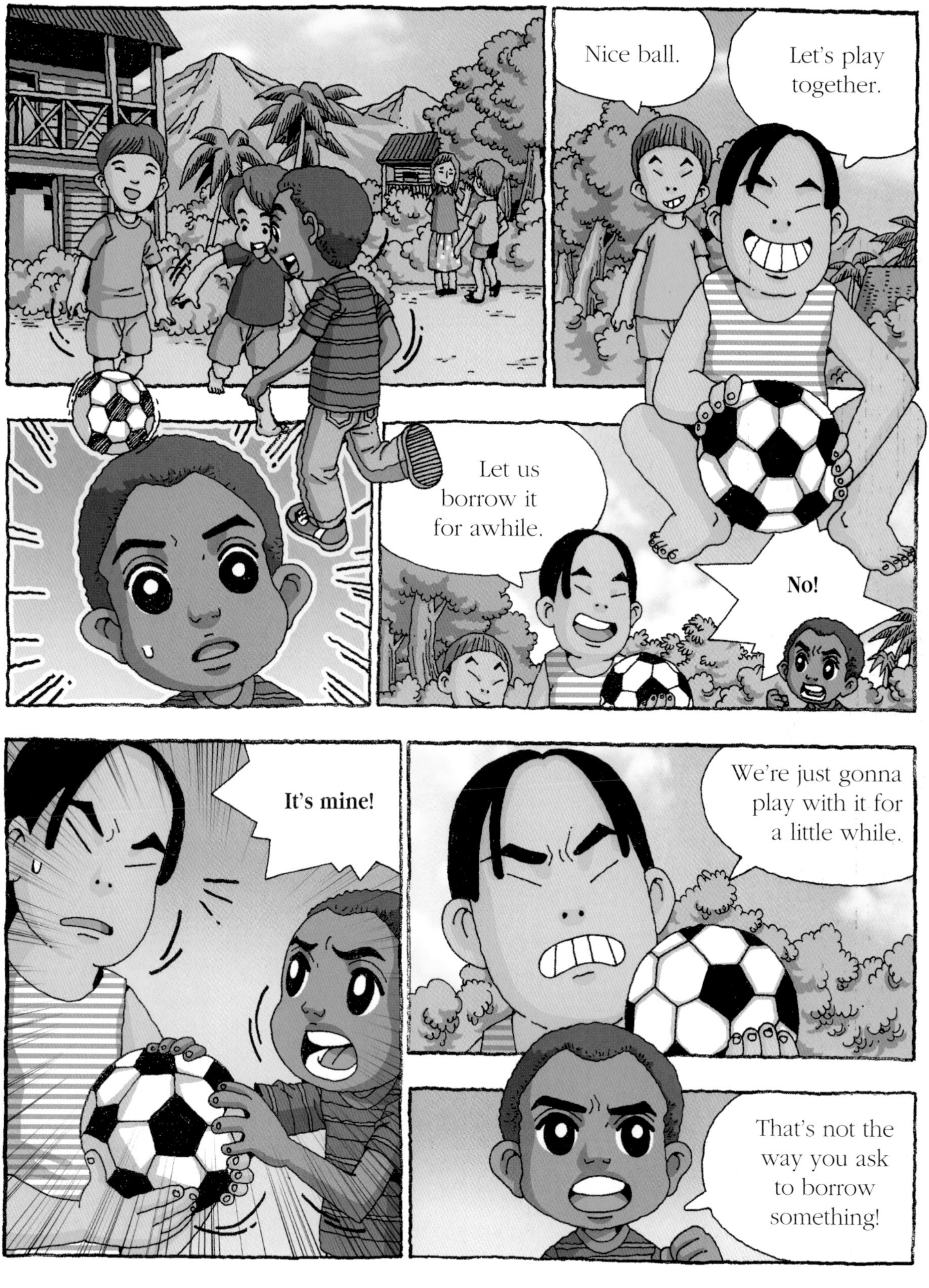
Nice ball.
Let's play together.
Let us borrow it for awhile.
No!
It's mine!
We're just gonna play with it for a little while.
That's not the way you ask to borrow something!

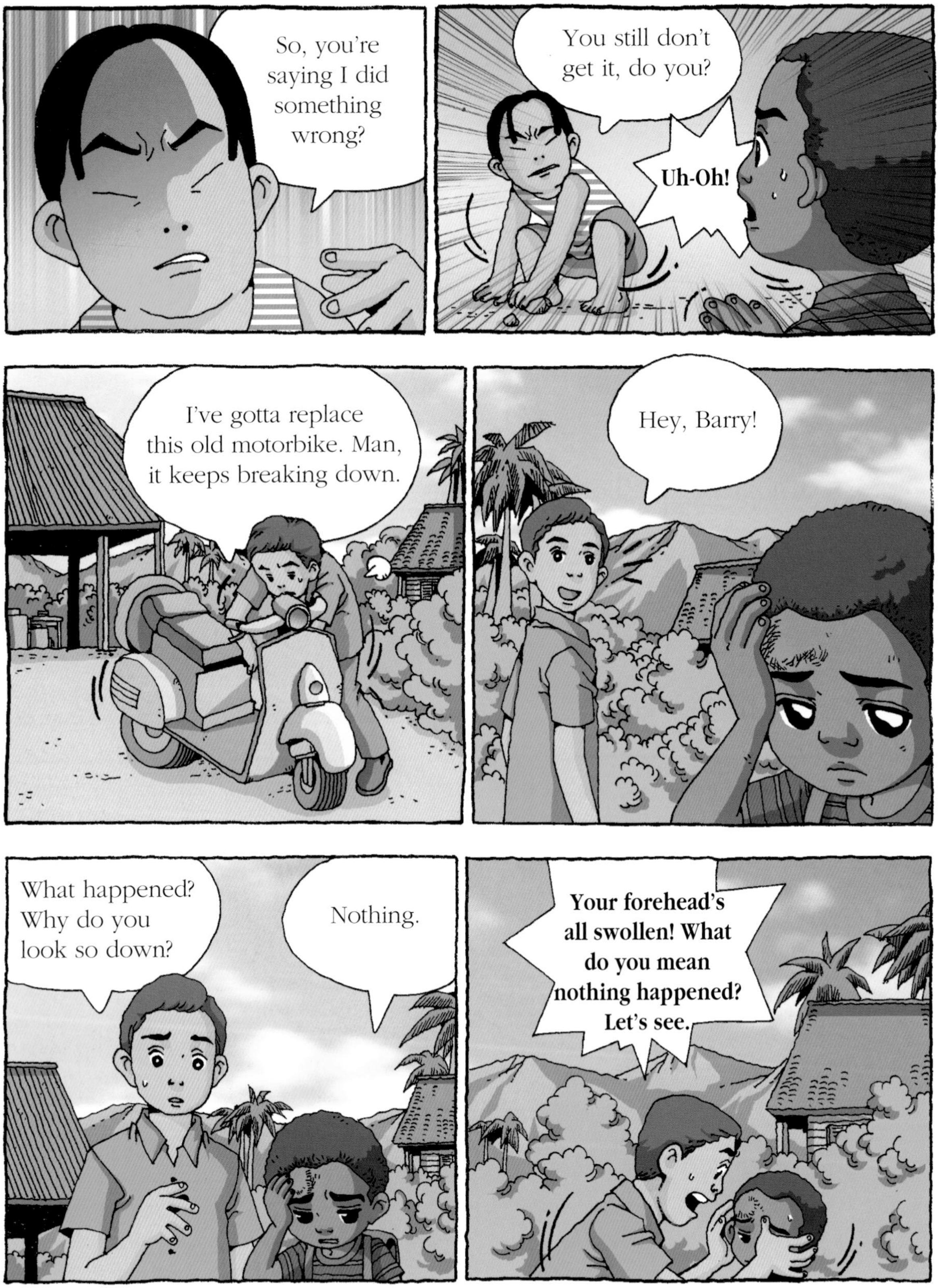
So, you're saying I did something wrong?
You still don't get it, do you?
Uh-Oh!
I've gotta replace this old motorbike. Man, it keeps breaking down.
Hey, Barry!
What happened? Why do you look so down?
Nothing.
Your forehead's all swollen! What do you mean nothing happened? Let's see.

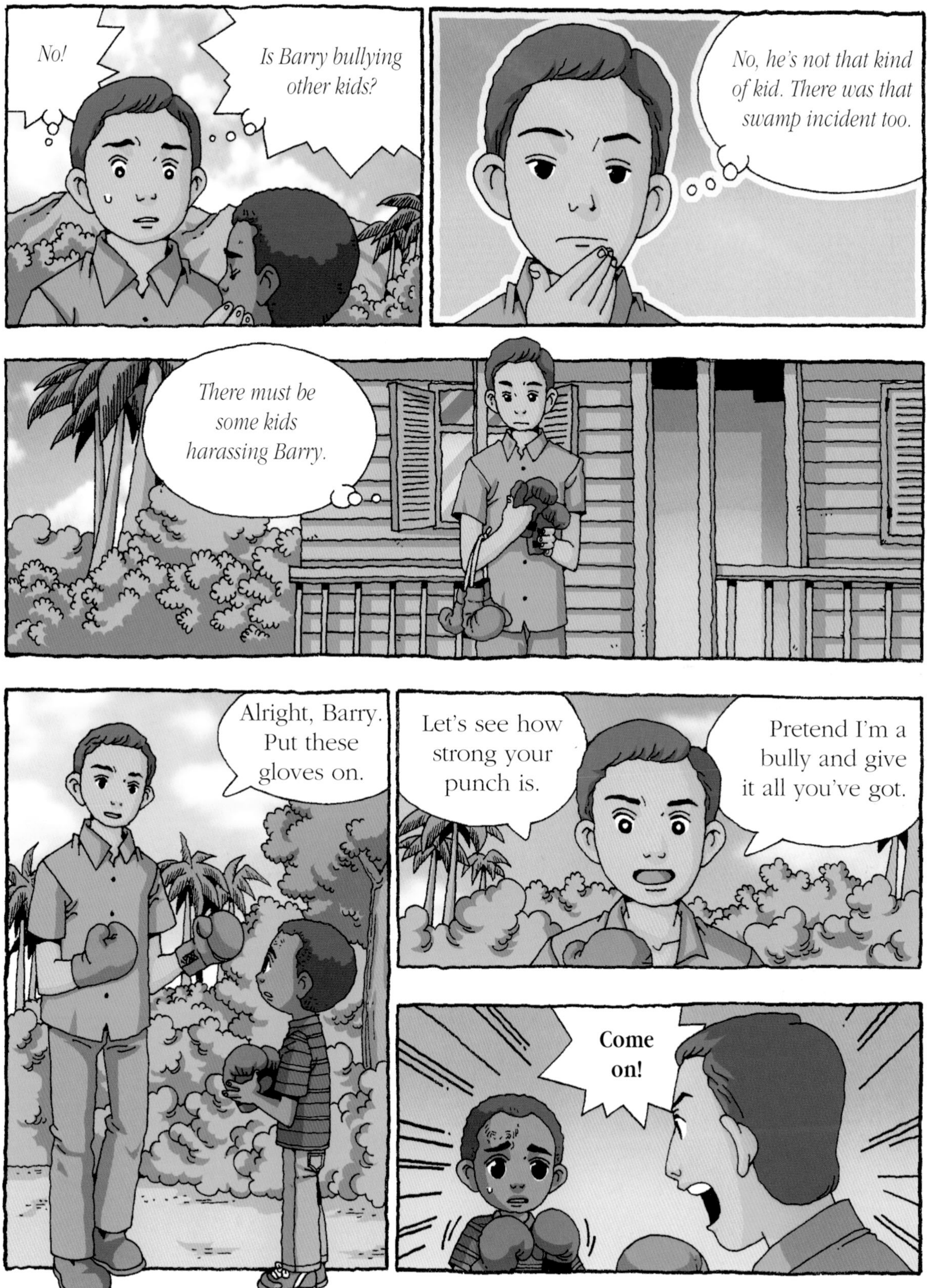
No!
Is Barry bullying other kids?
No, he's not that kind of kid. There was that swamp incident too.
There must be some kids harassing Barry.
Alright, Barry. Put these gloves on.
Let's see how strong your punch is.
Pretend I'm a bully and give it all you've got.
Come on!

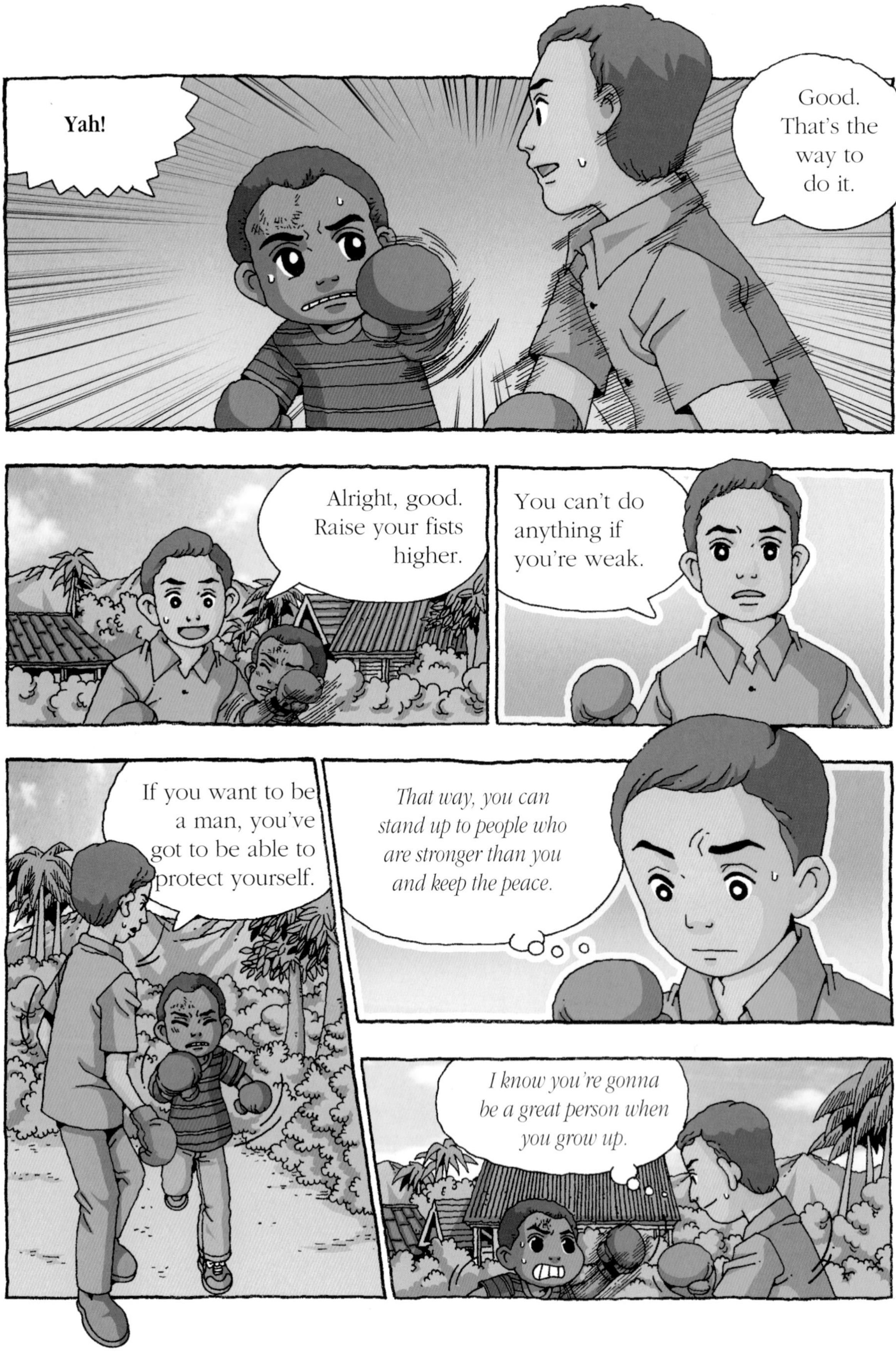

Yah!
Good. That's the way to do it.
Alright, good. Raise your fists higher.
You can't do anything if you're weak.
If you want to be a man, you've got to be able to protect yourself.
That way, you can stand up to people who are stronger than you and keep the peace.
I know you're gonna be a great person when you grow up.

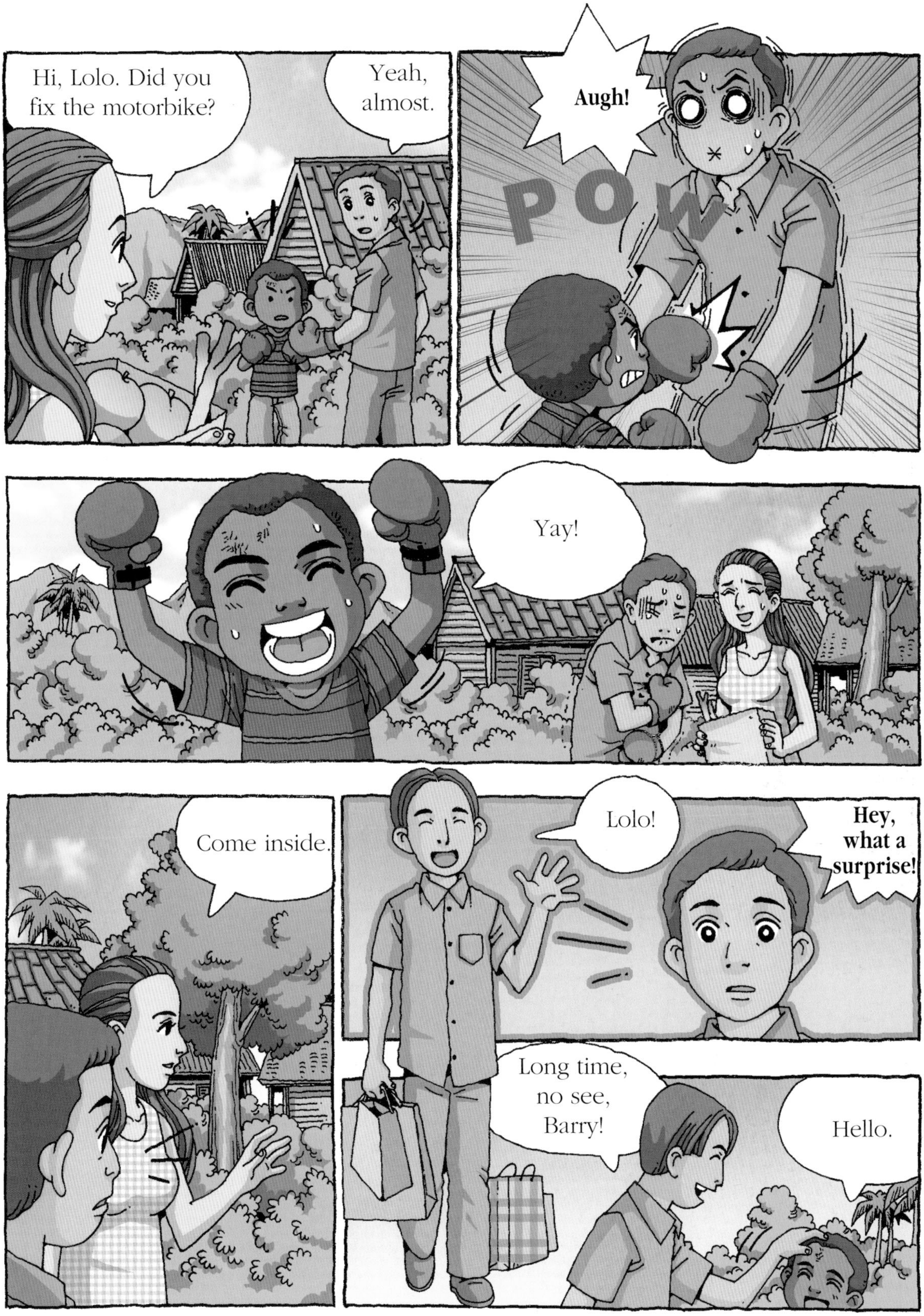

Hi, Lolo. Did you fix the motorbike?
Yeah, almost.
Augh!
POW
Yay!
Come inside.
Lolo!
Hey, what a surprise!
Long time, no see, Barry!
Hello.

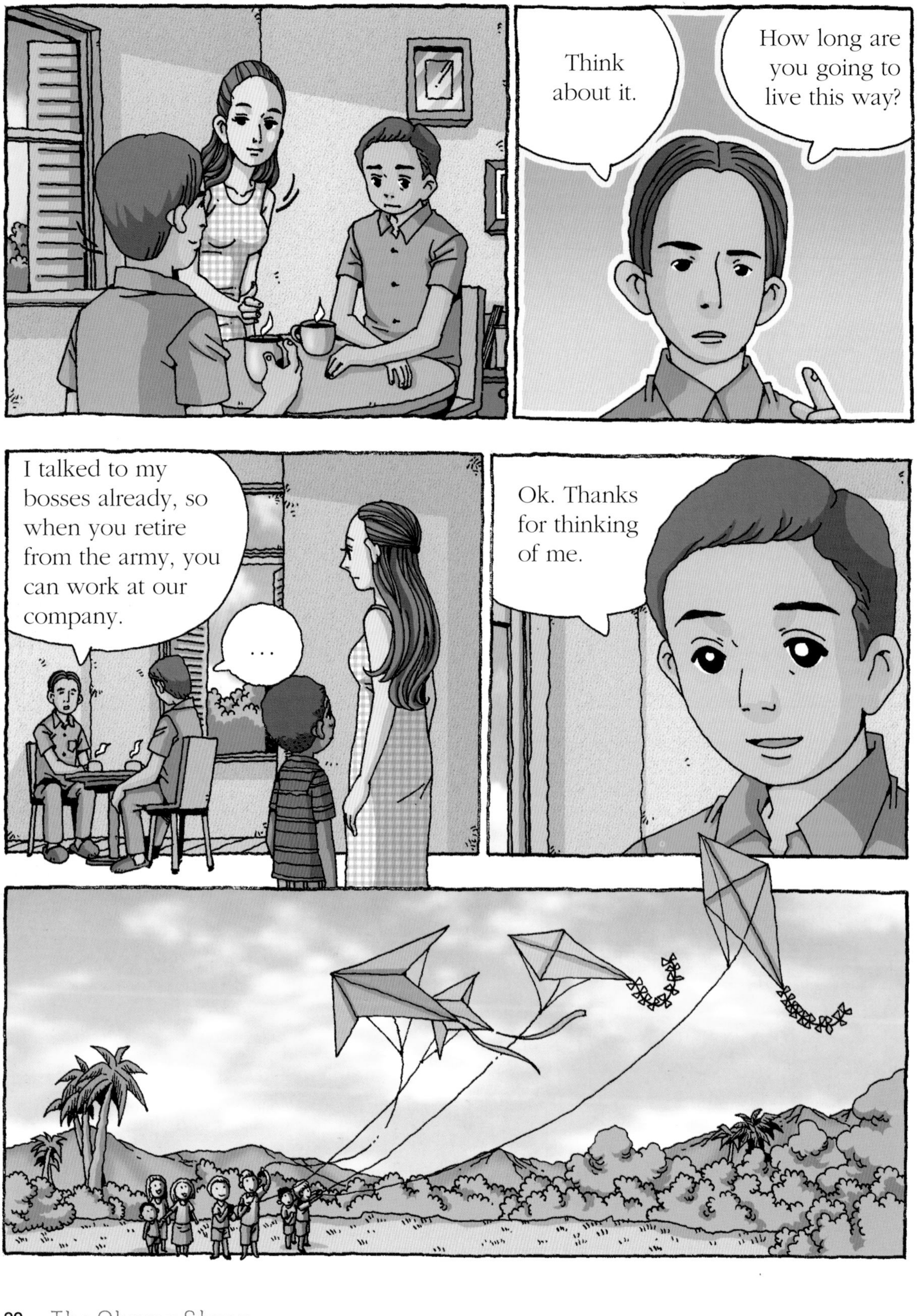
Think about it.
How long are you going to live this way?
I talked to my bosses already, so when you retire from the army, you can work at our company.
...
Ok. Thanks for thinking of me.

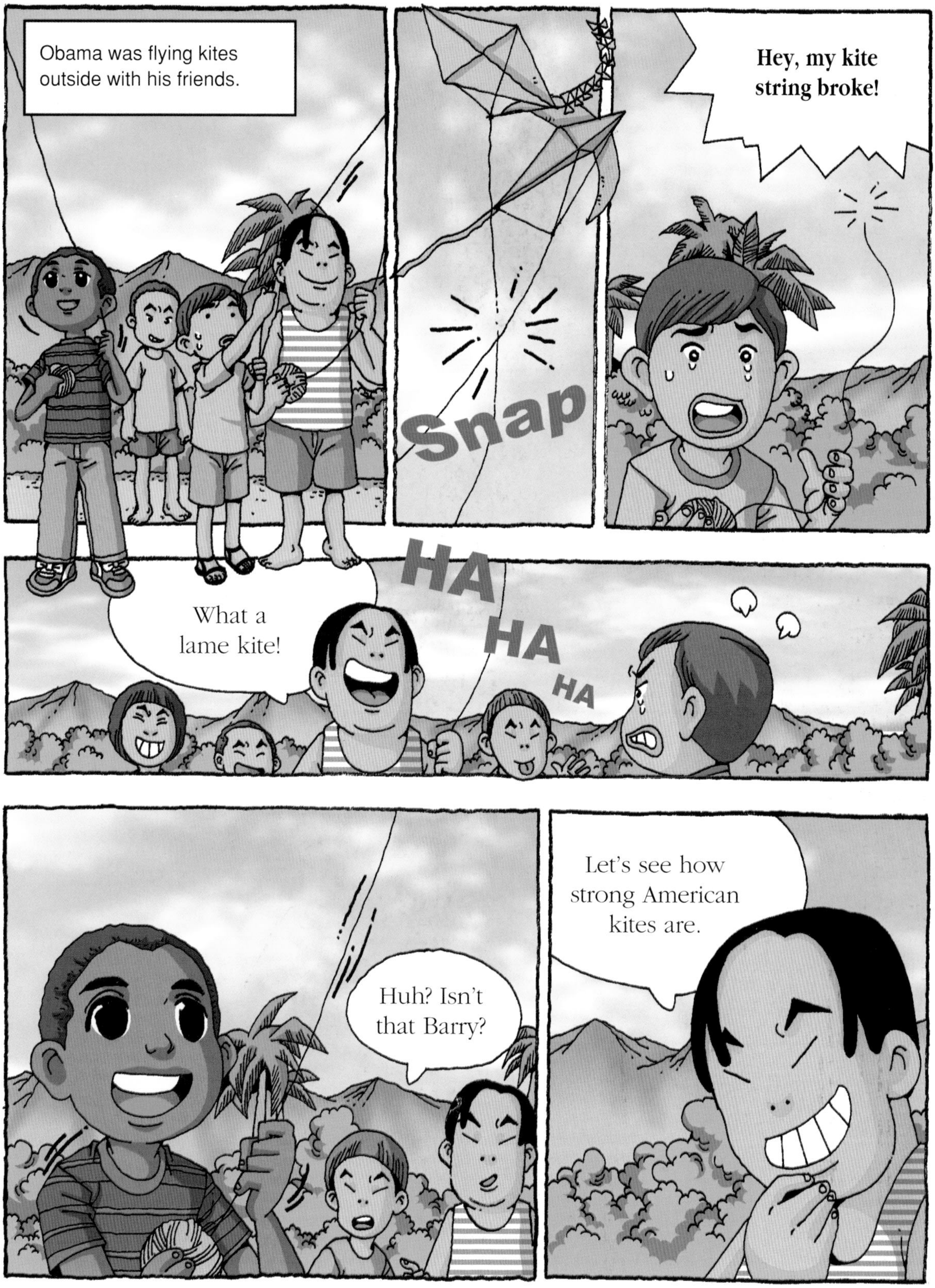
Obama was flying kites outside with his friends.
Snap
Hey, my kite string broke!
What a lame kite!
HA
HA
HA
Huh? Isn't that Barry?
Let's see how strong American kites are.

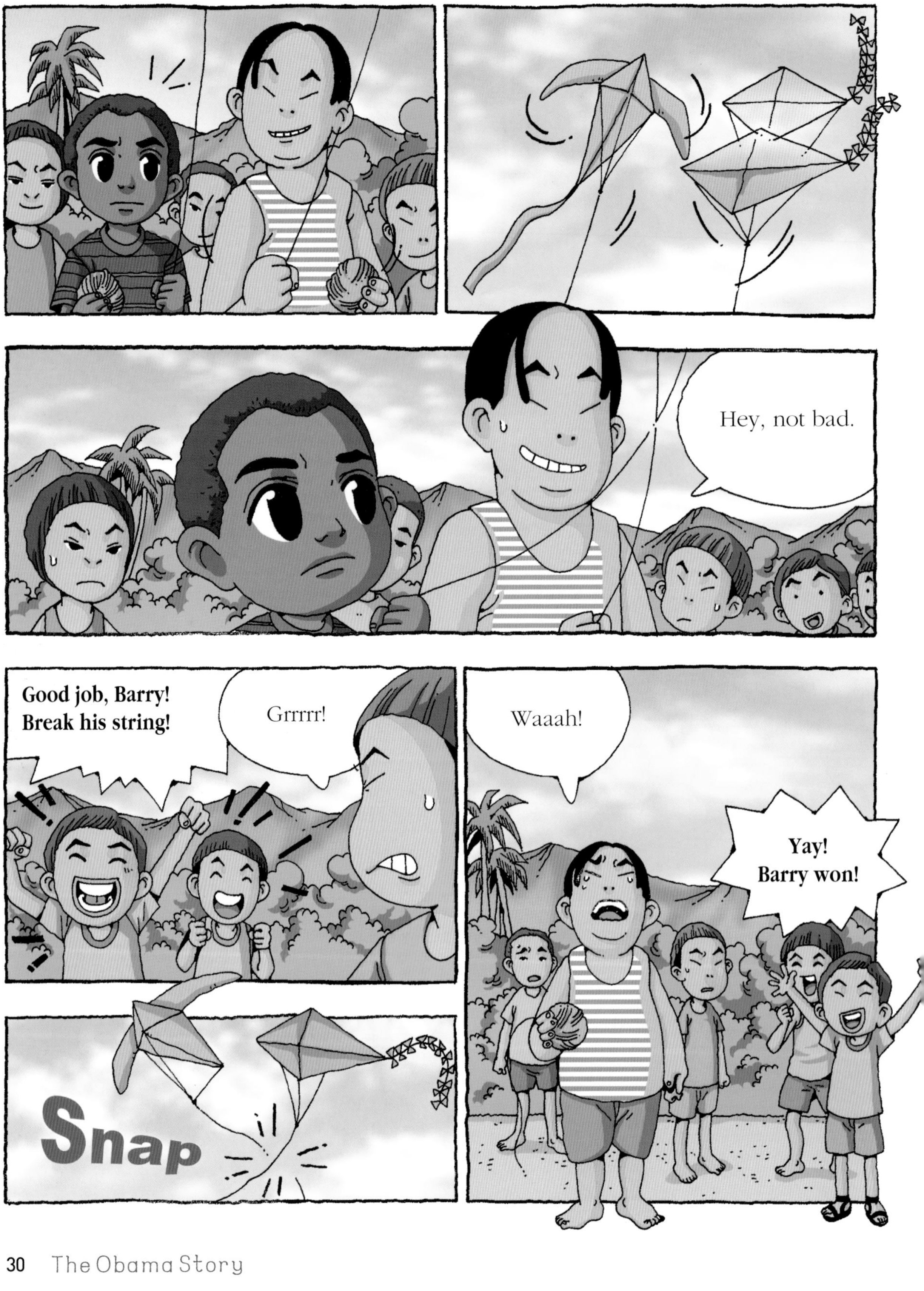
Hey, not bad.
Good job, Barry! Break his string!
Grrrr!
Snap
Waaah!
Yay! Barry won!

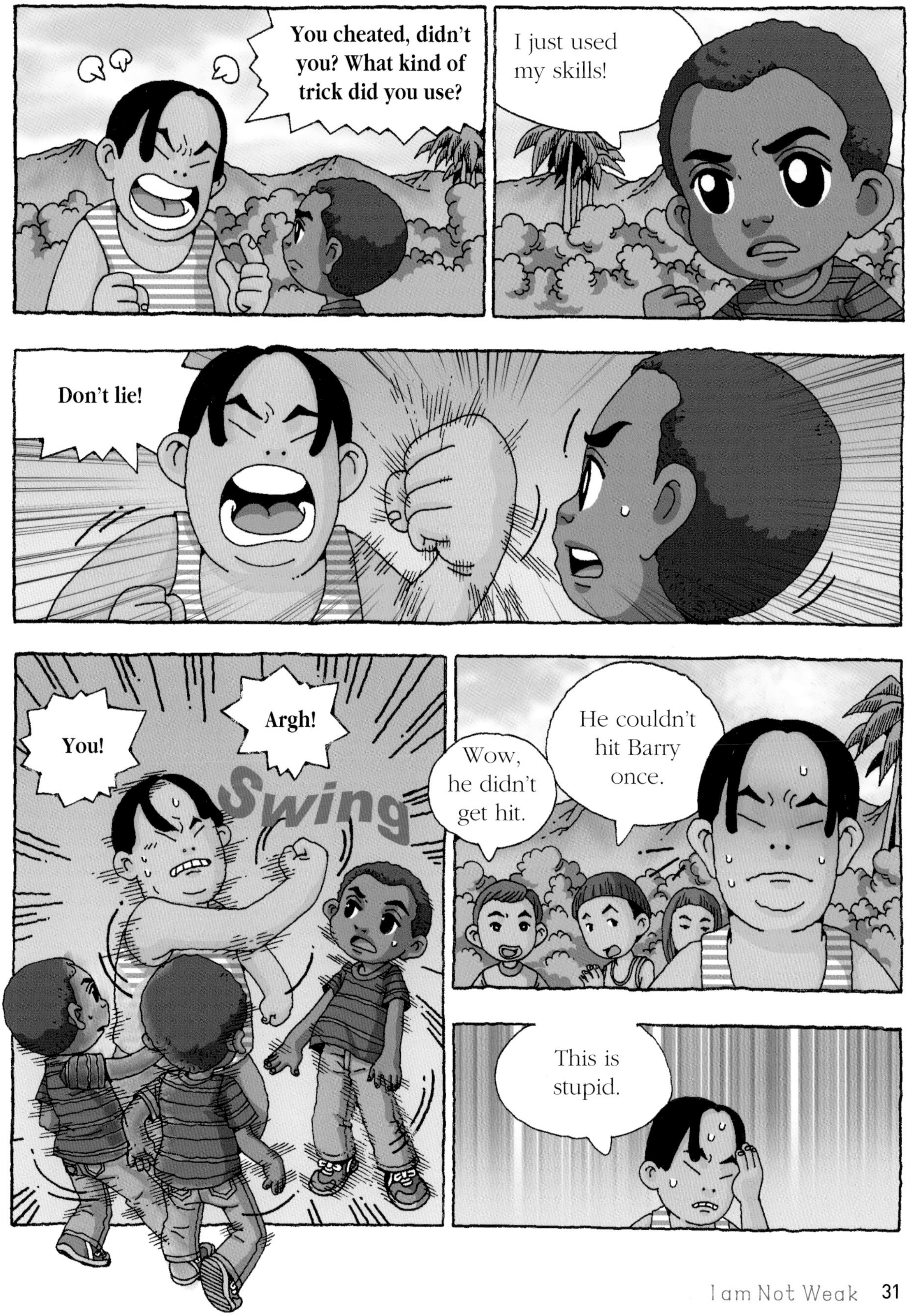
You cheated, didn't you? What kind of trick did you use?
I just used my skills!
Don't lie!
You!
Argh!
Swing
Wow, he didn't get hit.
He couldn't hit Barry once.
This is stupid.

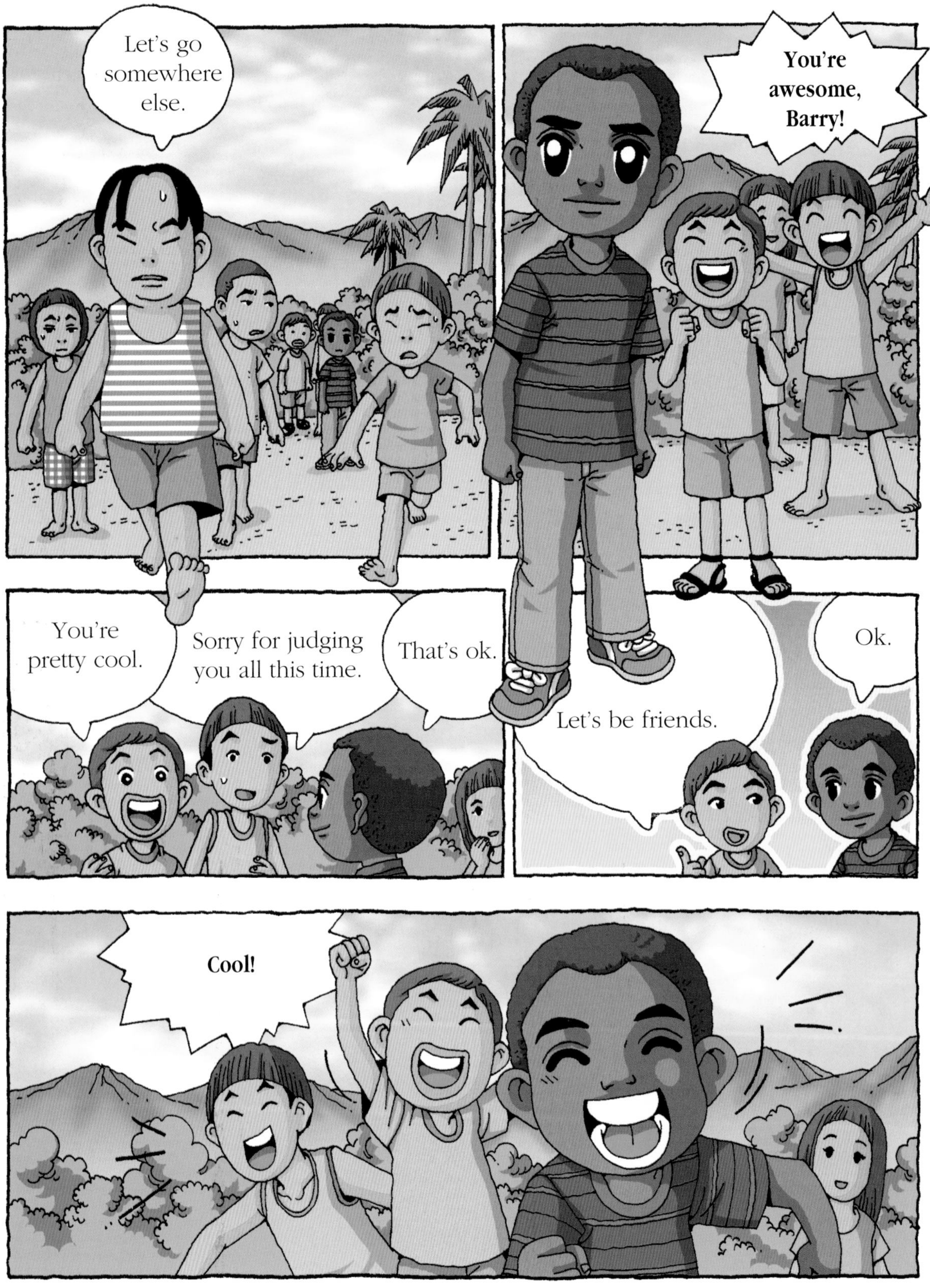
Let's go somewhere else.
You're awesome, Barry!
You're pretty cool.
Sorry for judging you all this time.
That's ok.
Ok.
Let's be friends.
Cool!

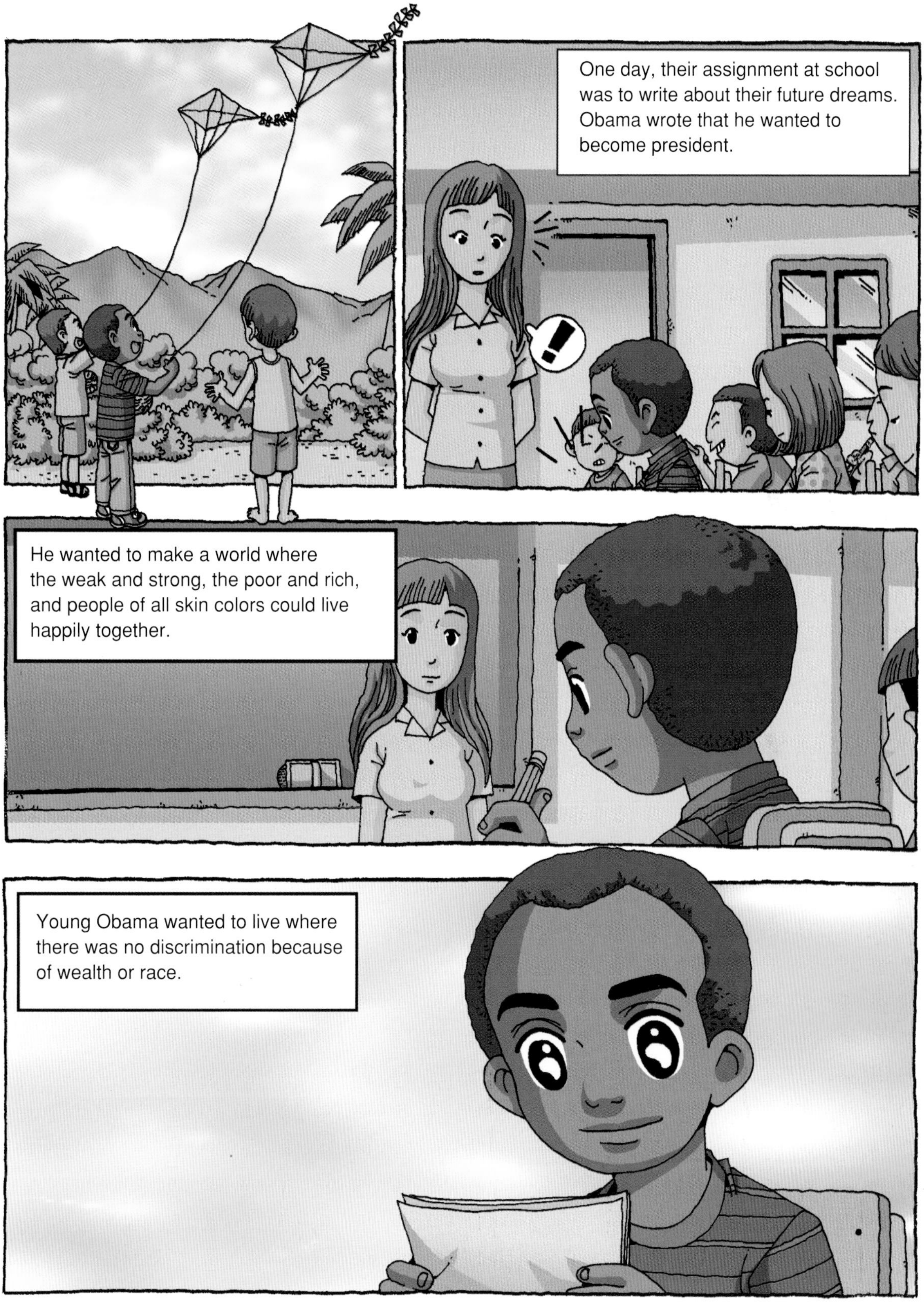
One day, their assignment at school was to write about their future dreams. Obama wrote that he wanted to become president.
!
He wanted to make a world where the weak and strong, the poor and rich, and people of all skin colors could live happily together.
Young Obama wanted to live where there was no discrimination because of wealth or race.

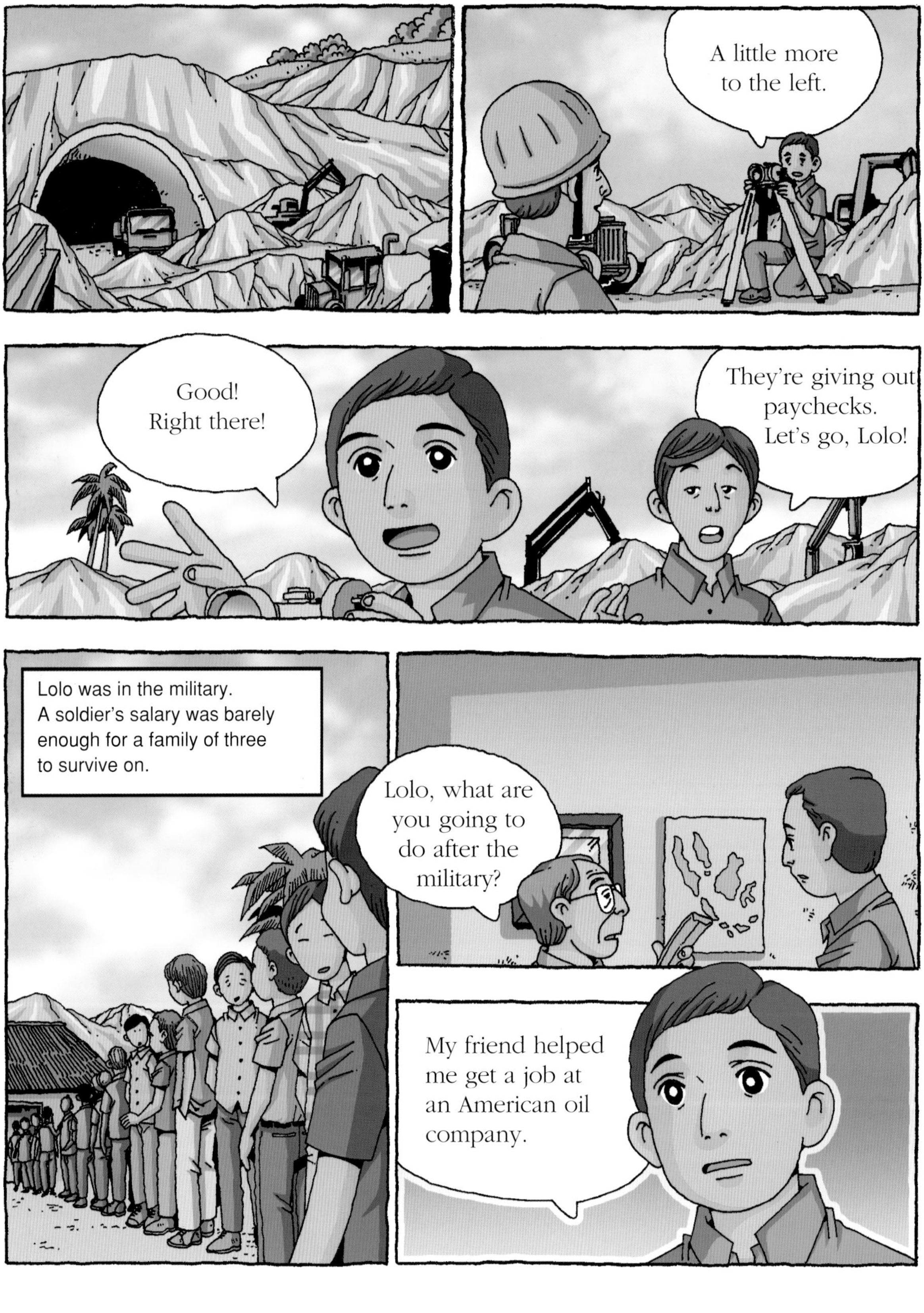
A little more
to the left.
Good!
Right there!
They're giving out paychecks.
Let's go, Lolo!
Lolo was in the military.
A soldier's salary was barely enough for a family of three to survive on.
Lolo, what are you going to do after the military?
My friend helped me get a job at an American oil company.

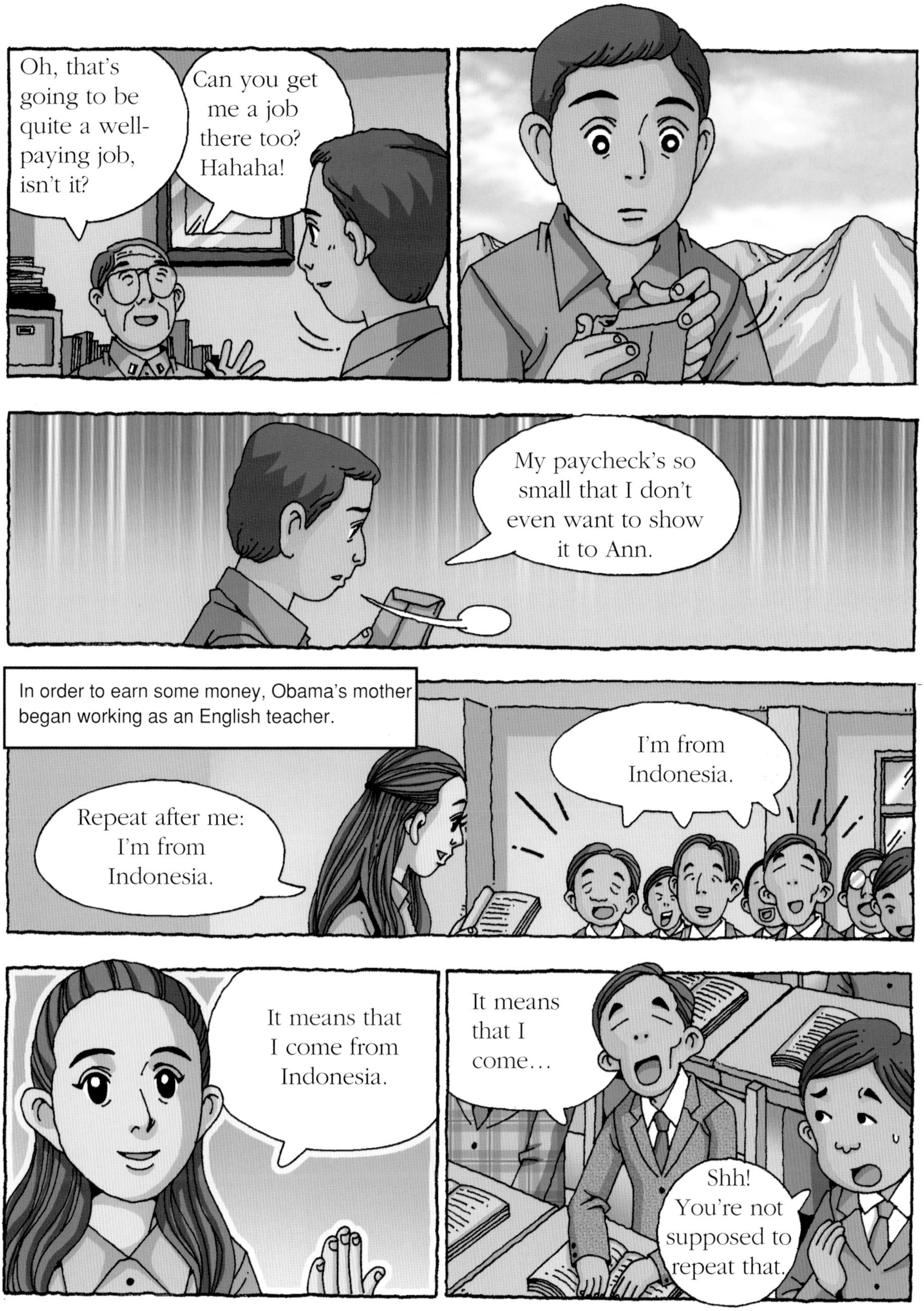

Oh, that's going to be quite a well-paying job, isn't it?
Can you get me a job there too? Hahaha!
My paycheck's so small that I don't even want to show it to Ann.
In order to earn some money, Obama's mother began working as an English teacher.
Repeat after me: I'm from Indonesia.
I'm from Indonesia.
It means that I come from Indonesia.
It means that I come…
Shh! You're not supposed to repeat that.

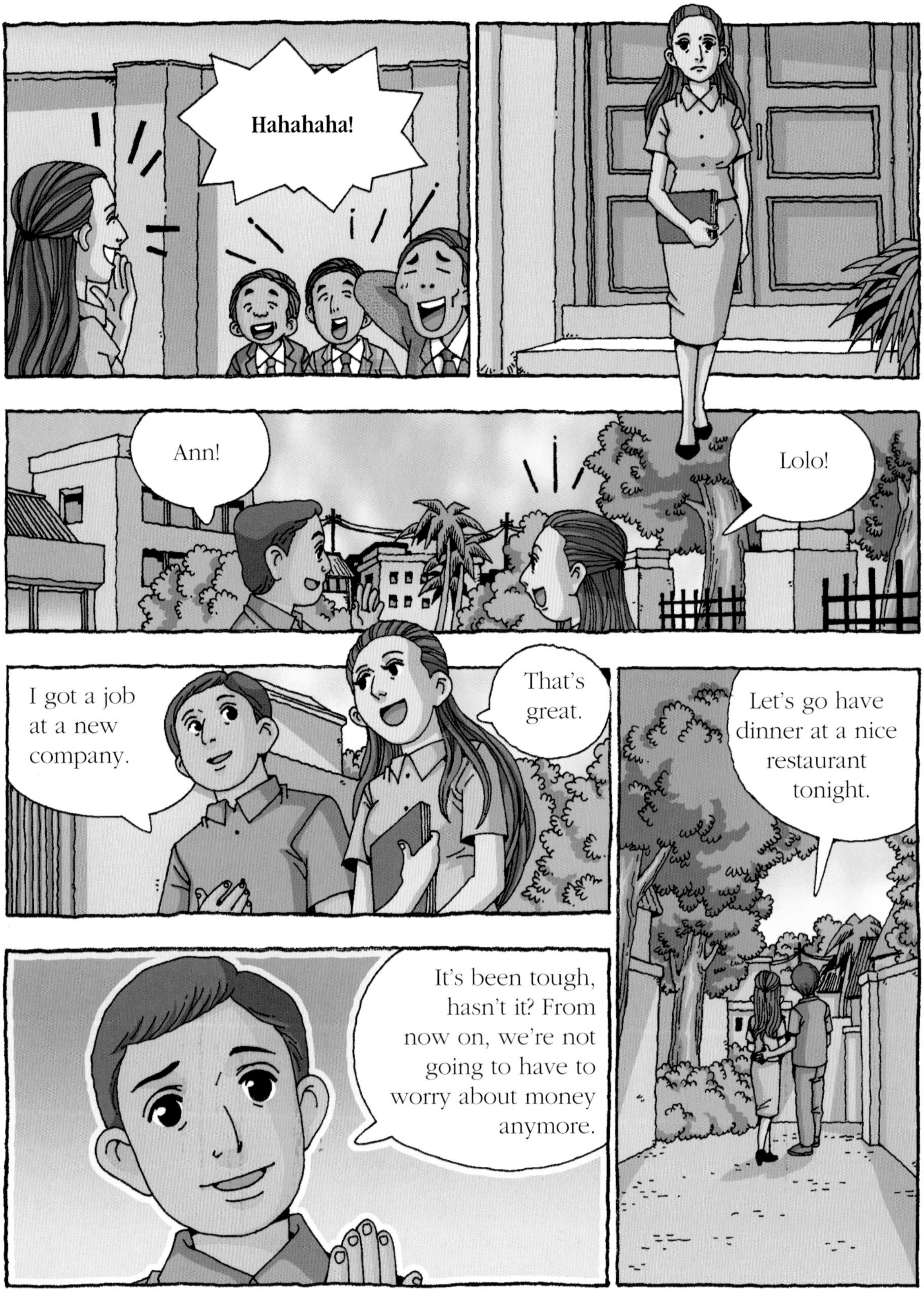
Hahahaha!
Ann!
Lolo!
I got a job at a new company.
That's great.
Let's go have dinner at a nice restaurant tonight.
It's been tough, hasn't it? From now on, we're not going to have to worry about money anymore.

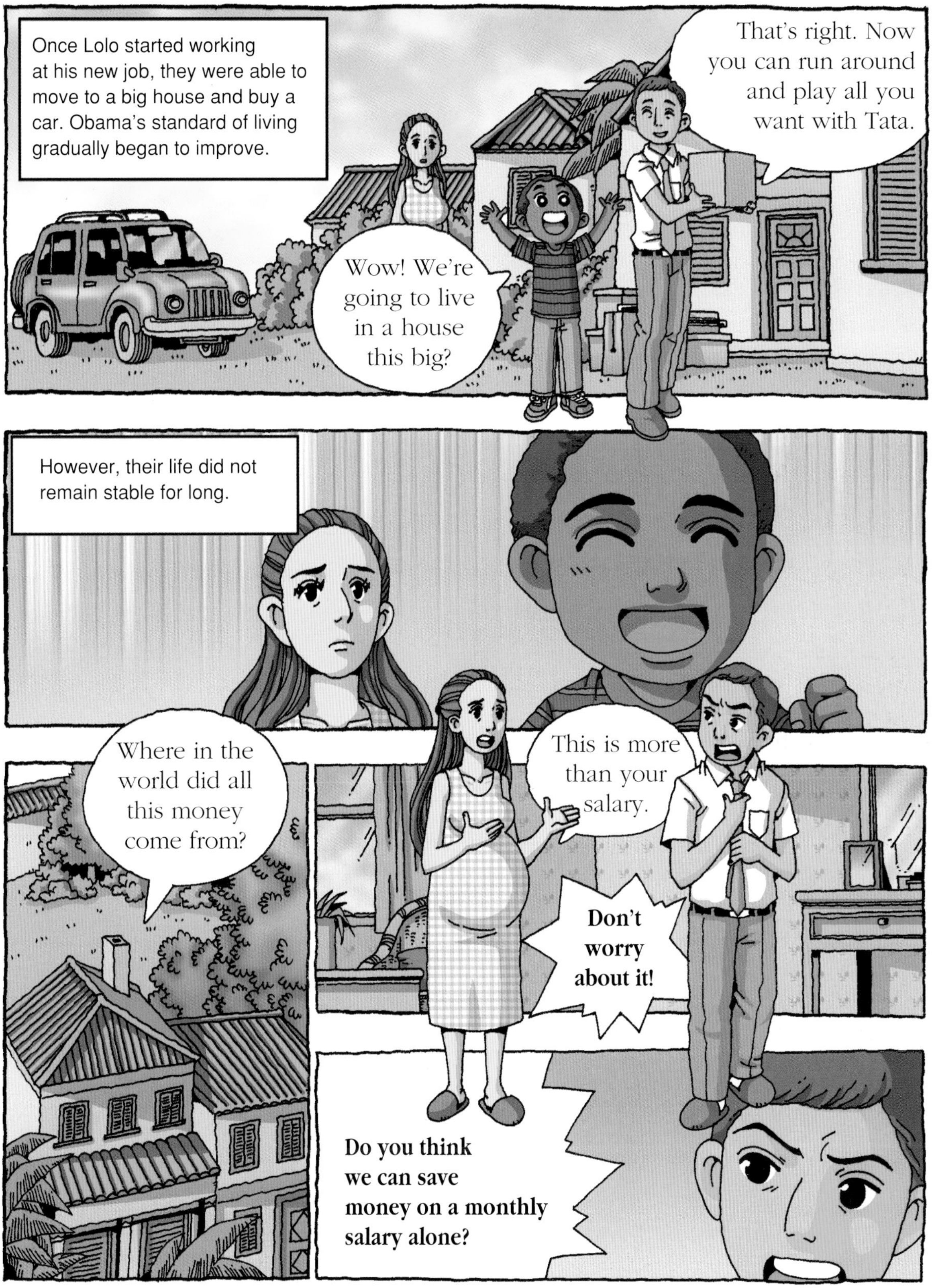
Once Lolo started working at his new job, they were able to move to a big house and buy a car. Obama's standard of living gradually began to improve.
That's right. Now you can run around and play all you want with Tata.
Wow! We're going to live in a house this big?
However, their life did not remain stable for long.
Where in the world did all this money come from?
This is more than your salary.
Don't worry about it!
Do you think we can save money on a monthly salary alone?

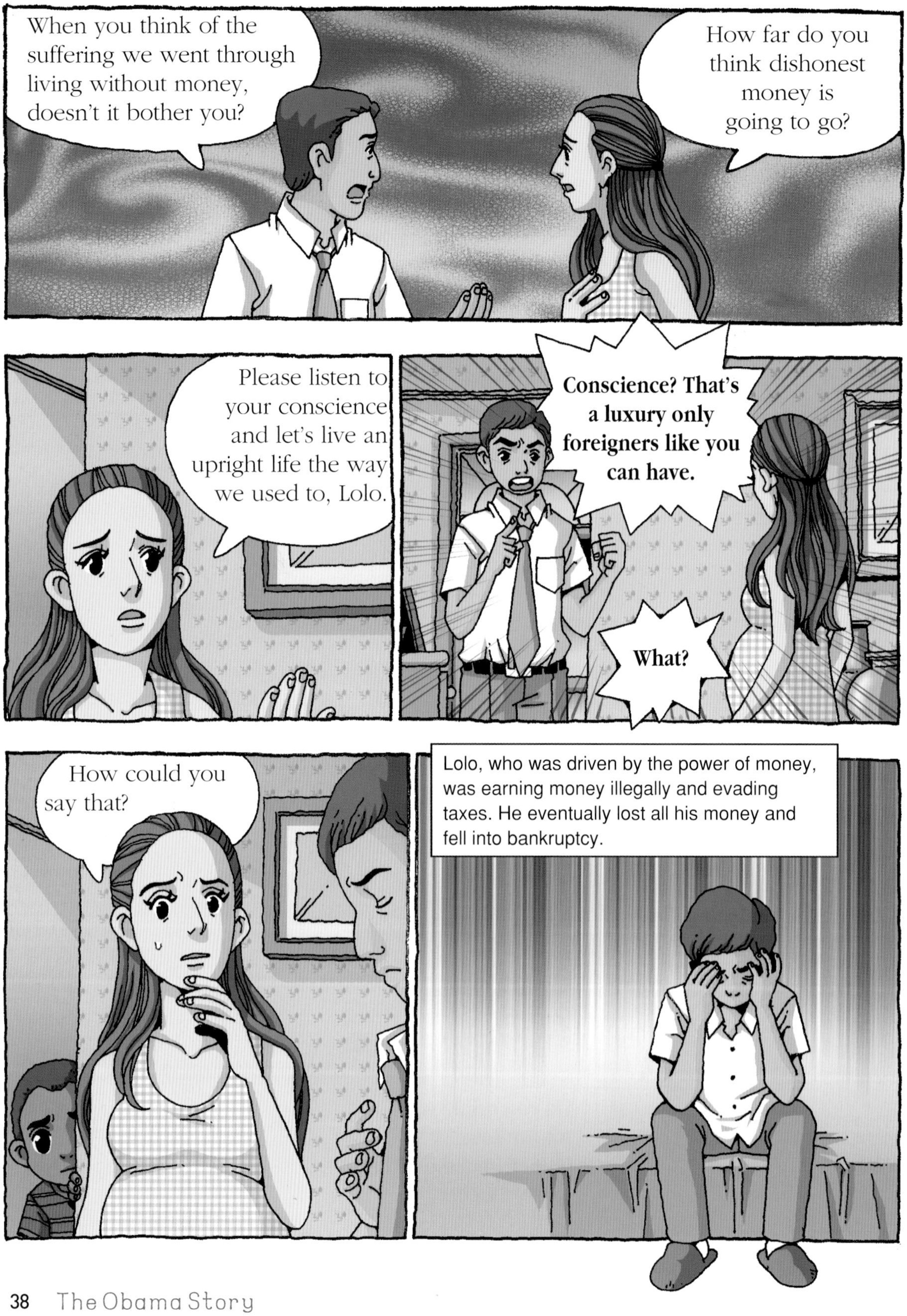

When you think of the suffering we went through living without money, doesn't it bother you?
How far do you think dishonest money is going to go?
Please listen to your conscience and let's live an upright life the way we used to, Lolo.
Conscience? That's a luxury only foreigners like you can have.
What?
How could you say that?
Lolo, who was driven by the power of money, was earning money illegally and evading taxes. He eventually lost all his money and fell into bankruptcy.

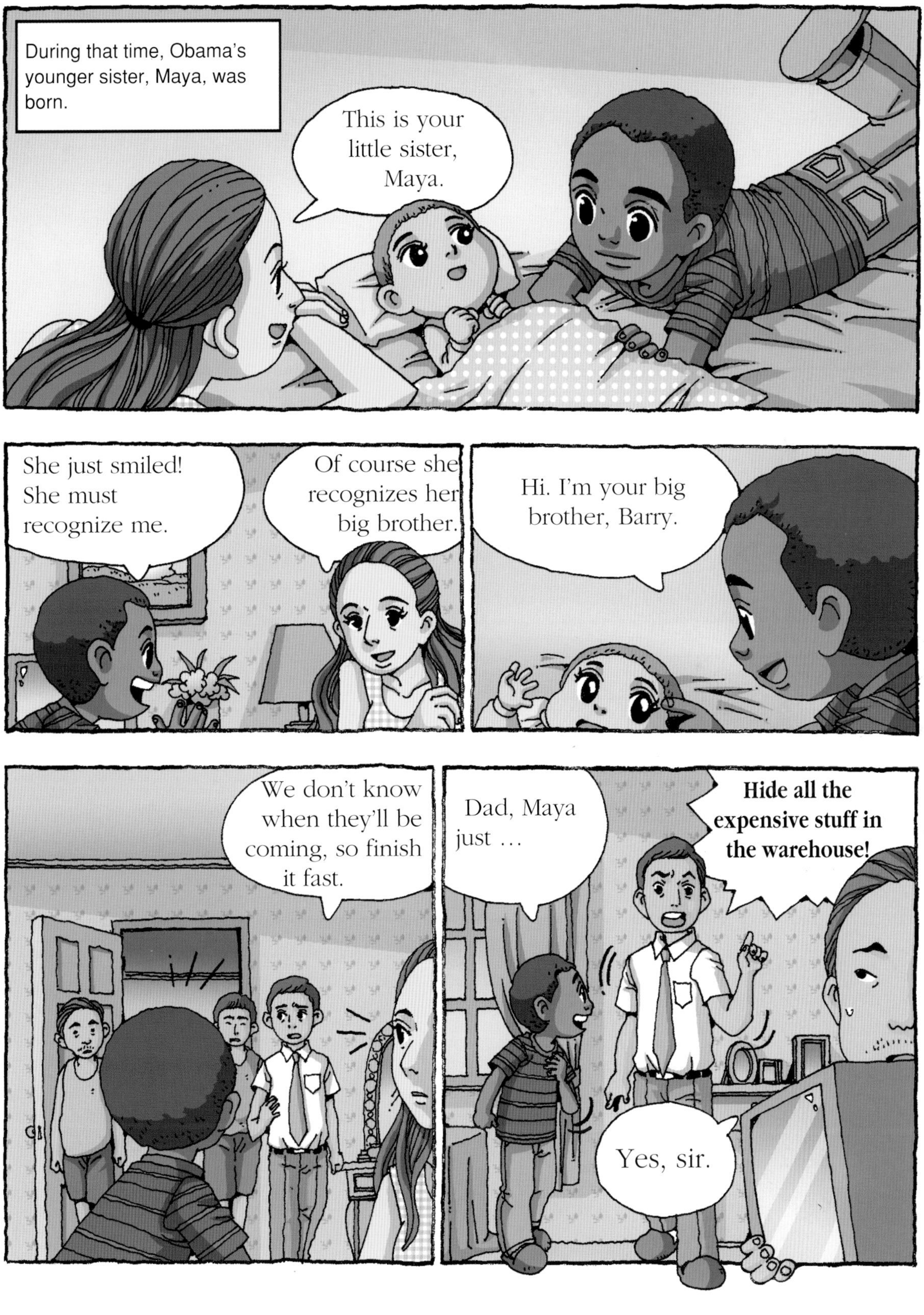
During that time, Obama's younger sister, Maya, was born.
This is your little sister, Maya.
She just smiled! She must recognize me.
Of course she recognizes her big brother.
Hi. I'm your big brother, Barry.
We don't know when they'll be coming, so finish it fast.
Dad, Maya just …
Hide all the expensive stuff in the warehouse!
Yes, sir.

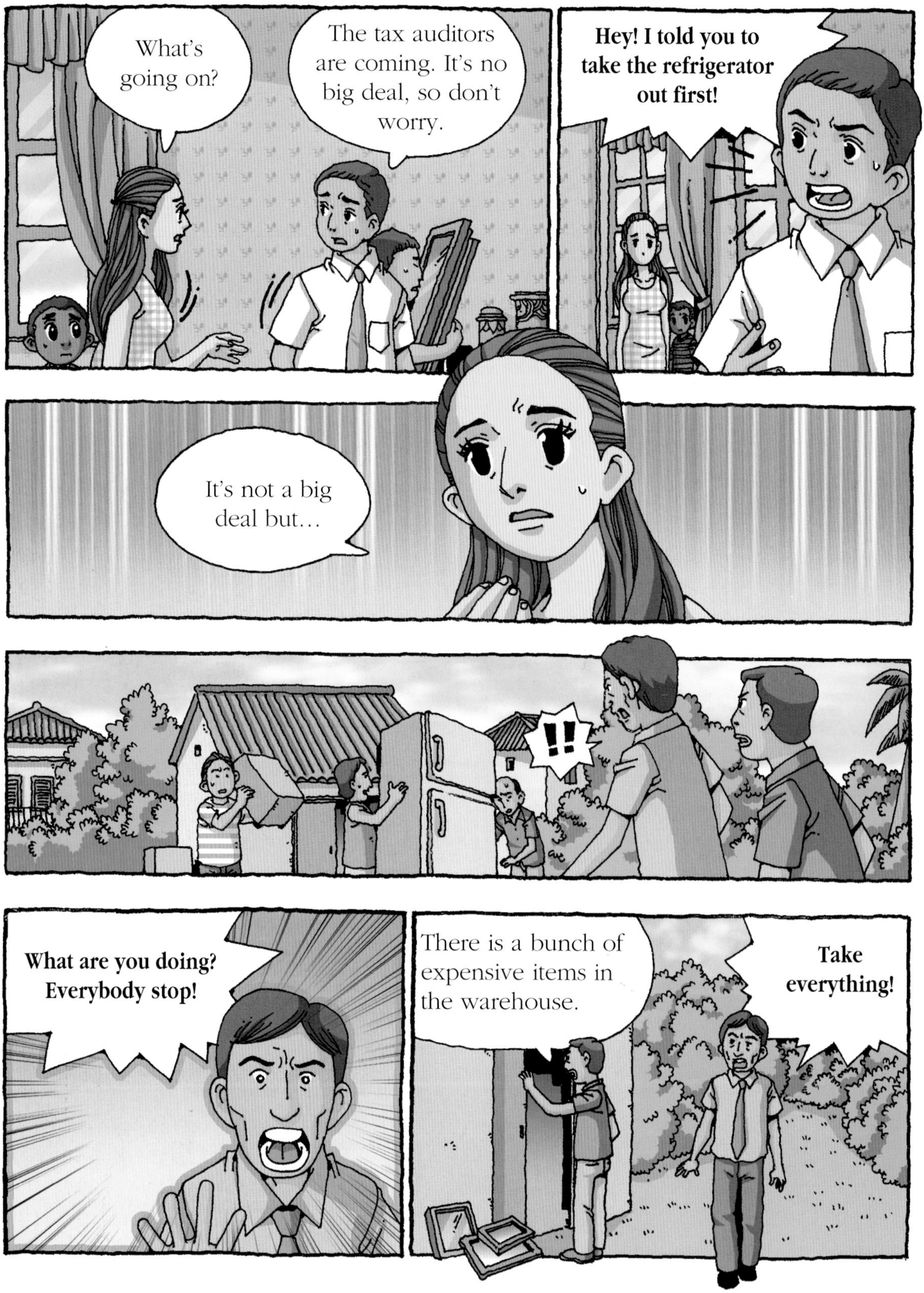

What's going on?
The tax auditors are coming. It's no big deal, so don't worry.
Hey! I told you to take the refrigerator out first!
It's not a big deal but…
!!
What are you doing? Everybody stop!
There is a bunch of expensive items in the warehouse.
Take everything!

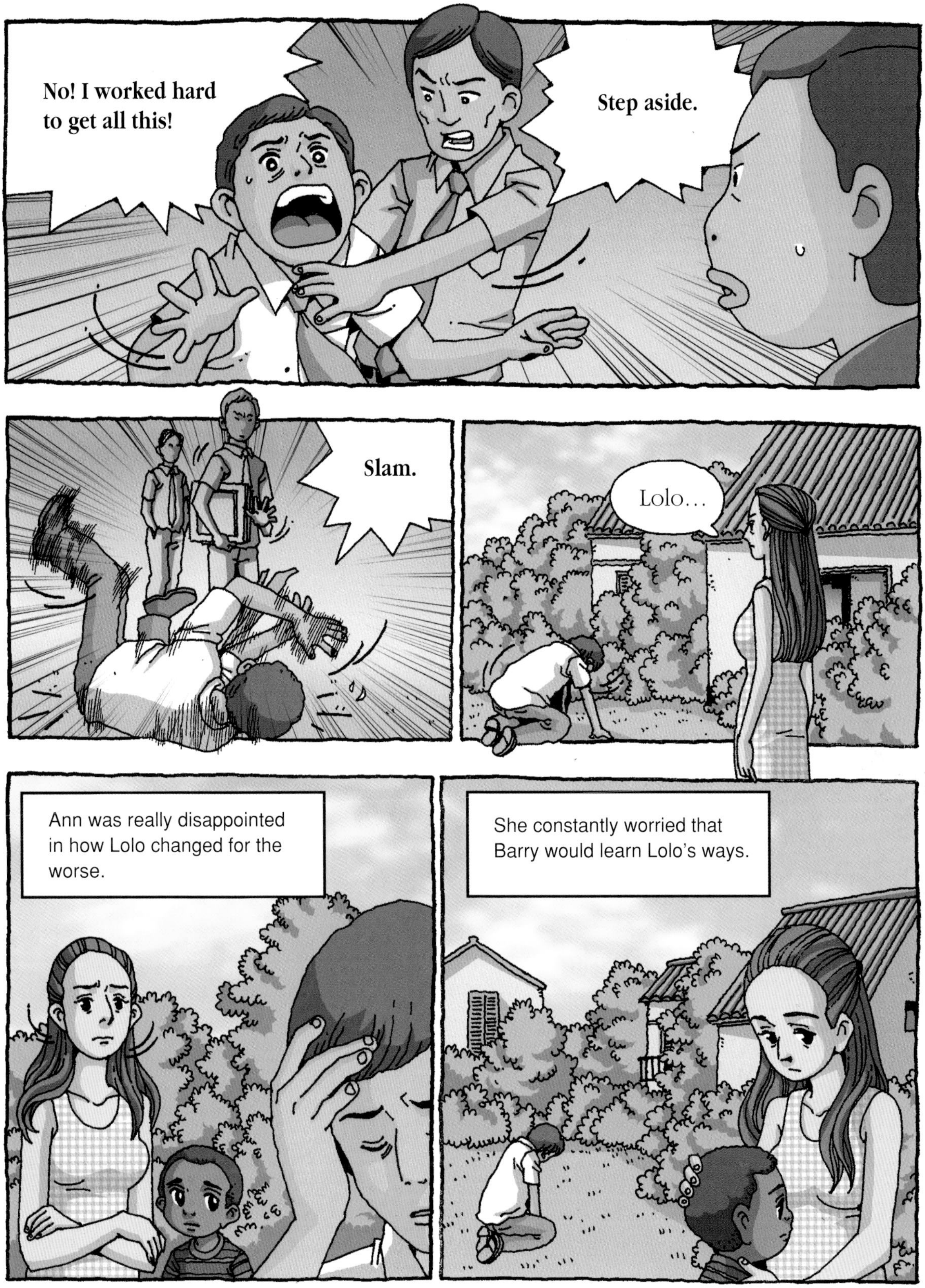

No! I worked hard
to get all this!
Step aside.
Slam.
Lolo...
Ann was really disappointed in how Lolo changed for the worse.
She constantly worried that Barry would learn Lolo's ways.

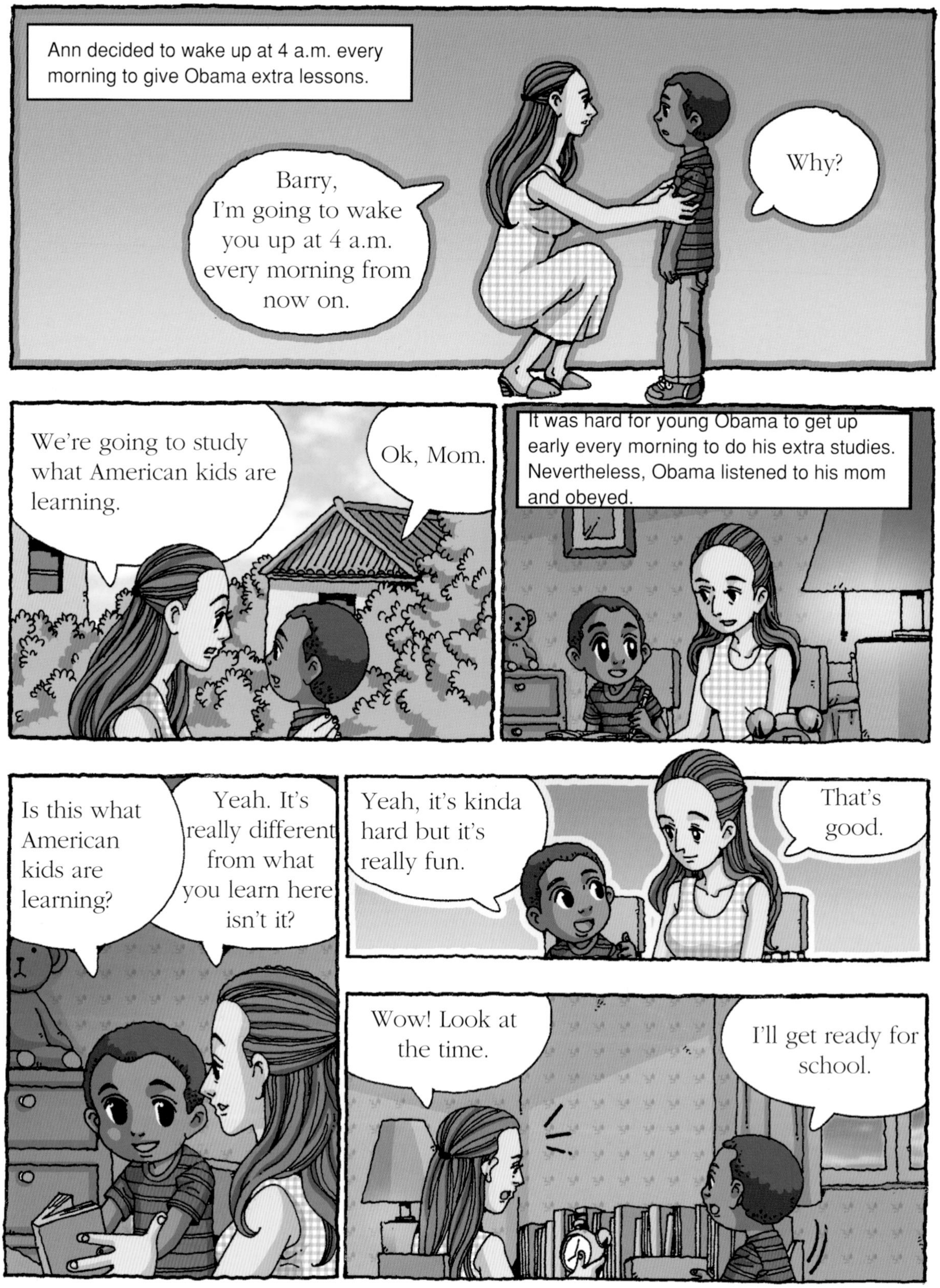
Ann decided to wake up at 4 a.m. every morning to give Obama extra lessons.
Barry, I'm going to wake you up at 4 a.m. every morning from now on.
Why?
We're going to study what American kids are learning.
Ok, Mom.
It was hard for young Obama to get up early every morning to do his extra studies. Nevertheless, Obama listened to his mom and obeyed.
Is this what American kids are learning?
Yeah. It's really different from what you learn here isn't it?
Yeah, it's kinda hard but it's really fun.
That's good.
Wow! Look at the time.
I'll get ready for school.

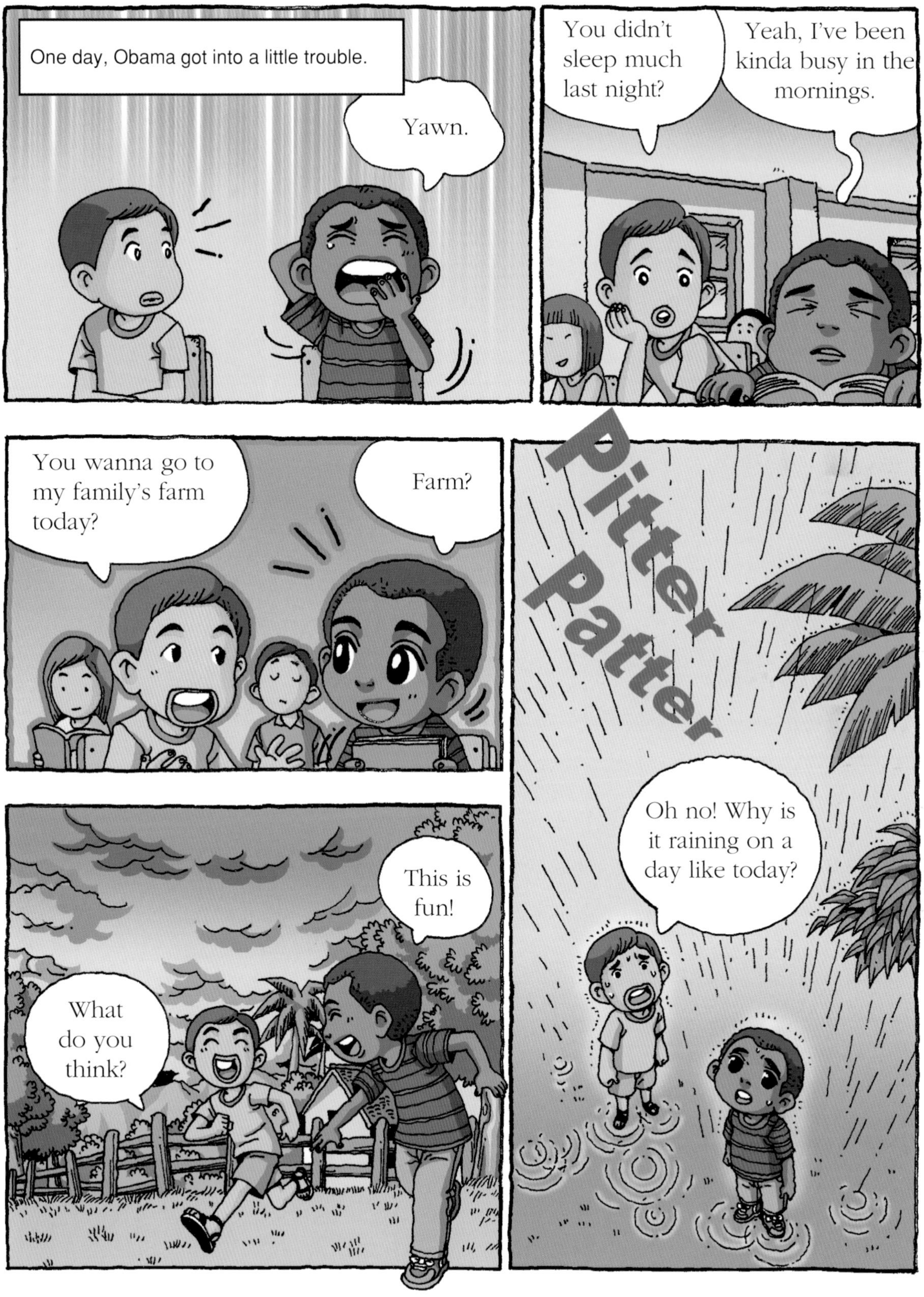
One day, Obama got into a little trouble.
Yawn.
You didn't sleep much last night?
Yeah, I've been kinda busy in the mornings.
You wanna go to my family's farm today?
Farm?
This is fun!
What do you think?
Pitter Patter
Oh no! Why is it raining on a day like today?

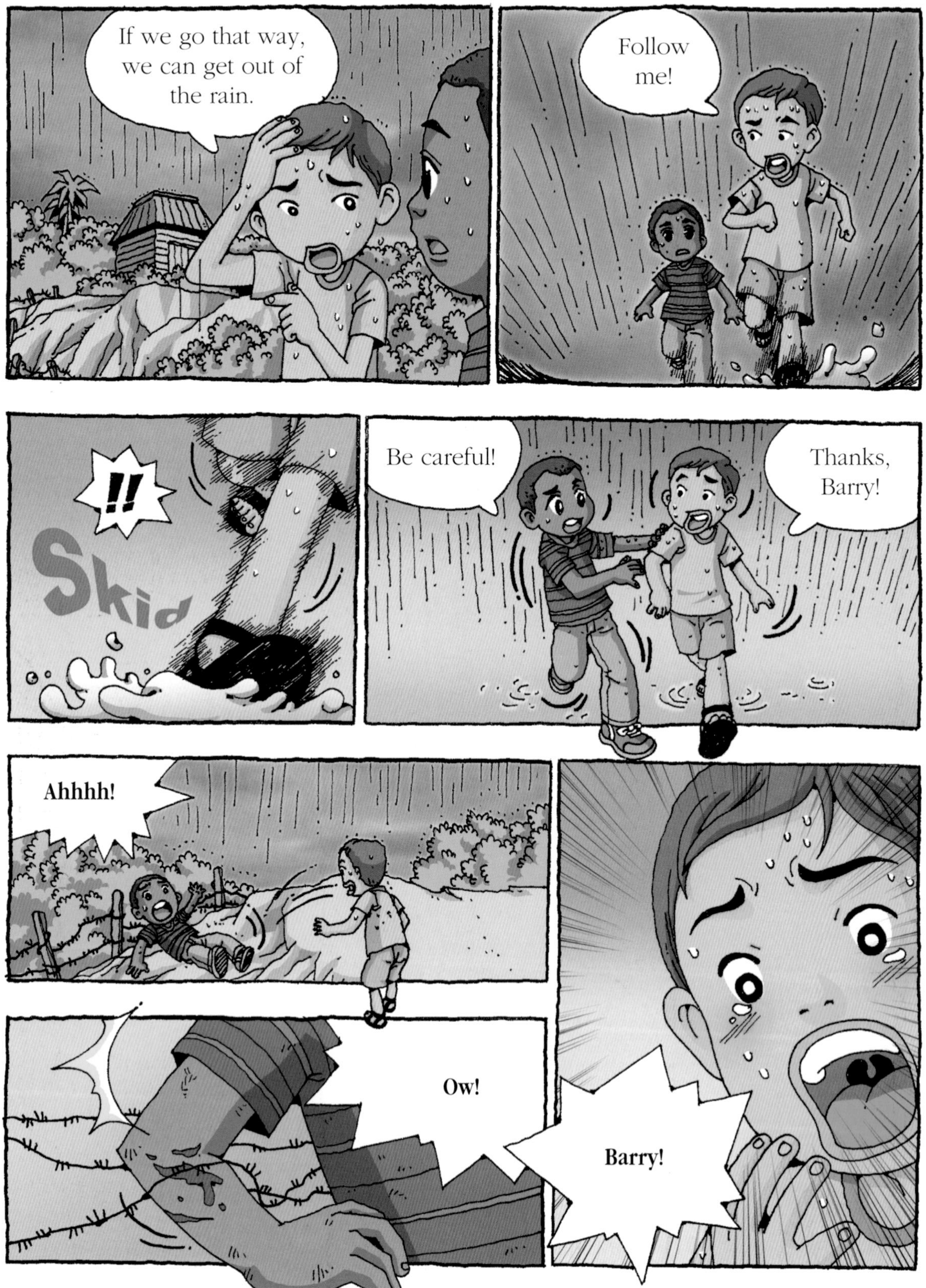

If we go that way, we can get out of the rain.
Follow me!
!!
Skid
Be careful!
Thanks, Barry!
Ahhhh!
Ow!
Barry!

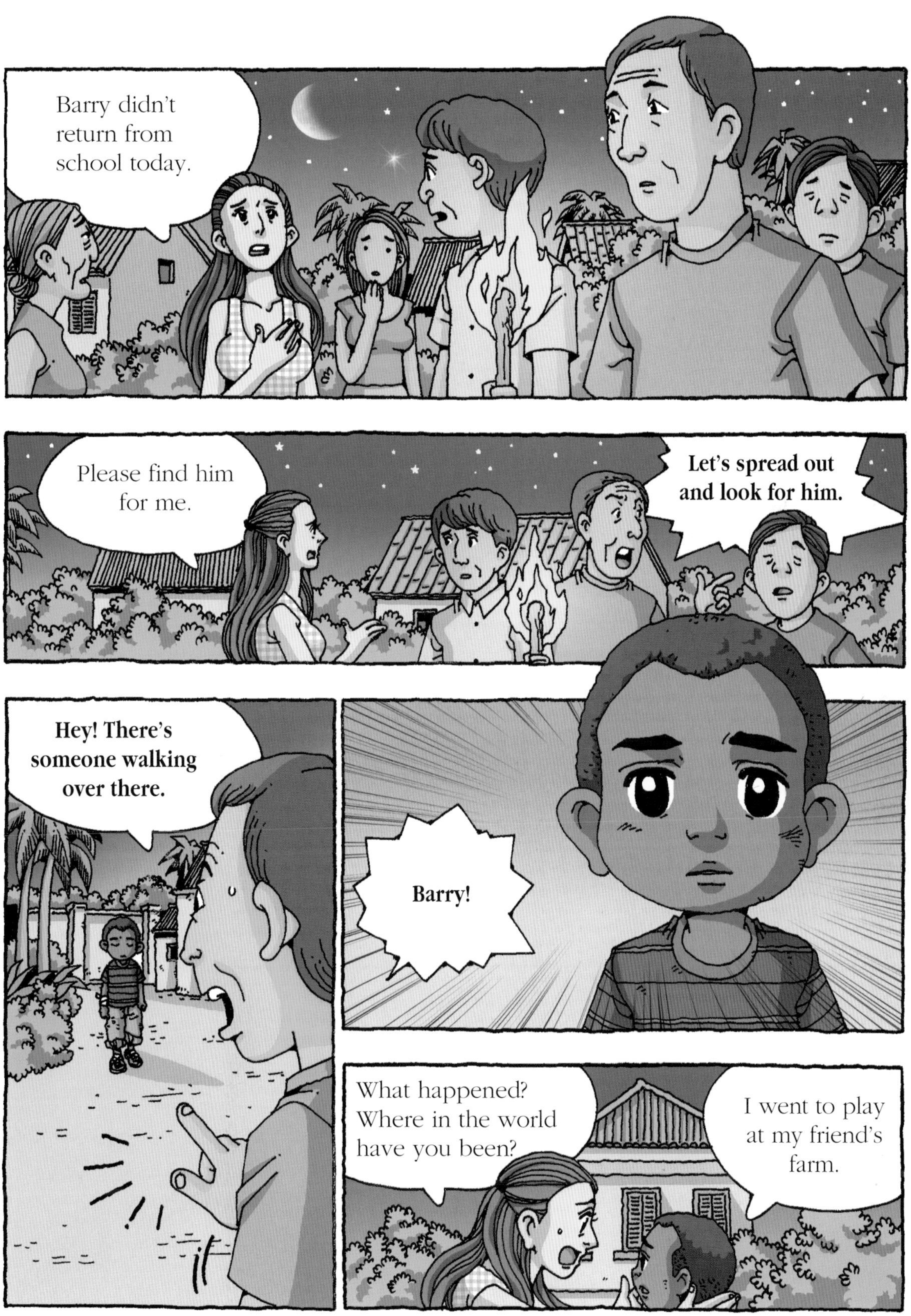
Barry didn't return from school today.
Please find him for me.
Let's spread out and look for him.
Hey! There's someone walking over there.
Barry!
What happened? Where in the world have you been?
I went to play at my friend's farm.

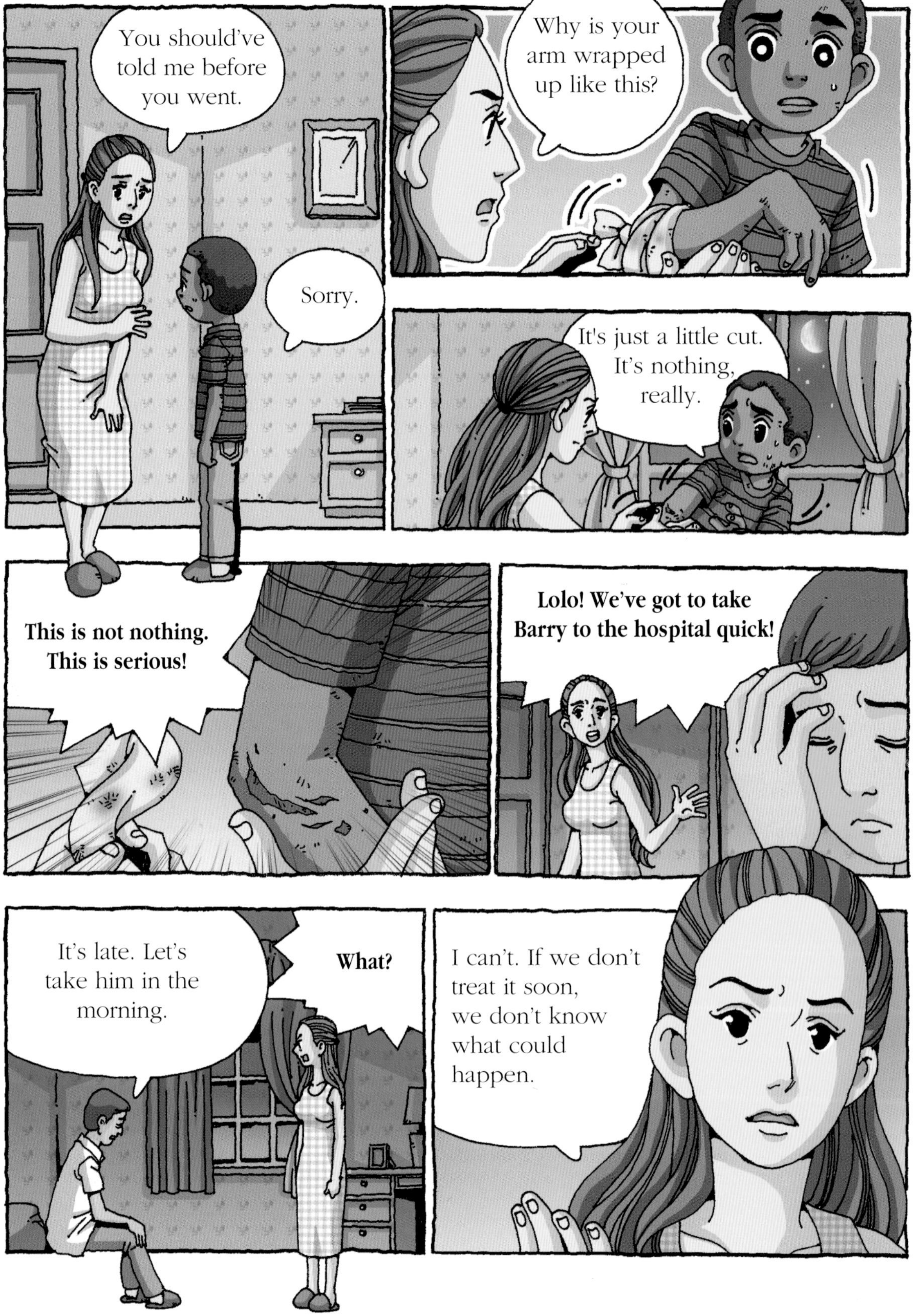

You should've told me before you went.
Sorry.
Why is your arm wrapped up like this?
It's just a little cut. It's nothing, really.
This is not nothing. This is serious!
Lolo! We've got to take Barry to the hospital quick!
It's late. Let's take him in the morning.
What?
I can't. If we don't treat it soon, we don't know what could happen.

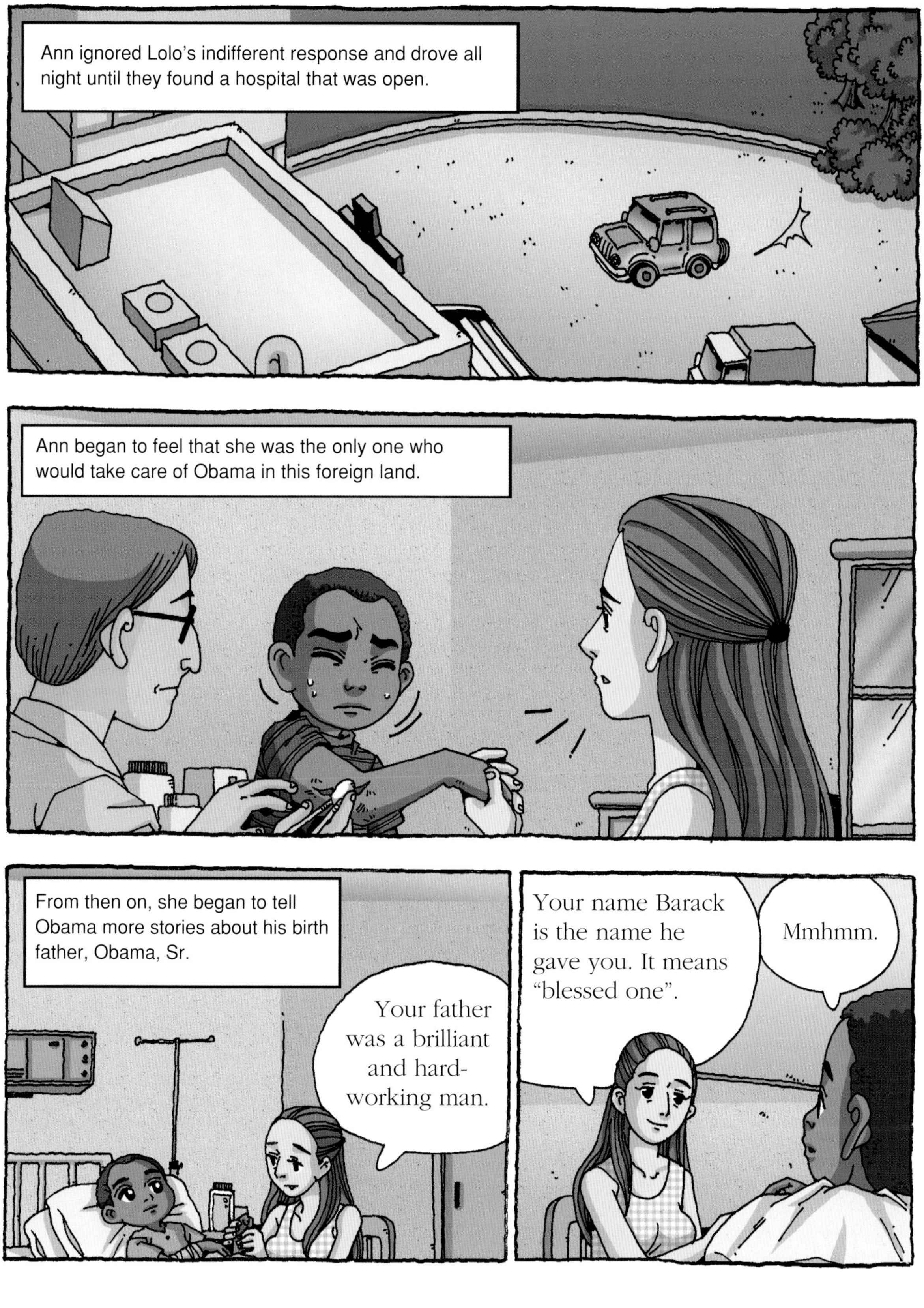
Ann ignored Lolo's indifferent response and drove all night until they found a hospital that was open.
Ann began to feel that she was the only one who would take care of Obama in this foreign land.
From then on, she began to tell Obama more stories about his birth father, Obama, Sr.
Your father was a brilliant and hard-working man.
Your name Barack is the name he gave you. It means "blessed one".
Mmhmm.

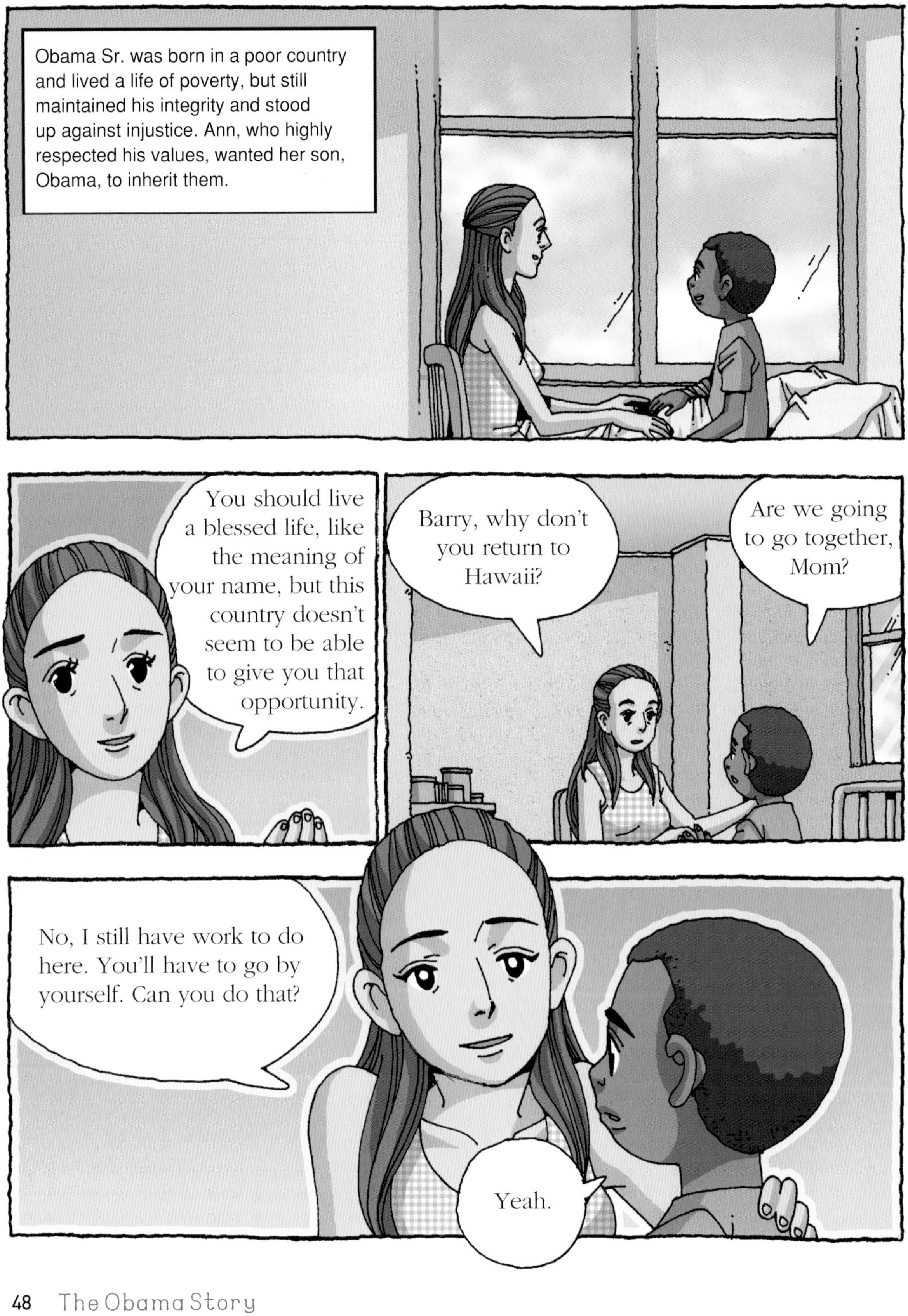
Obama Sr. was born in a poor country and lived a life of poverty, but still maintained his integrity and stood up against injustice. Ann, who highly respected his values, wanted her son, Obama, to inherit them.
You should live a blessed life, like the meaning of your name, but this country doesn't seem to be able to give you that opportunity.
Barry, why don't you return to Hawaii?
Are we going to go together, Mom?
No, I still have work to do here. You'll have to go by yourself. Can you do that?
Yeah.

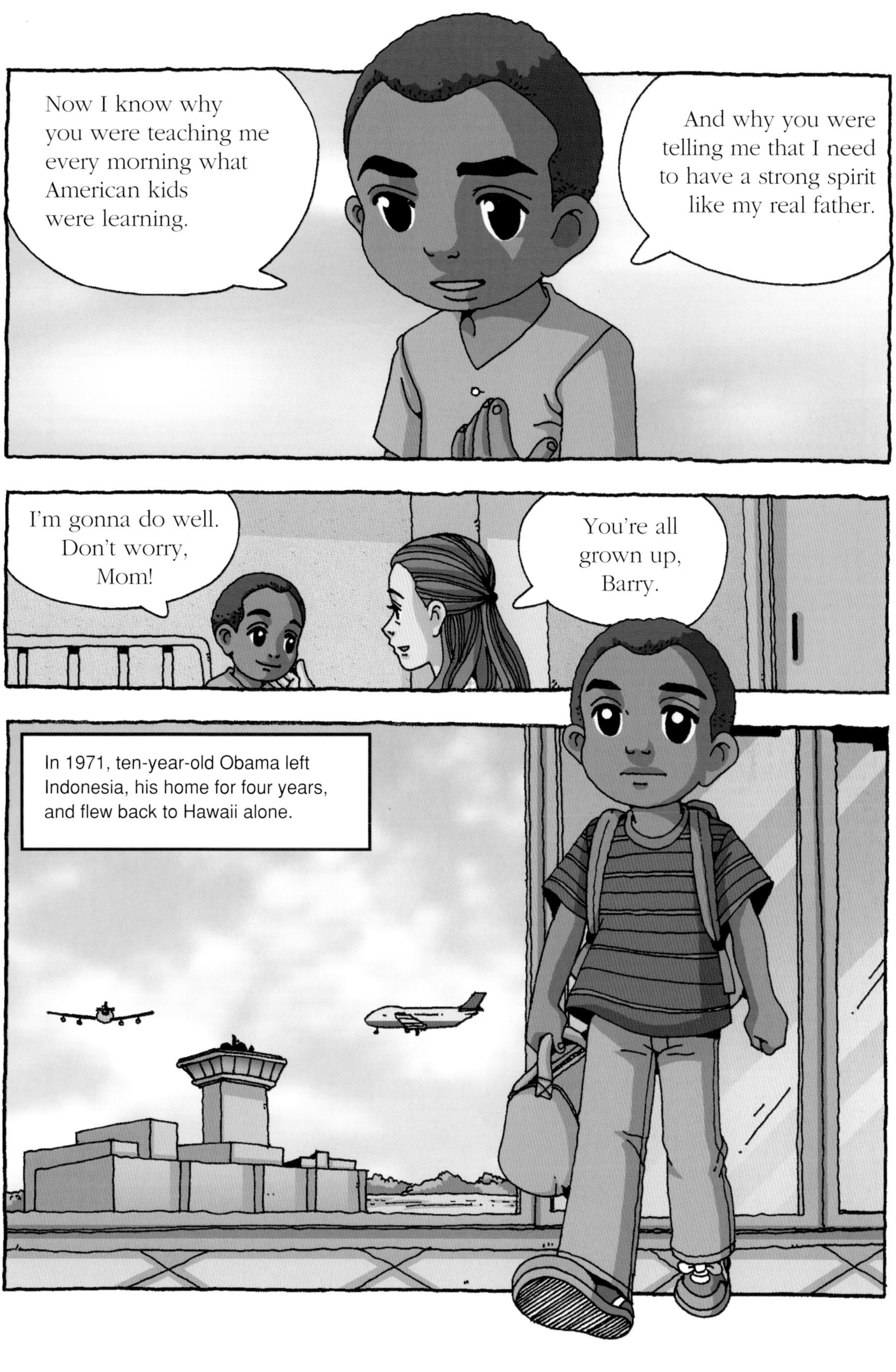
Now I know why you were teaching me every morning what American kids were learning.
And why you were telling me that I need to have a strong spirit like my real father.
I'm gonna do well. Don't worry, Mom!
You're all grown up, Barry.
In 1971, ten-year-old Obama left Indonesia, his home for four years, and flew back to Hawaii alone.

People who have influenced Obama 2

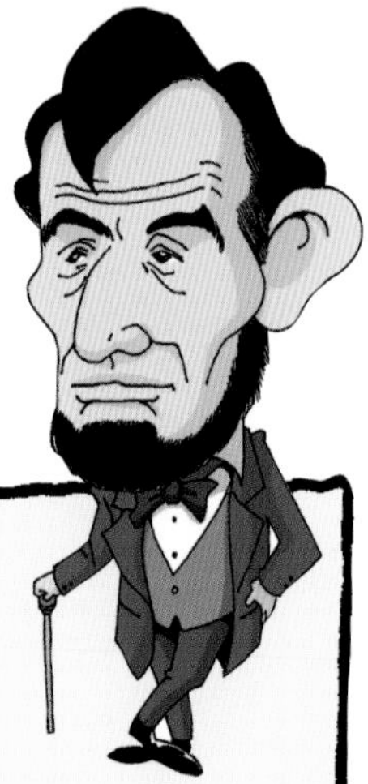

Abraham Lincoln

Abraham Lincoln is one of the most beloved presidents of the American people. He was born on February 12, 1809 in a small log cabin in Kentucky to a poor shoemaker. He was so poor that he couldn't even finish elementary school. Since he couldn't go to school, he studied diligently on his own. He even walked several hours to a distant town once in order to get a book for his studies.

Although Lincoln never had a formal education, he was able to pass the bar exam because of the extensive reading he had done on his own. In 1834, he started his political career when he won a seat in the Illinois Senate. And in March, 1861, he was elected America's 16th president.

If one examines the life of someone as successful as Lincoln, one would find a series of failures in the beginning of his life. Lincoln failed in business and lost many elections. But these setbacks did not get Lincoln down. He was able to overcome them with his endless efforts, integrity and faith.

Overcoming difficulties and eventually becoming president, Abraham Lincoln accomplished much in his life. Believing that all people were created equal, he abolished slavery, laid the foundation for American democracy, and improved the administration of many government organizations. Abraham Lincoln is America's most beloved president and a model for many politicians.

Chapter 3

Facing Discrimination

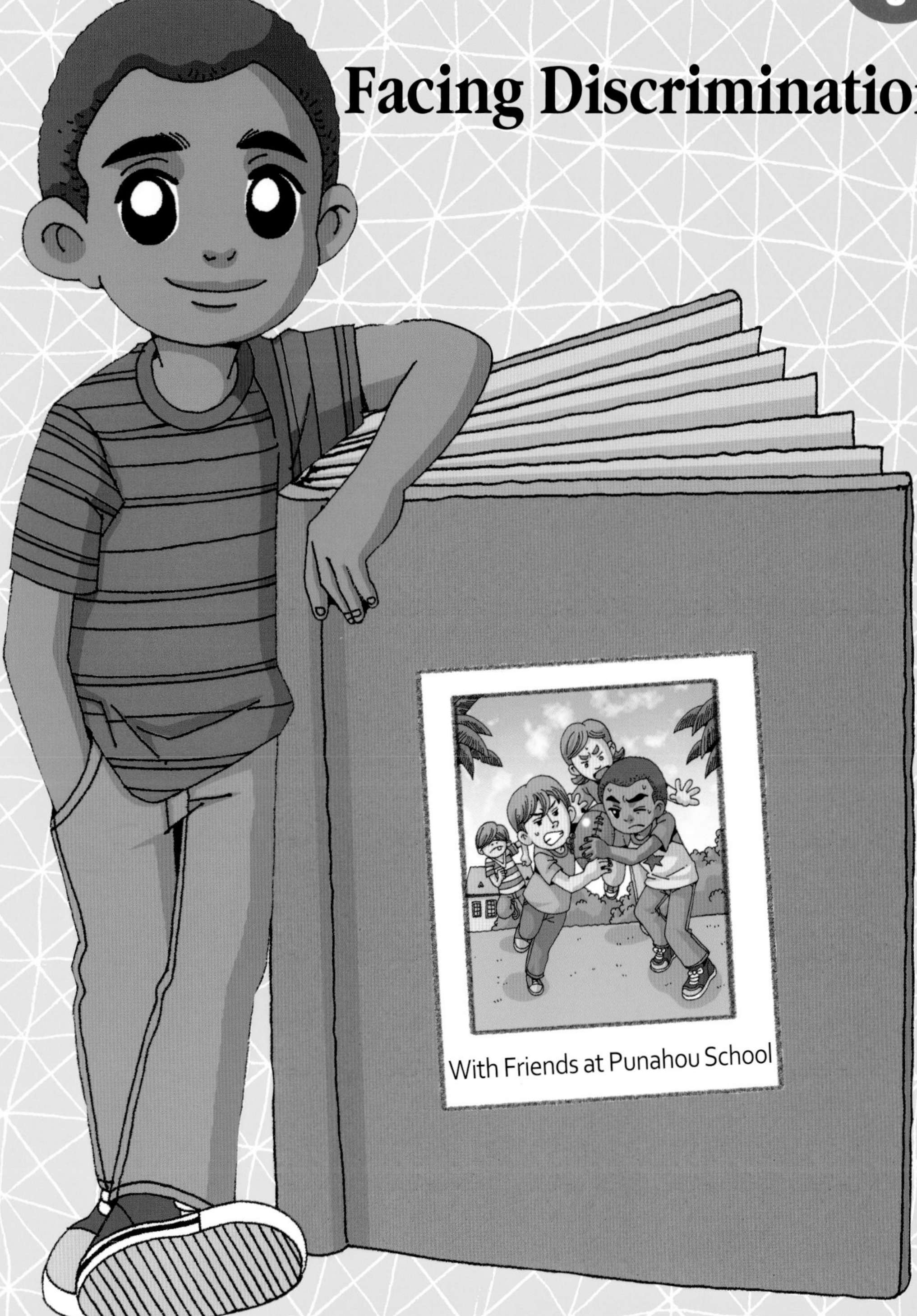
With Friends at Punahou School

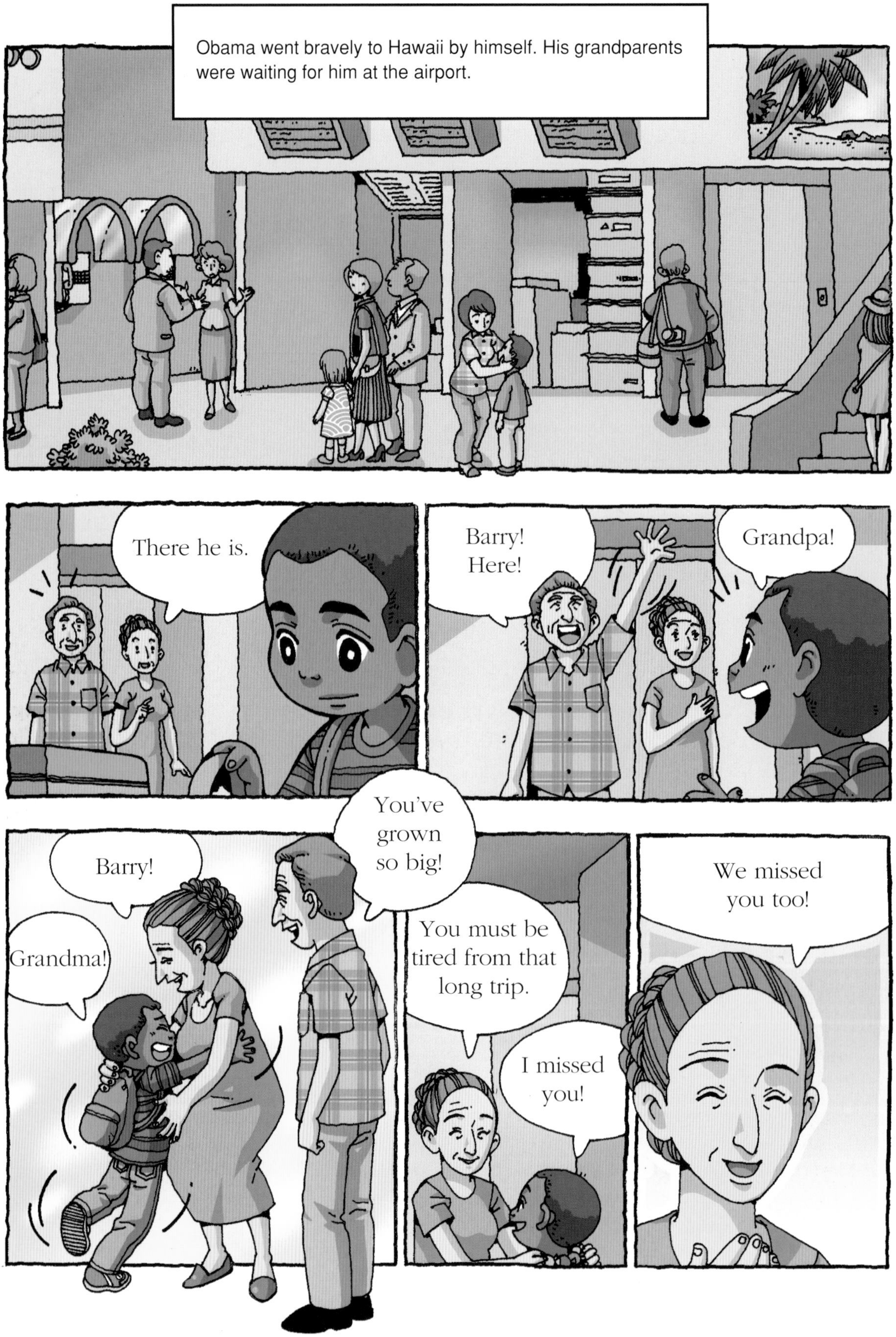
Obama went bravely to Hawaii by himself. His grandparents were waiting for him at the airport.
There he is.
Barry! Here!
Grandpa!
Barry!
Grandma!
You've grown so big!
You must be tired from that long trip.
I missed you!
We missed you too!

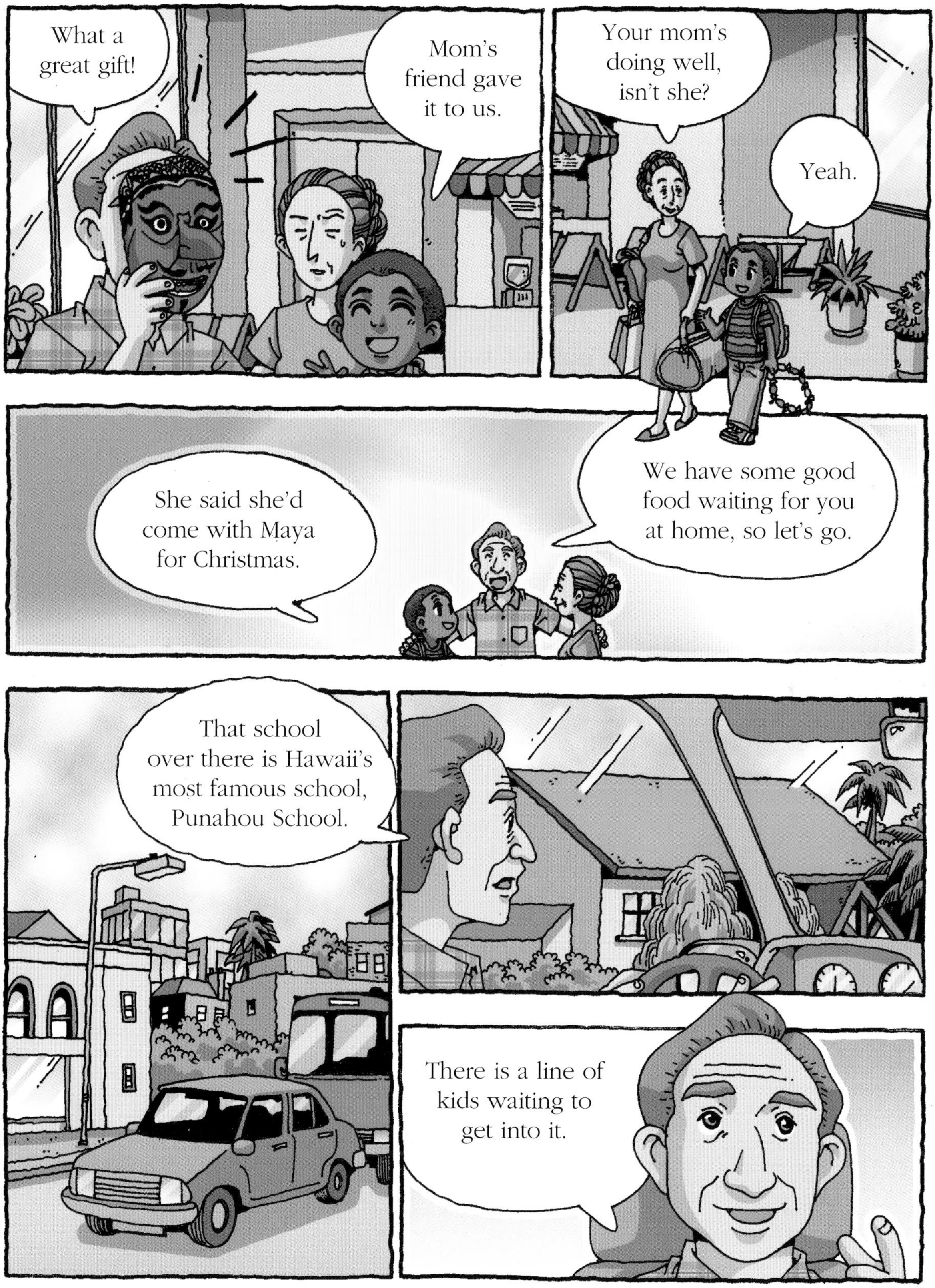
What a great gift!
Mom's friend gave it to us.
Your mom's doing well, isn't she?
Yeah.
We have some good food waiting for you at home, so let's go.
She said she'd come with Maya for Christmas.
That school over there is Hawaii's most famous school, Punahou School.
There is a line of kids waiting to get into it.

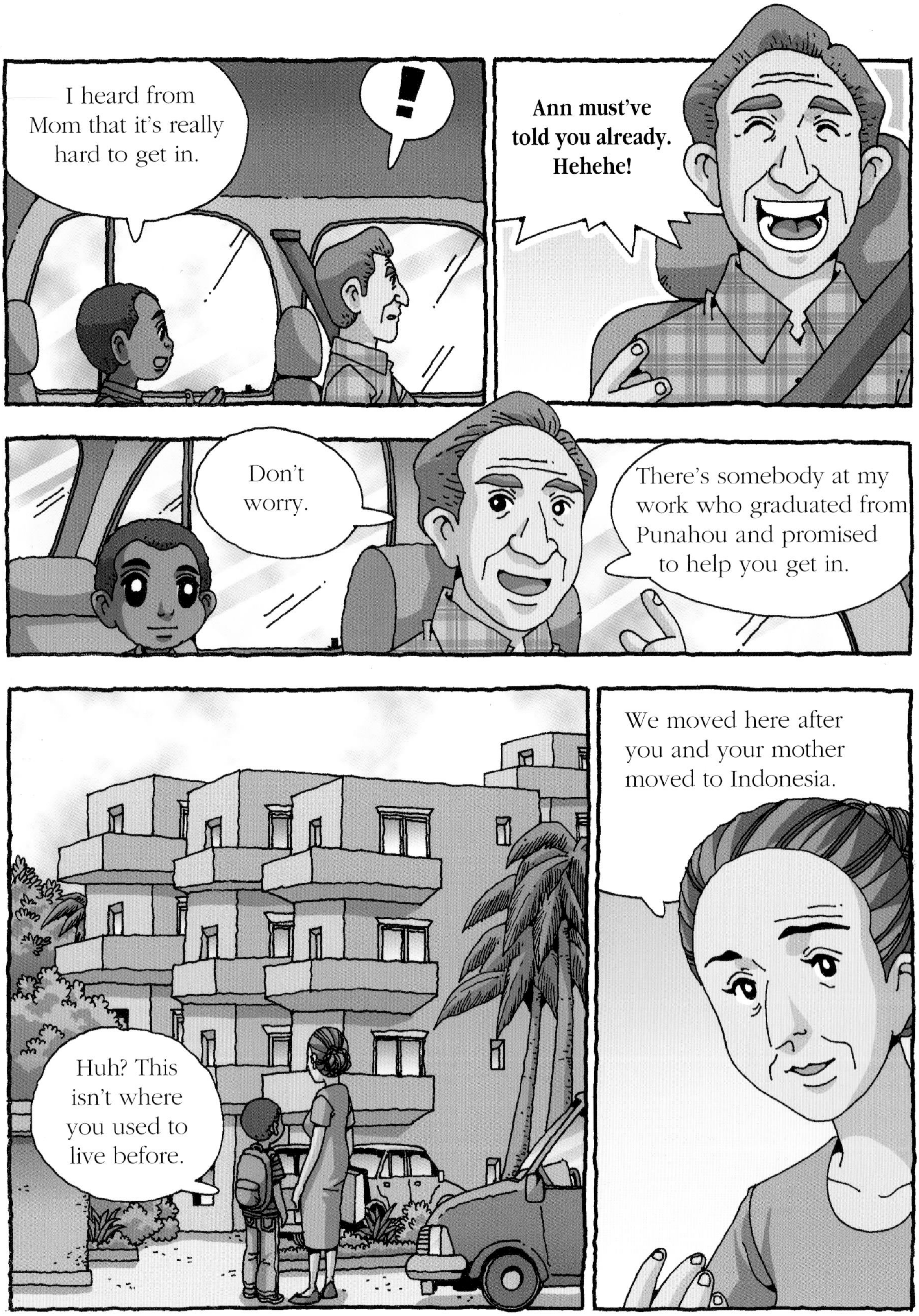
I heard from Mom that it's really hard to get in.
!
Ann must've told you already. Hehehe!
Don't worry.
There's somebody at my work who graduated from Punahou and promised to help you get in.
Huh? This isn't where you used to live before.
We moved here after you and your mother moved to Indonesia.

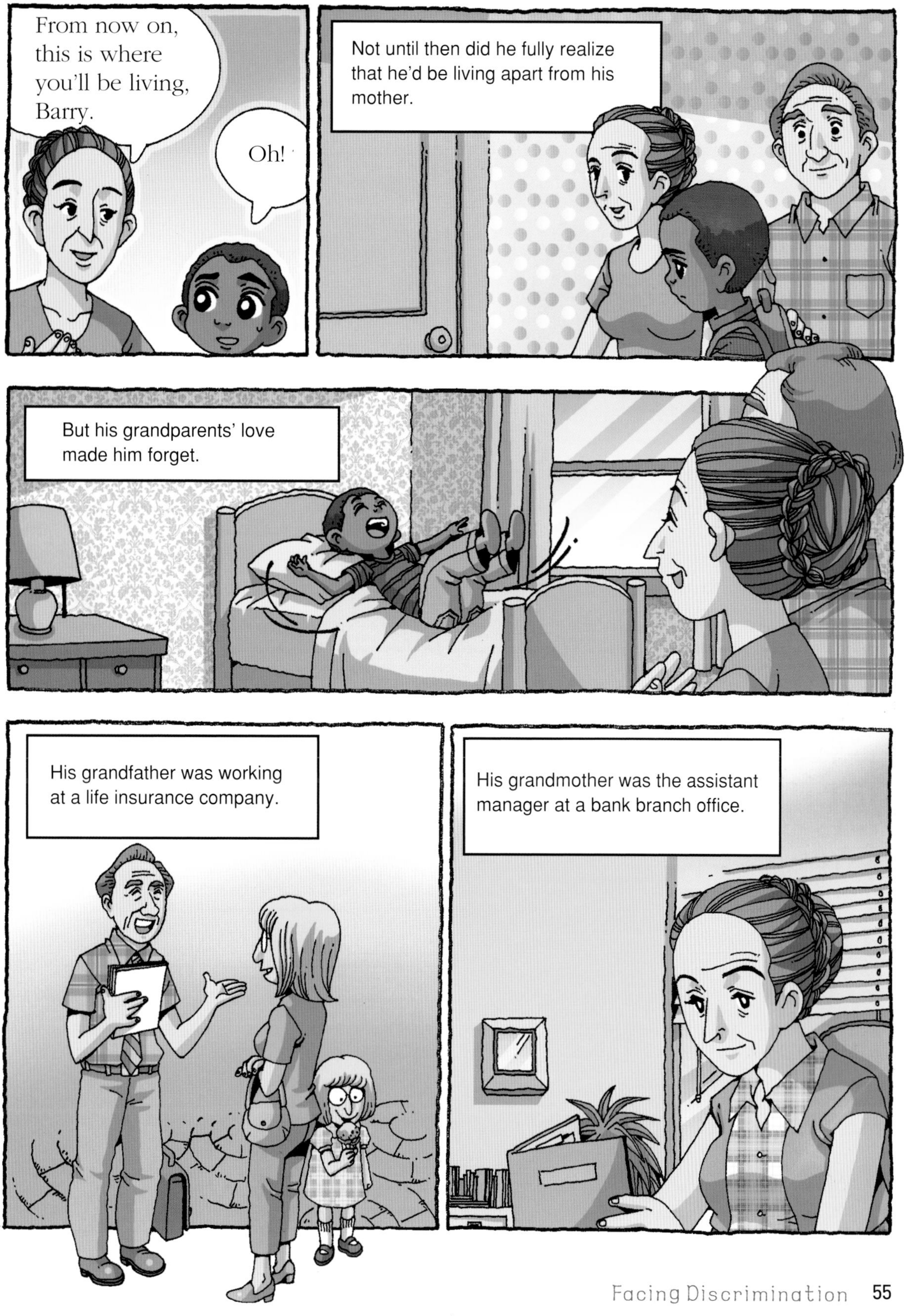

From now on, this is where you'll be living, Barry.
Oh!
Not until then did he fully realize that he'd be living apart from his mother.
But his grandparents' love made him forget.
His grandfather was working at a life insurance company.
His grandmother was the assistant manager at a bank branch office.

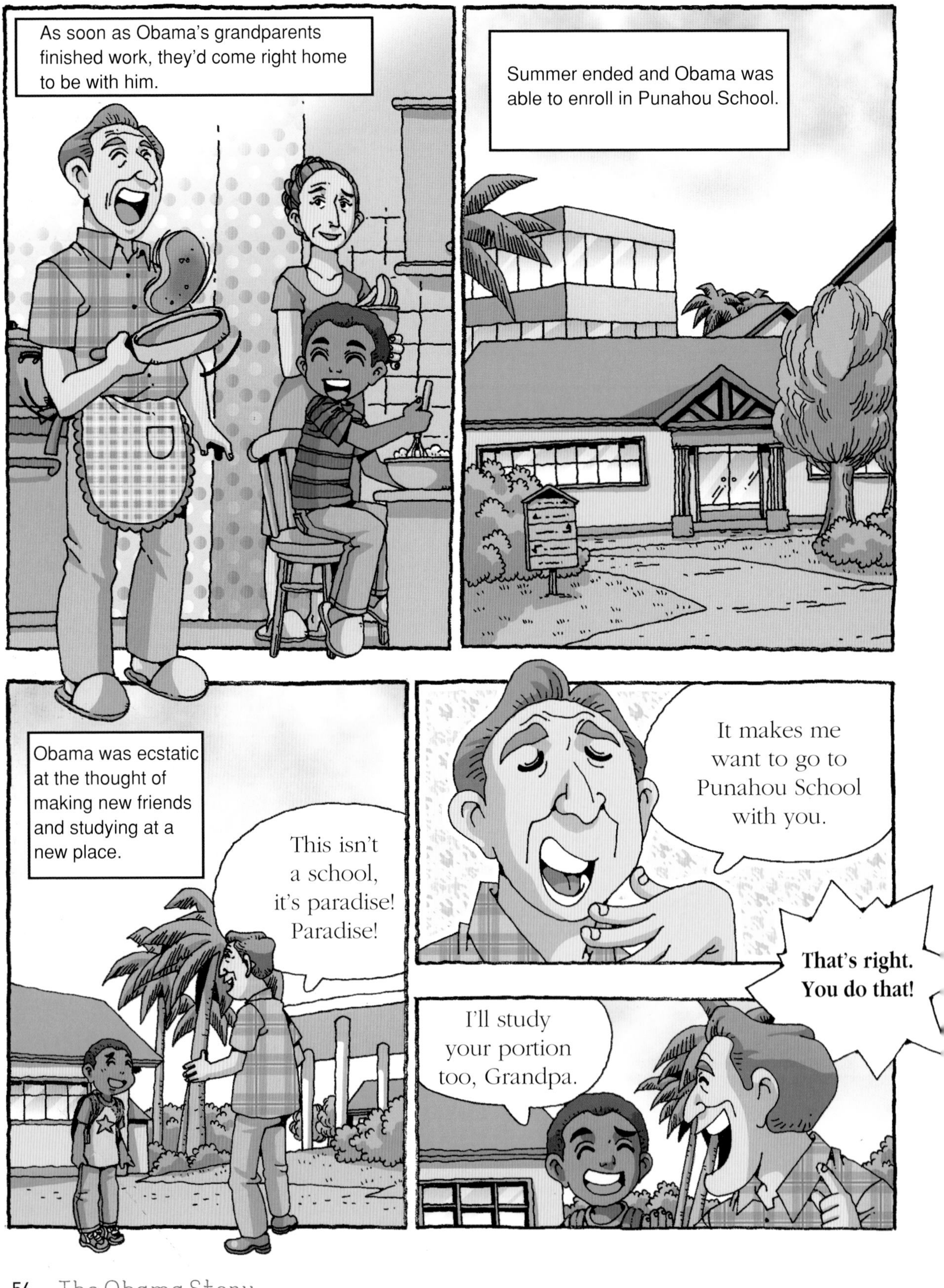
As soon as Obama's grandparents finished work, they'd come right home to be with him.
Summer ended and Obama was able to enroll in Punahou School.
Obama was ecstatic at the thought of making new friends and studying at a new place.
This isn't a school, it's paradise! Paradise!
It makes me want to go to Punahou School with you.
I'll study your portion too, Grandpa.
That's right. You do that!

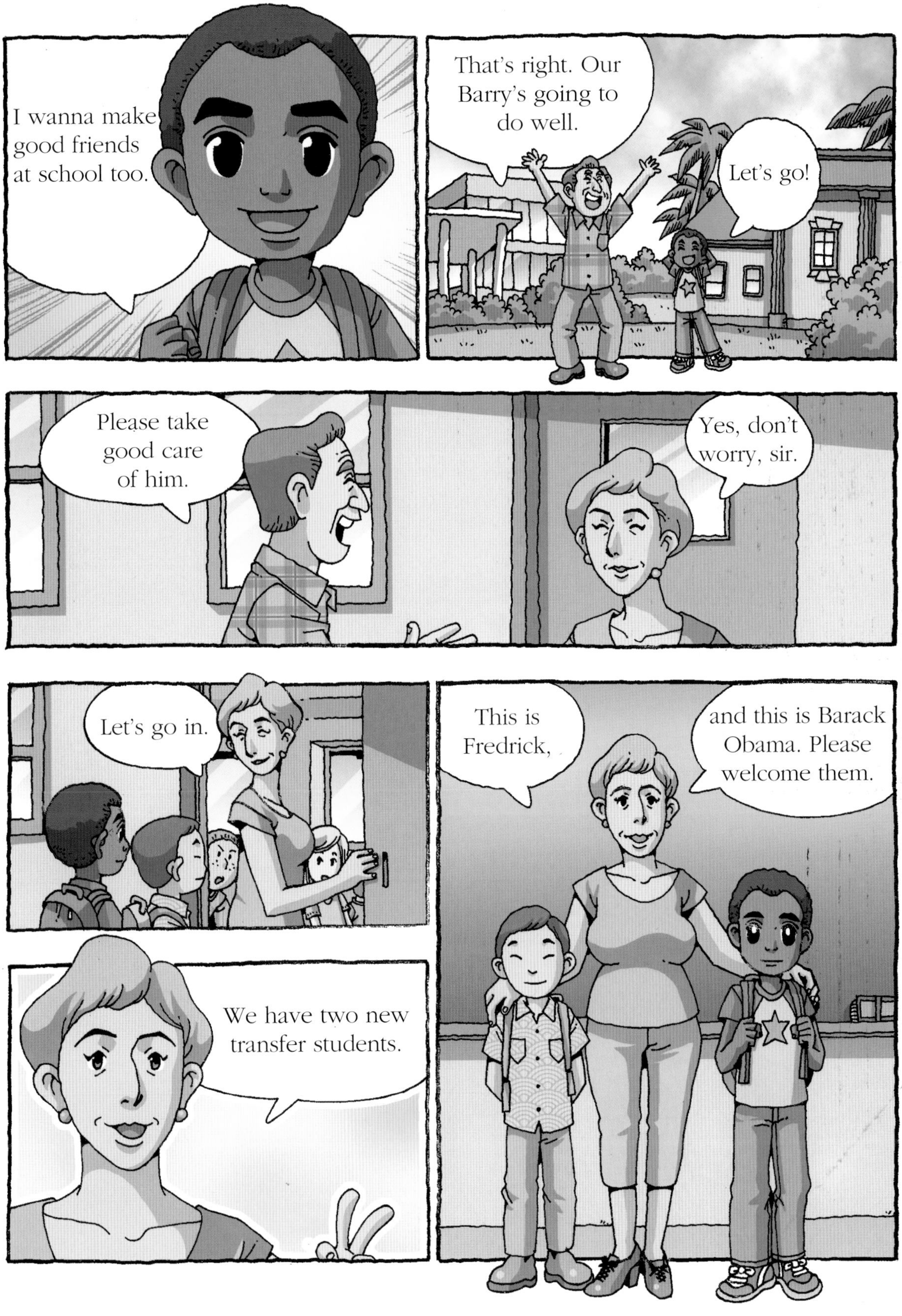
I wanna make good friends at school too.
That's right. Our Barry's going to do well.
Let's go!
Please take good care of him.
Yes, don't worry, sir.
Let's go in.
We have two new transfer students.
This is Fredrick,
and this is Barack Obama. Please welcome them.

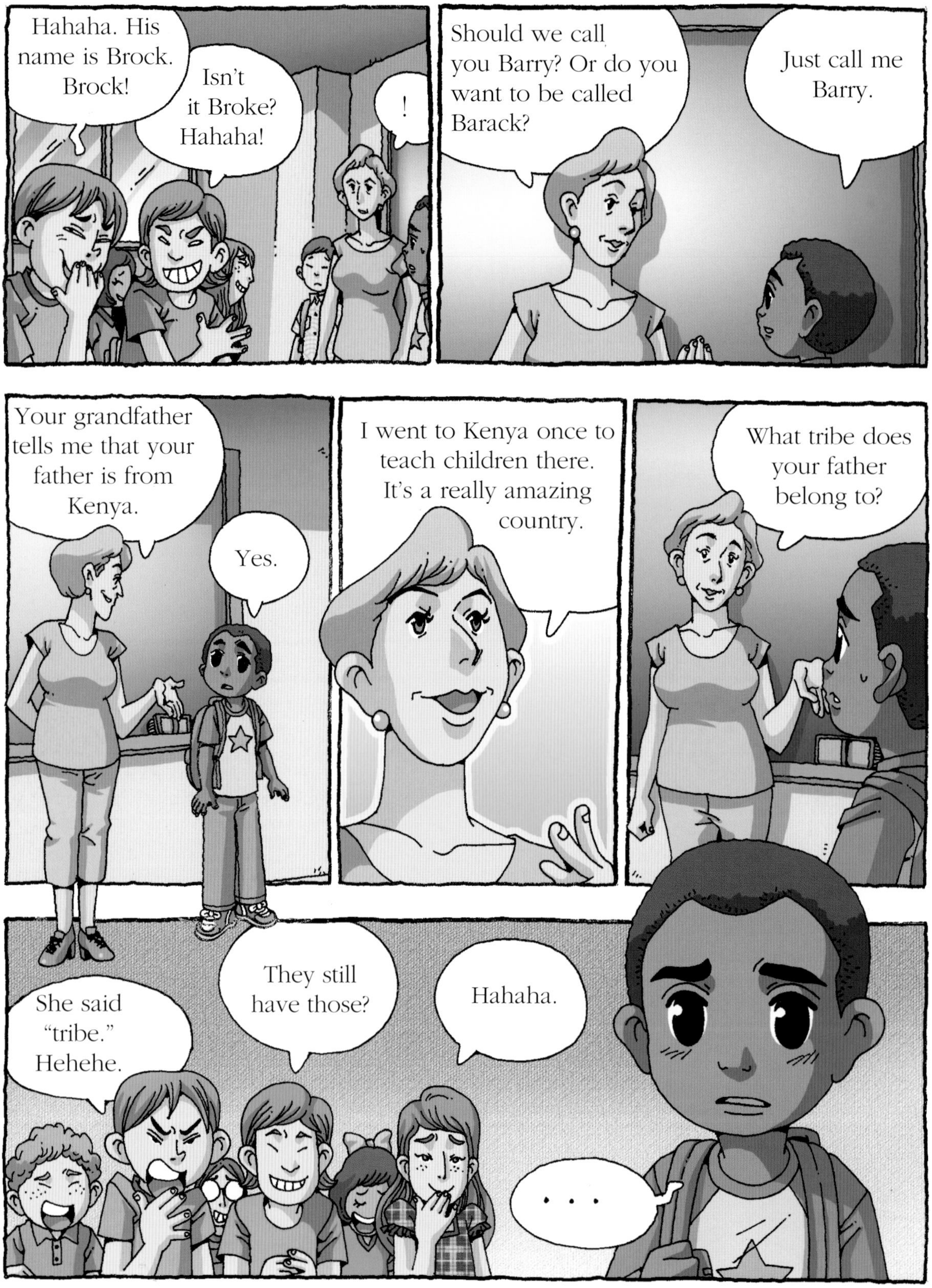

Hahaha. His name is Brock. Brock!
Isn't it Broke? Hahaha!
!
Should we call you Barry? Or do you want to be called Barack?
Just call me Barry.
Your grandfather tells me that your father is from Kenya.
Yes.
I went to Kenya once to teach children there. It's a really amazing country.
What tribe does your father belong to?
She said "tribe." Hehehe.
They still have those?
Hahaha.
. . .

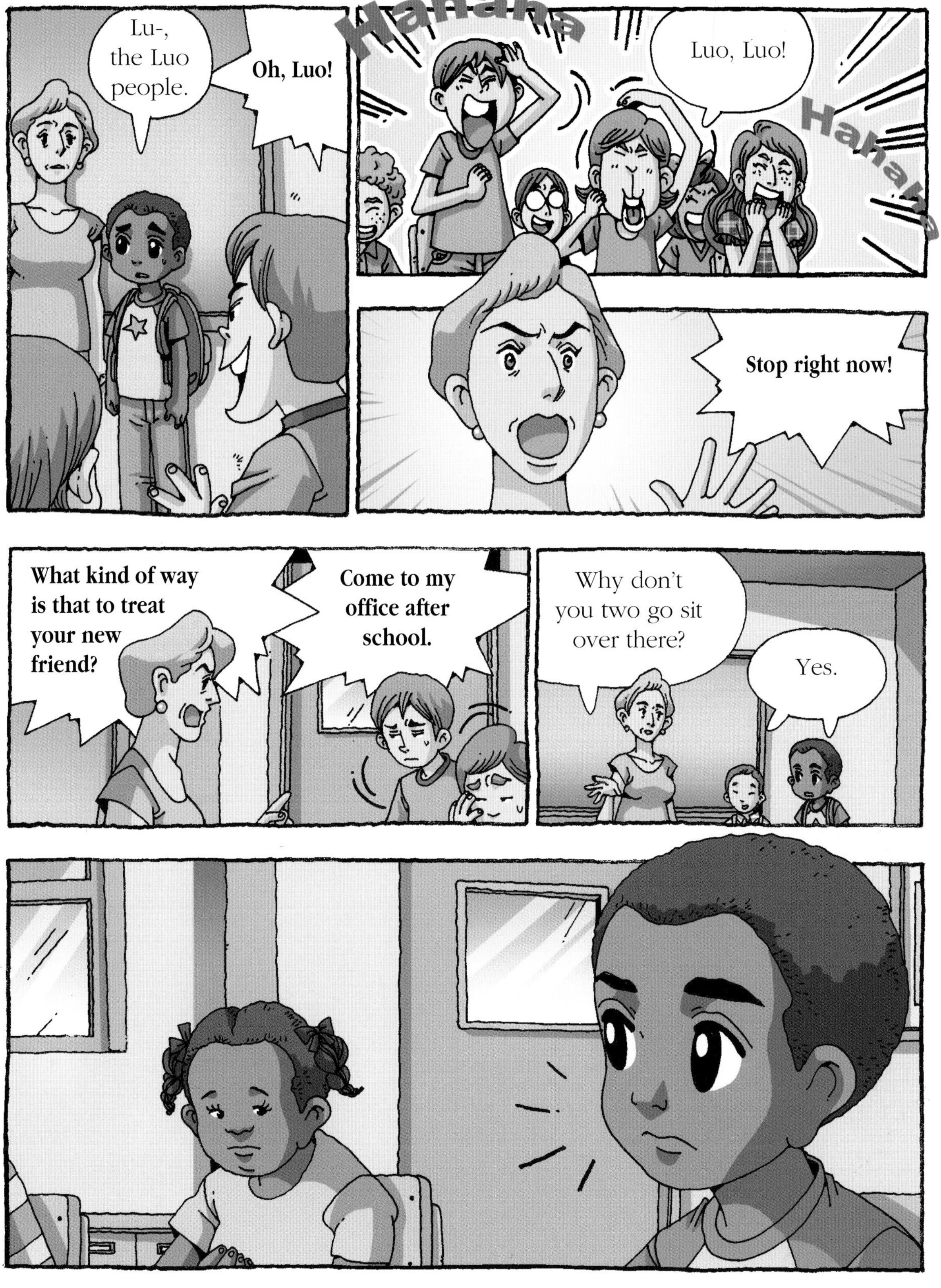
Lu-, the Luo people.
Oh, Luo!
Hahaha
Luo, Luo!
Hahaha
Stop right now!
What kind of way is that to treat your new friend?
Come to my office after school.
Why don't you two go sit over there?
Yes.

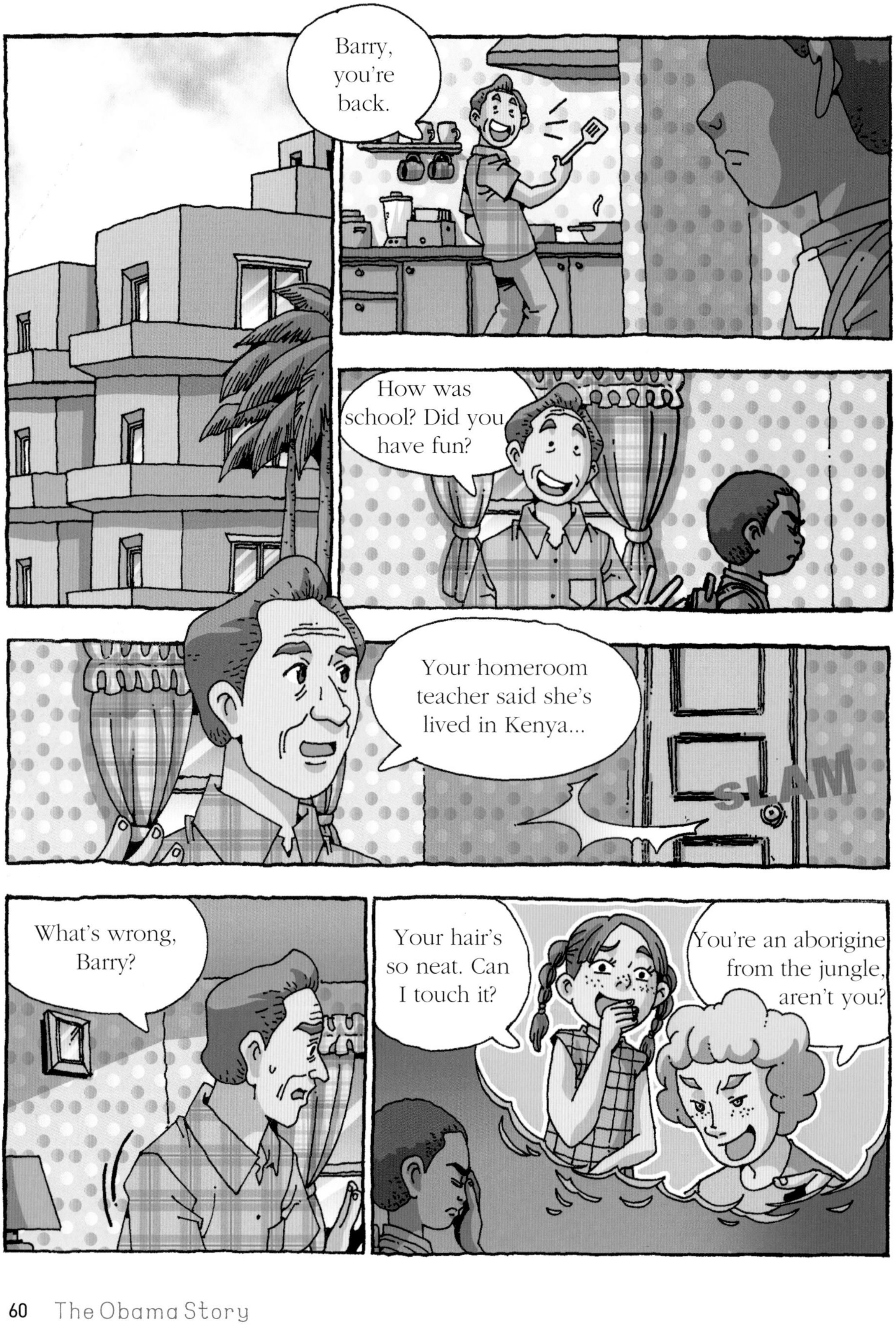
Barry, you're back.
How was school? Did you have fun?
Your homeroom teacher said she's lived in Kenya...
SLAM
What's wrong, Barry?
Your hair's so neat. Can I touch it?
You're an aborigine from the jungle, aren't you?

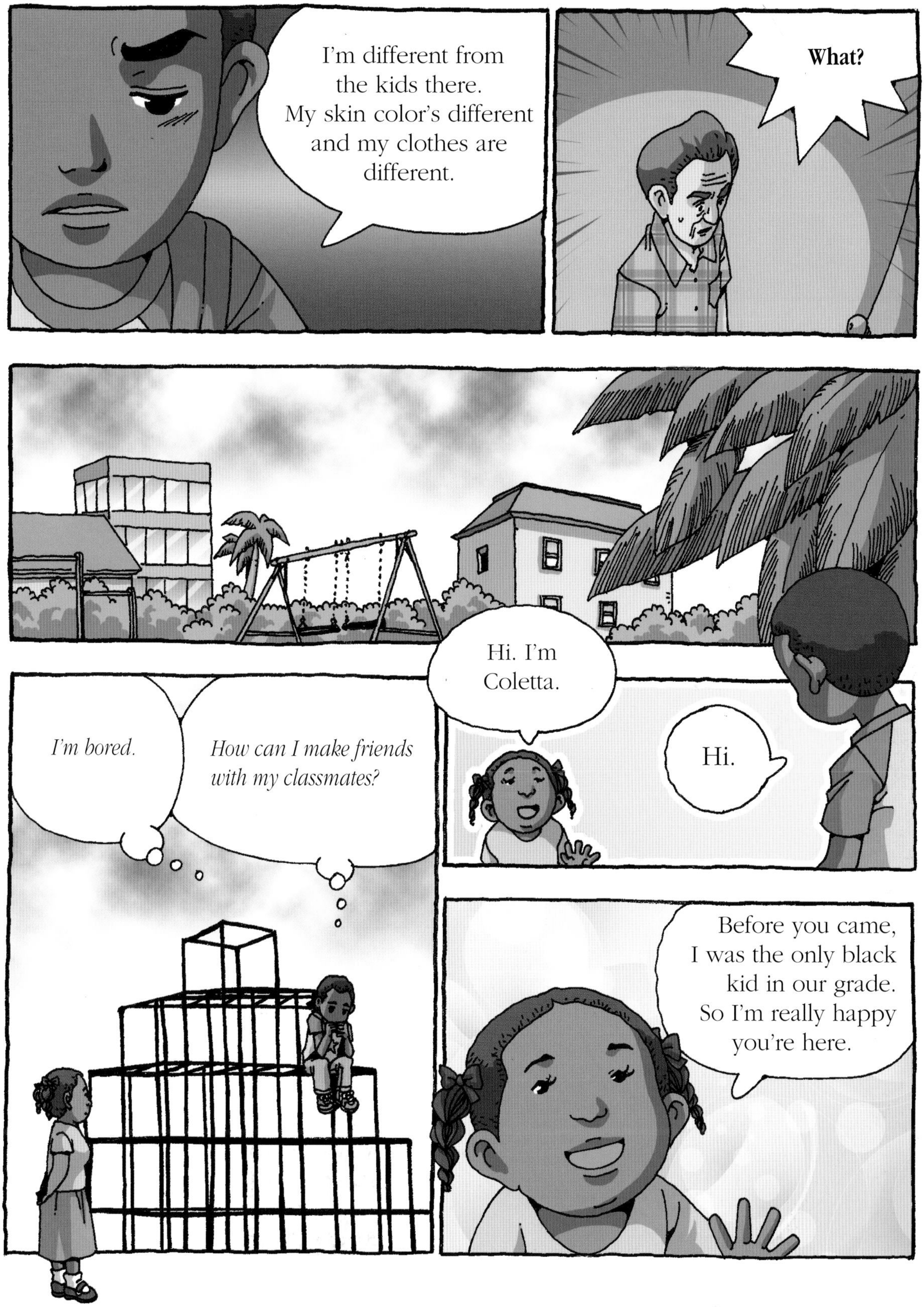
I'm different from the kids there. My skin color's different and my clothes are different.
What?
I'm bored.
How can I make friends with my classmates?
Hi. I'm Coletta.
Hi.
Before you came, I was the only black kid in our grade. So I'm really happy you're here.

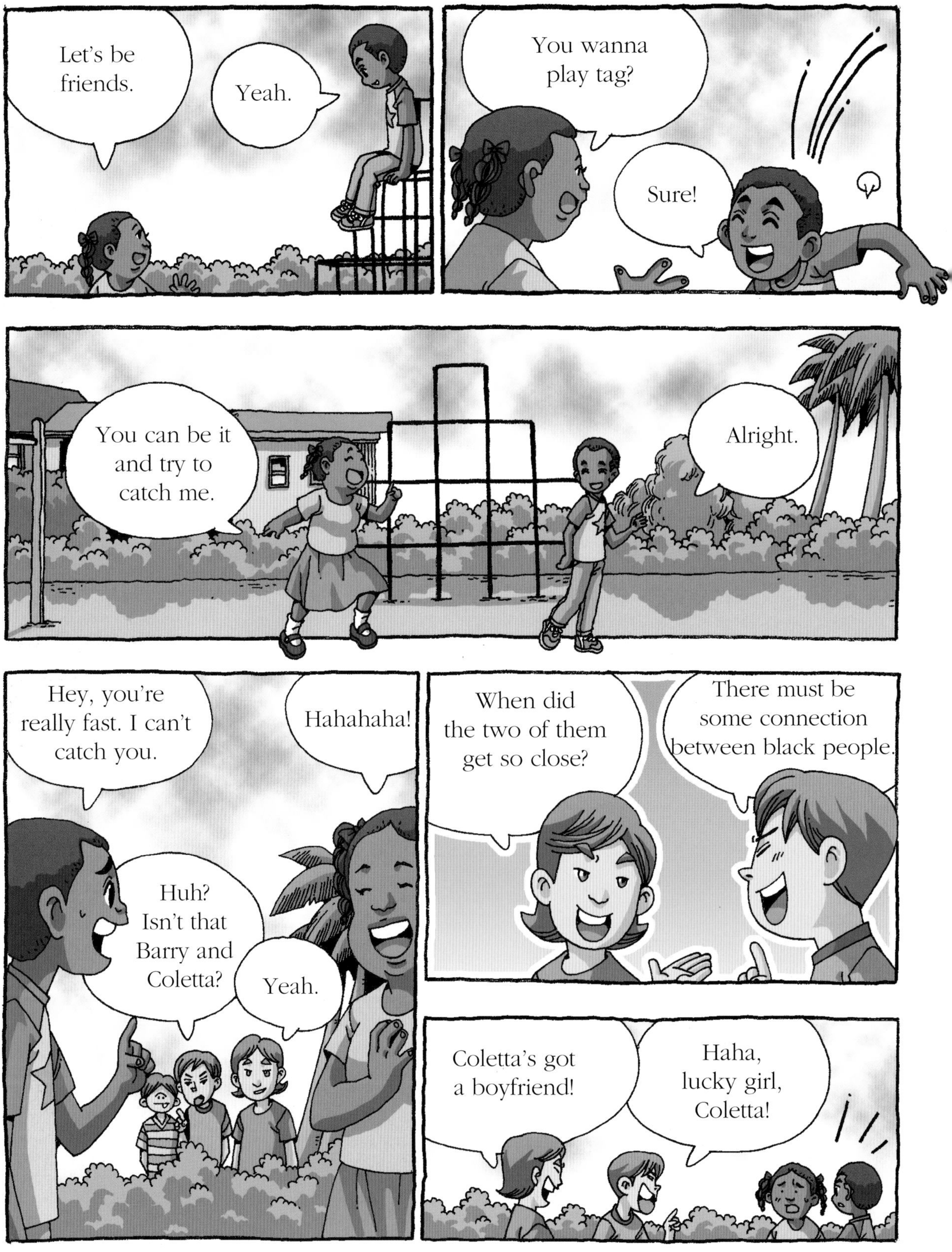
Let's be friends.
Yeah.
You wanna play tag?
Sure!
You can be it and try to catch me.
Alright.
Hey, you're really fast. I can't catch you.
Hahahaha!
Huh? Isn't that Barry and Coletta?
Yeah.
When did the two of them get so close?
There must be some connection between black people.
Coletta's got a boyfriend!
Haha, lucky girl, Coletta!

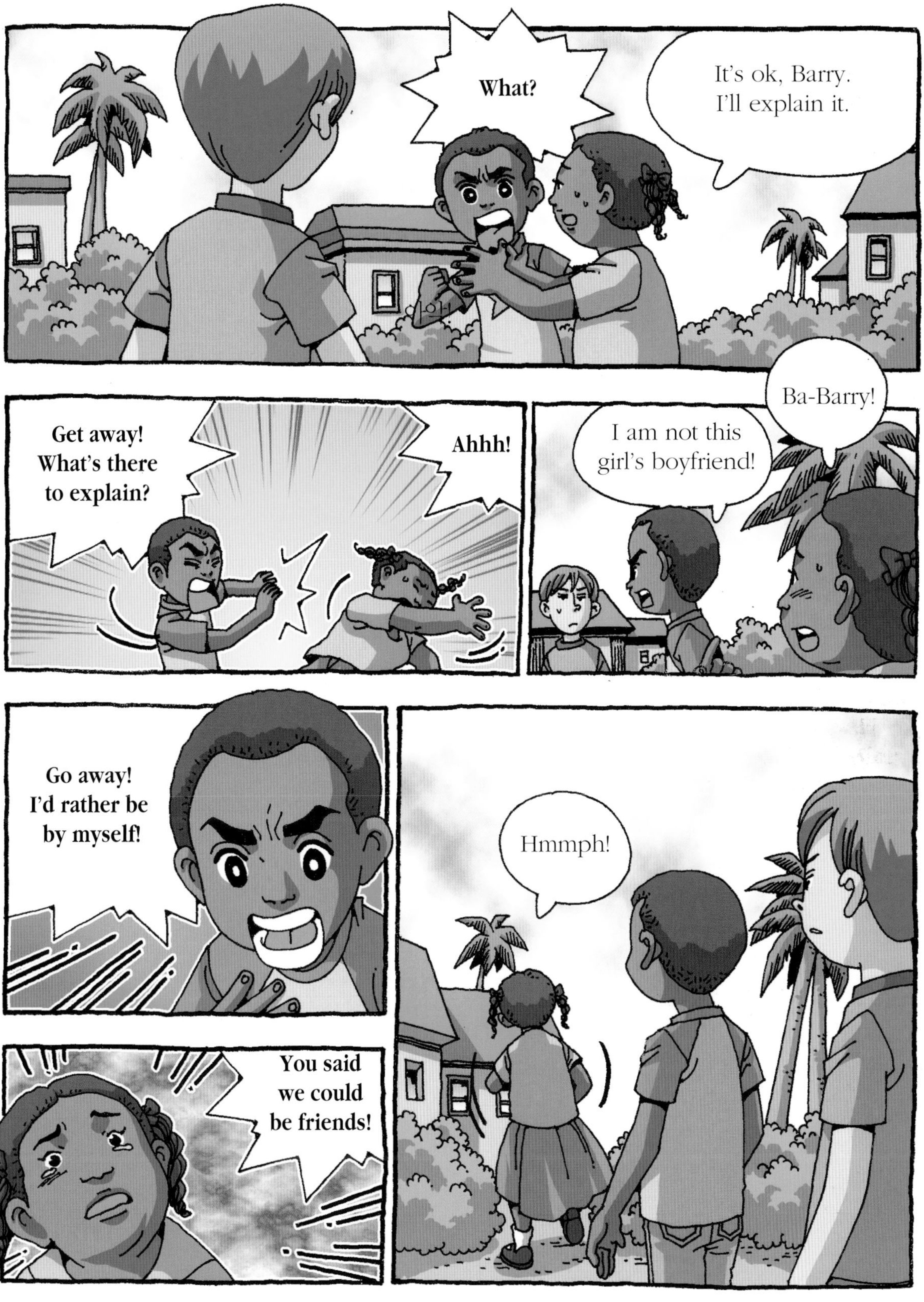
What?
It's ok, Barry. I'll explain it.
Get away! What's there to explain?
Ahhh!
Ba-Barry!
I am not this girl's boyfriend!
Go away! I'd rather be by myself!
You said we could be friends!
Hmmph!

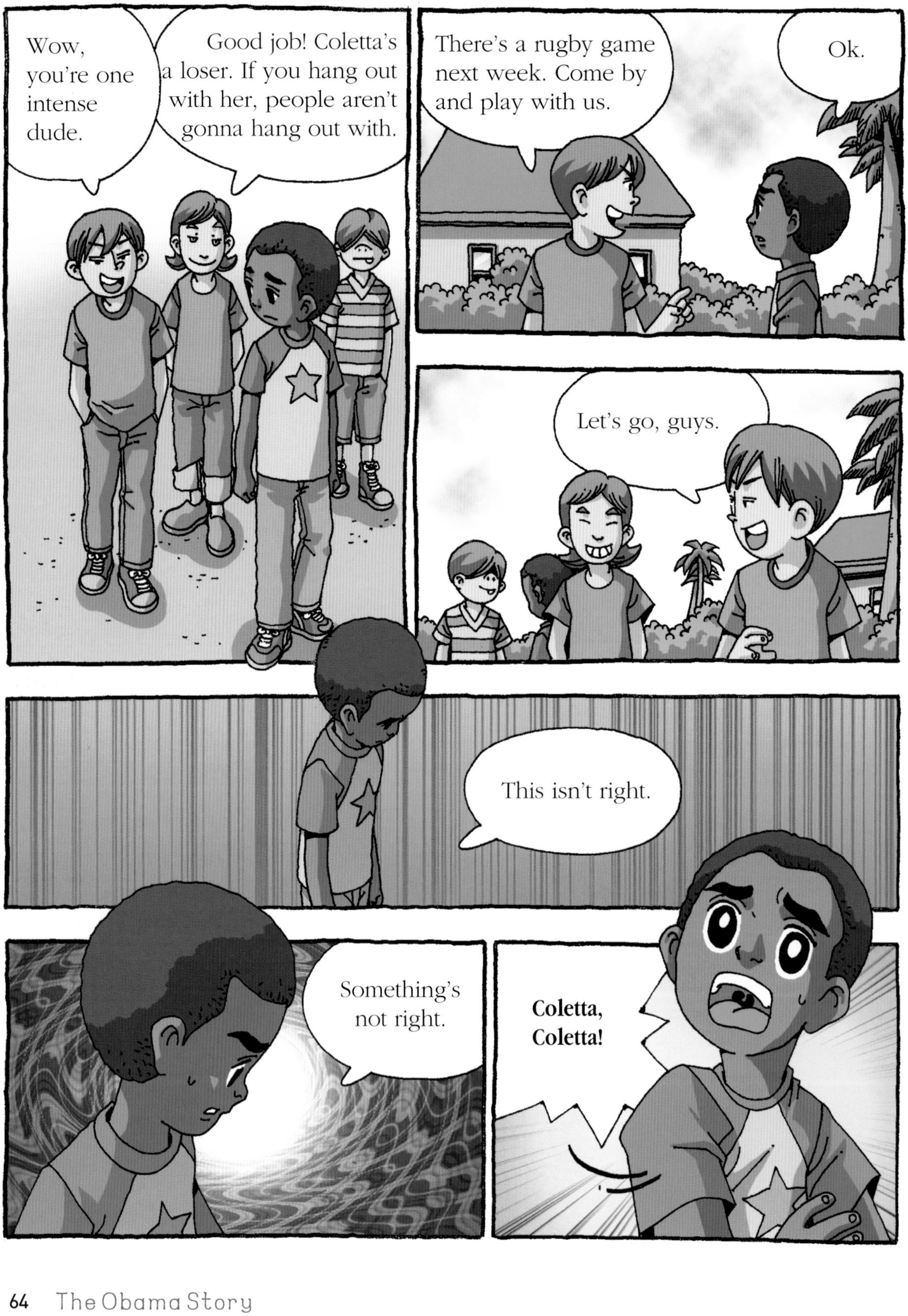
Wow, you're one intense dude.
Good job! Coletta's a loser. If you hang out with her, people aren't gonna hang out with.
There's a rugby game next week. Come by and play with us.
Ok.
Let's go, guys.
This isn't right.
Something's not right.
Coletta, Coletta!

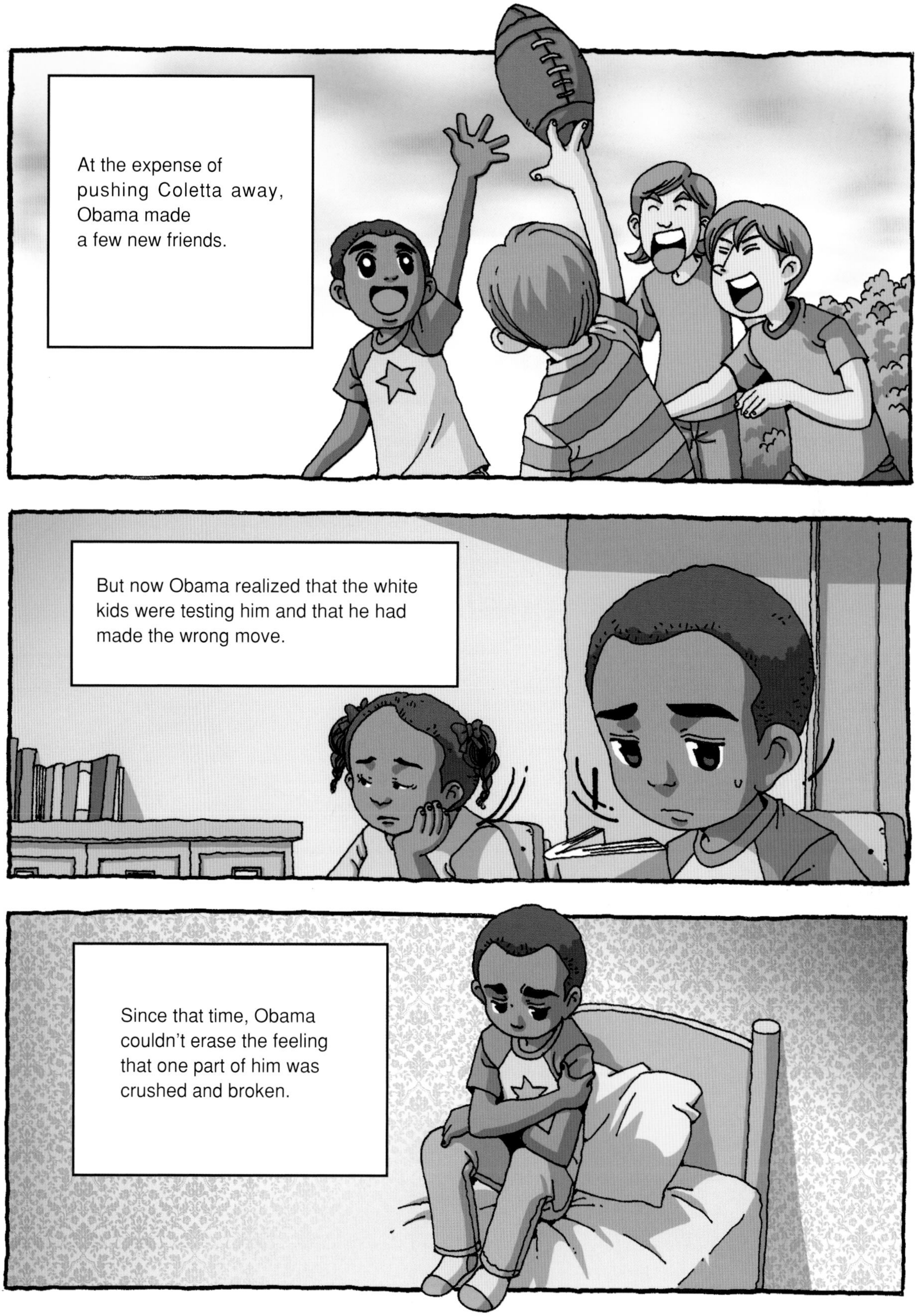
At the expense of pushing Coletta away, Obama made a few new friends.
But now Obama realized that the white kids were testing him and that he had made the wrong move.
Since that time, Obama couldn't erase the feeling that one part of him was crushed and broken.

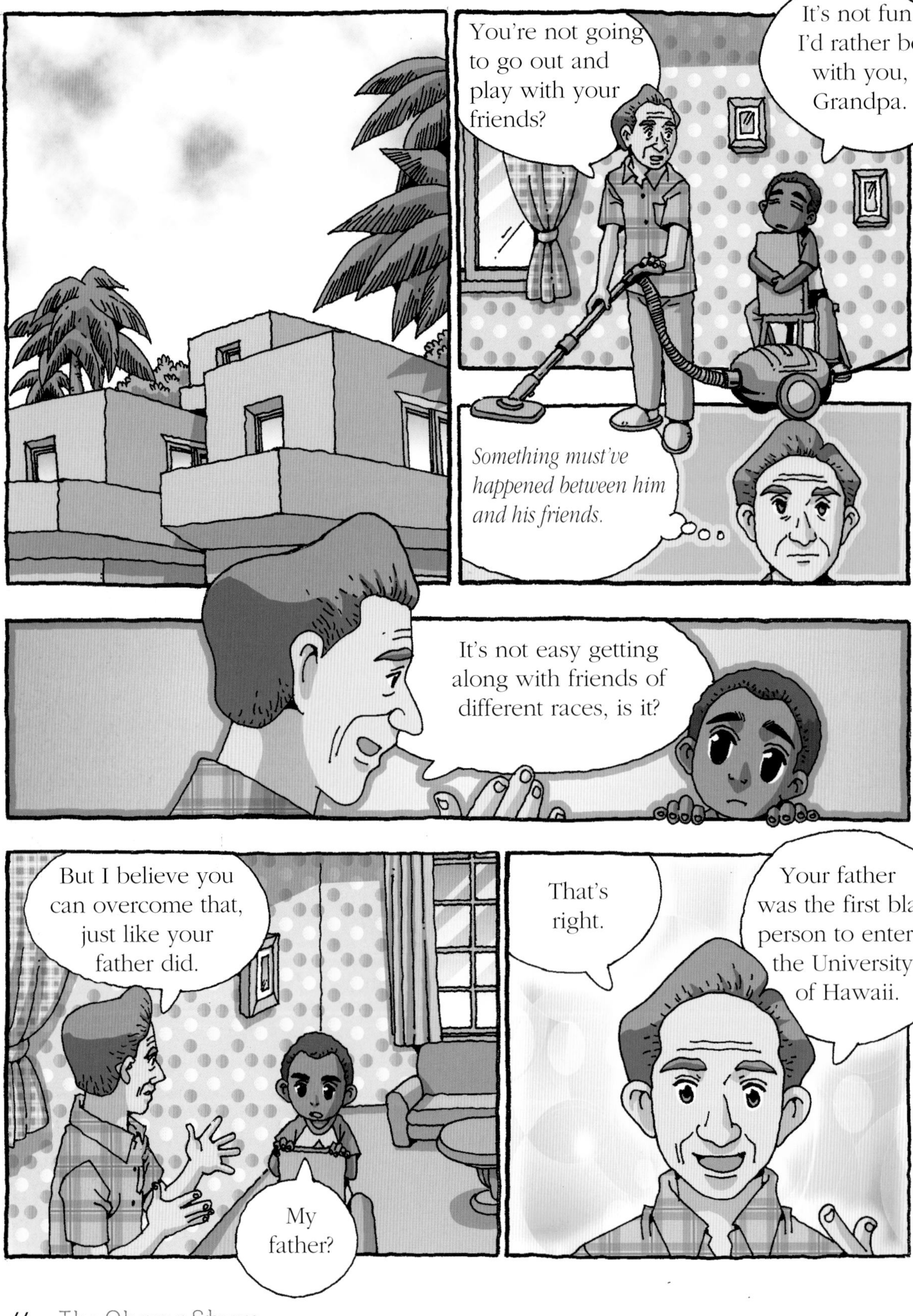
You're not going to go out and play with your friends?
It's not fun. I'd rather be with you, Grandpa.
Something must've happened between him and his friends.
It's not easy getting along with friends of different races, is it?
But I believe you can overcome that, just like your father did.
My father?
That's right.
Your father was the first black person to enter the University of Hawaii.

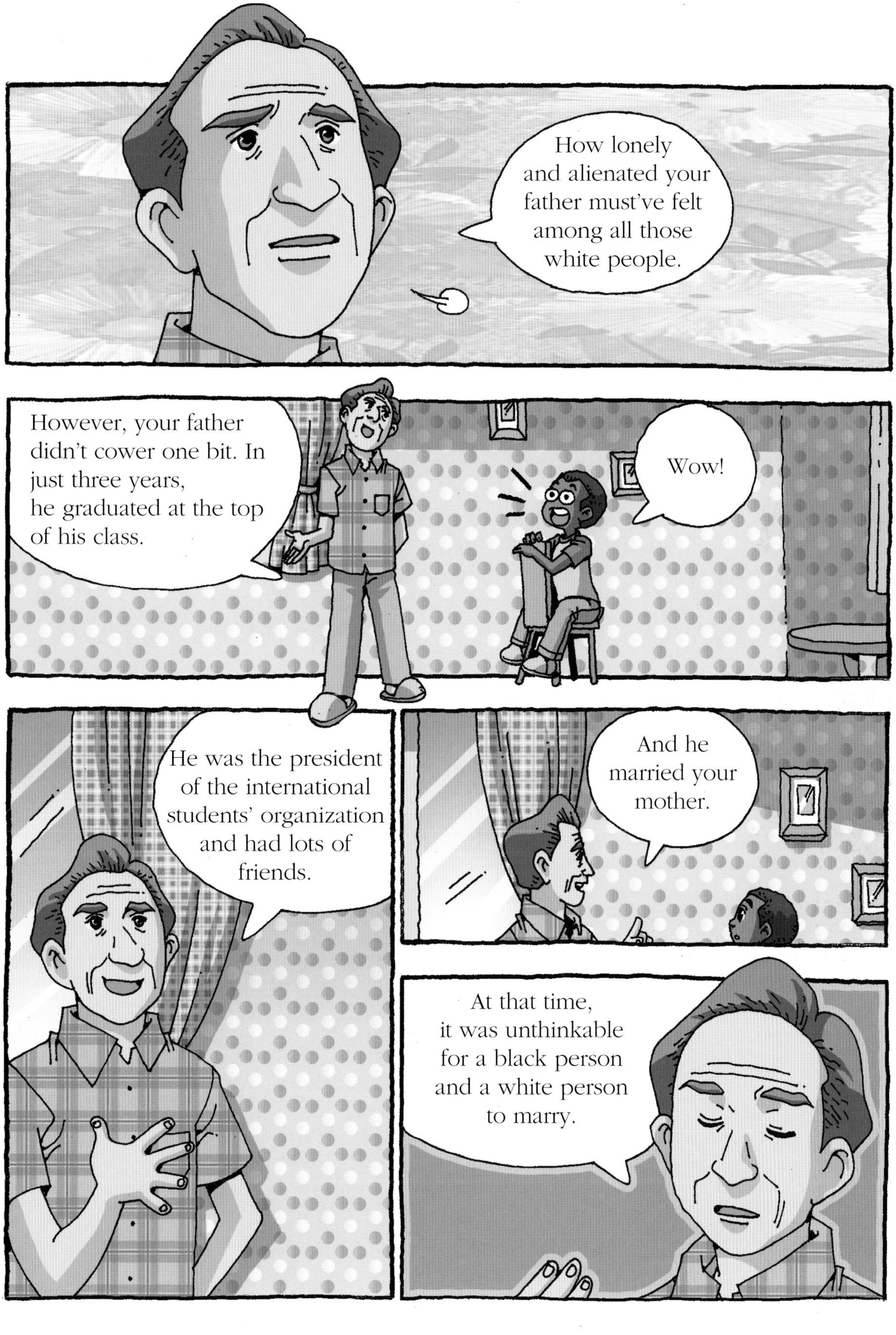
How lonely and alienated your father must've felt among all those white people.
However, your father didn't cower one bit. In just three years, he graduated at the top of his class.
Wow!
He was the president of the international students' organization and had lots of friends.
And he married your mother.
At that time, it was unthinkable for a black person and a white person to marry.

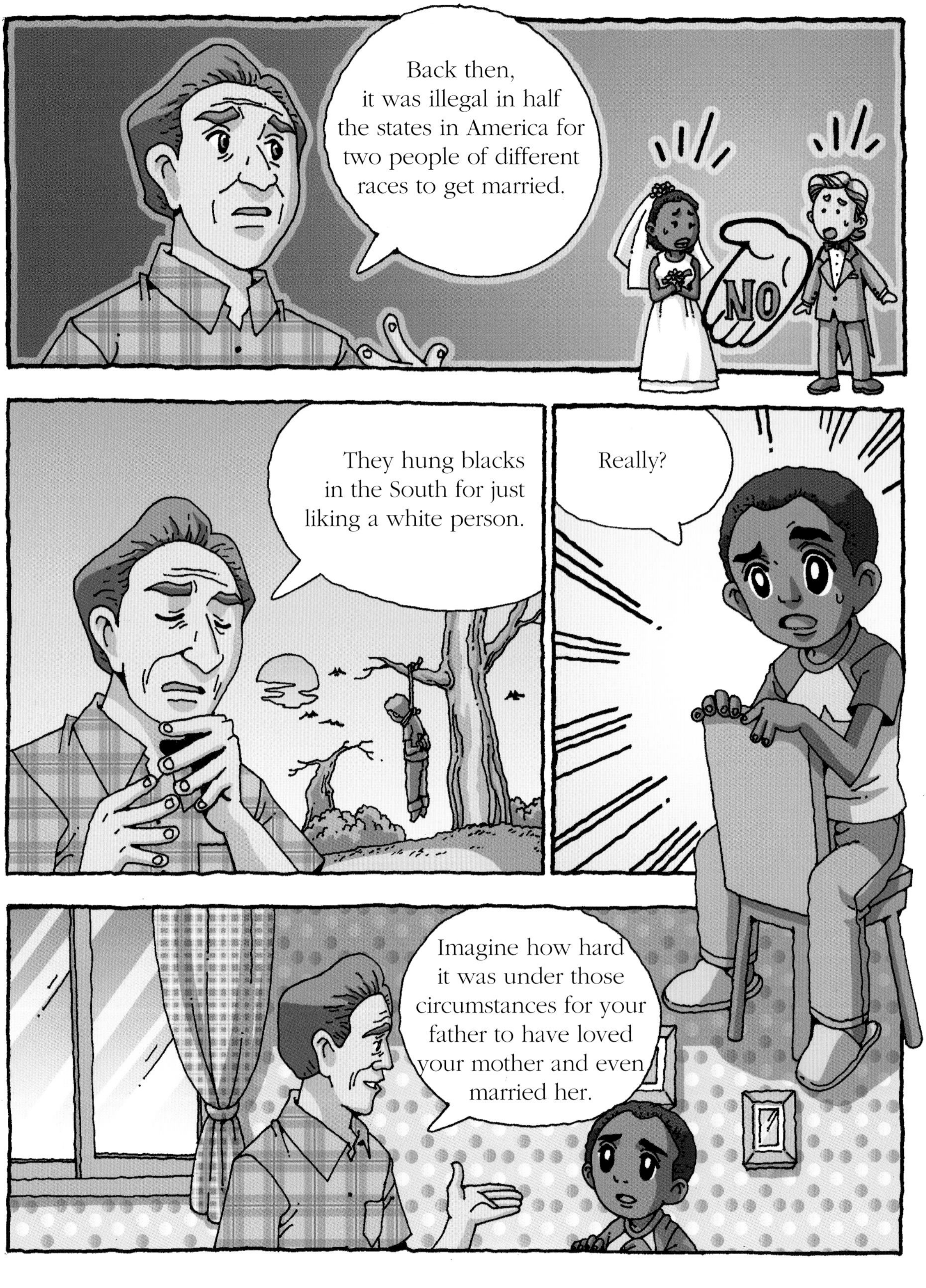
Back then, it was illegal in half the states in America for two people of different races to get married.
NO
They hung blacks in the South for just liking a white person.
Really?
Imagine how hard it was under those circumstances for your father to have loved your mother and even married her.

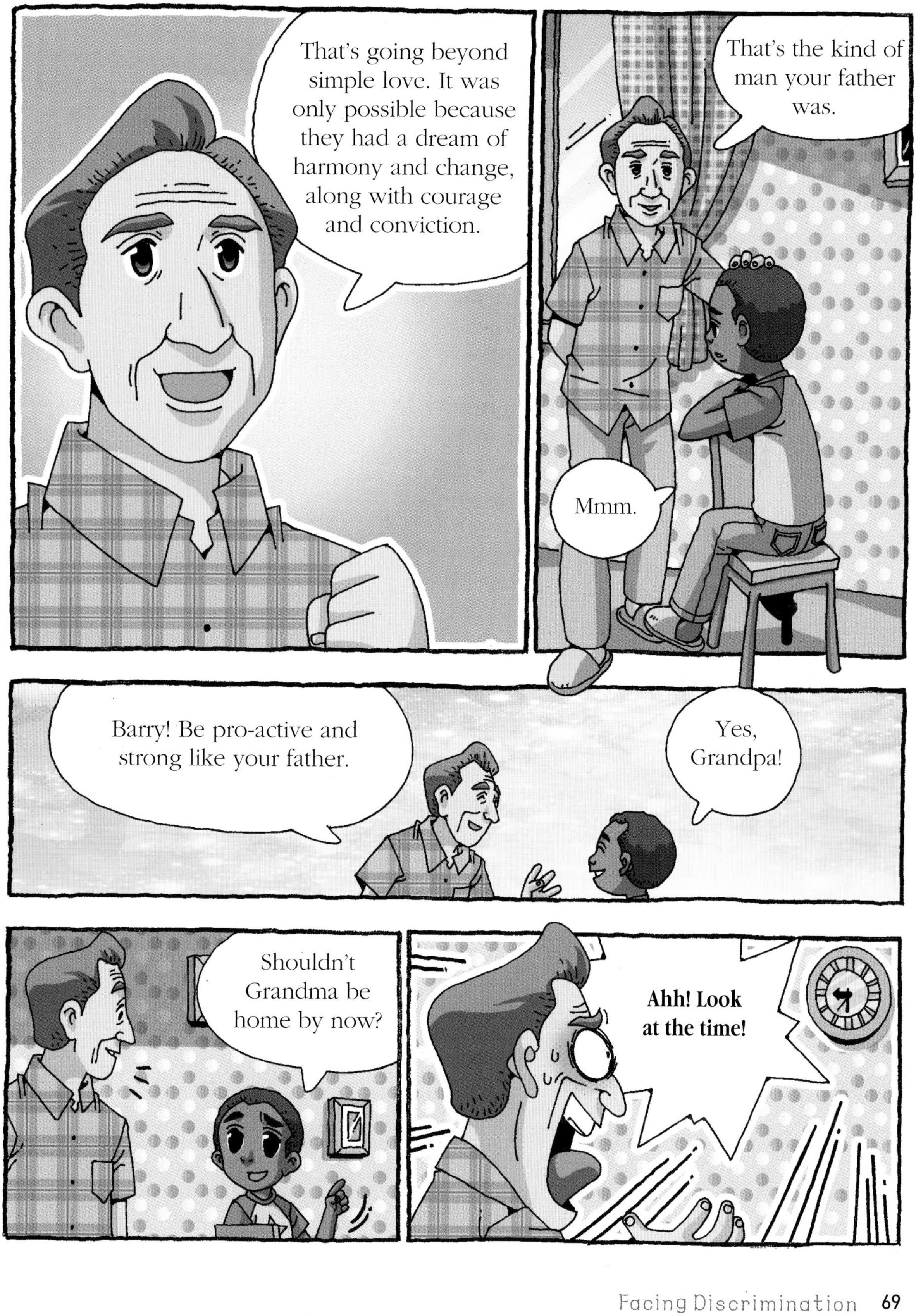
That's going beyond simple love. It was only possible because they had a dream of harmony and change, along with courage and conviction.
That's the kind of man your father was.
Mmm.
Barry! Be pro-active and strong like your father.
Yes, Grandpa!
Shouldn't Grandma be home by now?
Ahh! Look at the time!

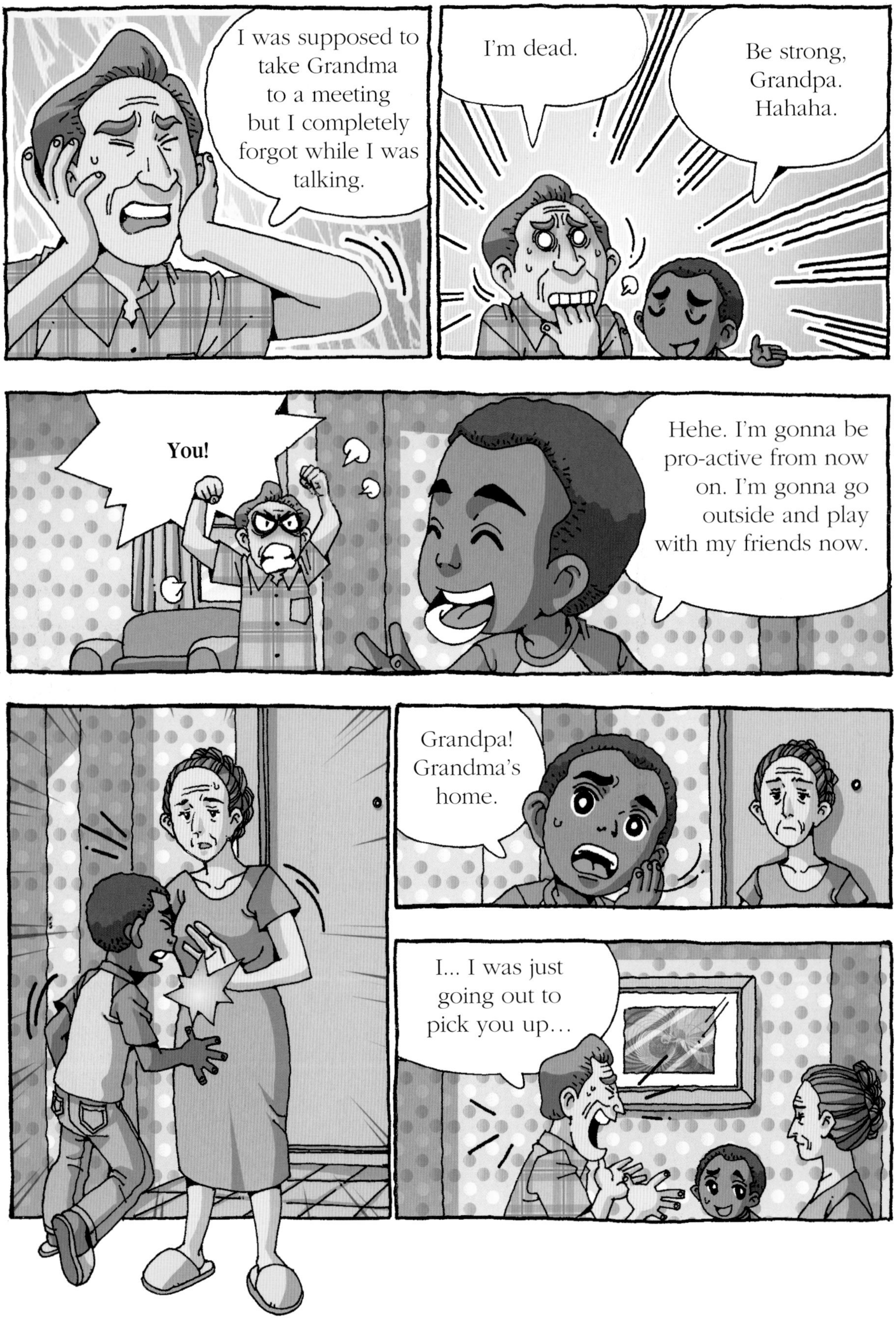
I was supposed to take Grandma to a meeting but I completely forgot while I was talking.
I'm dead.
Be strong, Grandpa. Hahaha.
You!
Hehe. I'm gonna be pro-active from now on. I'm gonna go outside and play with my friends now.
Grandpa! Grandma's home.
I... I was just going out to pick you up...

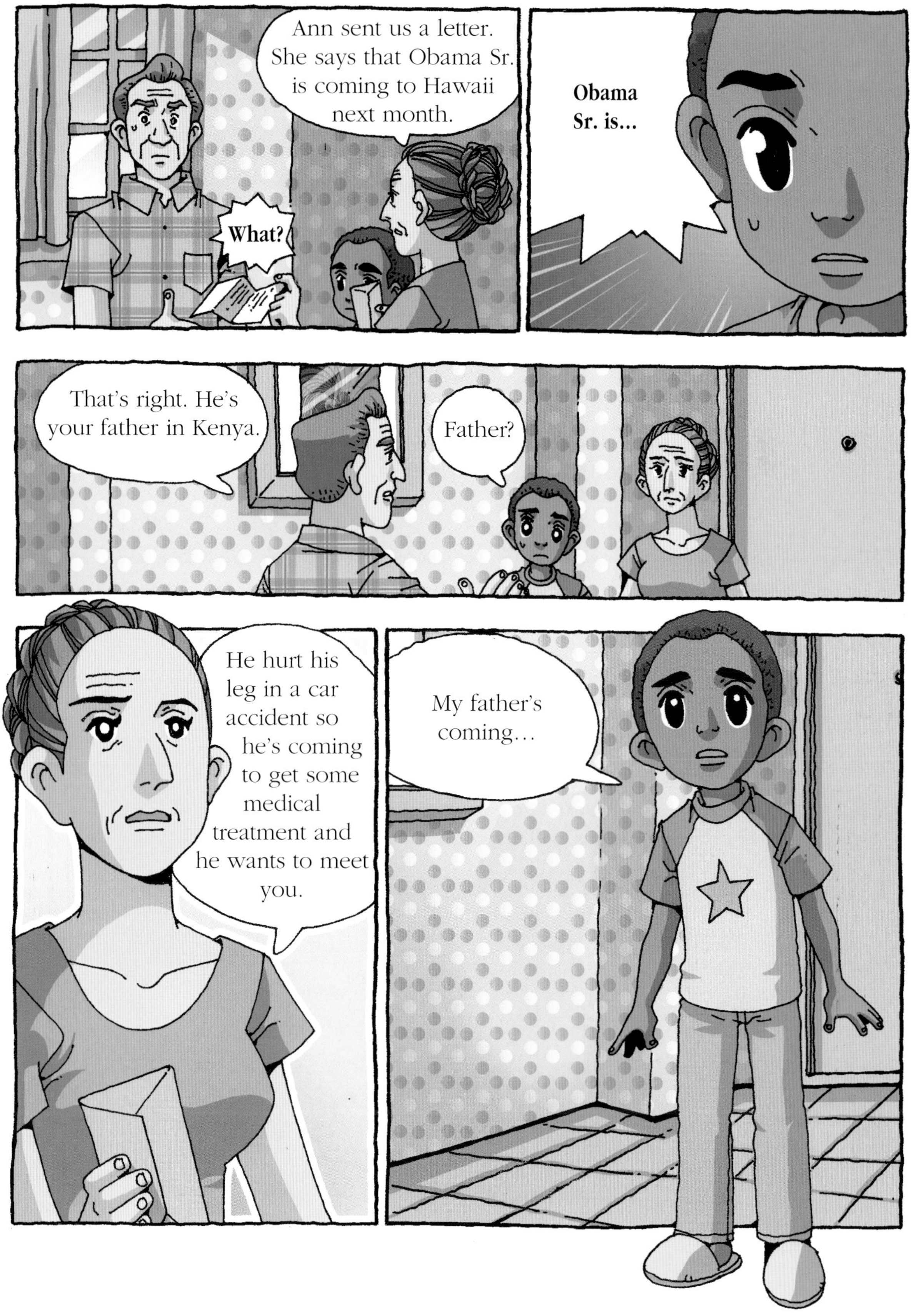
Ann sent us a letter. She says that Obama Sr. is coming to Hawaii next month.
What?
Obama Sr. is...
That's right. He's your father in Kenya.
Father?
He hurt his leg in a car accident so he's coming to get some medical treatment and he wants to meet you.
My father's coming...

Getting to know Obama 1

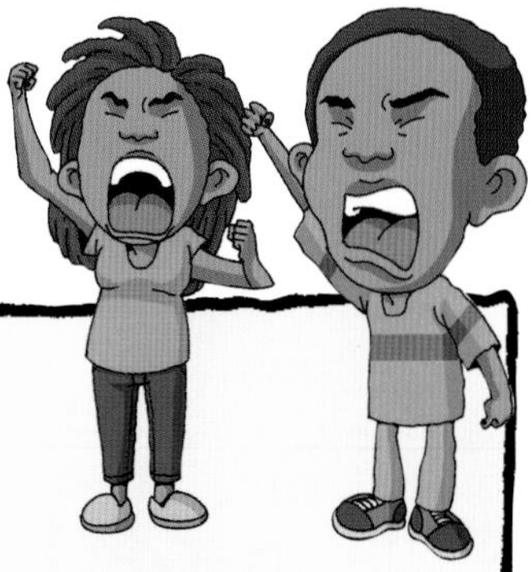

Racial discrimination in America

As recently as 50 years ago, African-Americans had been living under harsh discrimination. They did not have the right to vote in their own country and were forced into segregation. Places like trains, theaters, restaurants and bathrooms were all designated areas to be used by whites and other areas to be used by blacks. In addition, blacks were altogether banned from using beaches and parks. Marriage between blacks and whites was also illegal.

Blacks began to form city alliances and liberation movement organizations to combat the discrimination. Finally, in 1954, the Supreme Court ruled that racial segregation in schools was unconstitutional. Since then, racial tensions have subsided in America.

However, when Martin Luther King Jr. was assassinated in 1968 by a white man, this enraged the African-American community and riots arose all over the country in 168 cities. As a result, a law was passed banning racial discrimination in housing, and blacks became eligible for welfare benefits, just as whites were.

The discrimination problem, however, continues to exist today in everyday life. Even in the 1990s, black and white discrimination continues to be a major problem in the United States. But the fact that African-American Barack Obama has been elected president of the United States shows that the perception of African-Americans has changed significantly.

Chapter 4

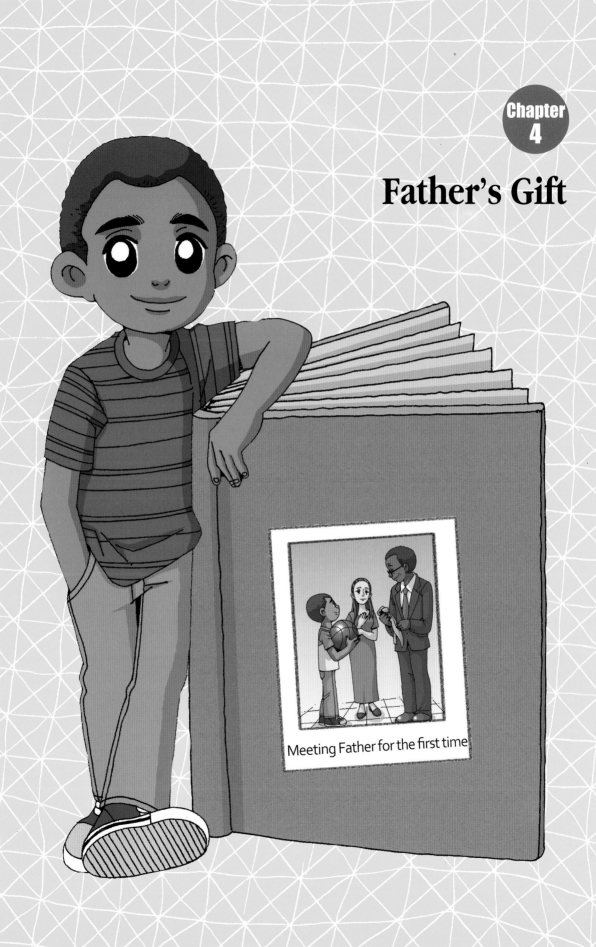

Father's Gift

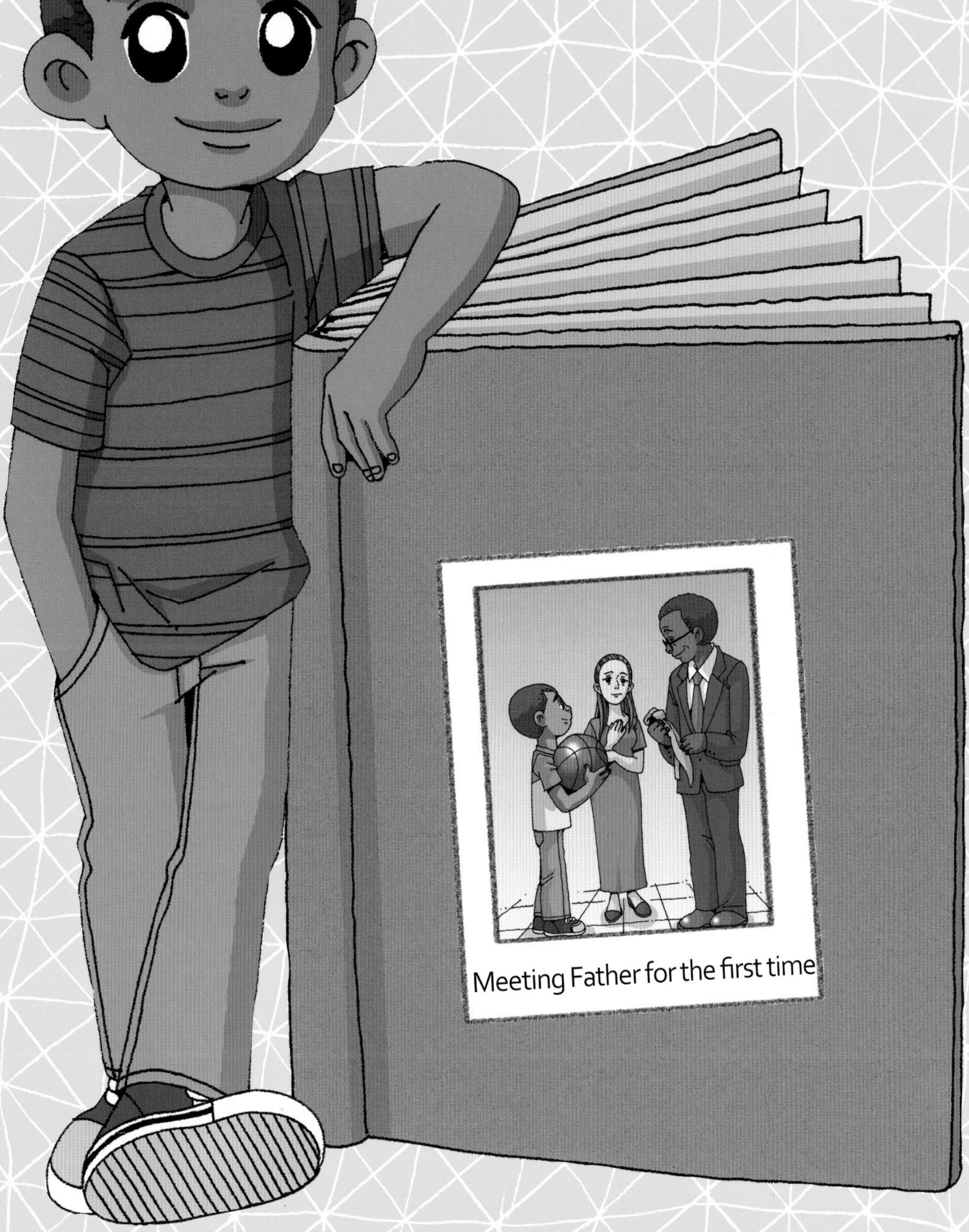
Meeting Father for the first time

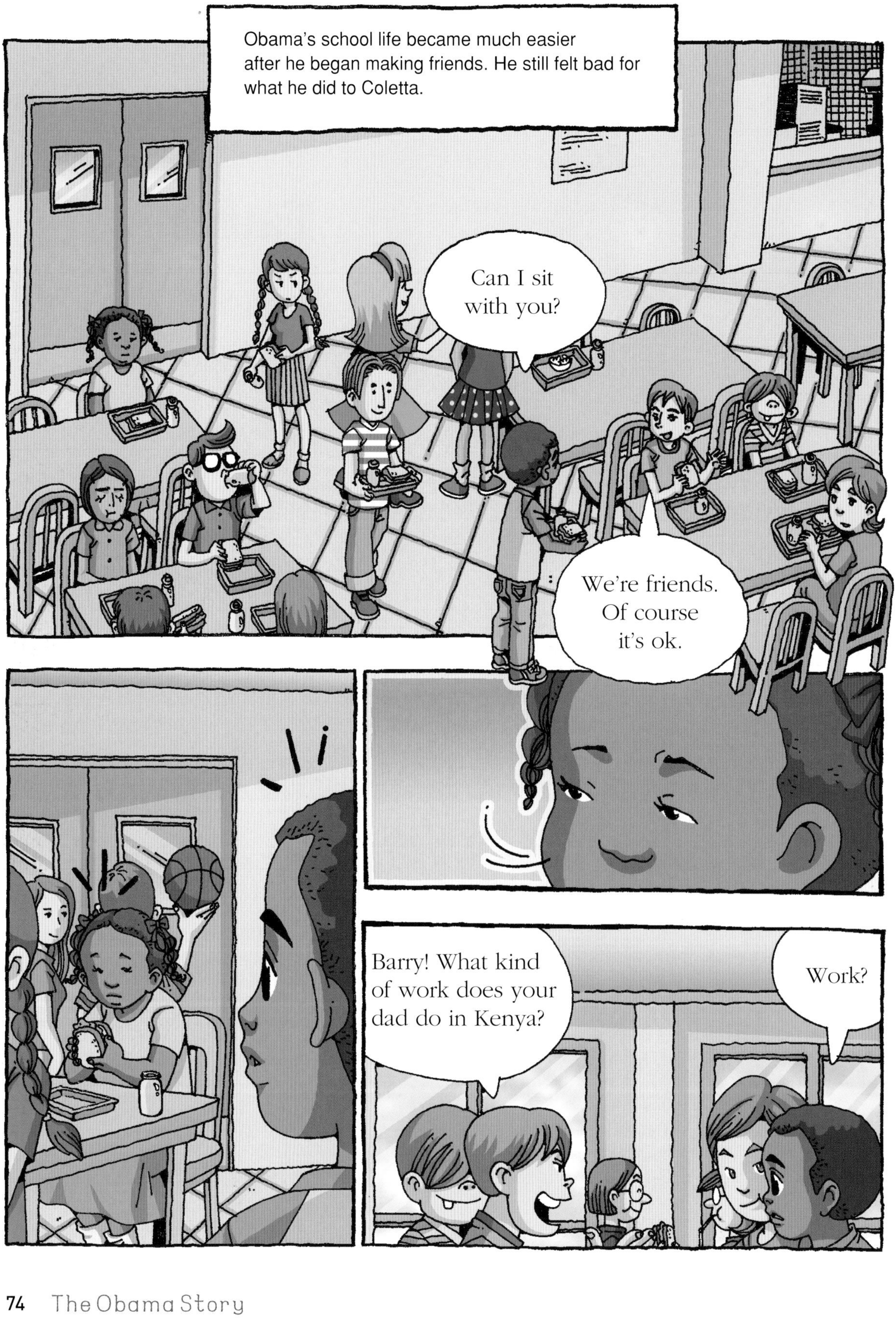
Obama's school life became much easier after he began making friends. He still felt bad for what he did to Coletta.
Can I sit with you?
We're friends. Of course it's ok.
Barry! What kind of work does your dad do in Kenya?
Work?

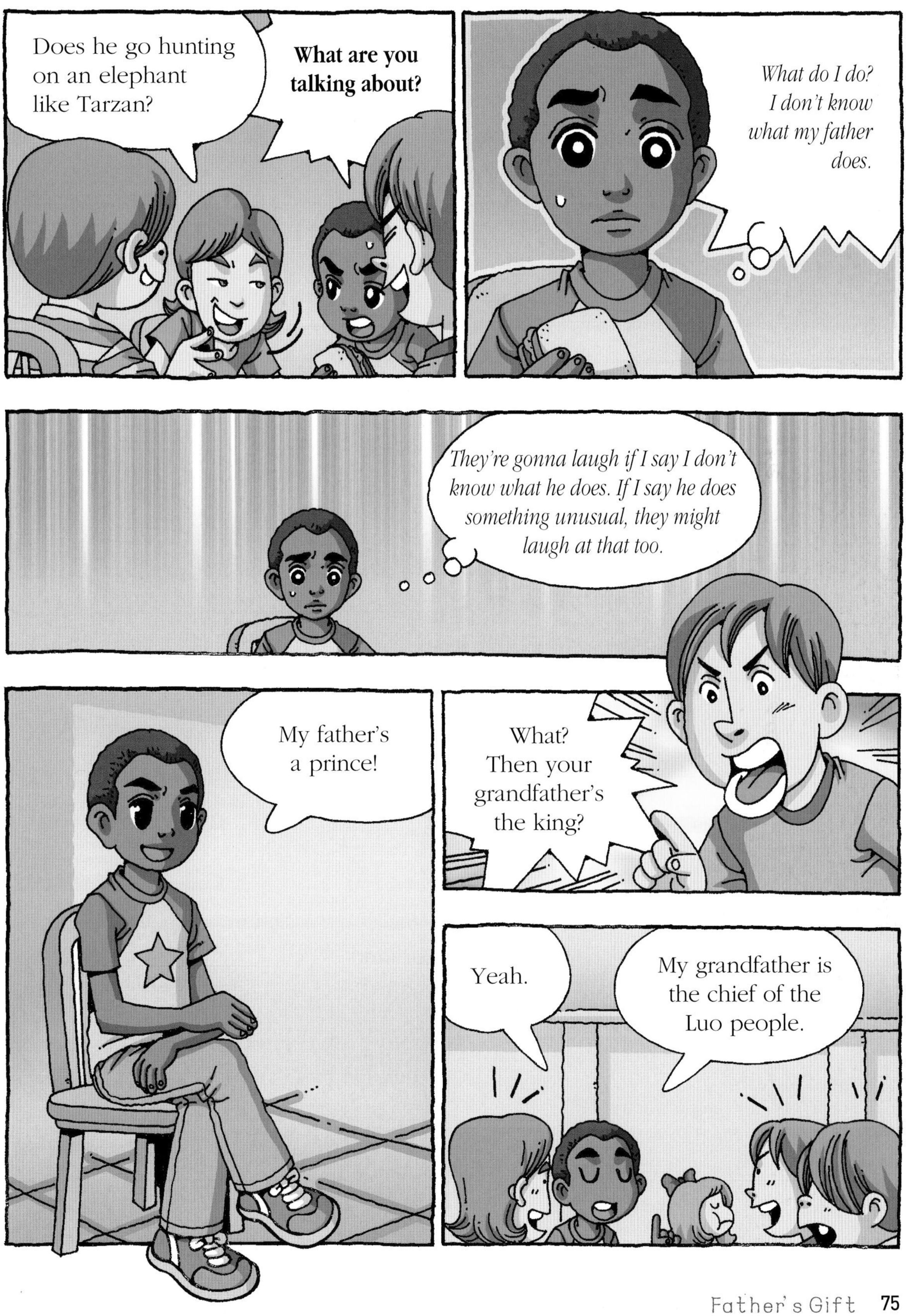
Does he go hunting on an elephant like Tarzan?
What are you talking about?
What do I do? I don't know what my father does.
They're gonna laugh if I say I don't know what he does. If I say he does something unusual, they might laugh at that too.
My father's a prince!
What? Then your grandfather's the king?
Yeah.
My grandfather is the chief of the Luo people.

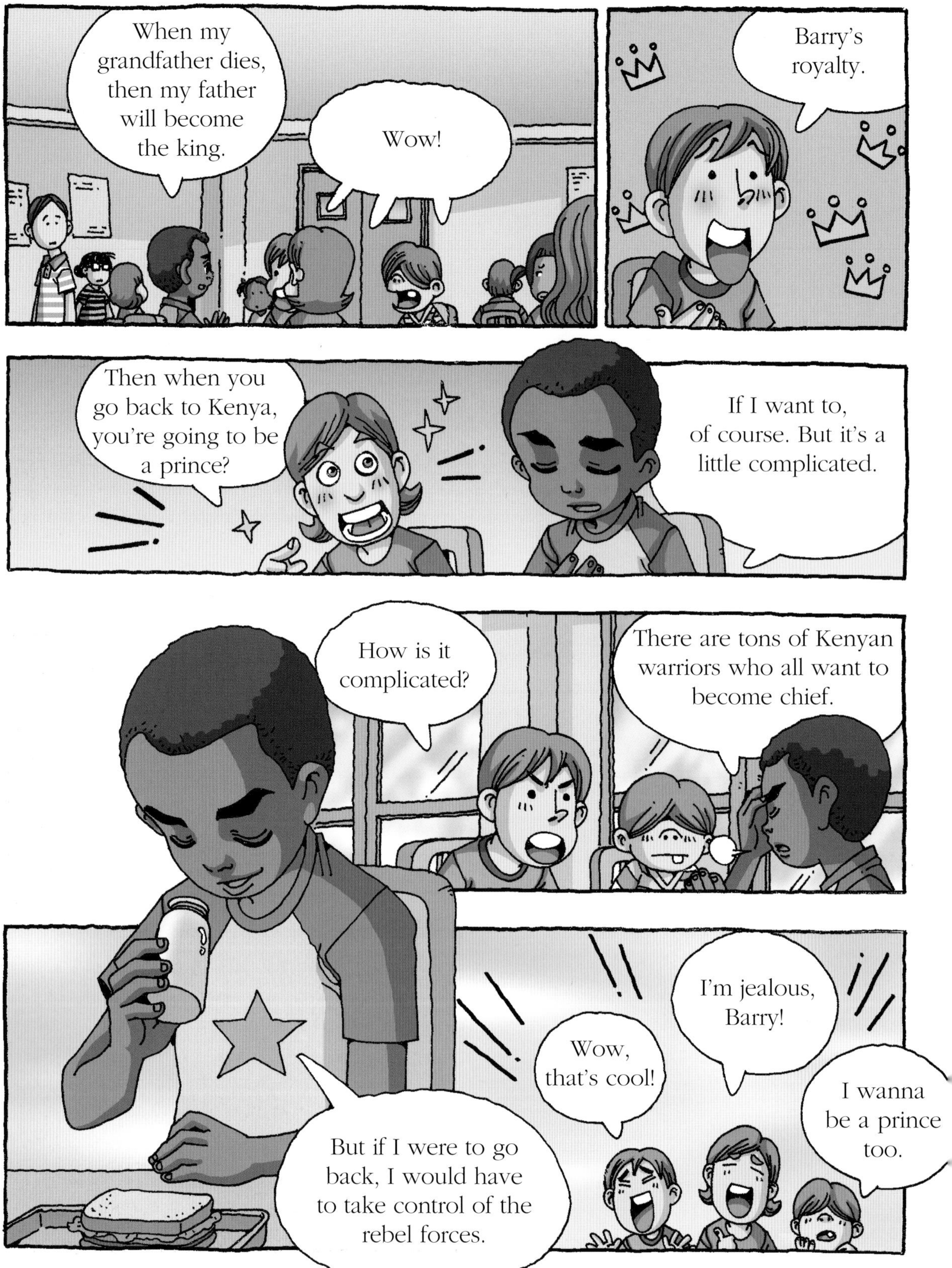
When my grandfather dies, then my father will become the king.
Wow!
Barry's royalty.
Then when you go back to Kenya, you're going to be a prince?
If I want to, of course. But it's a little complicated.
How is it complicated?
There are tons of Kenyan warriors who all want to become chief.
But if I were to go back, I would have to take control of the rebel forces.
Wow, that's cool!
I'm jealous, Barry!
I wanna be a prince too.

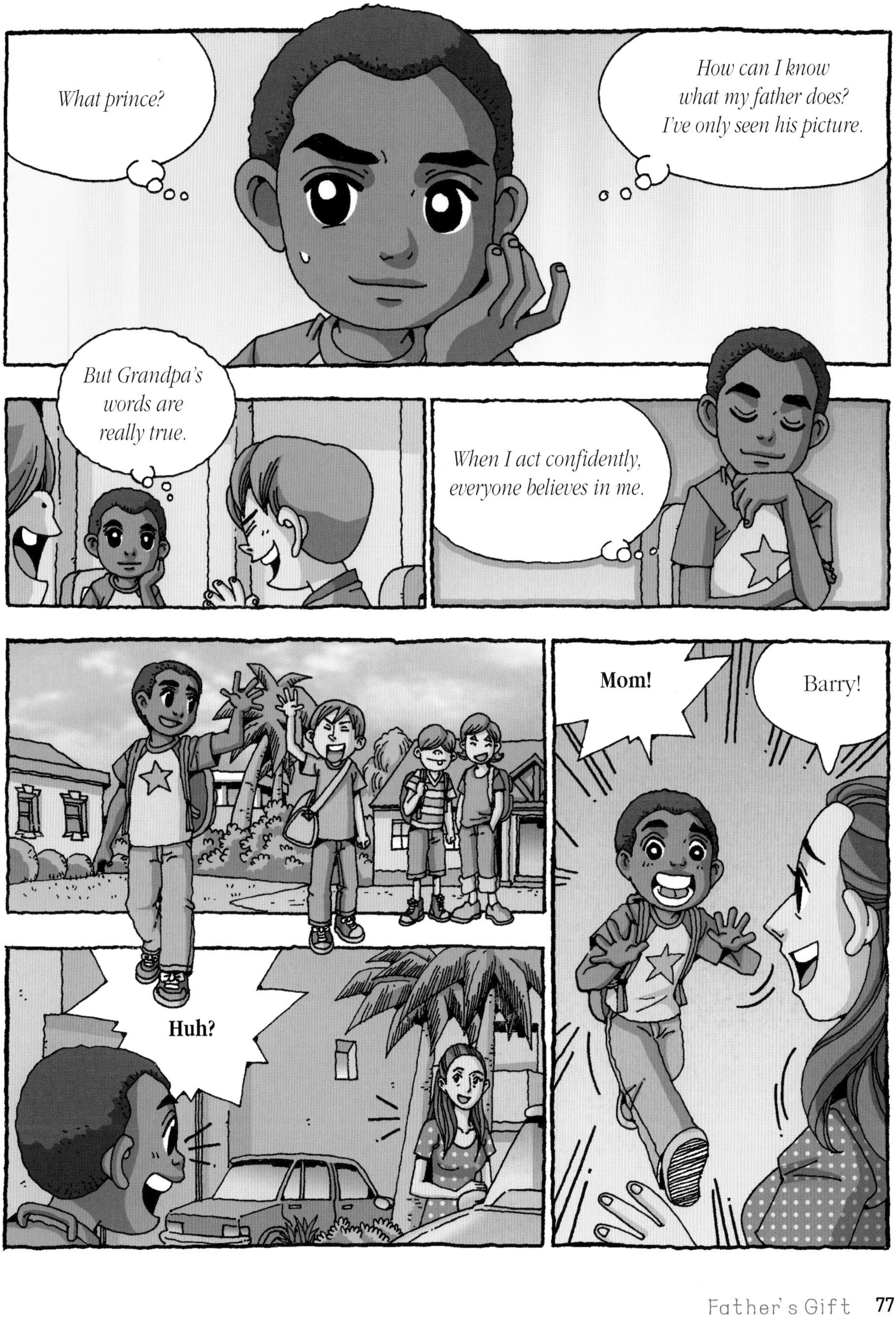
What prince?
How can I know what my father does? I've only seen his picture.
But Grandpa's words are really true.
When I act confidently, everyone believes in me.
Huh?
Mom!
Barry!

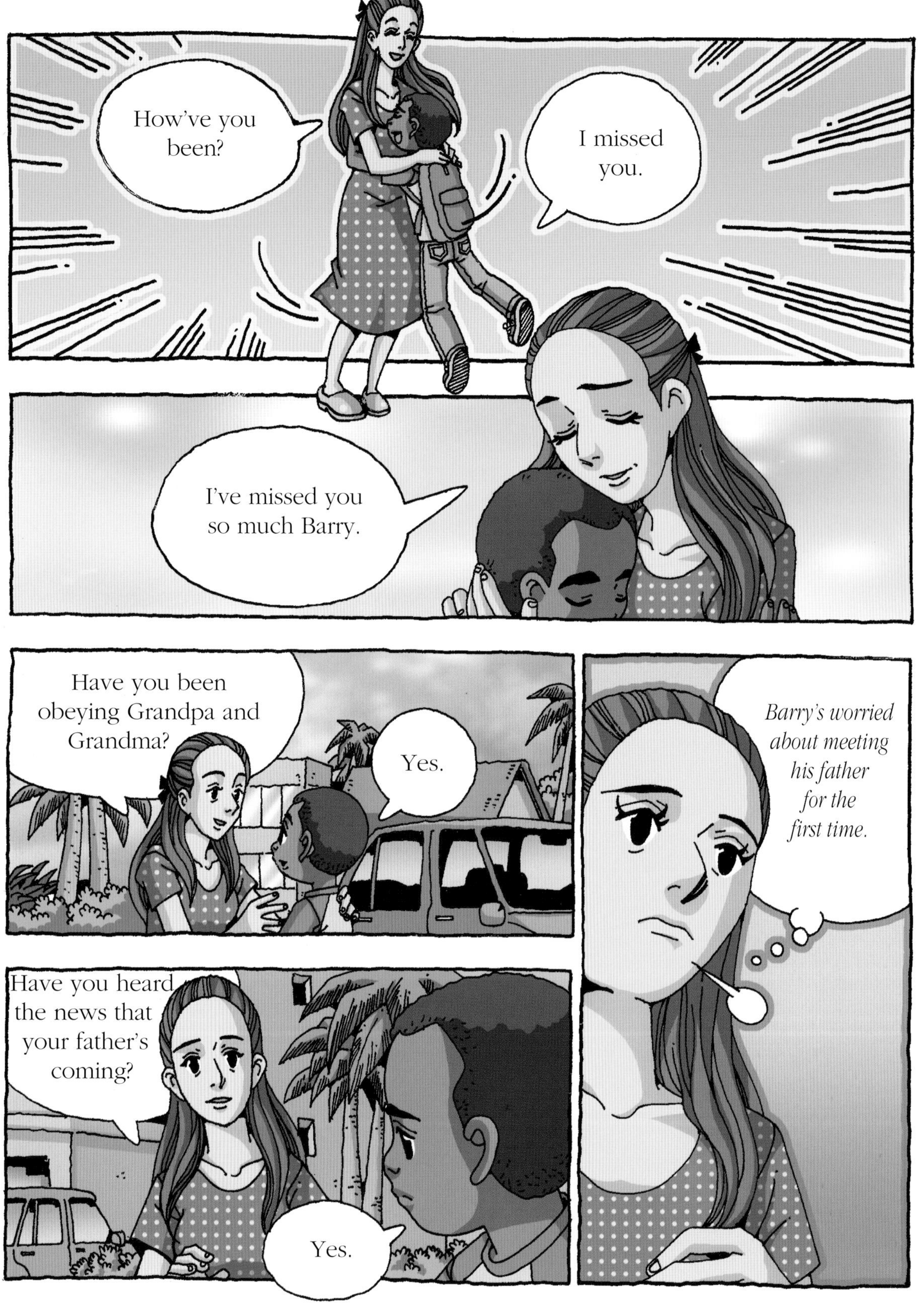
How've you been?
I missed you.
I've missed you so much Barry.
Have you been obeying Grandpa and Grandma?
Yes.
Barry's worried about meeting his father for the first time.
Have you heard the news that your father's coming?
Yes.

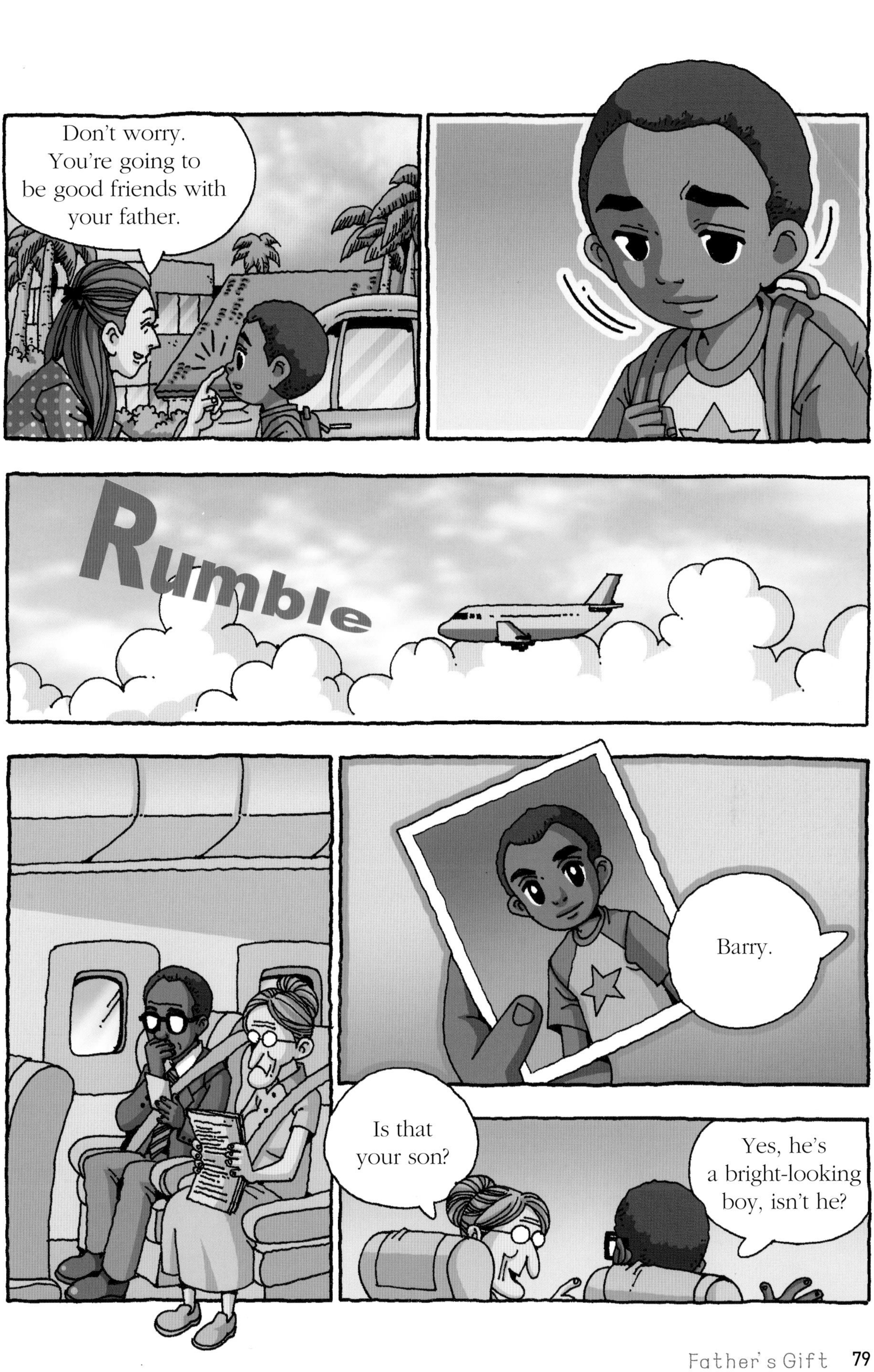
Don't worry. You're going to be good friends with your father.
Rumble
Barry.
Is that your son?
Yes, he's a bright-looking boy, isn't he?

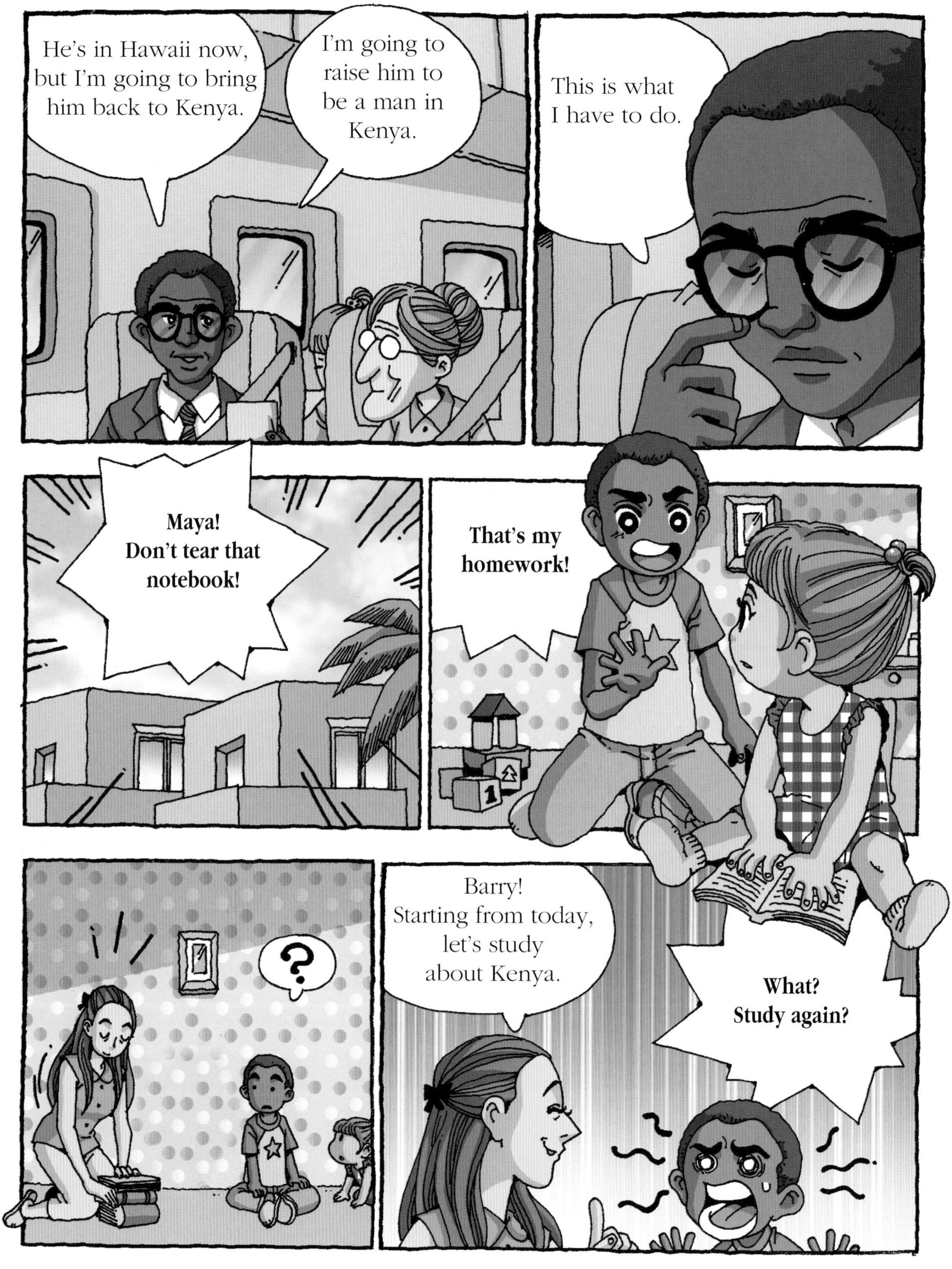
He's in Hawaii now, but I'm going to bring him back to Kenya.
I'm going to raise him to be a man in Kenya.
This is what I have to do.
Maya! Don't tear that notebook!
That's my homework!
Barry! Starting from today, let's study about Kenya.
What? Study again?

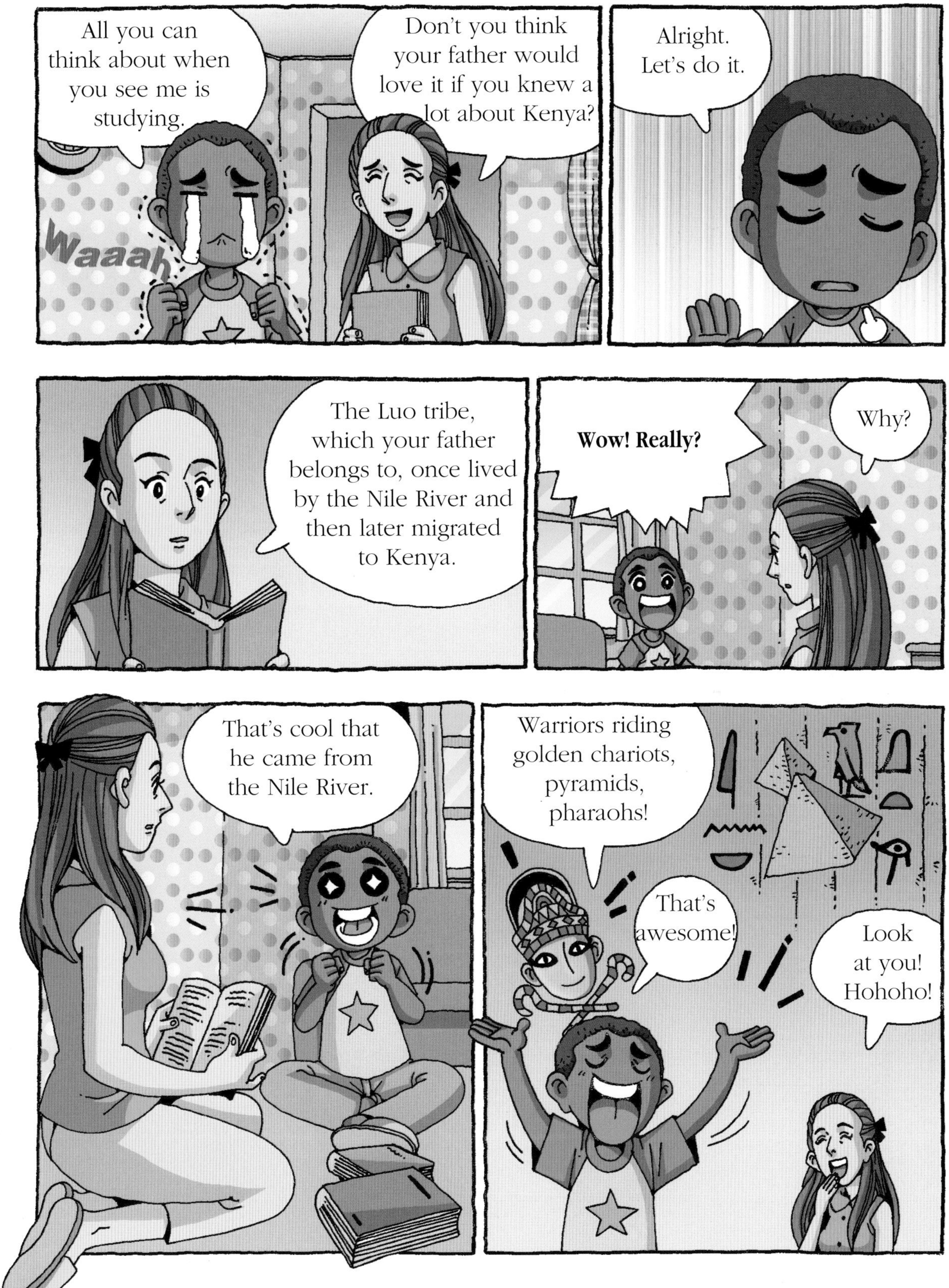
All you can think about when you see me is studying.
Waaah
Don't you think your father would love it if you knew a lot about Kenya?
Alright. Let's do it.
The Luo tribe, which your father belongs to, once lived by the Nile River and then later migrated to Kenya.
Wow! Really?
Why?
That's cool that he came from the Nile River.
Warriors riding golden chariots, pyramids, pharaohs!
That's awesome!
Look at you! Hohoho!

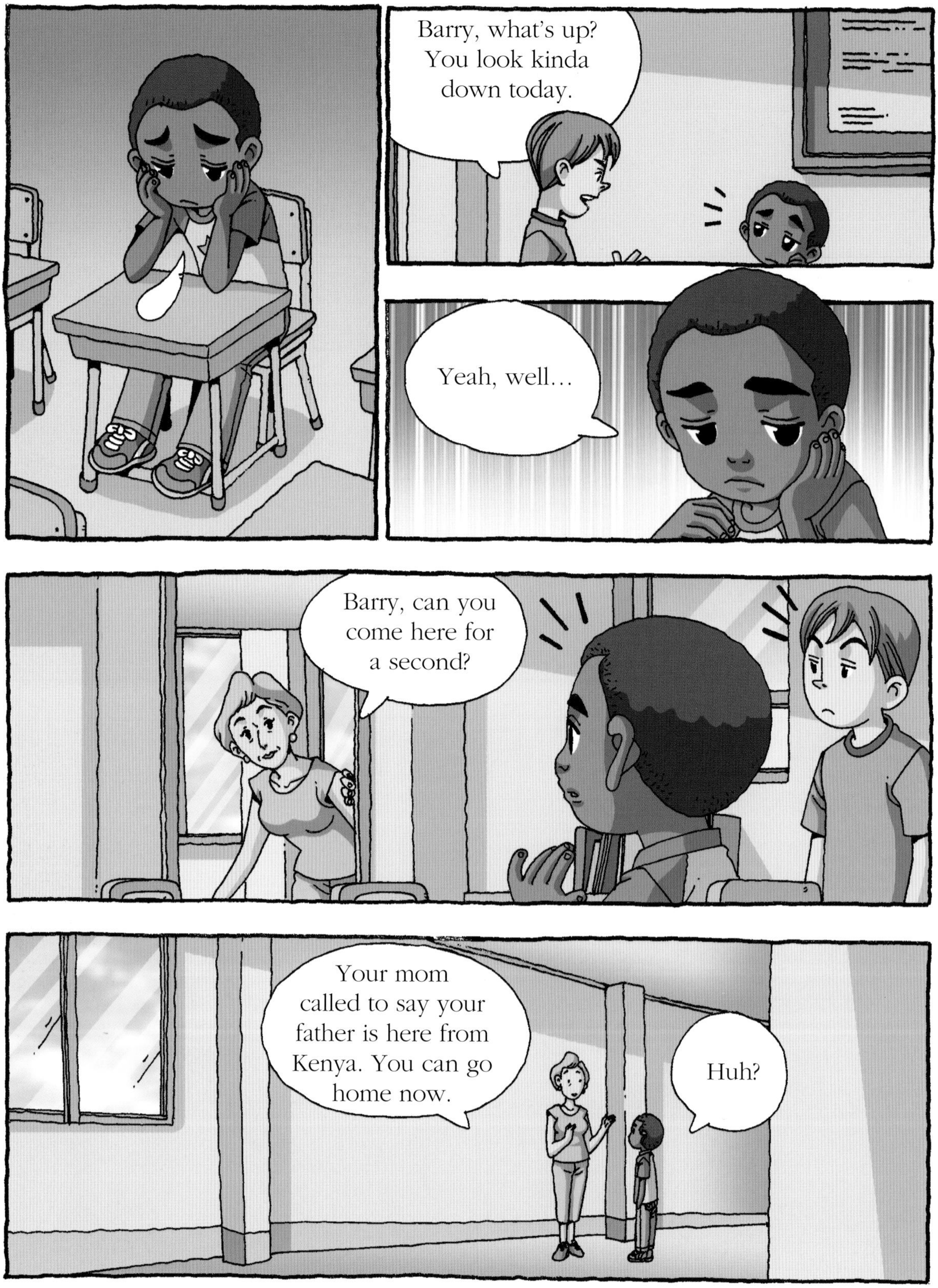
Barry, what's up? You look kinda down today.
Yeah, well…
Barry, can you come here for a second?
Your mom called to say your father is here from Kenya. You can go home now.
Huh?

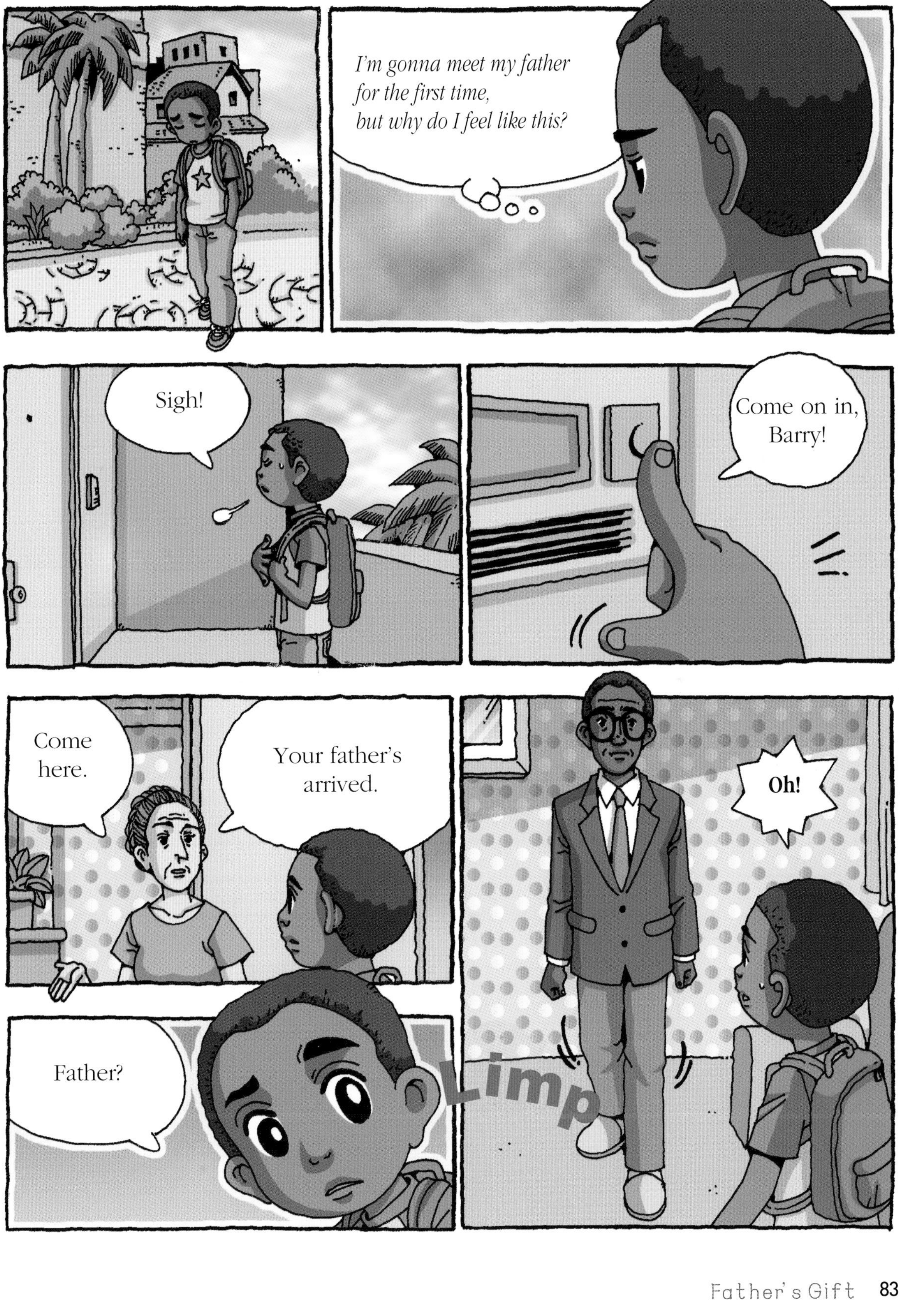
I'm gonna meet my father for the first time, but why do I feel like this?
Sigh!
Come on in, Barry!
Come here.
Your father's arrived.
Oh!
Father?
Limp

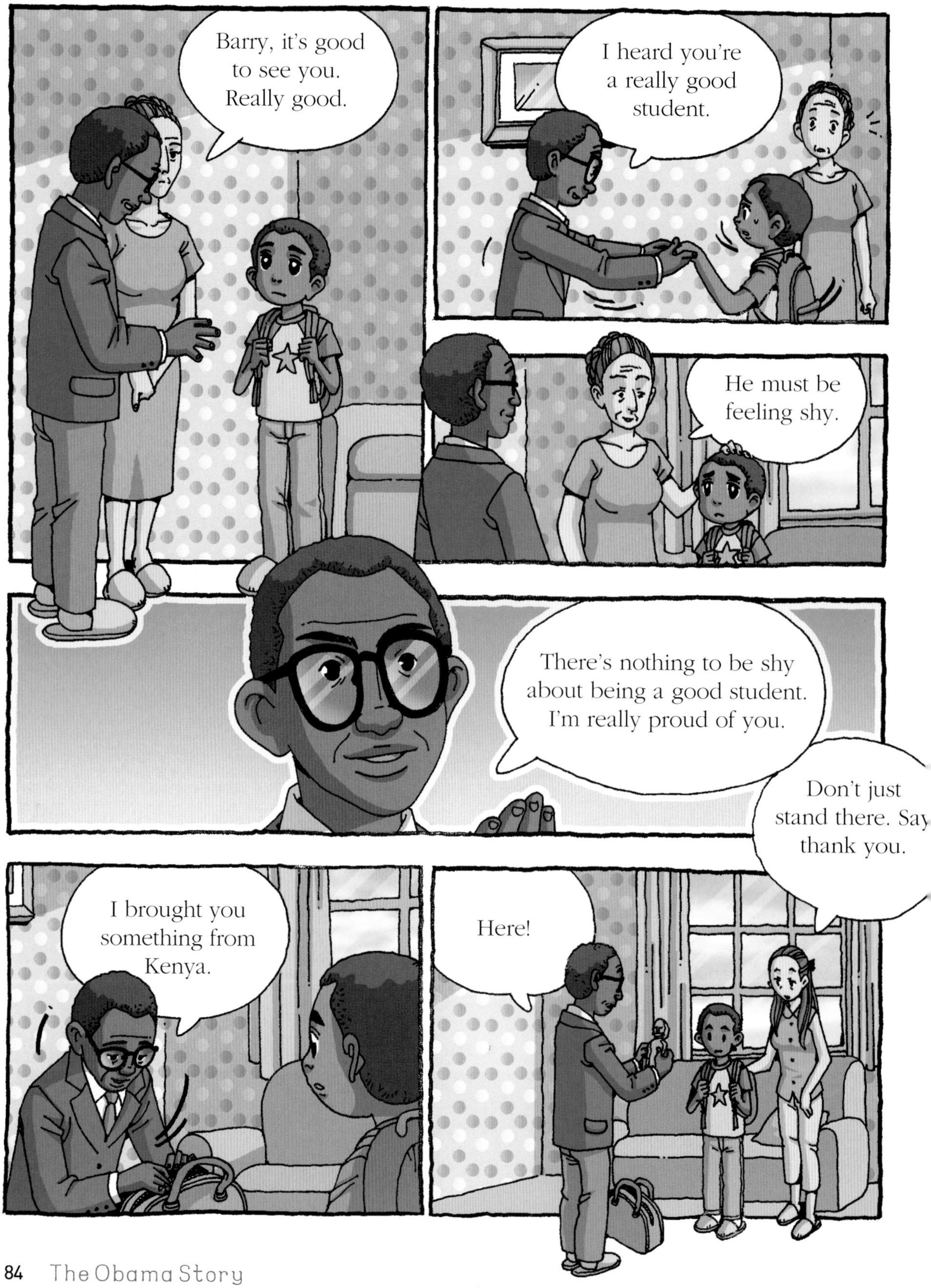
Barry, it's good to see you. Really good.
I heard you're a really good student.
He must be feeling shy.
There's nothing to be shy about being a good student. I'm really proud of you.
Don't just stand there. Say thank you.
I brought you something from Kenya.
Here!

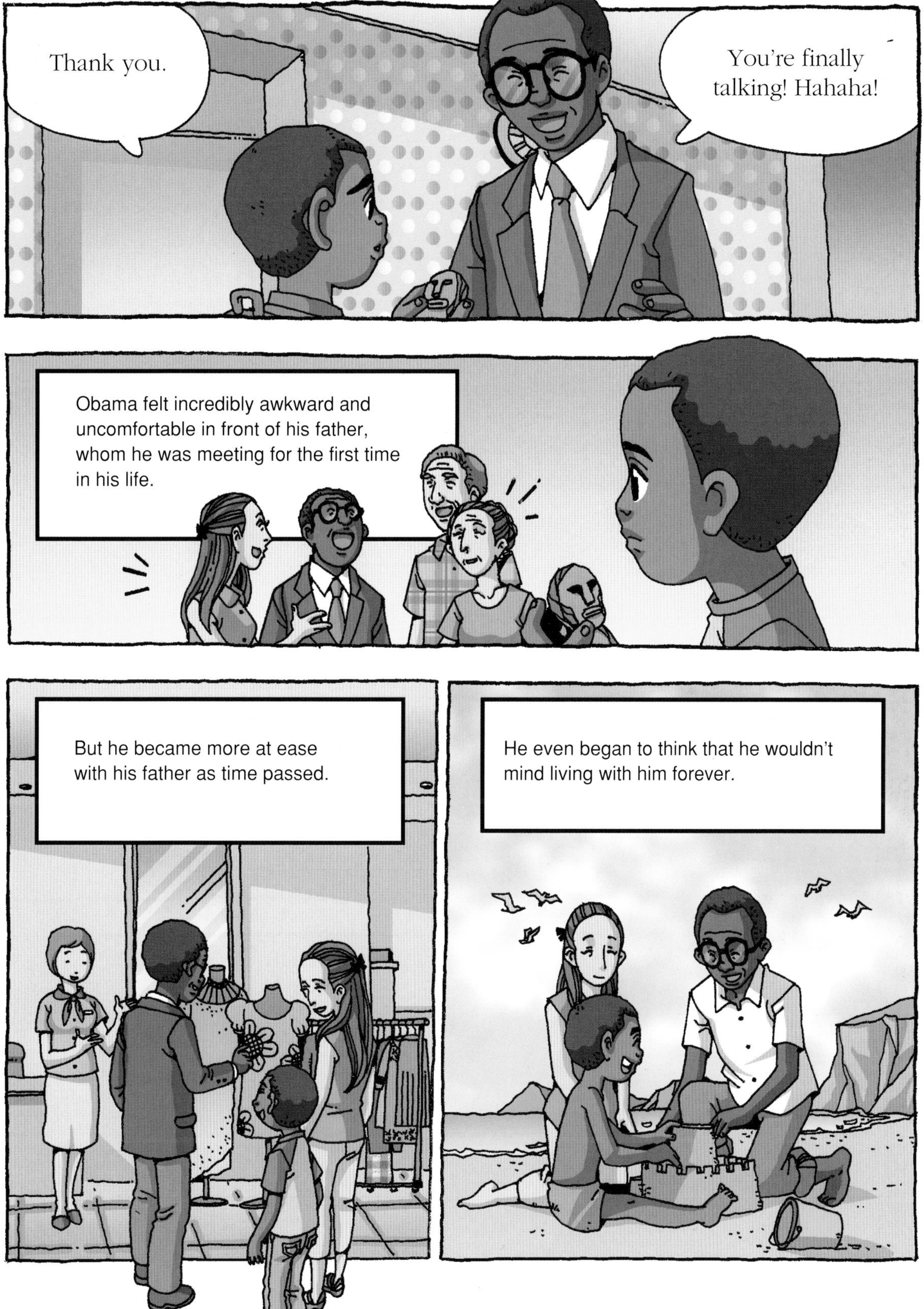
Thank you.
You're finally talking! Hahaha!
Obama felt incredibly awkward and uncomfortable in front of his father, whom he was meeting for the first time in his life.
But he became more at ease with his father as time passed.
He even began to think that he wouldn't mind living with him forever.

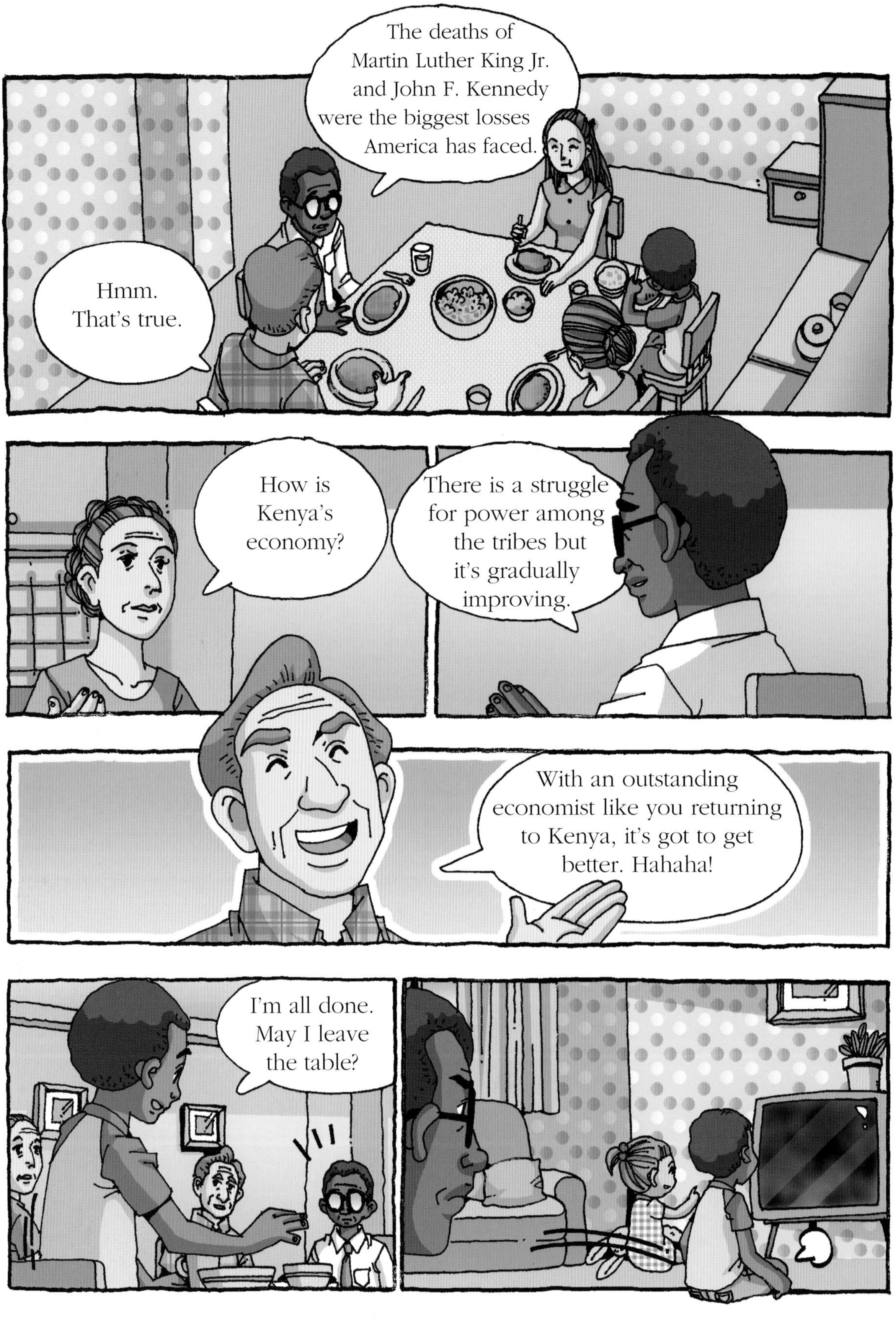
The deaths of Martin Luther King Jr. and John F. Kennedy were the biggest losses America has faced.
Hmm. That's true.
How is Kenya's economy?
There is a struggle for power among the tribes but it's gradually improving.
With an outstanding economist like you returning to Kenya, it's got to get better. Hahaha!
I'm all done. May I leave the table?

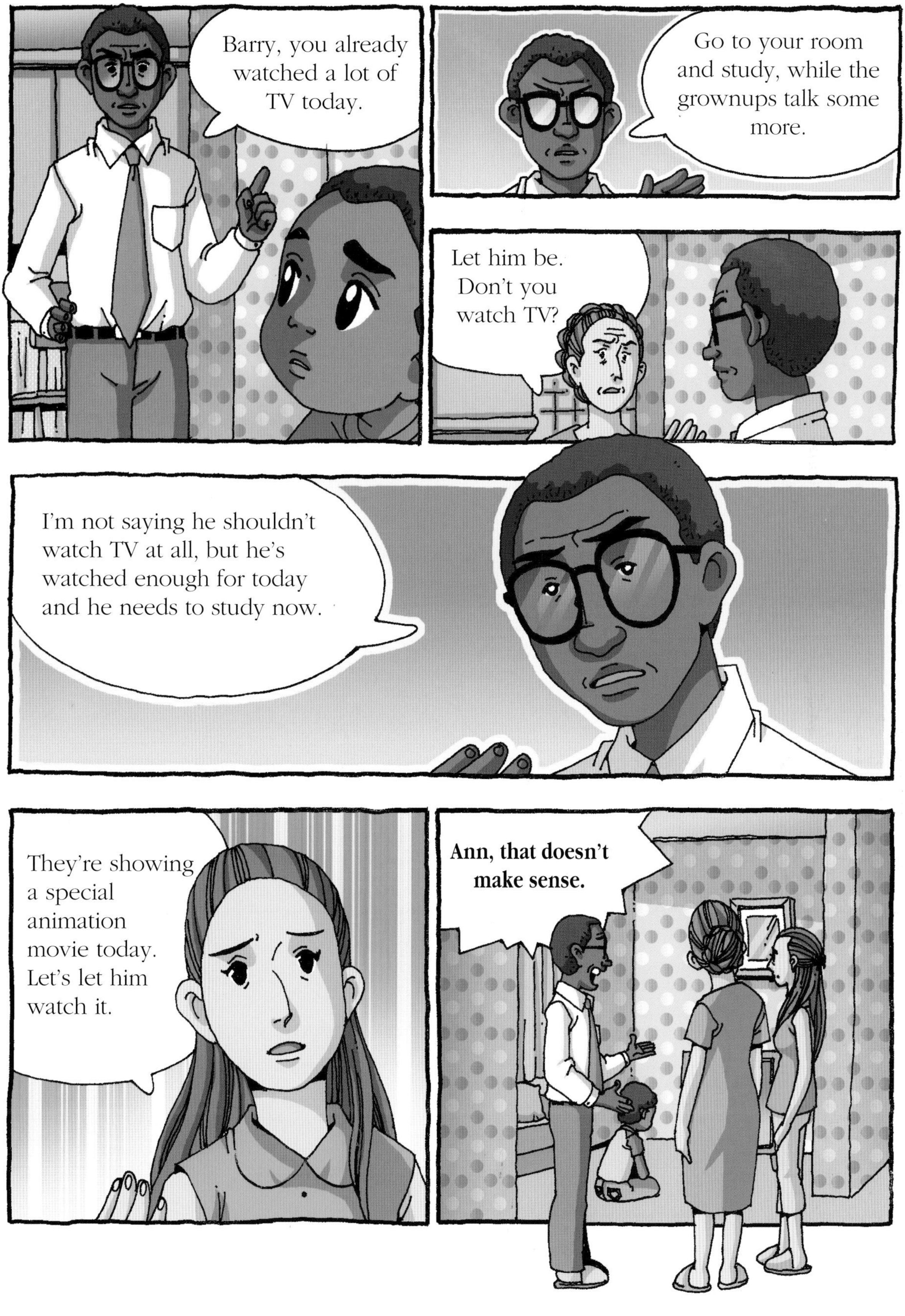
Barry, you already watched a lot of TV today.
Go to your room and study, while the grownups talk some more.
Let him be. Don't you watch TV?
I'm not saying he shouldn't watch TV at all, but he's watched enough for today and he needs to study now.
They're showing a special animation movie today. Let's let him watch it.
Ann, that doesn't make sense.

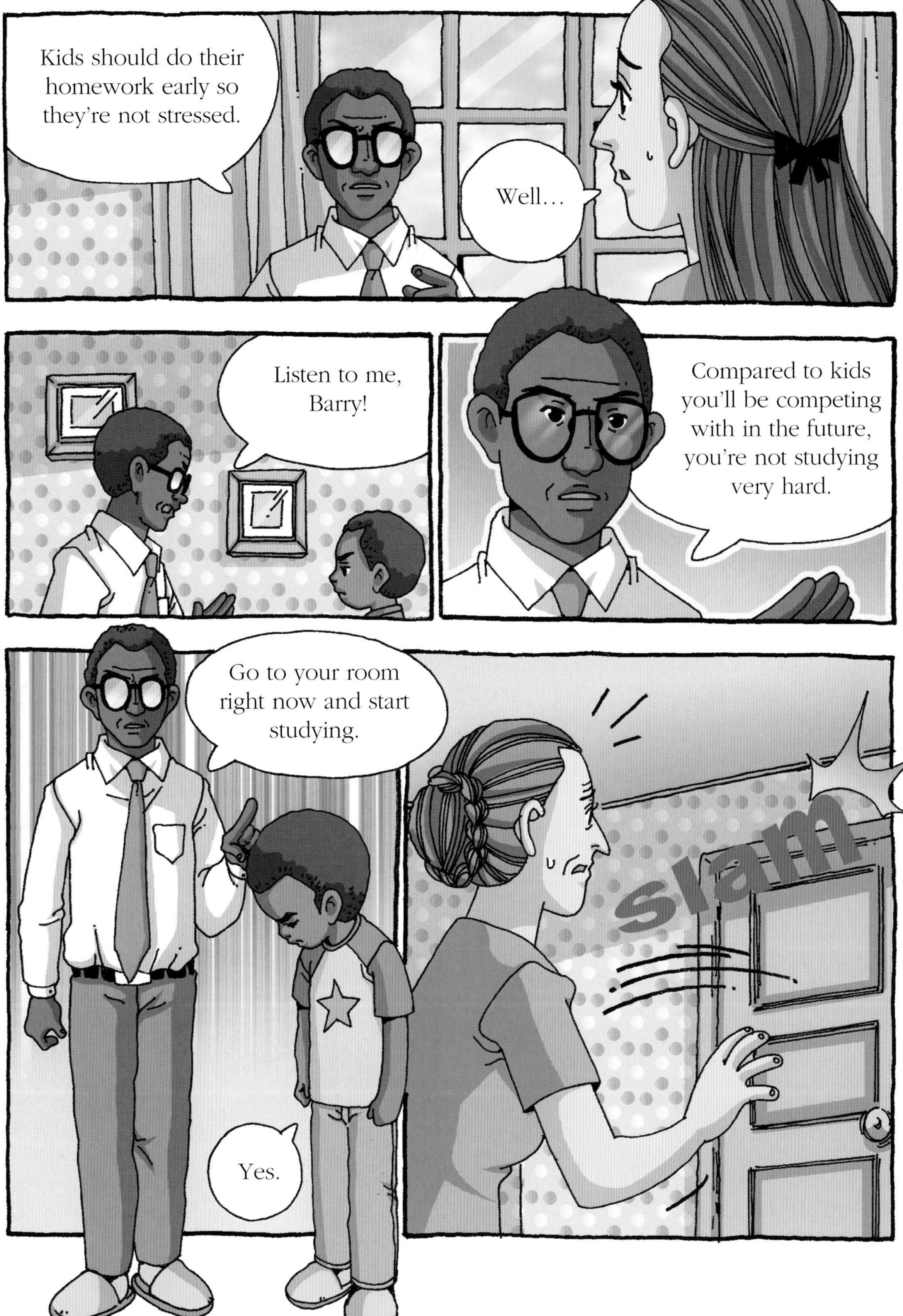
Kids should do their homework early so they're not stressed.
Well…
Listen to me, Barry!
Compared to kids you'll be competing with in the future, you're not studying very hard.
Go to your room right now and start studying.
Yes.
slam

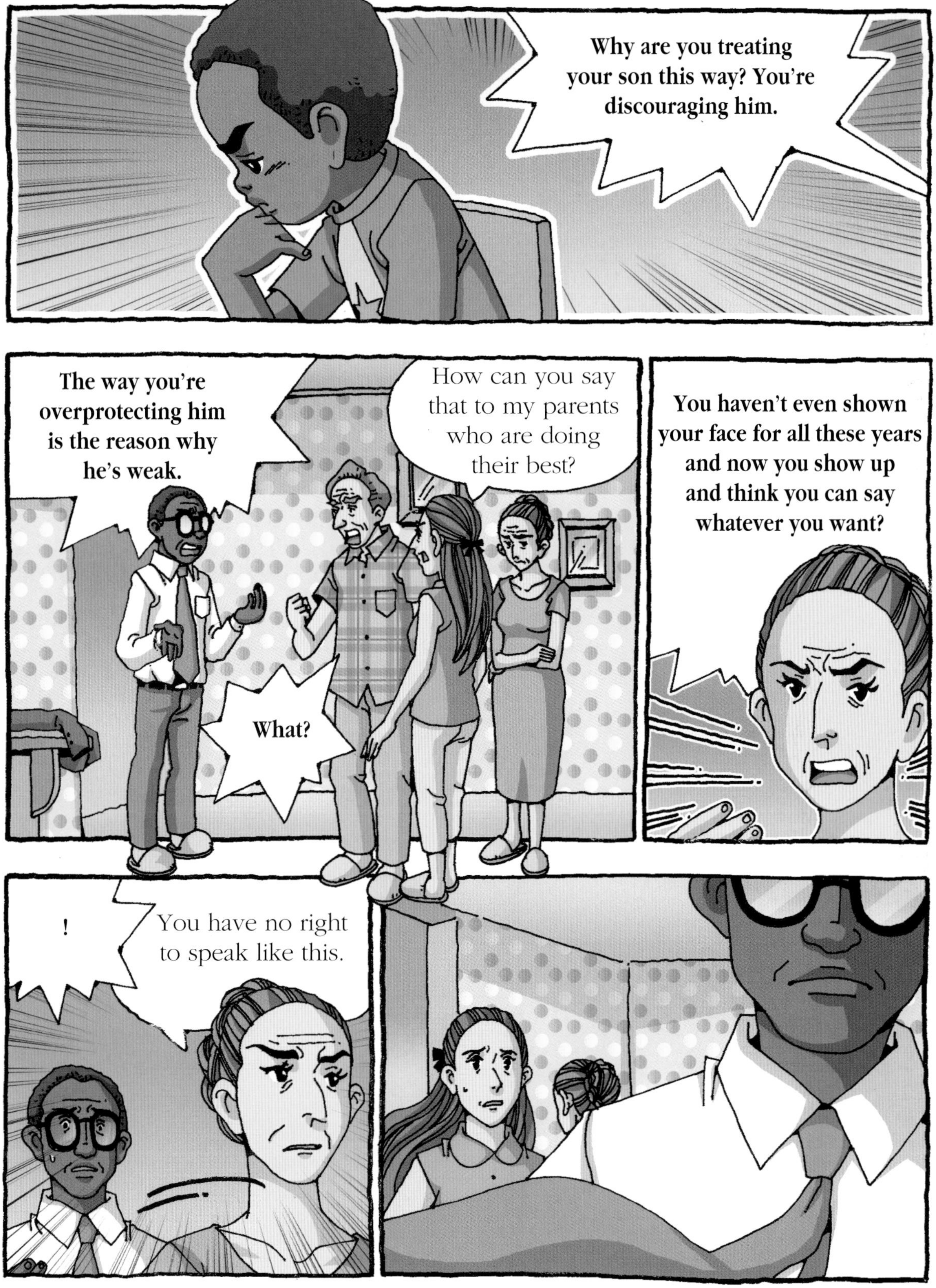
Why are you treating your son this way? You're discouraging him.
The way you're overprotecting him is the reason why he's weak.
How can you say that to my parents who are doing their best?
What?
You haven't even shown your face for all these years and now you show up and think you can say whatever you want?
!
You have no right to speak like this.

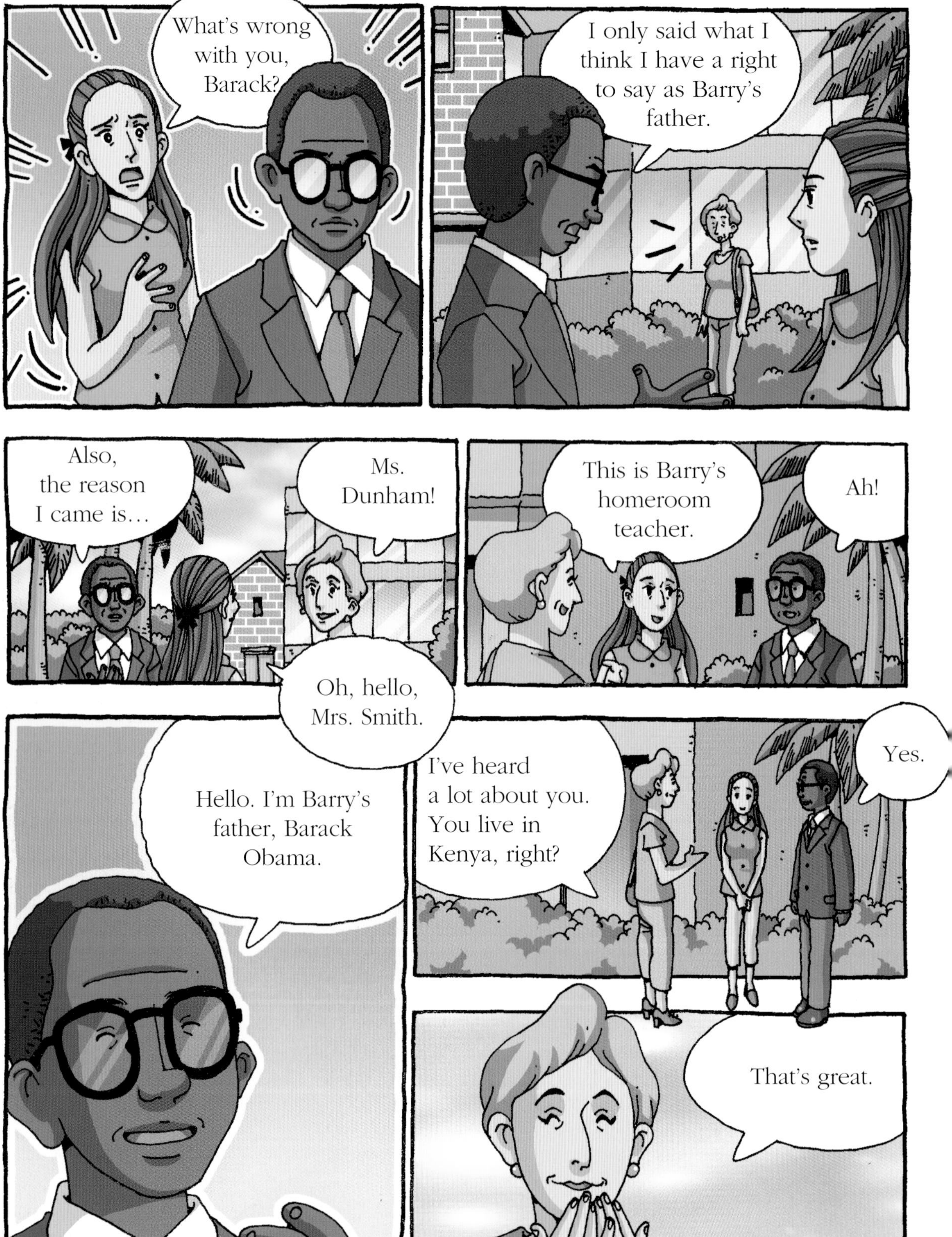

What's wrong with you, Barack?
I only said what I think I have a right to say as Barry's father.
Also, the reason I came is…
Ms. Dunham!
Oh, hello, Mrs. Smith.
This is Barry's homeroom teacher.
Ah!
Hello. I'm Barry's father, Barack Obama.
I've heard a lot about you. You live in Kenya, right?
Yes.
That's great.

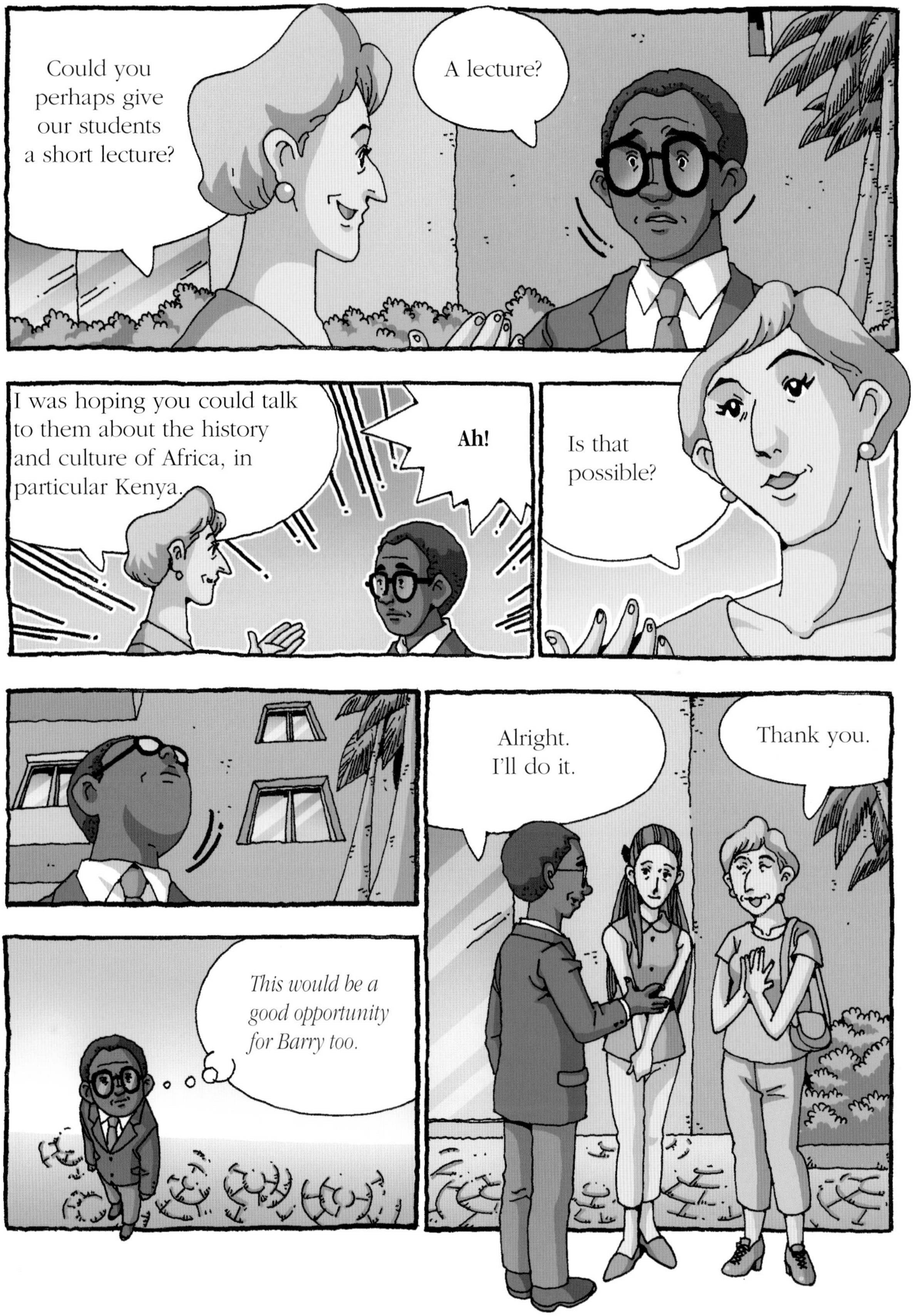
Could you perhaps give our students a short lecture?
A lecture?
I was hoping you could talk to them about the history and culture of Africa, in particular Kenya.
Ah!
Is that possible?
This would be a good opportunity for Barry too.
Alright. I'll do it.
Thank you.

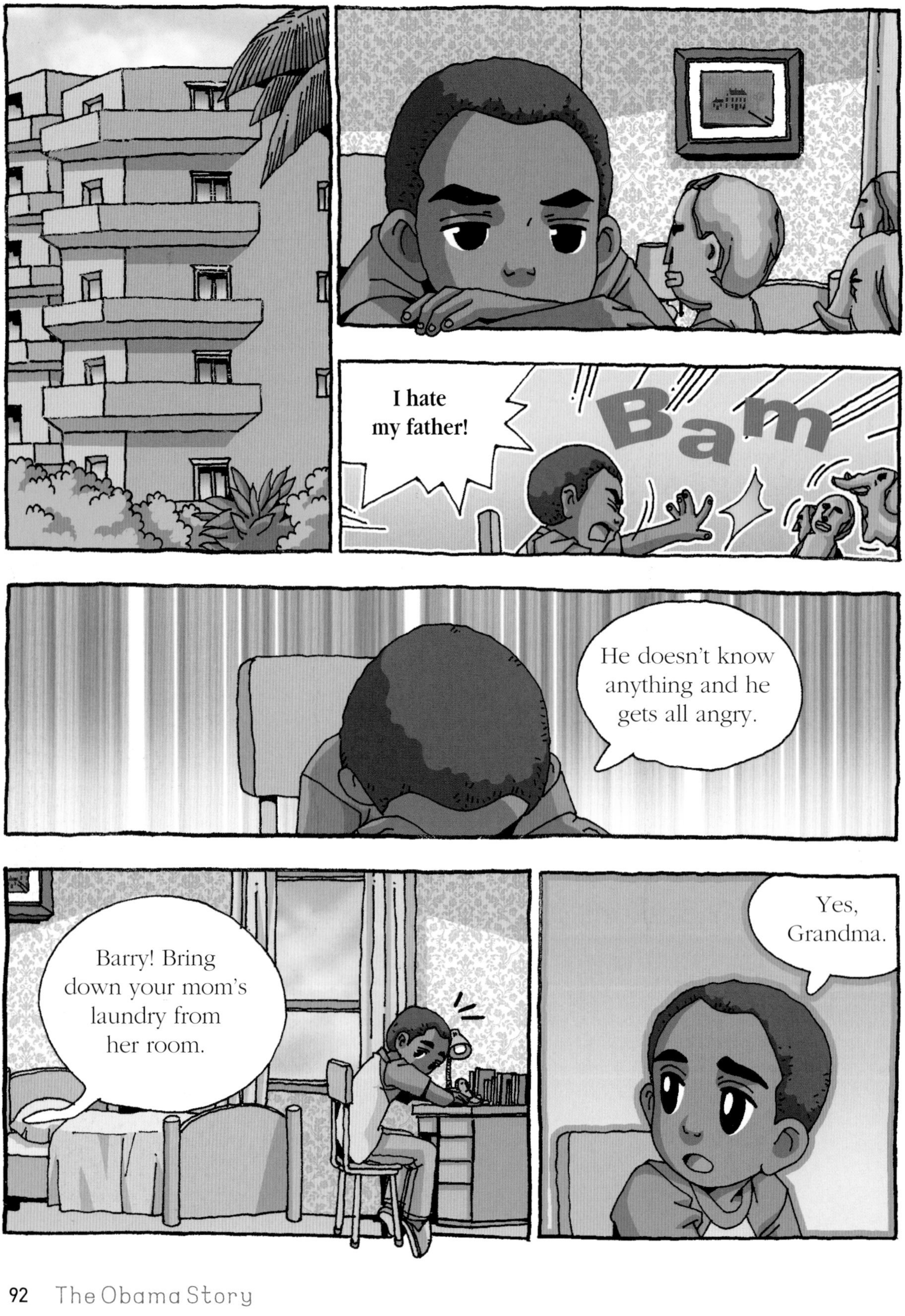
I hate my father!
Bam
He doesn't know anything and he gets all angry.
Barry! Bring down your mom's laundry from her room.
Yes, Grandma.

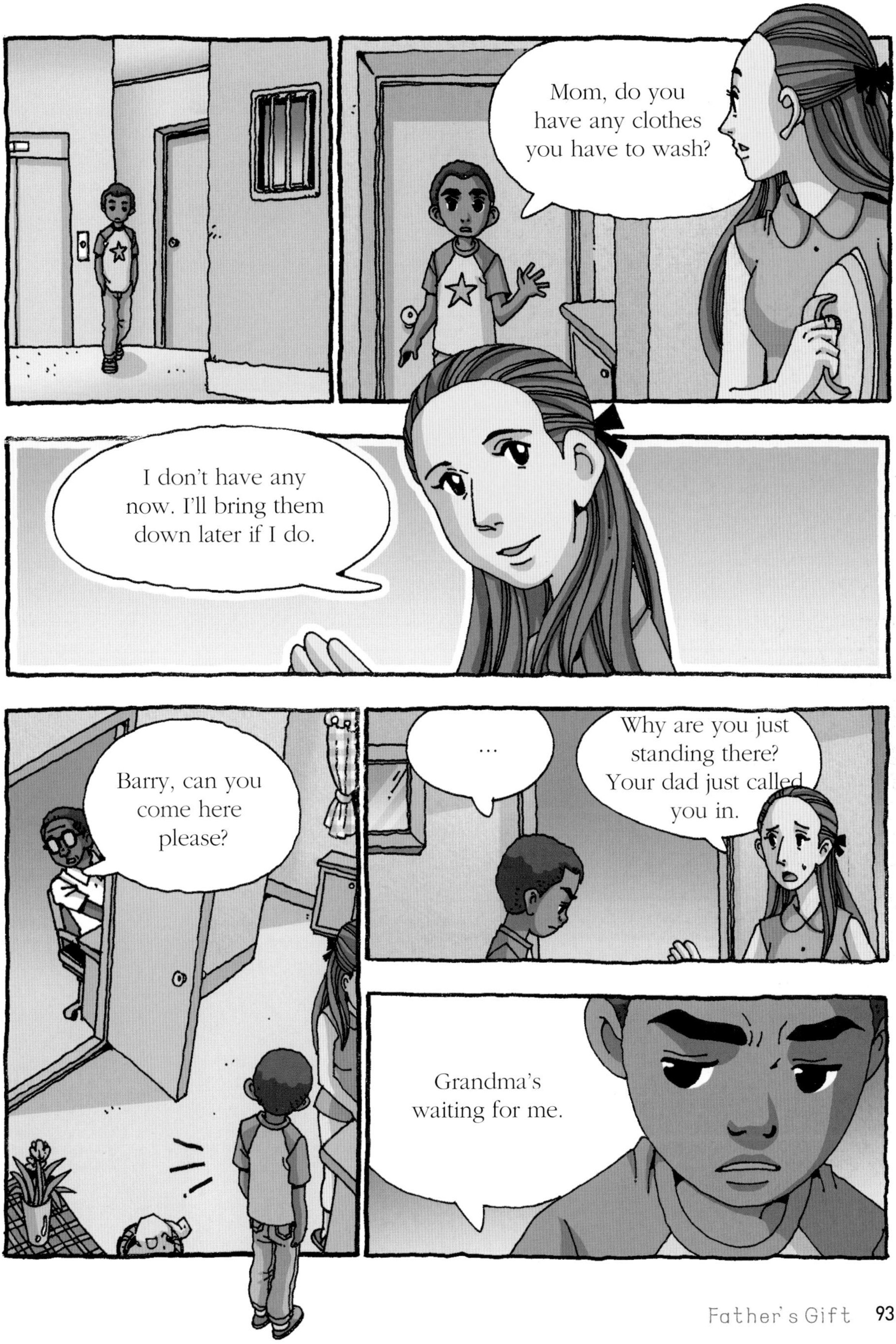
Mom, do you have any clothes you have to wash?
I don't have any now. I'll bring them down later if I do.
Barry, can you come here please?
...
Why are you just standing there? Your dad just called you in.
Grandma's waiting for me.

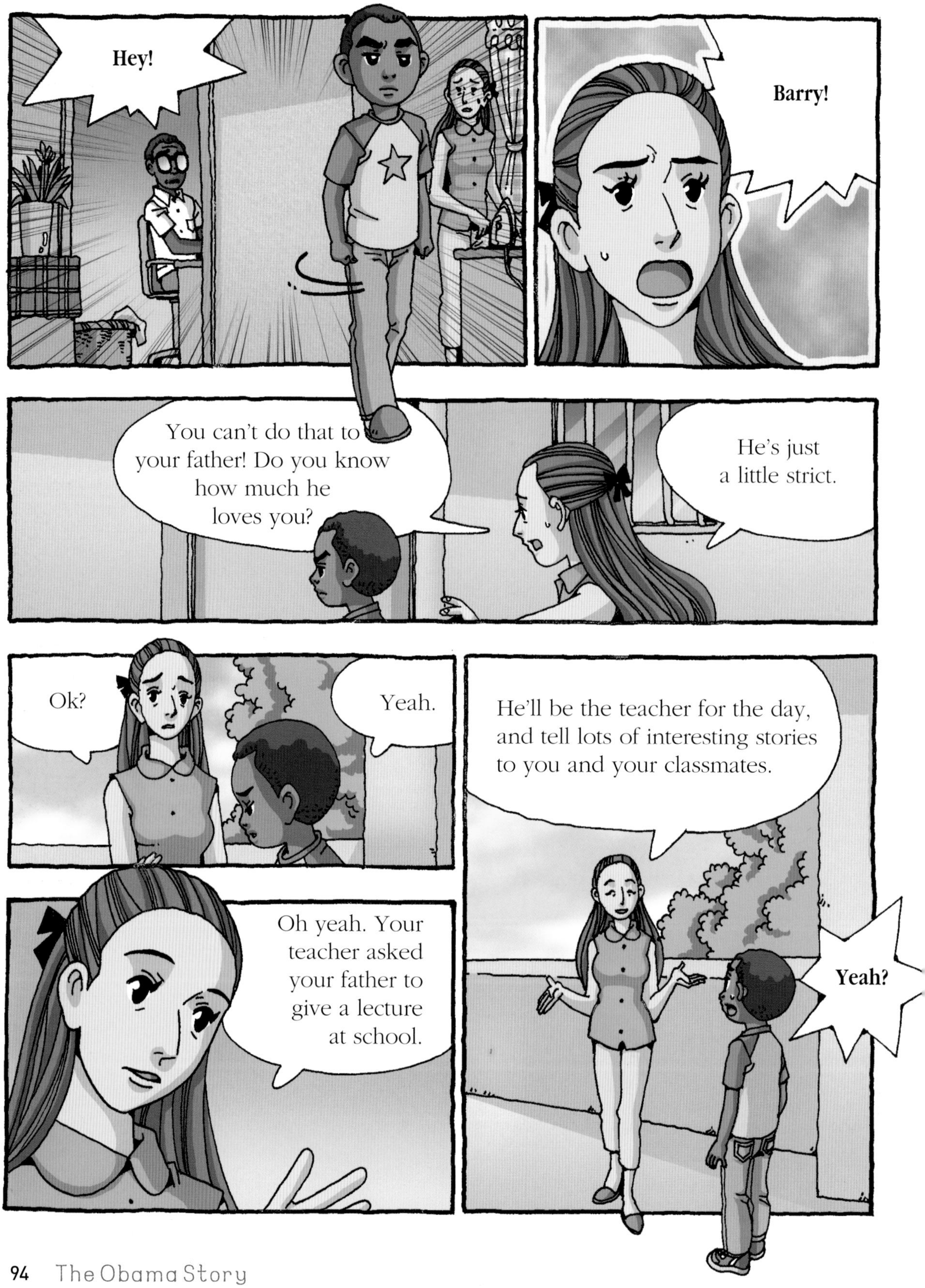
Hey!
Barry!
You can't do that to your father! Do you know how much he loves you?
He's just a little strict.
Ok?
Yeah.
Oh yeah. Your teacher asked your father to give a lecture at school.
He'll be the teacher for the day, and tell lots of interesting stories to you and your classmates.
Yeah?

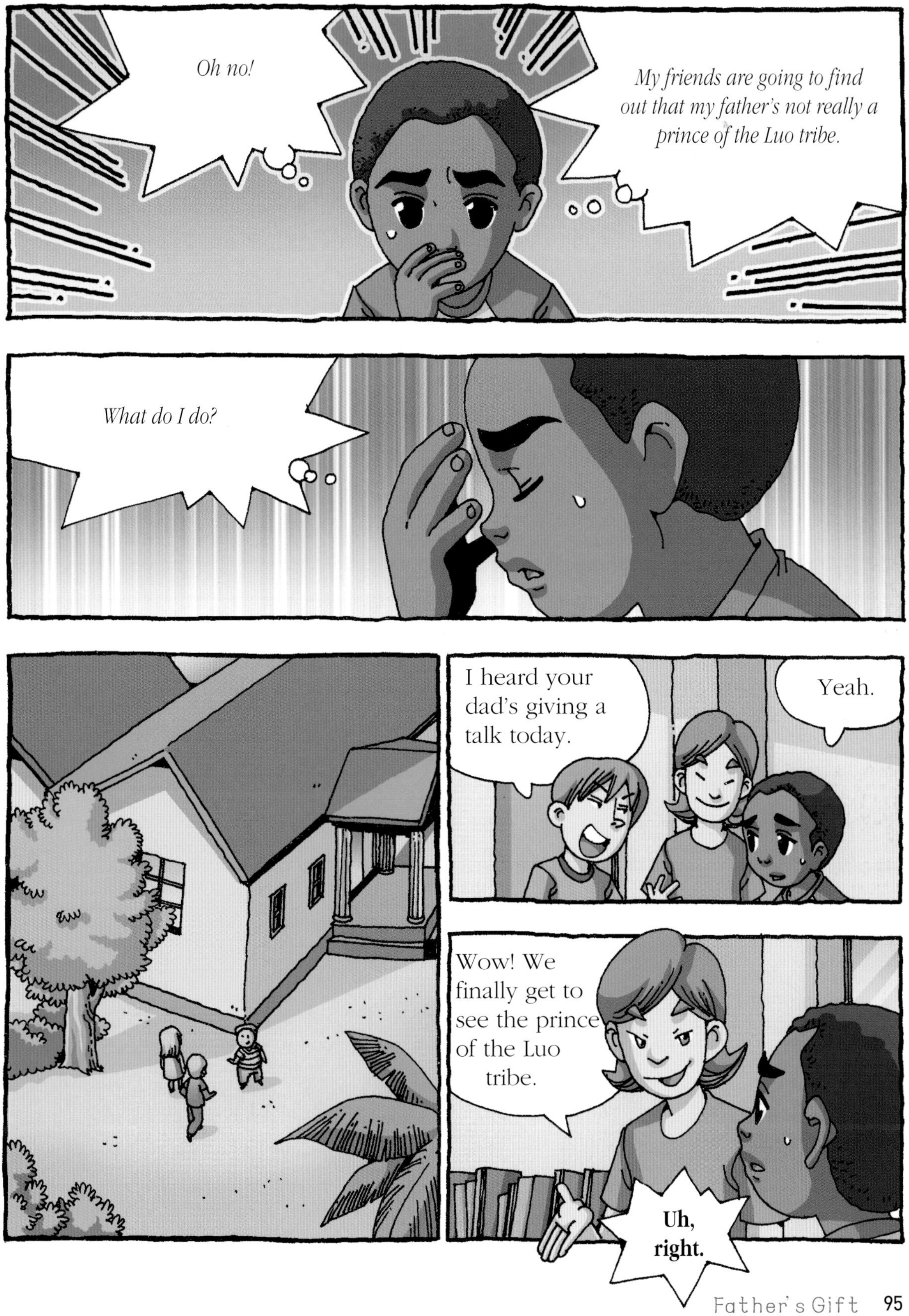
Oh no!
My friends are going to find out that my father's not really a prince of the Luo tribe.
What do I do?
I heard your dad's giving a talk today.
Yeah.
Wow! We finally get to see the prince of the Luo tribe.
Uh, right.

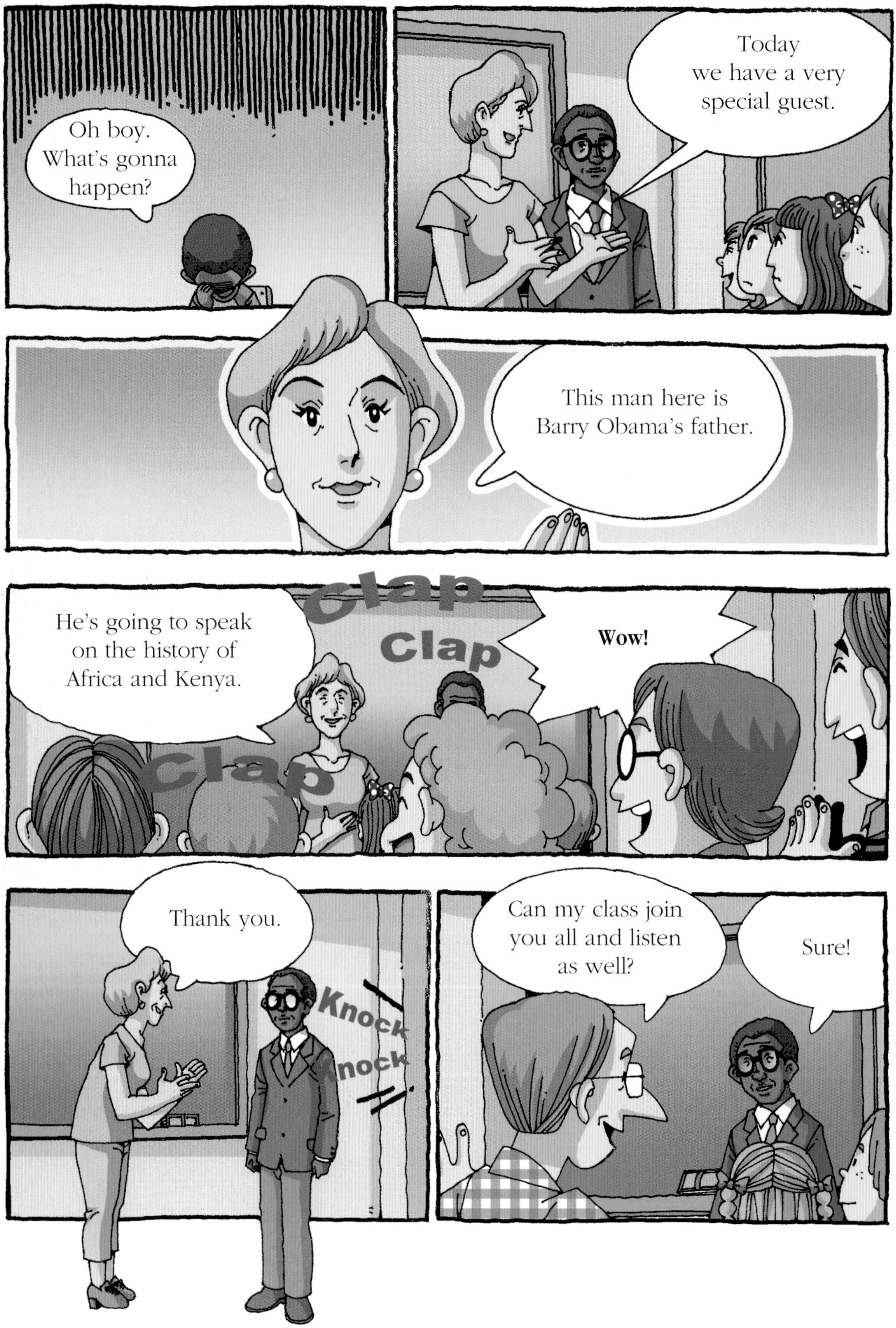

Oh boy. What's gonna happen?
Today we have a very special guest.
This man here is Barry Obama's father.
He's going to speak on the history of Africa and Kenya.
Clap
Clap
Clap
Wow!
Thank you.
Knock
Knock
Can my class join you all and listen as well?
Sure!

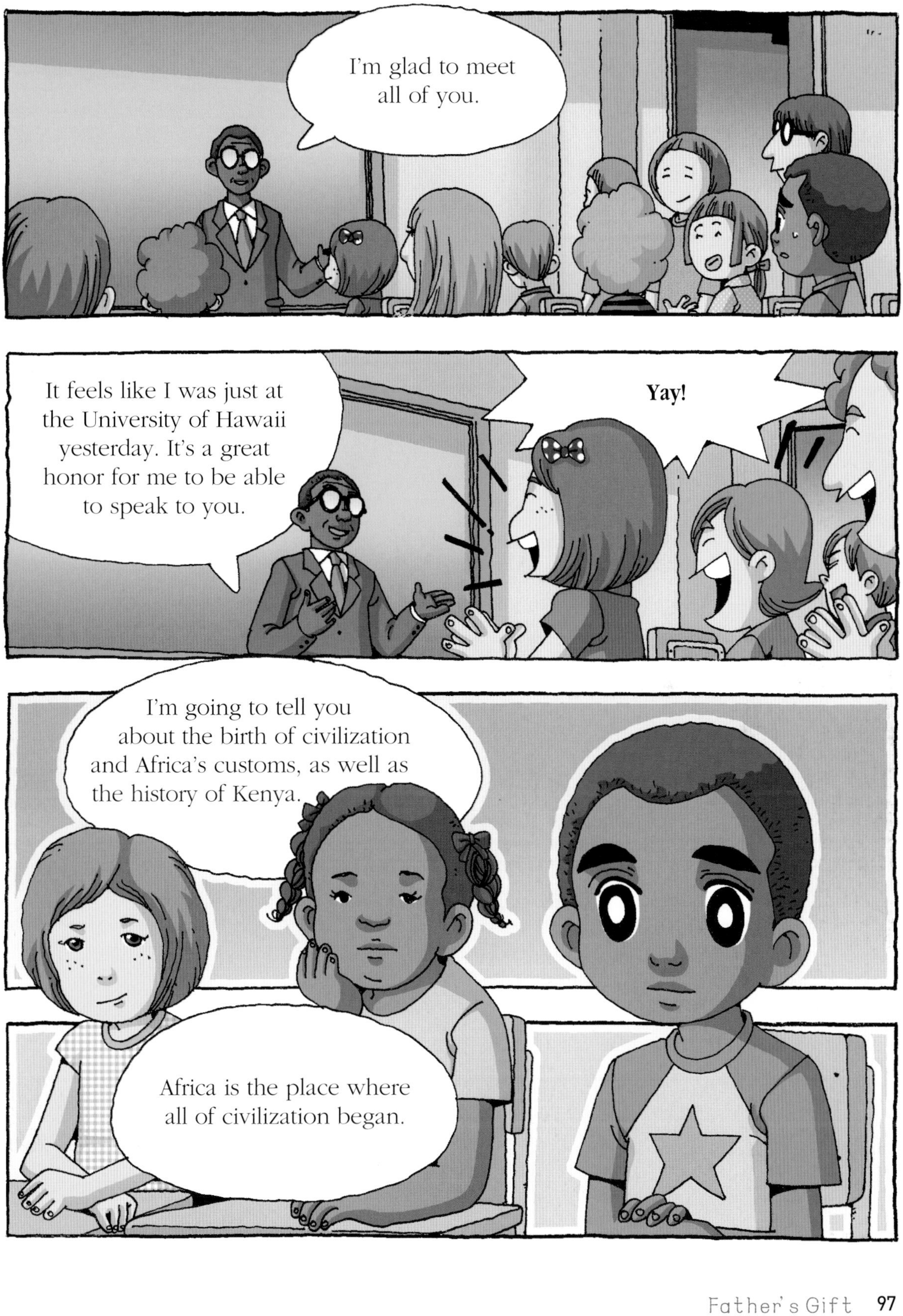
I'm glad to meet all of you.
It feels like I was just at the University of Hawaii yesterday. It's a great honor for me to be able to speak to you.
Yay!
I'm going to tell you about the birth of civilization and Africa's customs, as well as the history of Kenya.
Africa is the place where all of civilization began.

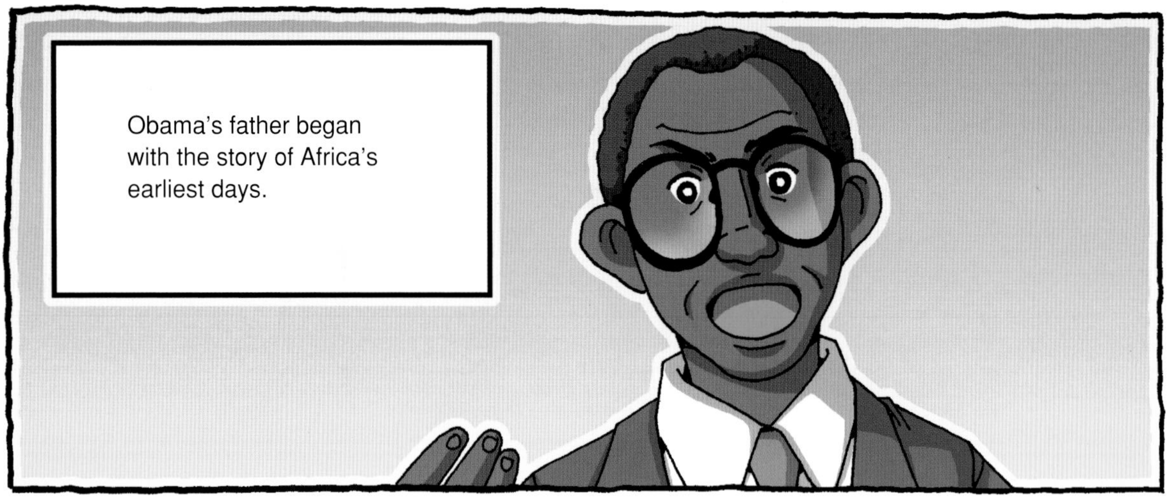
Obama's father began with the story of Africa's earliest days.

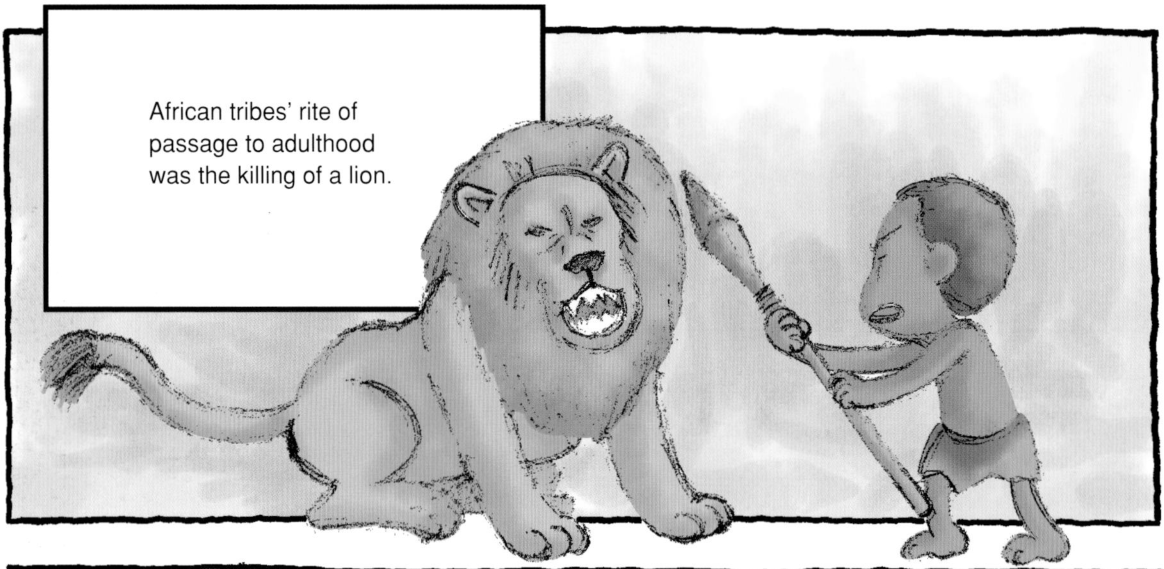
African tribes' rite of passage to adulthood was the killing of a lion.

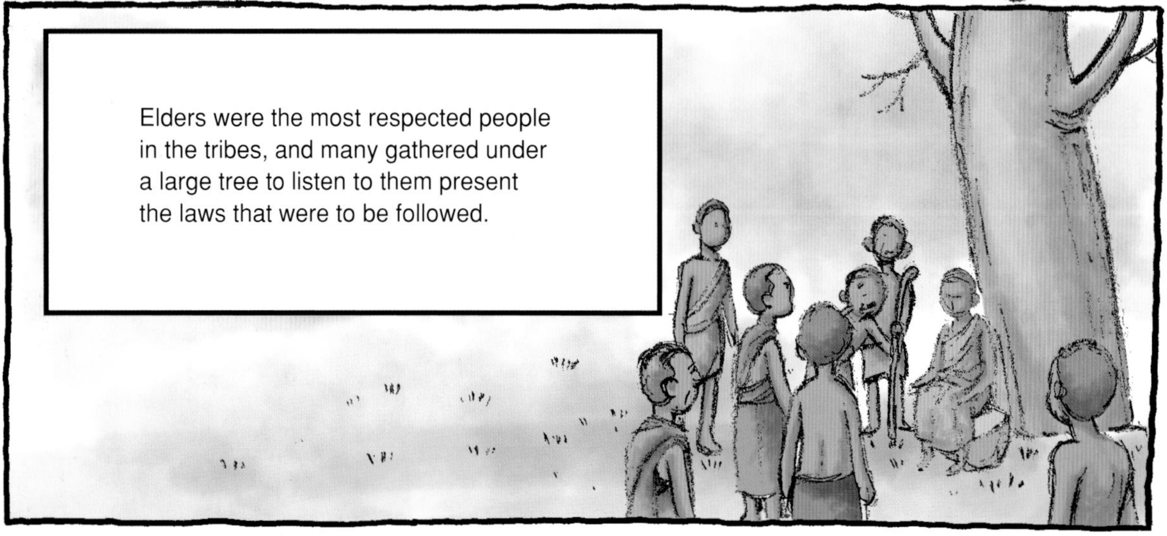
Elders were the most respected people in the tribes, and many gathered under a large tree to listen to them present the laws that were to be followed.

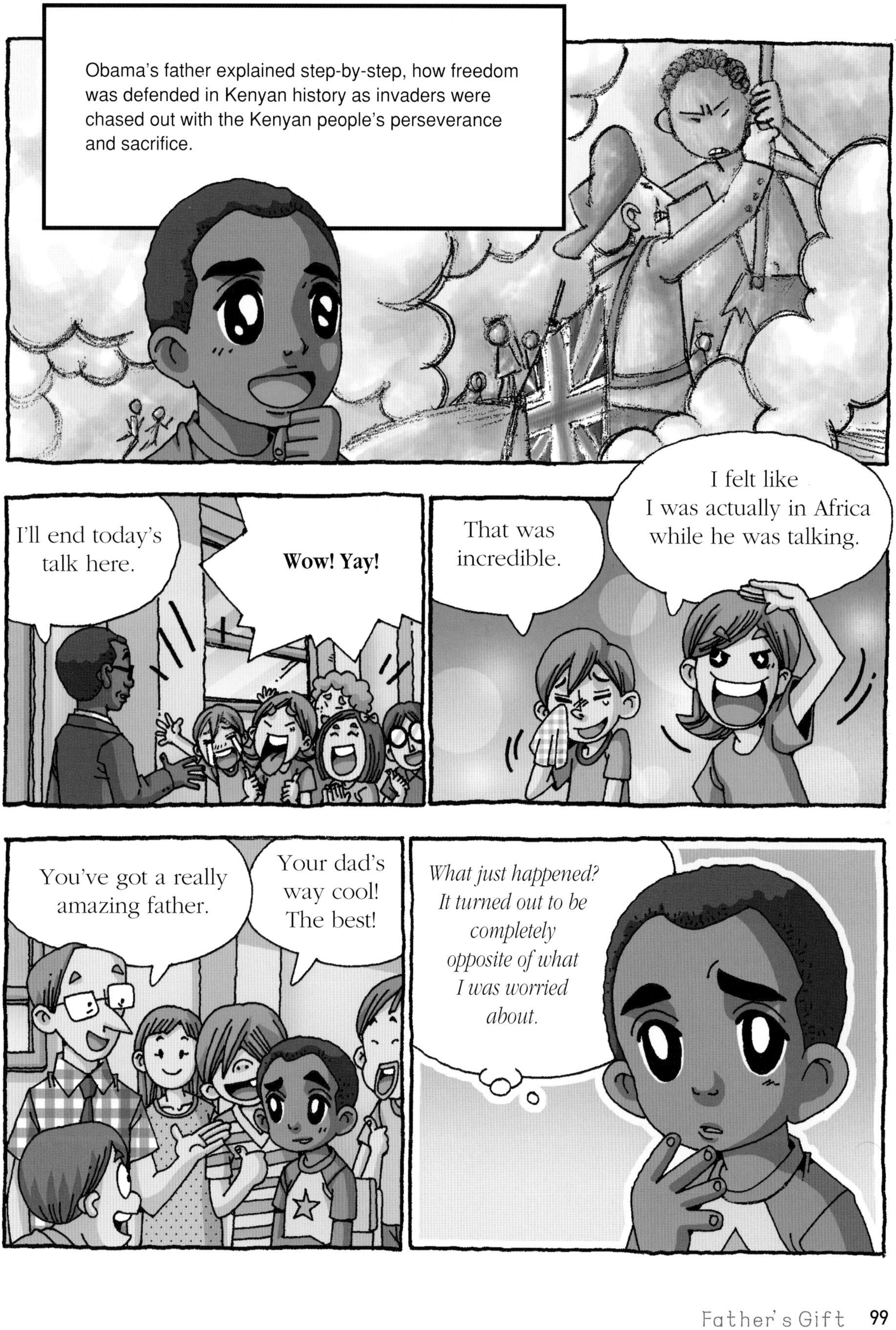
Obama's father explained step-by-step, how freedom was defended in Kenyan history as invaders were chased out with the Kenyan people's perseverance and sacrifice.
I'll end today's talk here.
Wow! Yay!
That was incredible.
I felt like I was actually in Africa while he was talking.
You've got a really amazing father.
Your dad's way cool! The best!
What just happened? It turned out to be completely opposite of what I was worried about.

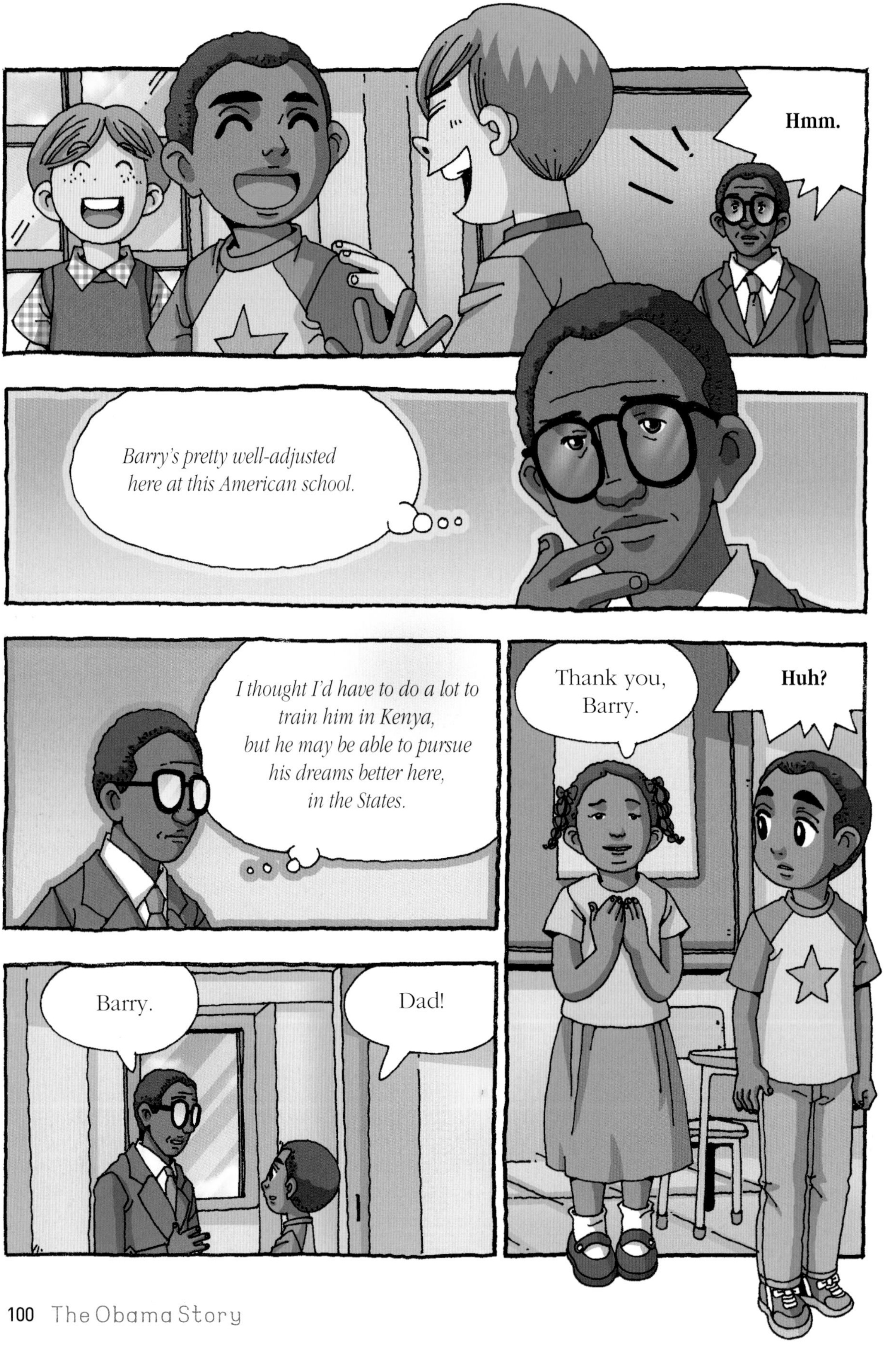
Hmm.
Barry's pretty well-adjusted here at this American school.
I thought I'd have to do a lot to train him in Kenya, but he may be able to pursue his dreams better here, in the States.
Barry.
Dad!
Thank you, Barry.
Huh?

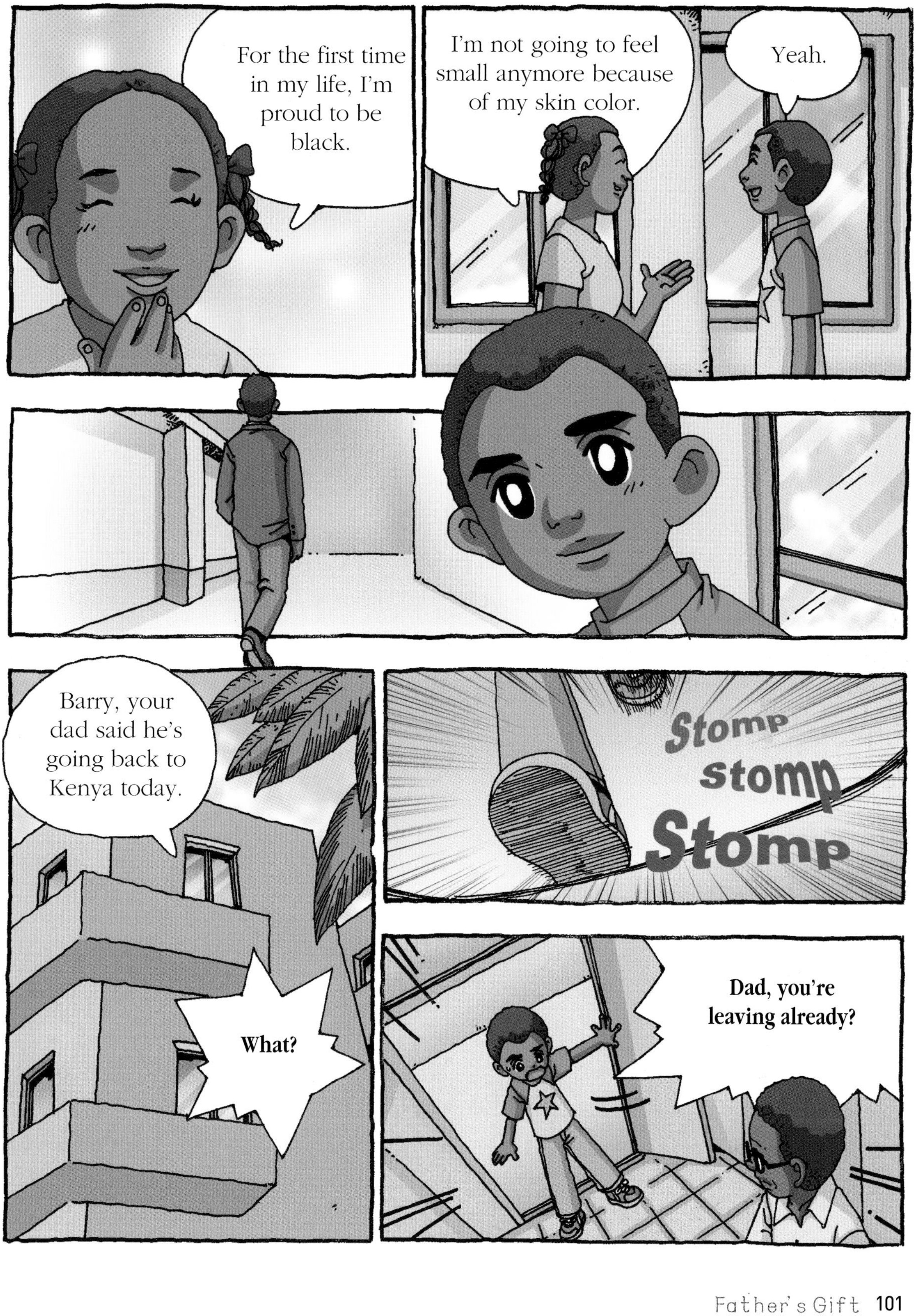
For the first time in my life, I'm proud to be black.
I'm not going to feel small anymore because of my skin color.
Yeah.
Barry, your dad said he's going back to Kenya today.
Stomp
stomp
Stomp
What?
Dad, you're leaving already?

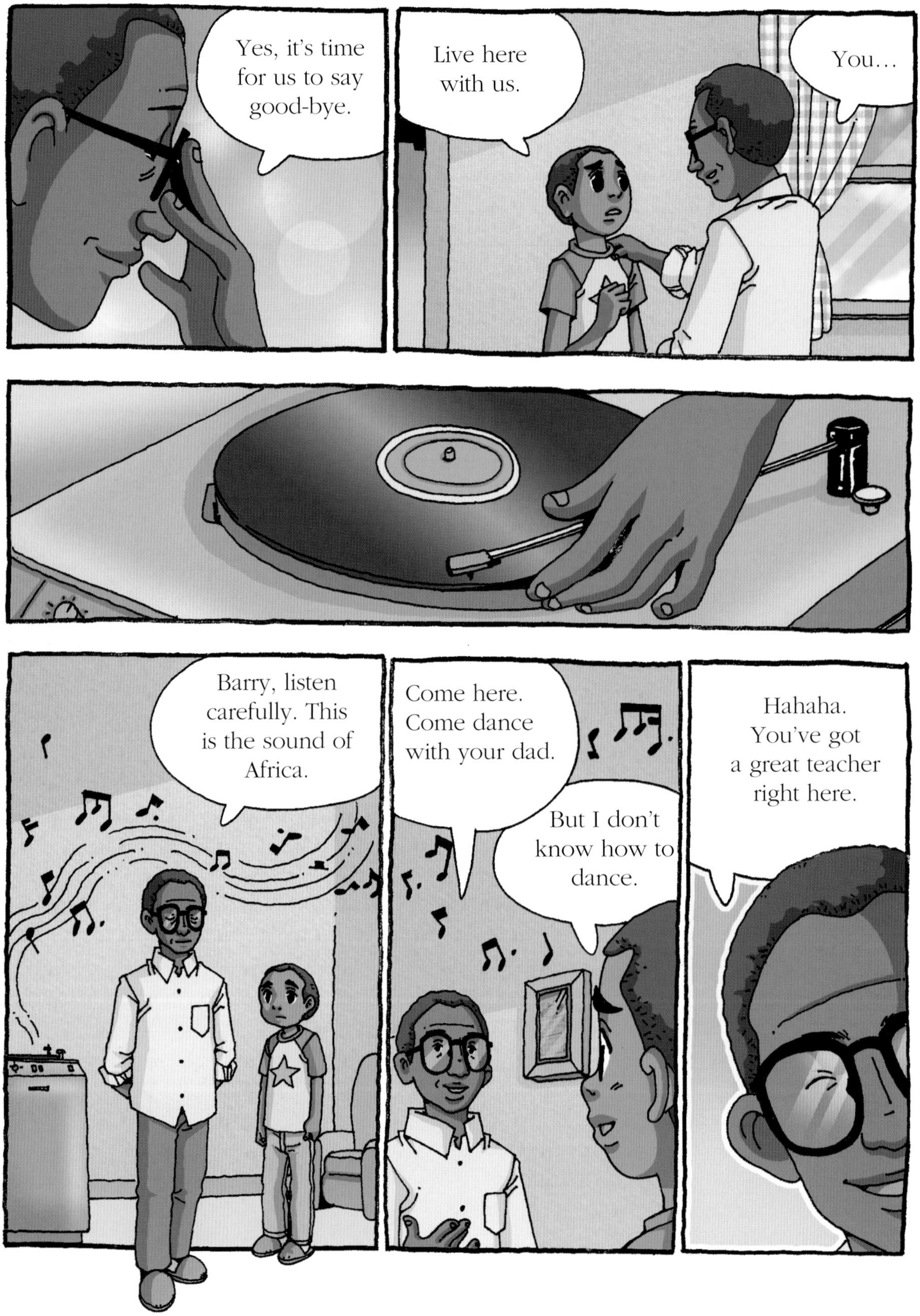
Yes, it's time for us to say good-bye.
Live here with us.
You…
Barry, listen carefully. This is the sound of Africa.
Come here. Come dance with your dad.
But I don't know how to dance.
Hahaha. You've got a great teacher right here.

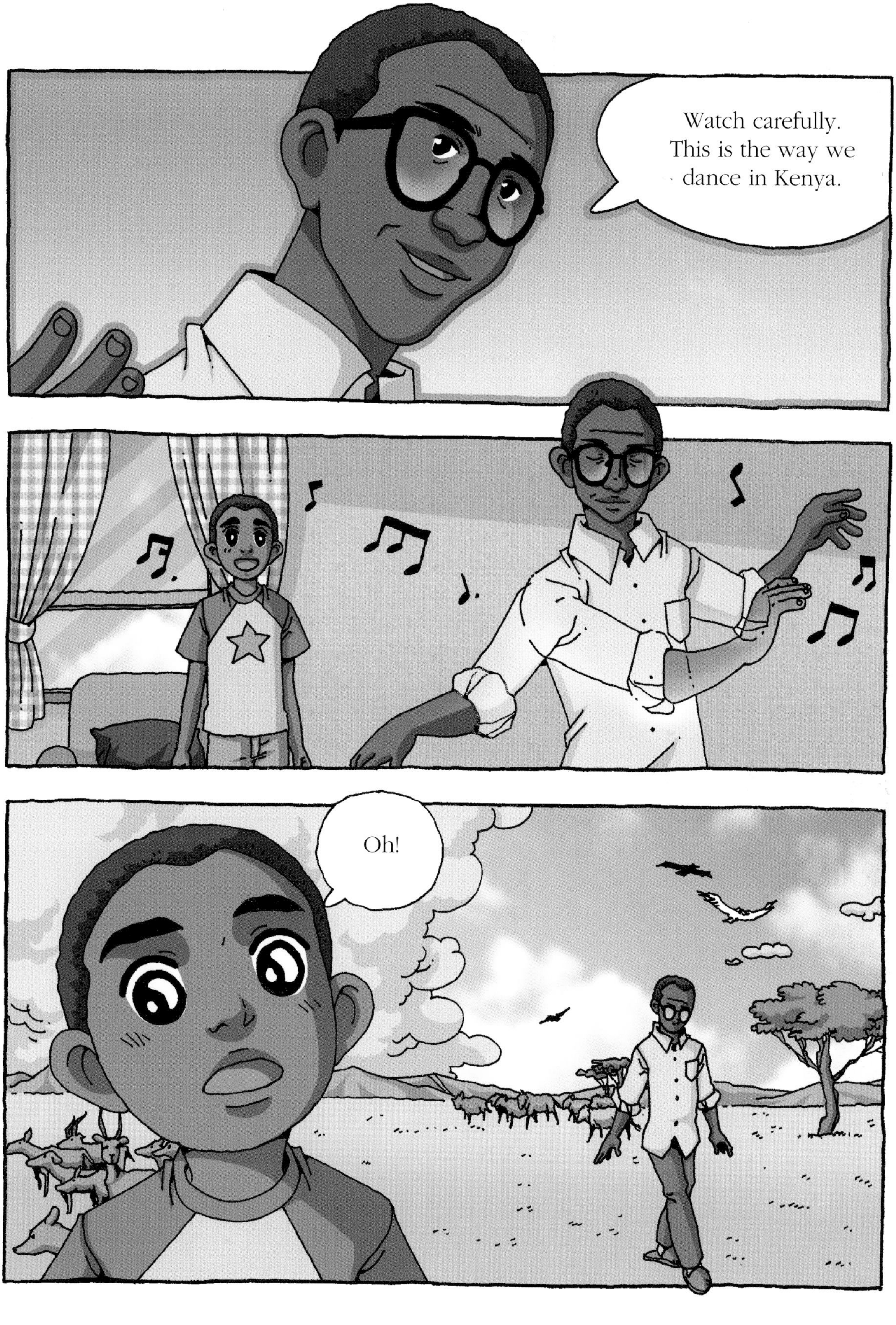
Watch carefully. This is the way we dance in Kenya.
Oh!

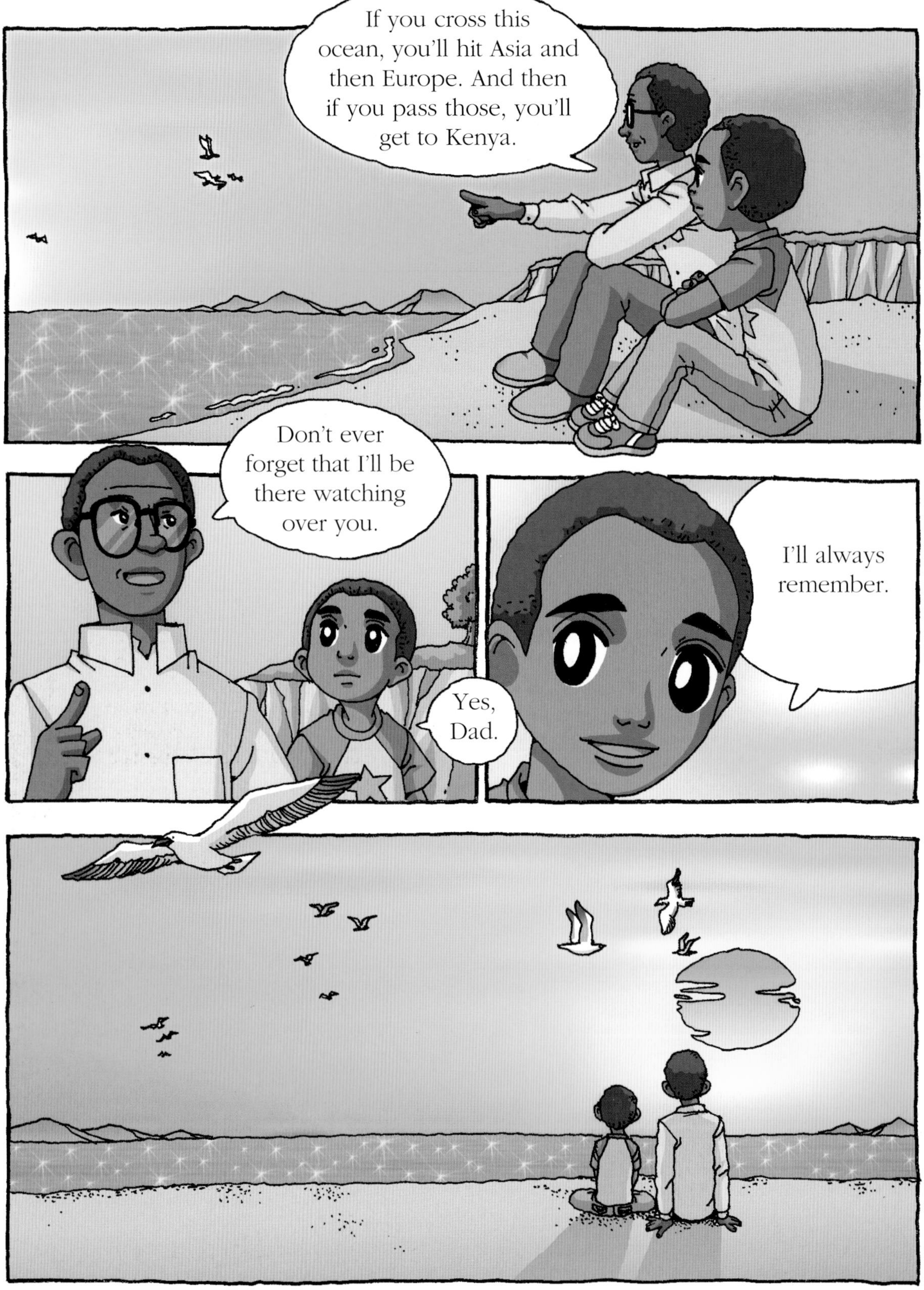
If you cross this ocean, you'll hit Asia and then Europe. And then if you pass those, you'll get to Kenya.
Don't ever forget that I'll be there watching over you.
Yes, Dad.
I'll always remember.

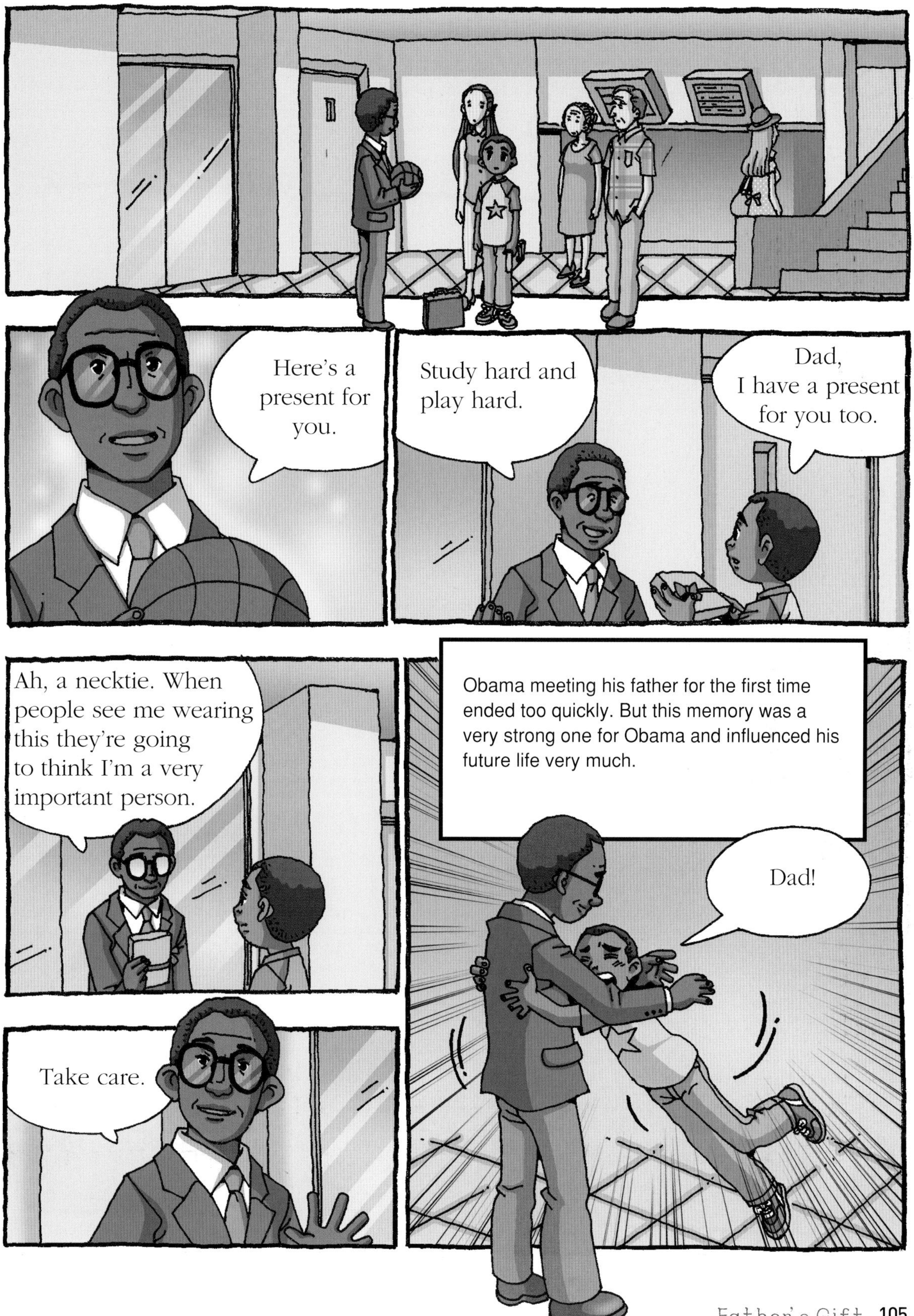
Here's a present for you.
Study hard and play hard.
Dad, I have a present for you too.
Ah, a necktie. When people see me wearing this they're going to think I'm a very important person.
Obama meeting his father for the first time ended too quickly. But this memory was a very strong one for Obama and influenced his future life very much.
Dad!
Take care.

People who have influenced Obama 3

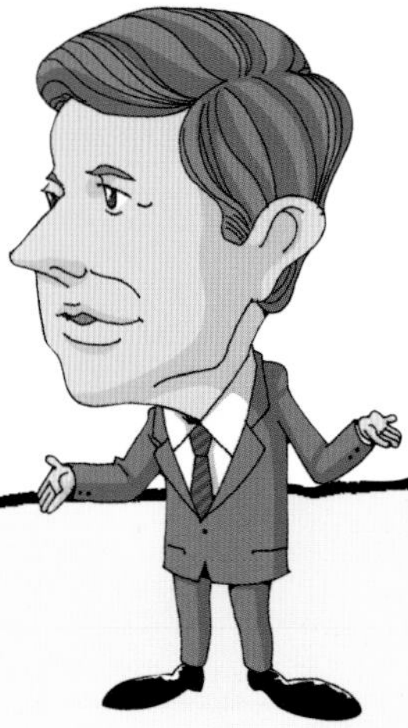

John F. Kennedy

Barack Obama is sometimes called “the black Kennedy” referring to the 35th president of the United States, John F. Kennedy. The reason for the comparison is that they were both young, relatively inexperienced politicians who advocated and brought in fresh change.

What makes Obama respect and resemble John F. Kennedy?

Kennedy was born in Massachusetts on May 29, 1917. He graduated from Harvard University with a degree in politics, and wrote a thesis called “Why was England sleeping?” This was published and became a bestseller. During World War II, Kennedy enlisted in the Navy. The ship he was on was attacked and sunk by the Japanese. His actions then as an admiral to save his subordinates made him a hero.

In 1946, Kennedy began his political career when he was elected to the Massachusetts House of Representatives. In 1952, he was elected to the Massachusetts Senate. And then in 1961, John F. Kennedy became the youngest and first Catholic to become president of the United States.

At that time, the U.S. and the Soviet Union were on very bad terms because of the Cuban missile crisis. But because of President Kennedy’s efforts to have talks with the Soviet head of state, despite the threat of nuclear war, the U.S. and the Soviet Union were able to reconcile.

Tragically, on November 22, 1963, Kennedy was assassinated by gunshot during a motorcade. However, he will always be remembered by many as a young, ambitious man who made a strong effort to achieve world peace.

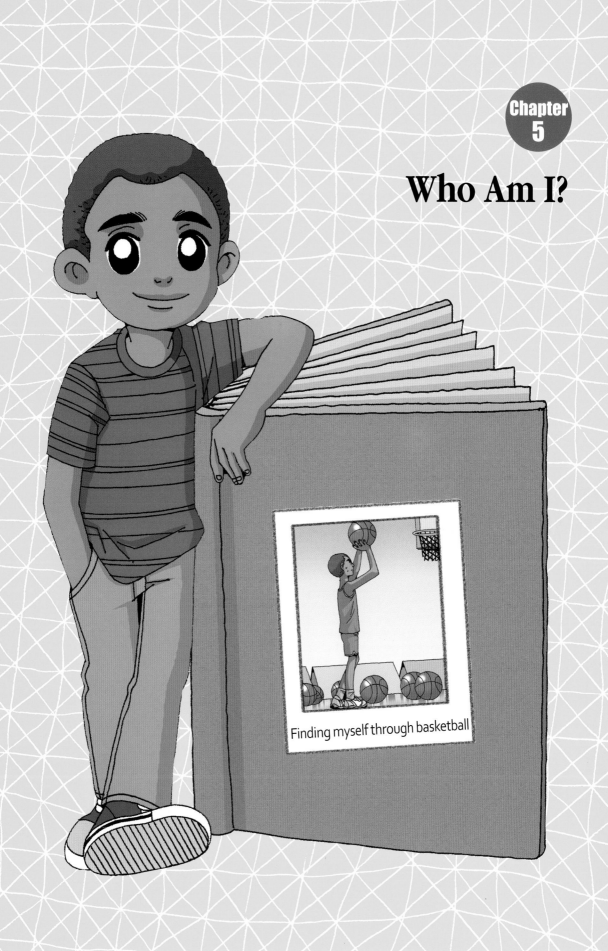

Who Am I?

Finding myself through basketball

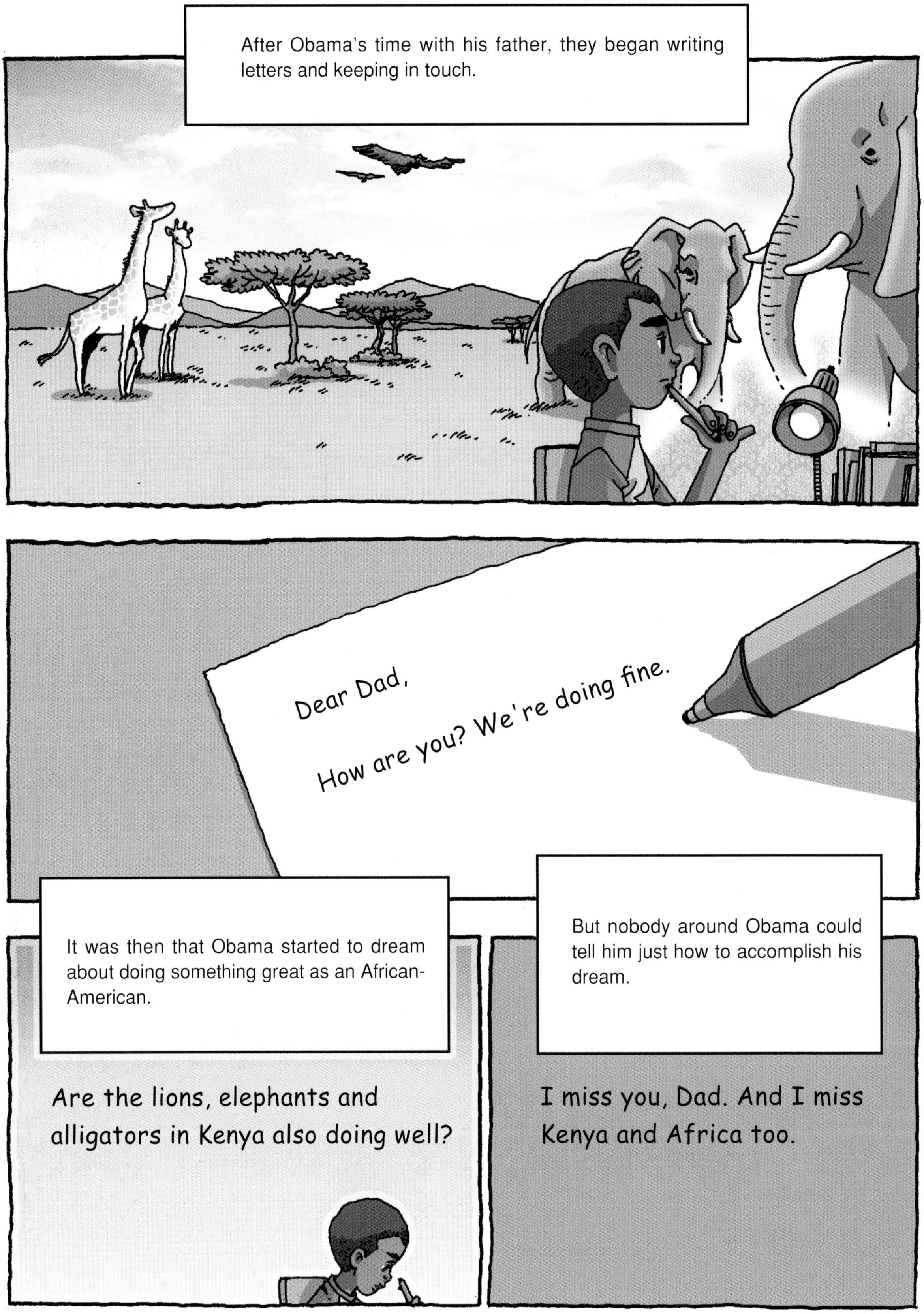
After Obama's time with his father, they began writing letters and keeping in touch.
Dear Dad,
How are you? We're doing fine.
It was then that Obama started to dream about doing something great as an African-American.
Are the lions, elephants and alligators in Kenya also doing well?
But nobody around Obama could tell him just how to accomplish his dream.
I miss you, Dad. And I miss Kenya and Africa too.

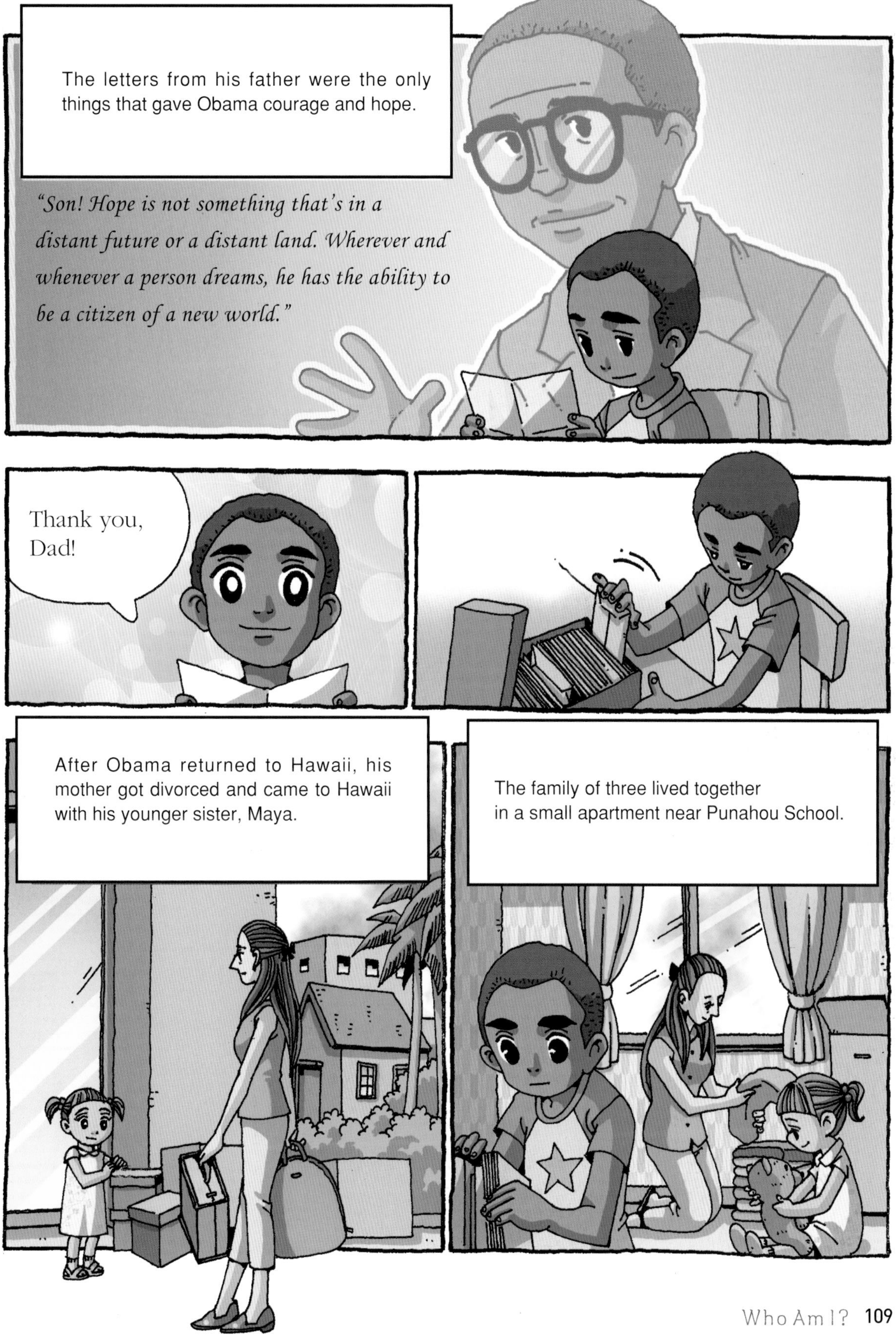

The letters from his father were the only things that gave Obama courage and hope.
"Son! Hope is not something that's in a distant future or a distant land. Wherever and whenever a person dreams, he has the ability to be a citizen of a new world."
Thank you, Dad!
After Obama returned to Hawaii, his mother got divorced and came to Hawaii with his younger sister, Maya.
The family of three lived together in a small apartment near Punahou School.

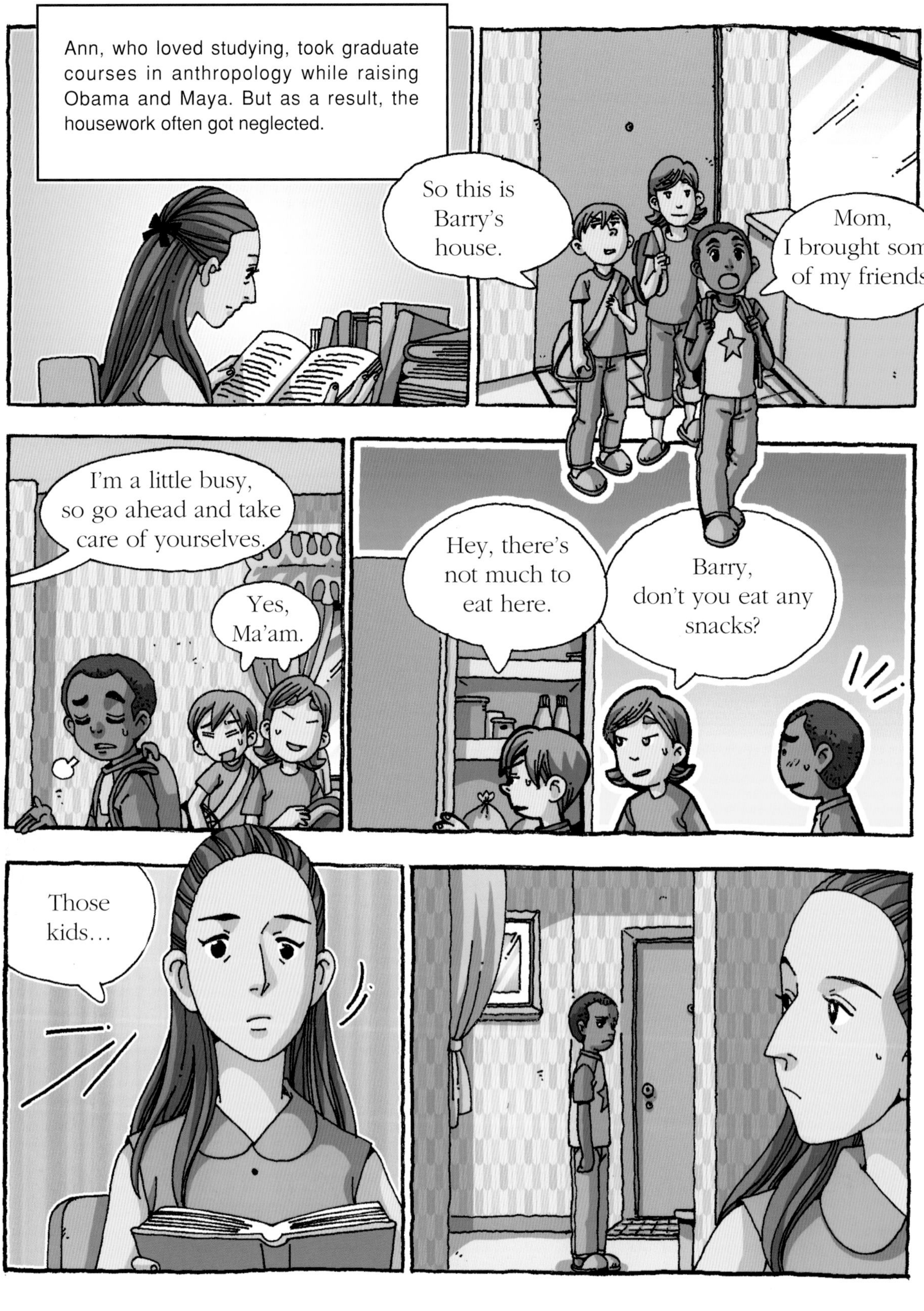

Ann, who loved studying, took graduate courses in anthropology while raising Obama and Maya. But as a result, the housework often got neglected.
So this is Barry's house.
Mom, I brought some of my friends.
I'm a little busy, so go ahead and take care of yourselves.
Yes, Ma'am.
Hey, there's not much to eat here.
Barry, don't you eat any snacks?
Those kids…

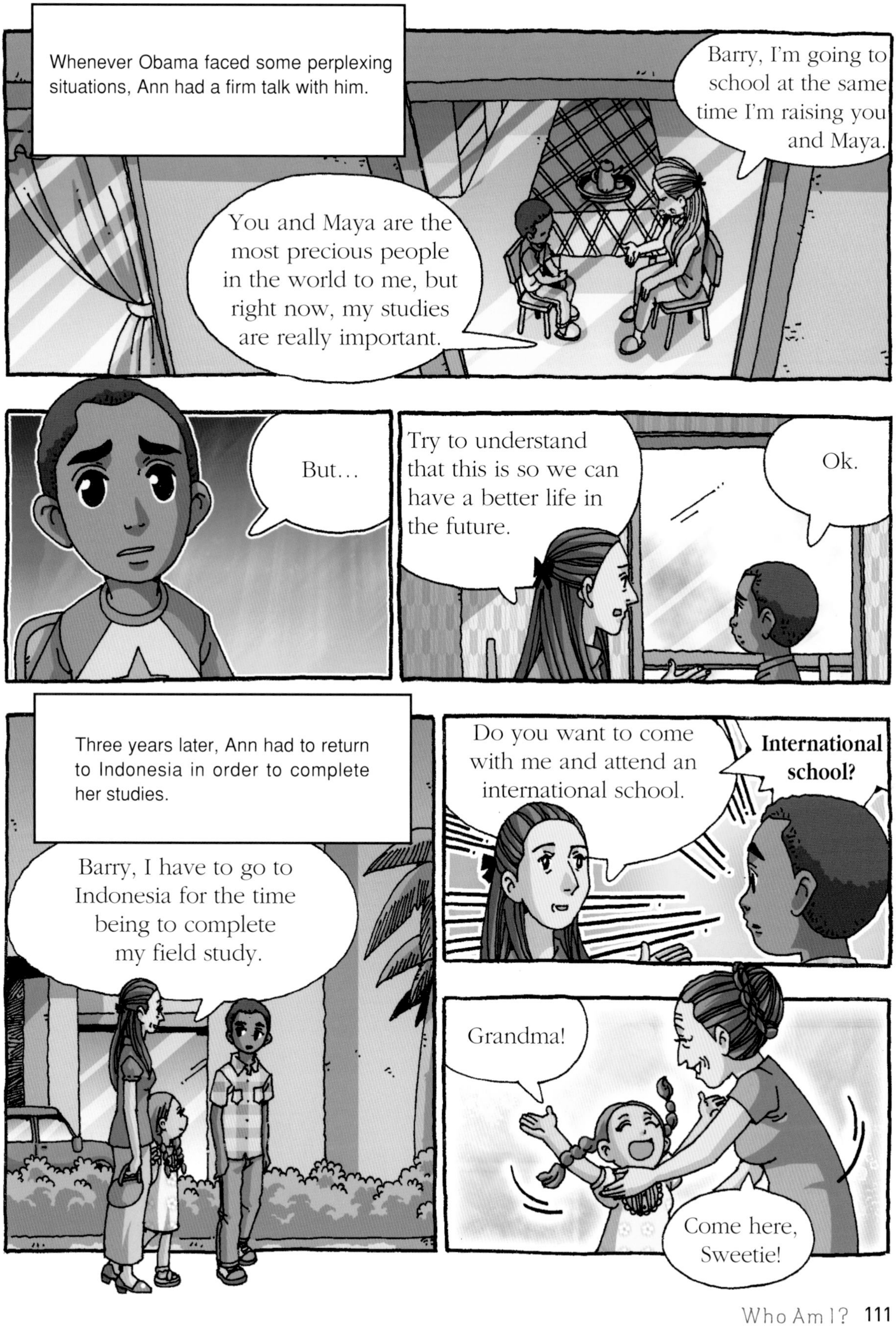
Whenever Obama faced some perplexing situations, Ann had a firm talk with him.
Barry, I'm going to school at the same time I'm raising you and Maya.
You and Maya are the most precious people in the world to me, but right now, my studies are really important.
But…
Try to understand that this is so we can have a better life in the future.
Ok.
Three years later, Ann had to return to Indonesia in order to complete her studies.
Barry, I have to go to Indonesia for the time being to complete my field study.
Do you want to come with me and attend an international school.
International school?
Grandma!
Come here, Sweetie!

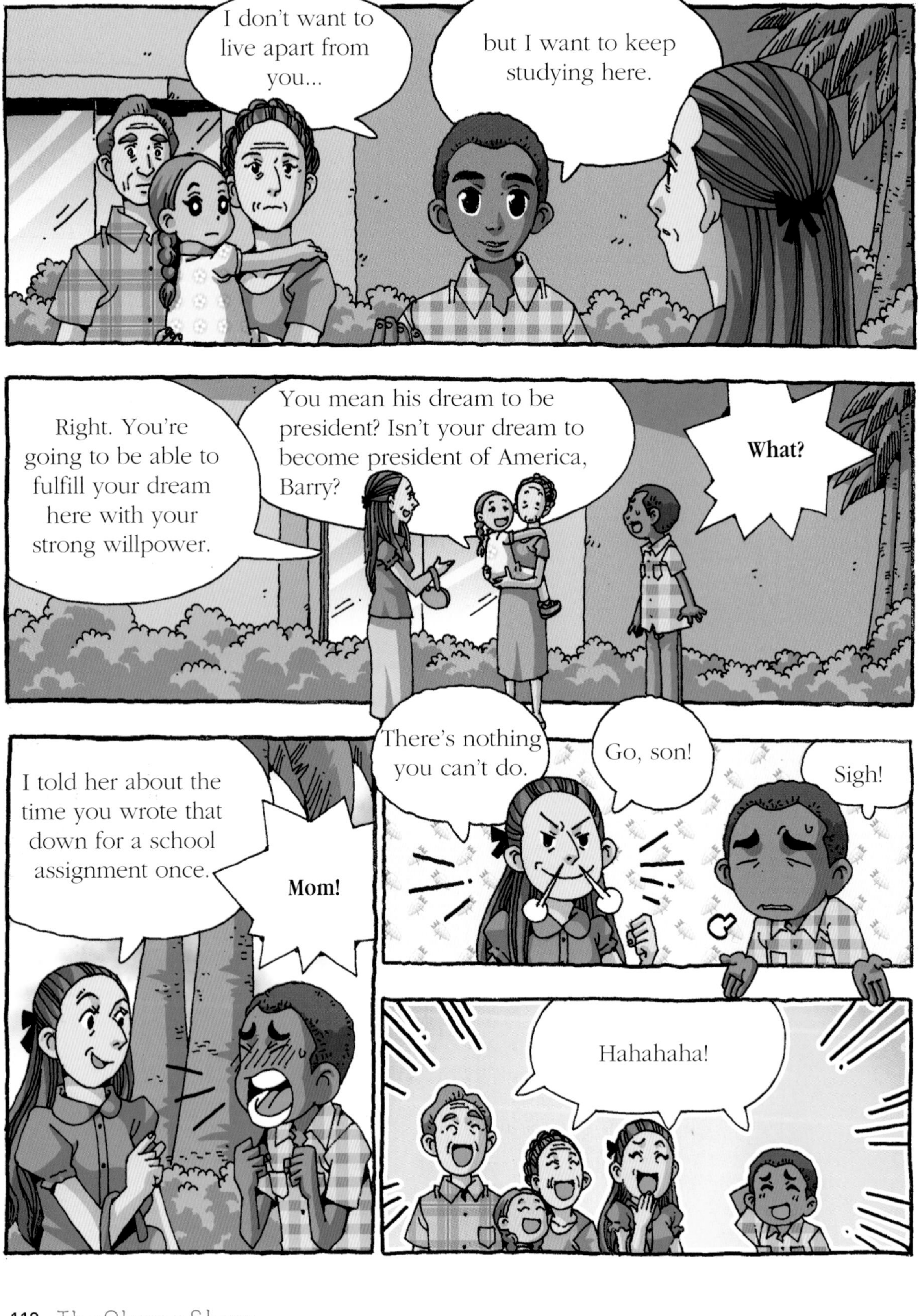
I don't want to live apart from you...
but I want to keep studying here.
Right. You're going to be able to fulfill your dream here with your strong willpower.
You mean his dream to be president? Isn't your dream to become president of America, Barry?
What?
I told her about the time you wrote that down for a school assignment once.
Mom!
There's nothing you can't do.
Go, son!
Sigh!
Hahahaha!

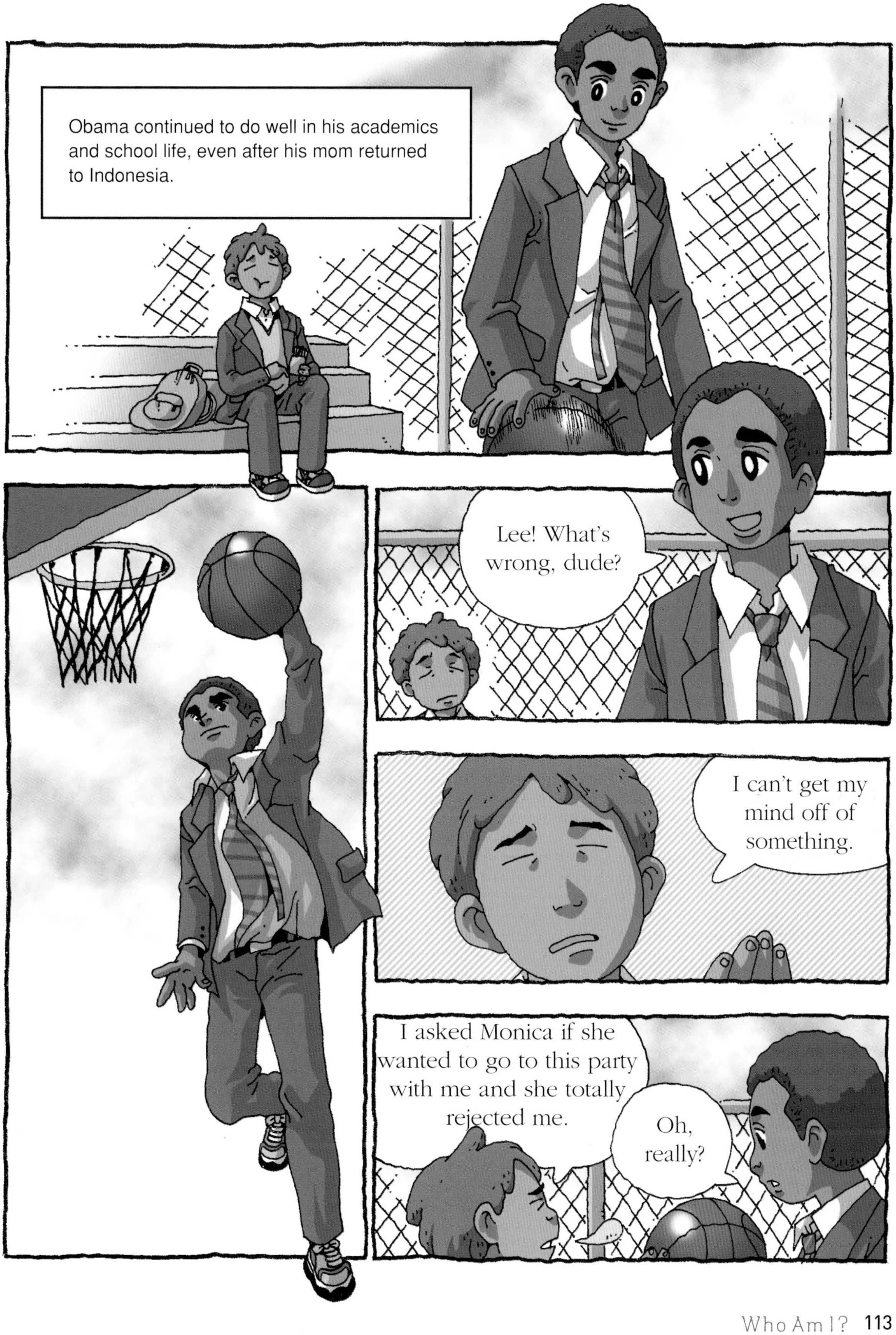
Obama continued to do well in his academics and school life, even after his mom returned to Indonesia.
Lee! What's wrong, dude?
I can't get my mind off of something.
I asked Monica if she wanted to go to this party with me and she totally rejected me.
Oh, really?

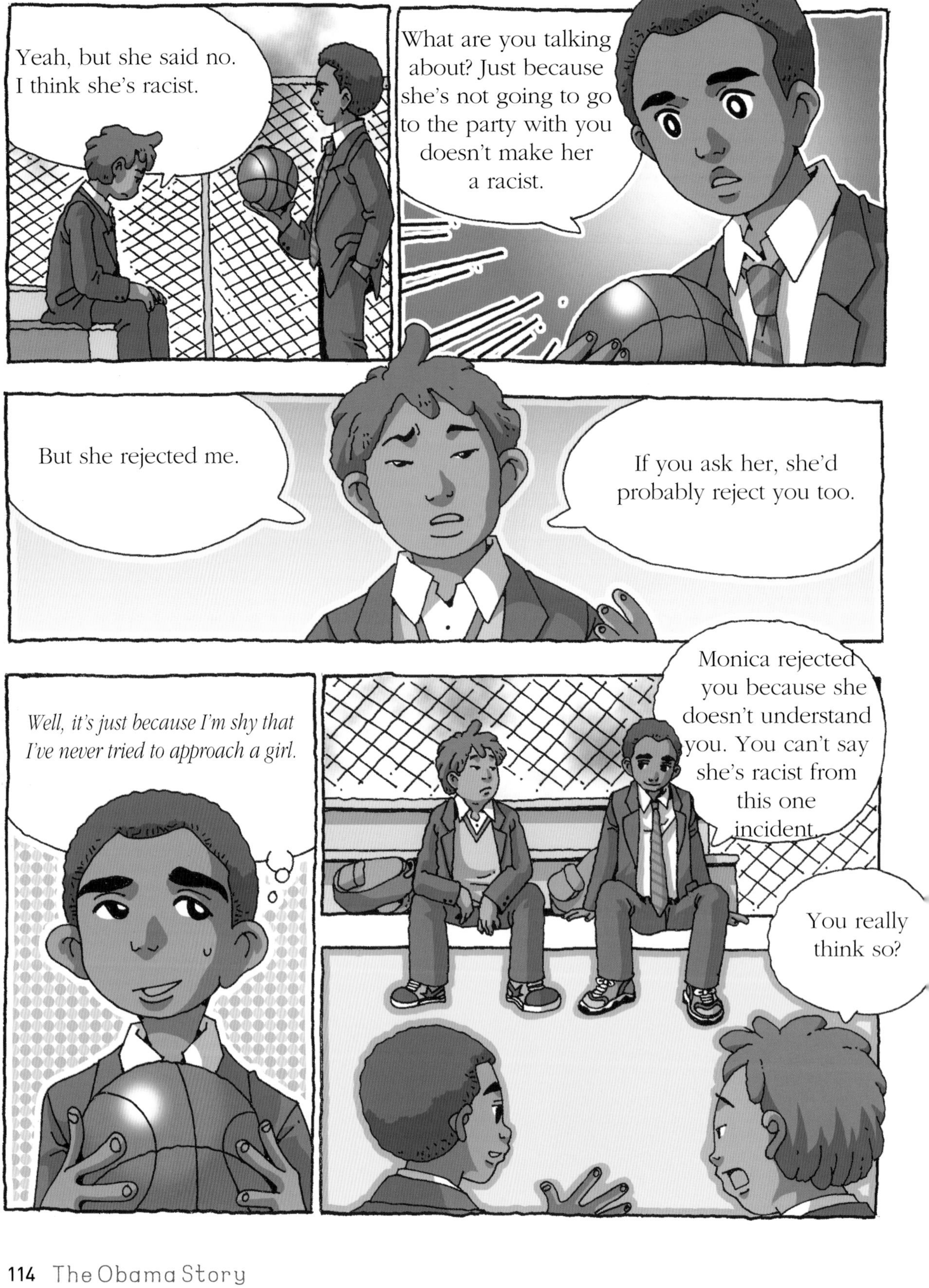
Yeah, but she said no. I think she's racist.
What are you talking about? Just because she's not going to go to the party with you doesn't make her a racist.
But she rejected me.
If you ask her, she'd probably reject you too.
Well, it's just because I'm shy that I've never tried to approach a girl.
Monica rejected you because she doesn't understand you. You can't say she's racist from this one incident.
You really think so?

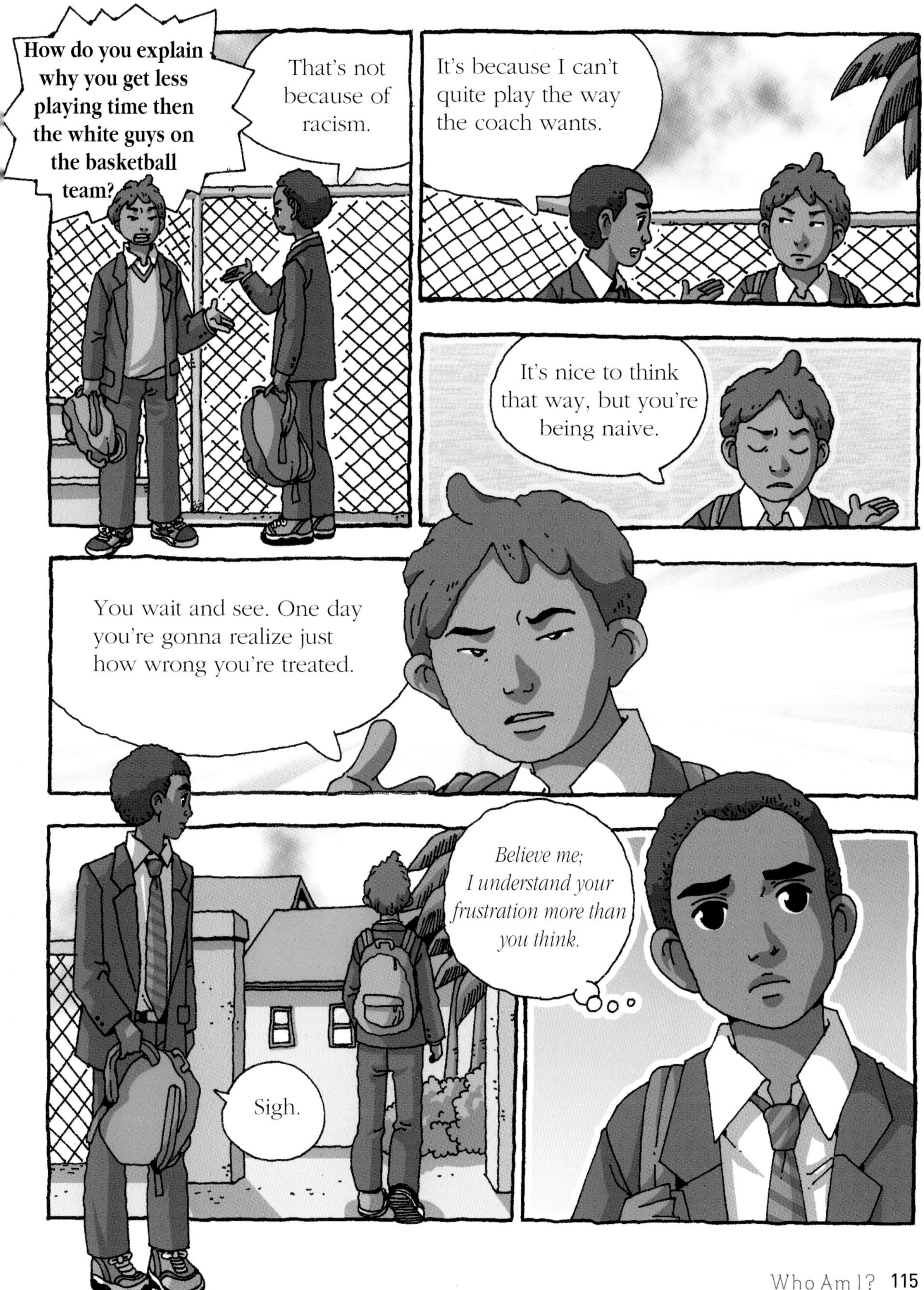
How do you explain why you get less playing time then the white guys on the basketball team?
That's not because of racism.
It's because I can't quite play the way the coach wants.
It's nice to think that way, but you're being naive.
You wait and see. One day you're gonna realize just how wrong you're treated.
Sigh.
Believe me; I understand your frustration more than you think.

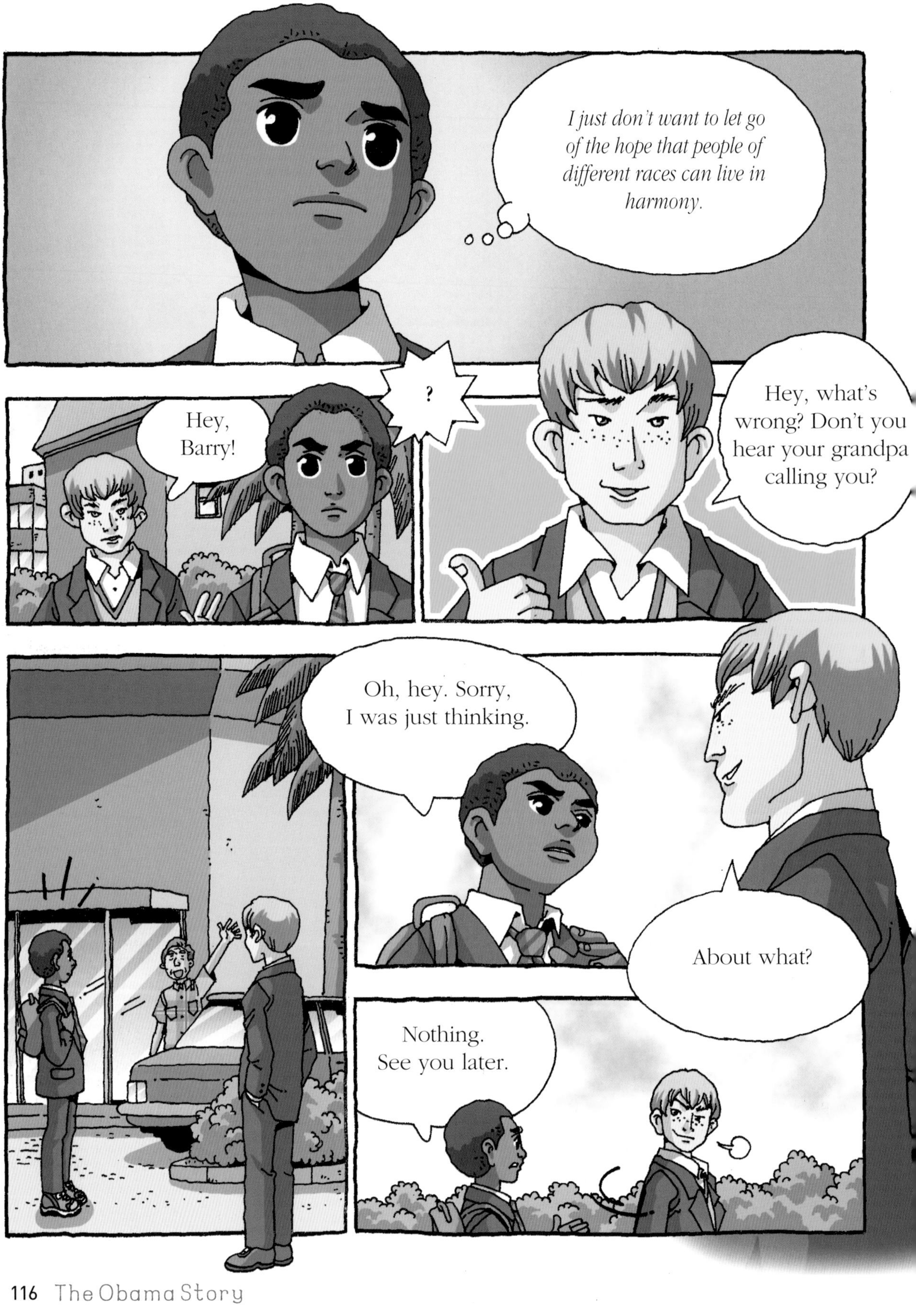
I just don't want to let go of the hope that people of different races can live in harmony.
Hey, Barry!
?
Hey, what's wrong? Don't you hear your grandpa calling you?
Oh, hey. Sorry, I was just thinking.
About what?
Nothing. See you later.

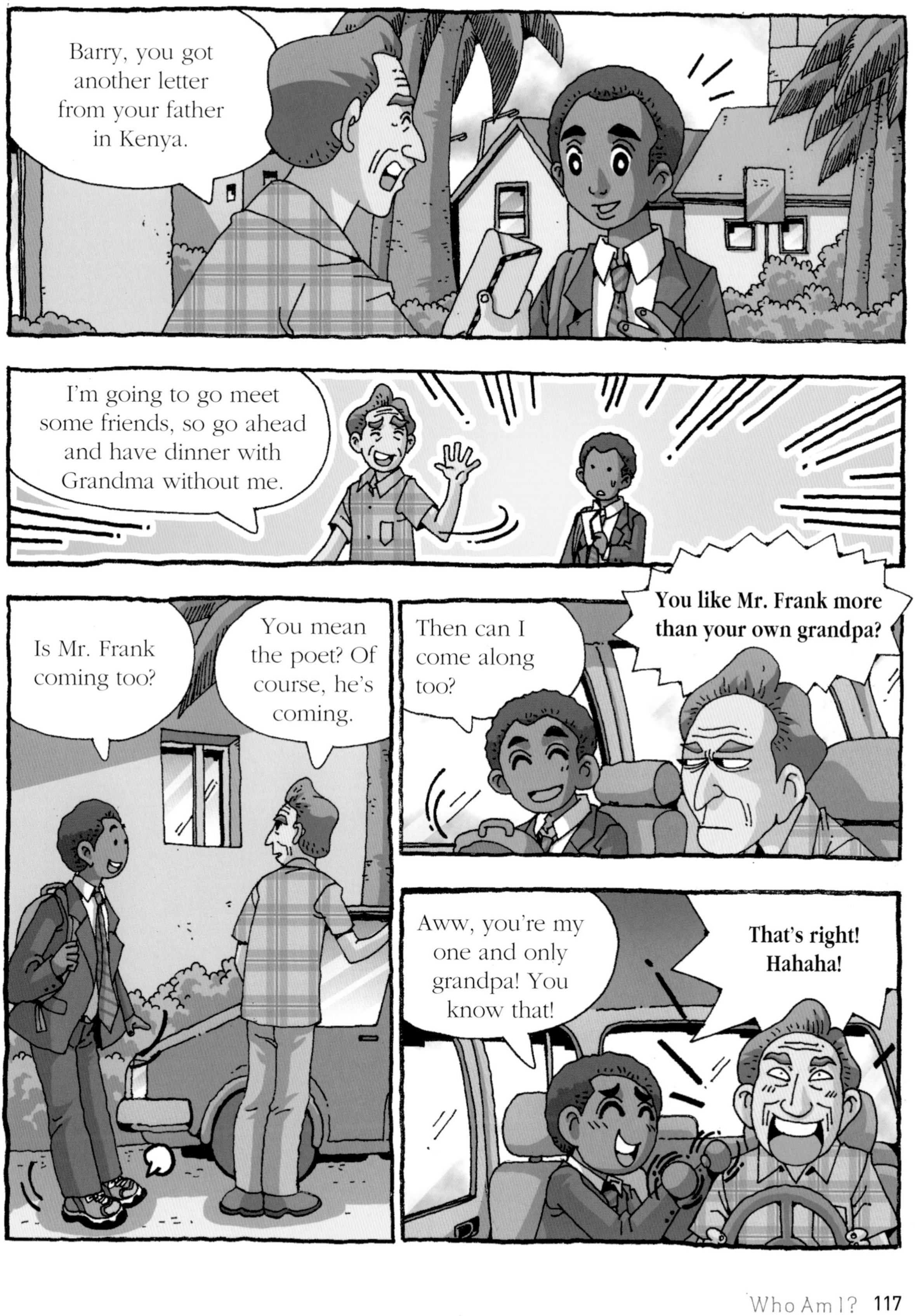
Barry, you got another letter from your father in Kenya.
I'm going to go meet some friends, so go ahead and have dinner with Grandma without me.
Is Mr. Frank coming too?
You mean the poet? Of course, he's coming.
Then can I come along too?
You like Mr. Frank more than your own grandpa?
Aww, you're my one and only grandpa! You know that!
That's right! Hahaha!

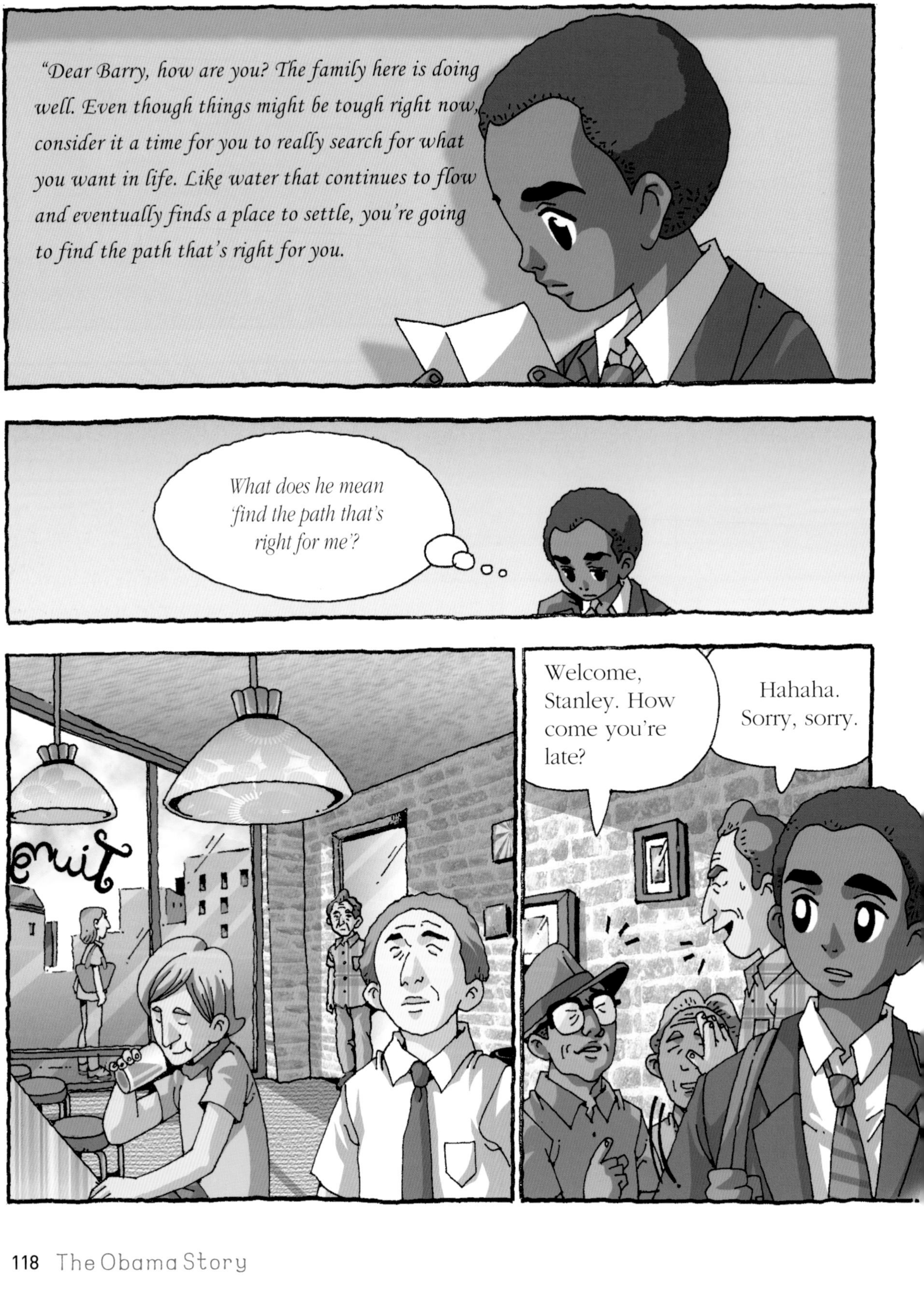
"Dear Barry, how are you? The family here is doing well. Even though things might be tough right now, consider it a time for you to really search for what you want in life. Like water that continues to flow and eventually finds a place to settle, you're going to find the path that's right for you.
What does he mean 'find the path that's right for me'?
Welcome, Stanley. How come you're late?
Hahaha. Sorry, sorry.

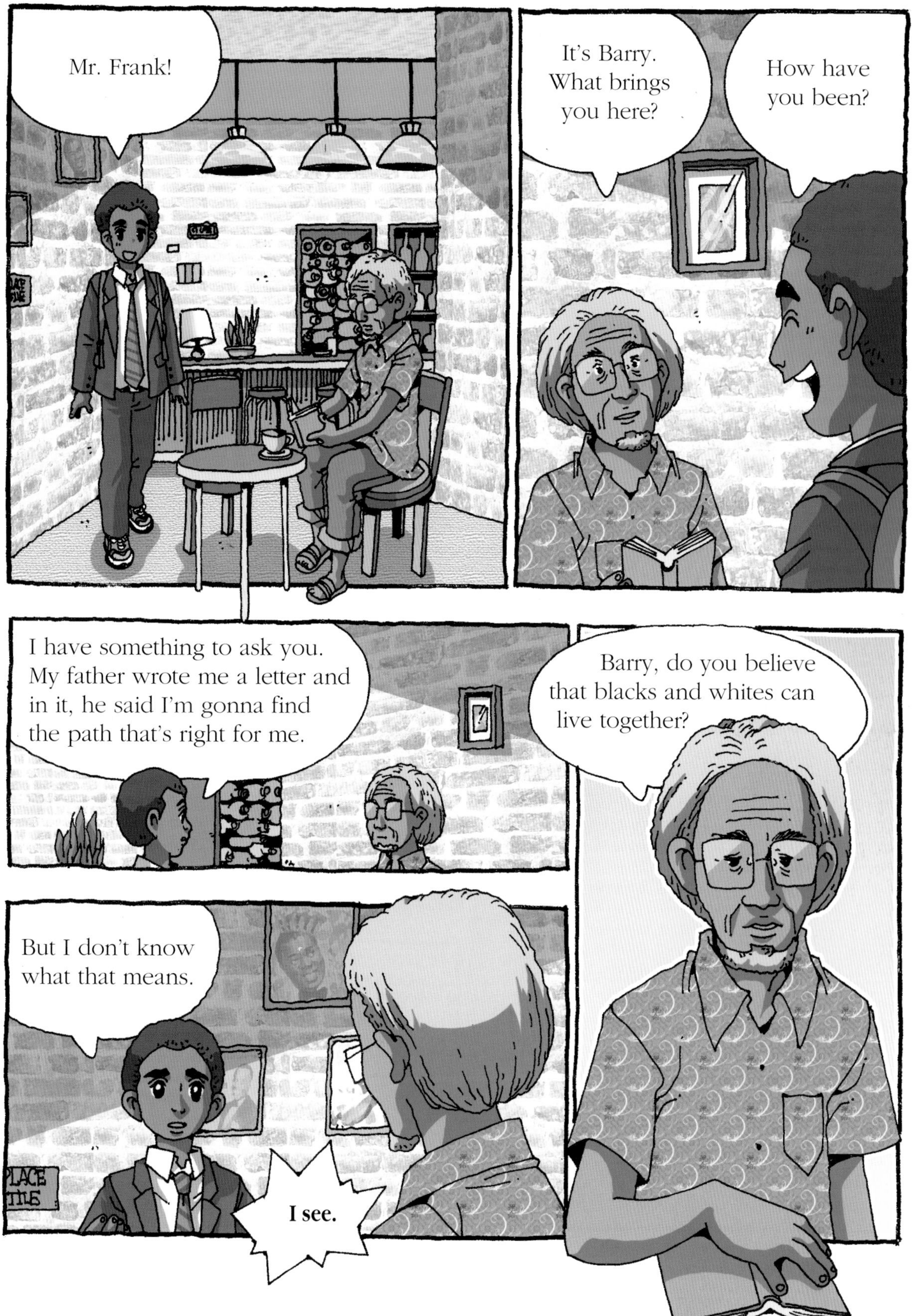
Mr. Frank!
It's Barry. What brings you here?
How have you been?
I have something to ask you. My father wrote me a letter and in it, he said I'm gonna find the path that's right for me.
But I don't know what that means.
I see.
Barry, do you believe that blacks and whites can live together?
PLACE TITLE

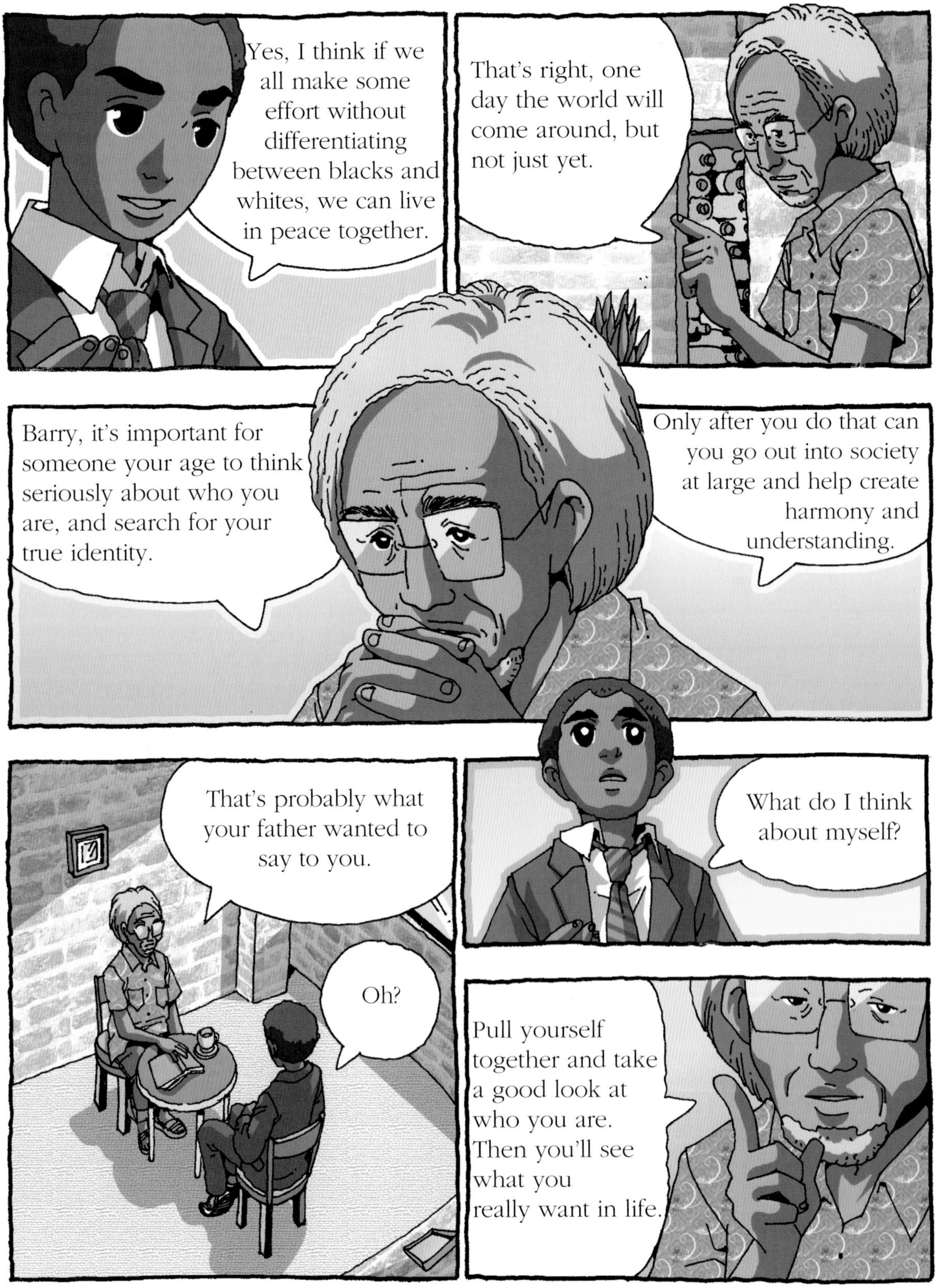
Yes, I think if we all make some effort without differentiating between blacks and whites, we can live in peace together.
That's right, one day the world will come around, but not just yet.
Barry, it's important for someone your age to think seriously about who you are, and search for your true identity.
Only after you do that can you go out into society at large and help create harmony and understanding.
That's probably what your father wanted to say to you.
Oh?
What do I think about myself?
Pull yourself together and take a good look at who you are. Then you'll see what you really want in life.

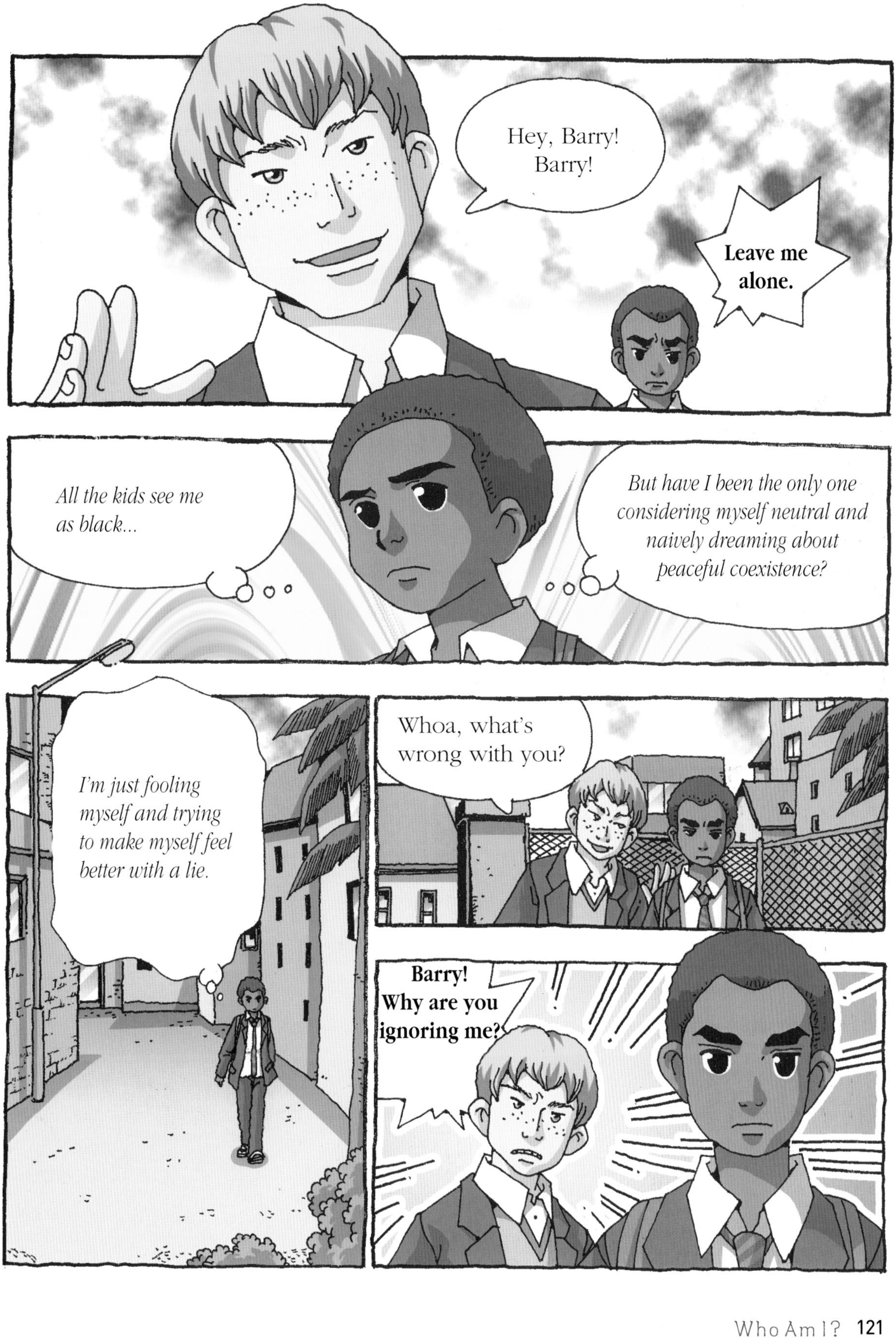
Hey, Barry! Barry!
Leave me alone.
All the kids see me as black...
But have I been the only one considering myself neutral and naively dreaming about peaceful coexistence?
I'm just fooling myself and trying to make myself feel better with a lie.
Whoa, what's wrong with you?
Barry! Why are you ignoring me?

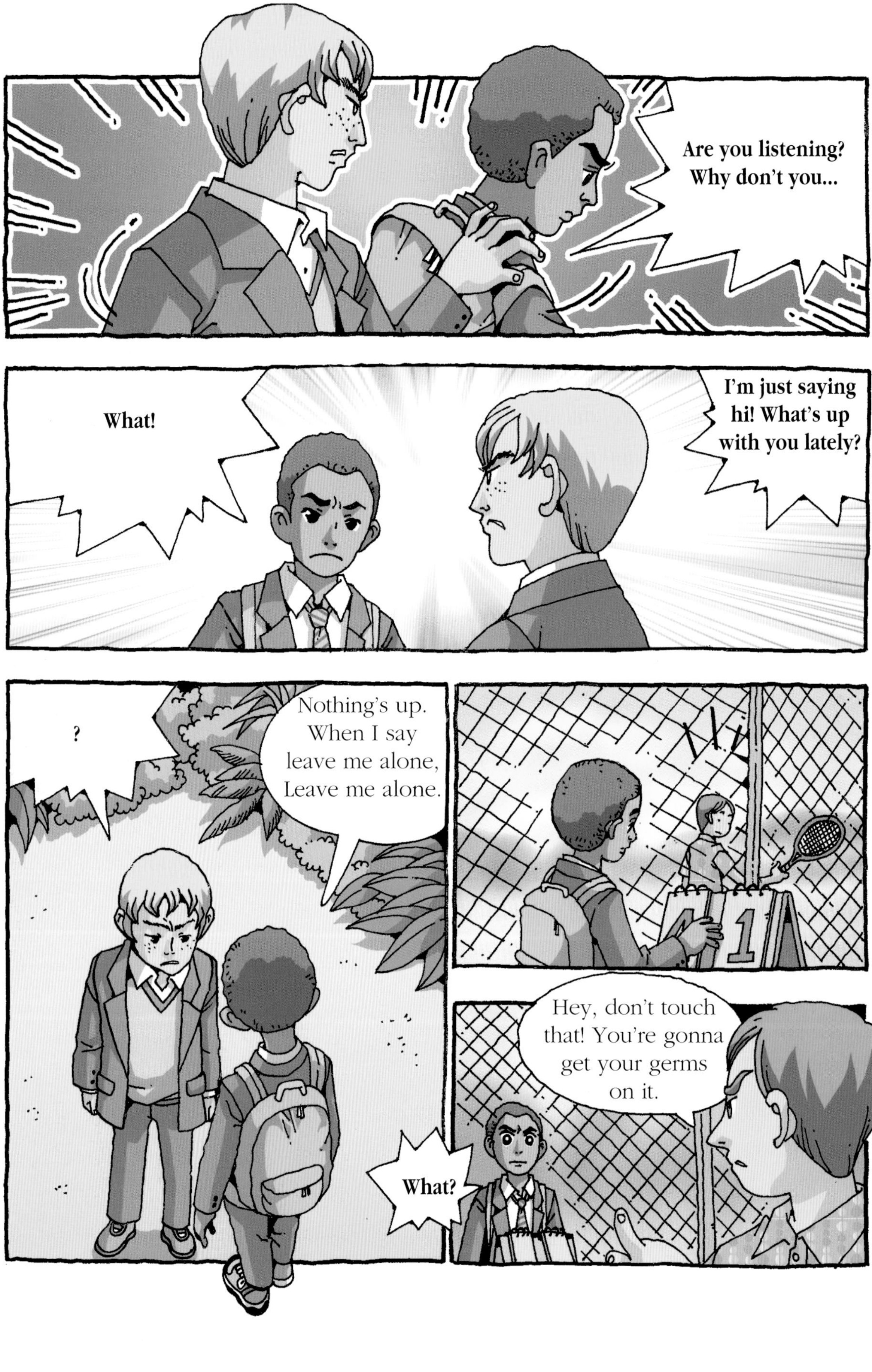

Are you listening? Why don't you...
What!
I'm just saying hi! What's up with you lately?
?
Nothing's up. When I say leave me alone, Leave me alone.
1
Hey, don't touch that! You're gonna get your germs on it.
What?

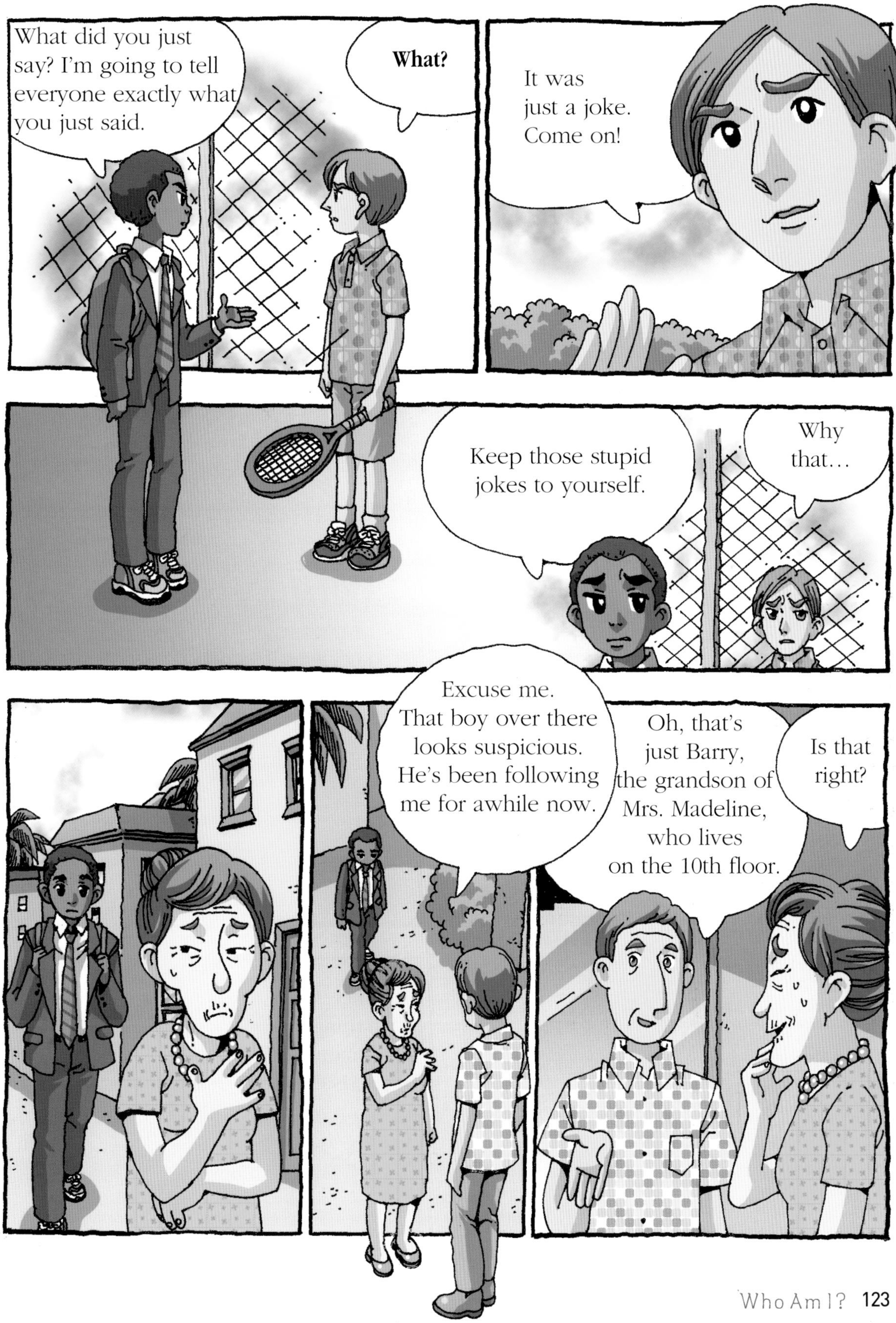
What did you just say? I'm going to tell everyone exactly what you just said.
What?
It was just a joke. Come on!
Keep those stupid jokes to yourself.
Why that…
Excuse me. That boy over there looks suspicious. He's been following me for awhile now.
Oh, that's just Barry, the grandson of Mrs. Madeline, who lives on the 10th floor.
Is that right?

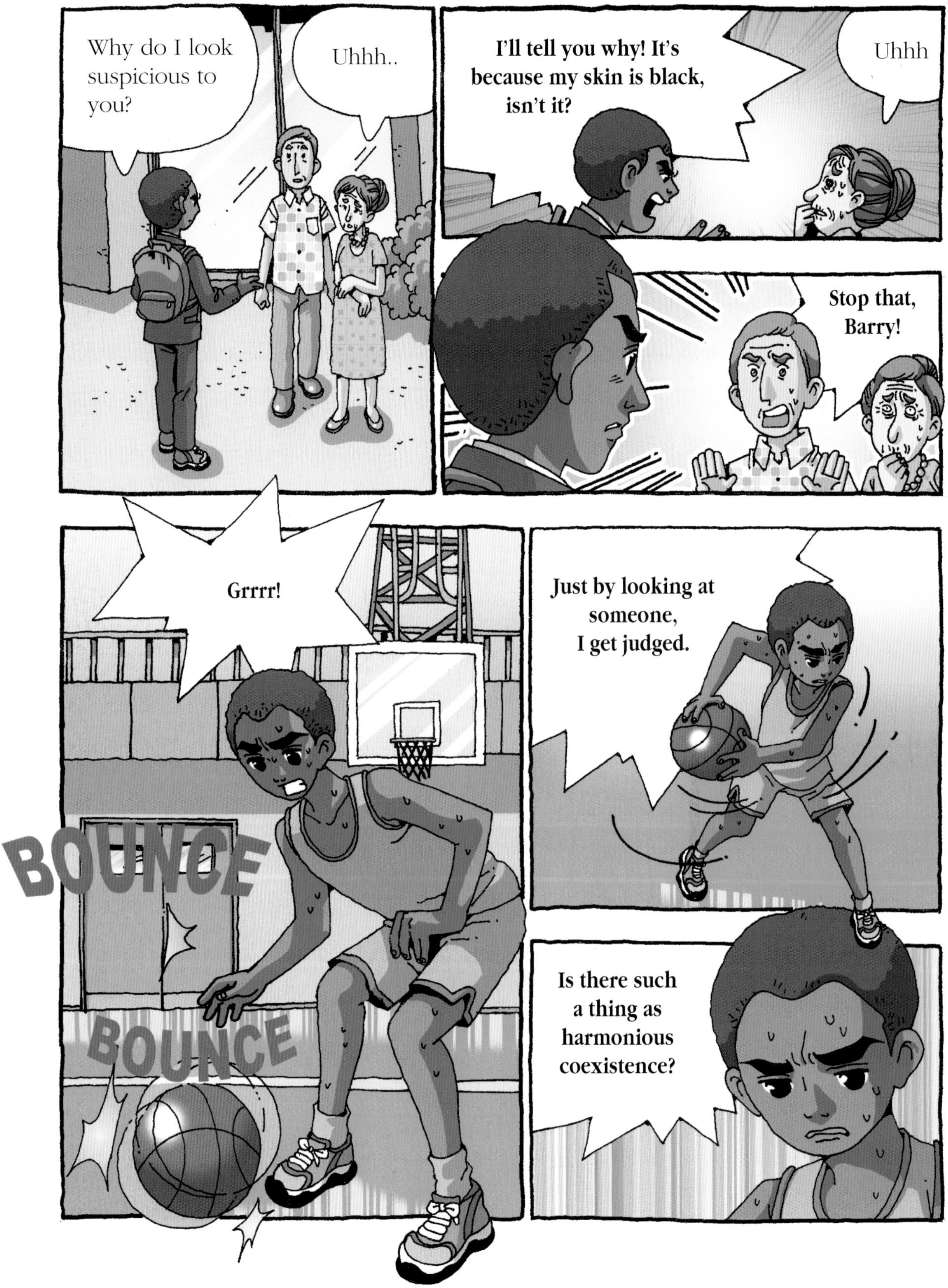
Why do I look suspicious to you?
Uhhh..
I'll tell you why! It's because my skin is black, isn't it?
Uhhh
Stop that, Barry!
Grrrr!
BOUNCE
BOUNCE
Just by looking at someone, I get judged.
Is there such a thing as harmonious coexistence?

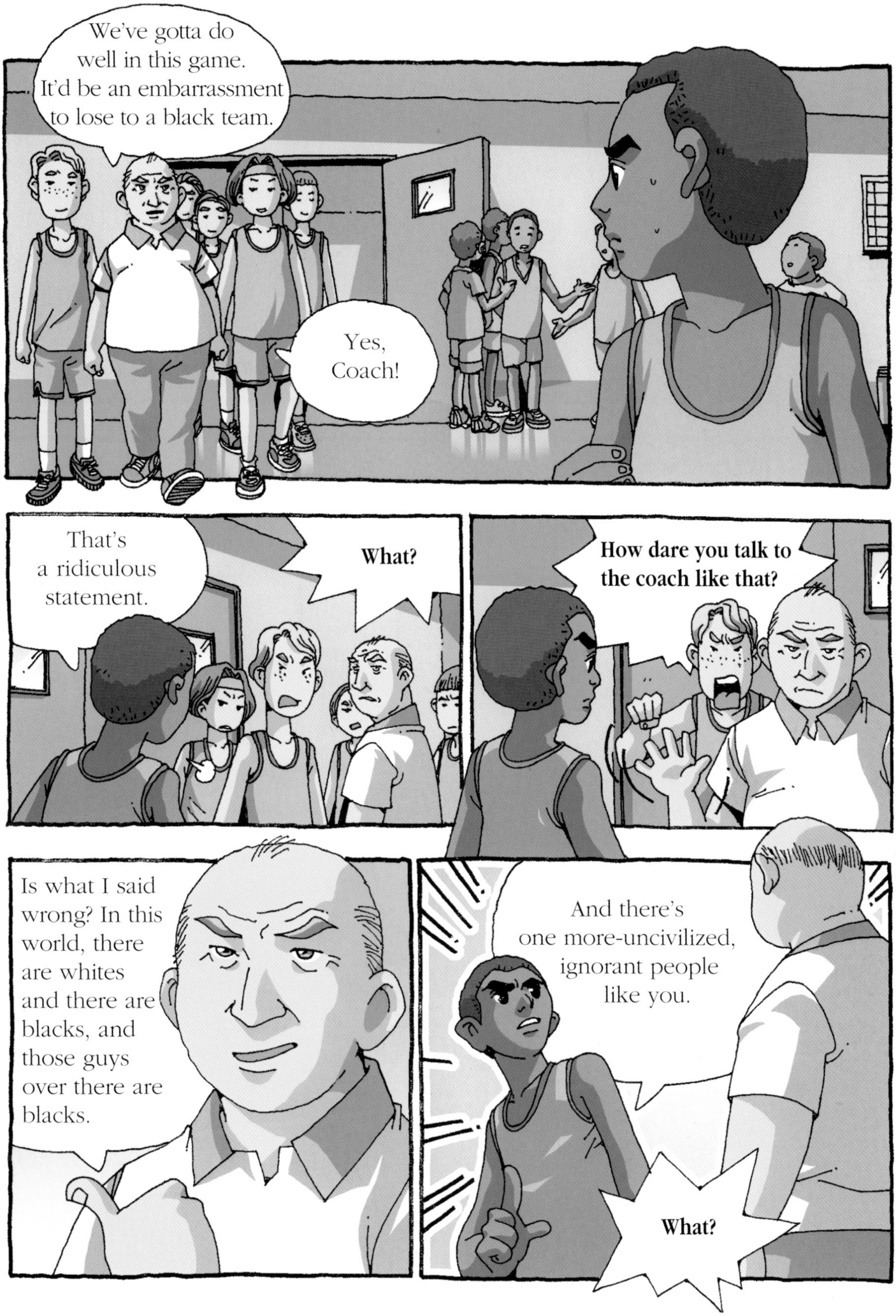

We've gotta do well in this game. It'd be an embarrassment to lose to a black team.
Yes, Coach!
That's a ridiculous statement.
What?
How dare you talk to the coach like that?
Is what I said wrong? In this world, there are whites and there are blacks, and those guys over there are blacks.
And there's one more-uncivilized, ignorant people like you.
What?

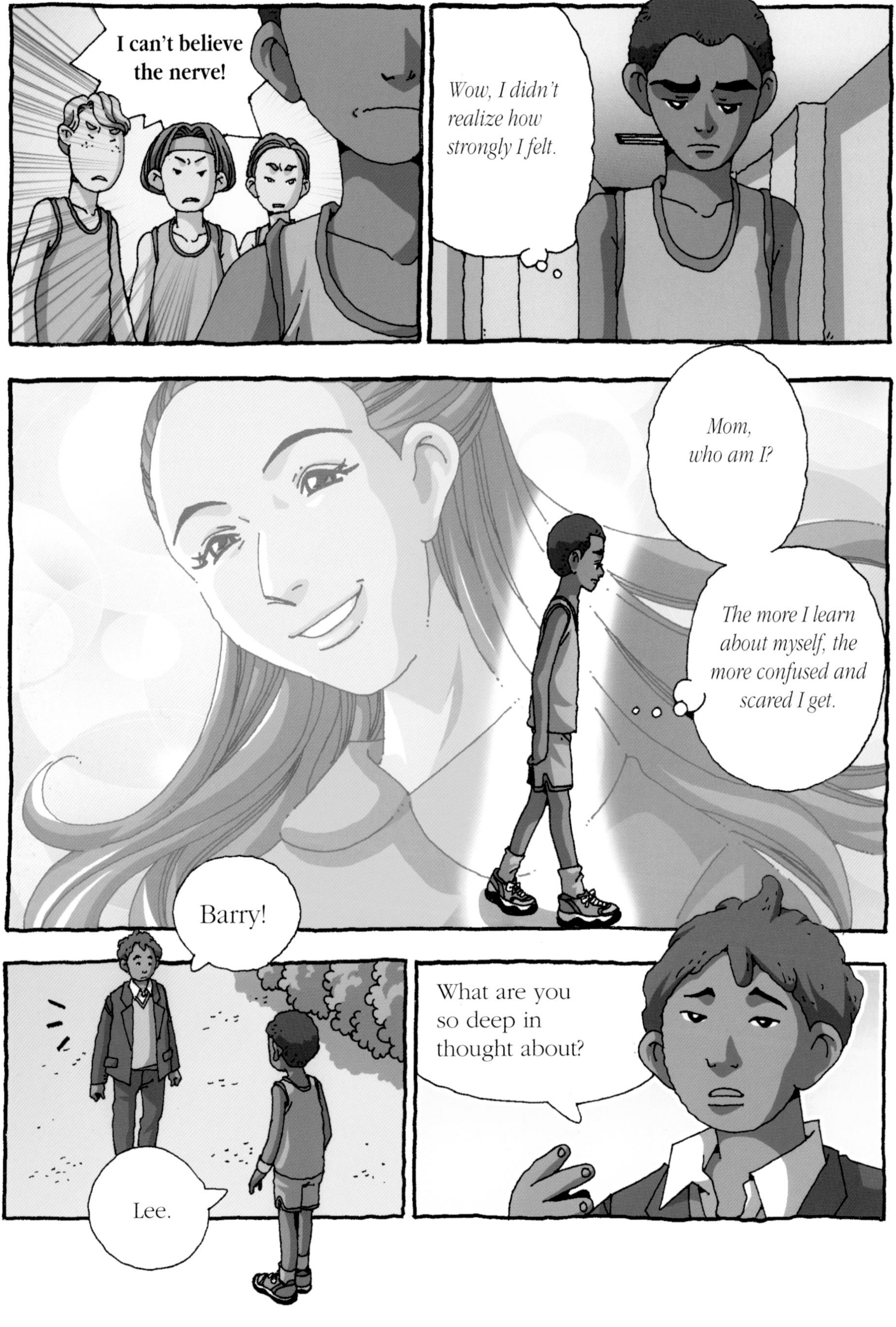
I can't believe the nerve!
Wow, I didn't realize how strongly I felt.
Mom, who am I?
The more I learn about myself, the more confused and scared I get.
Barry!
Lee.
What are you so deep in thought about?

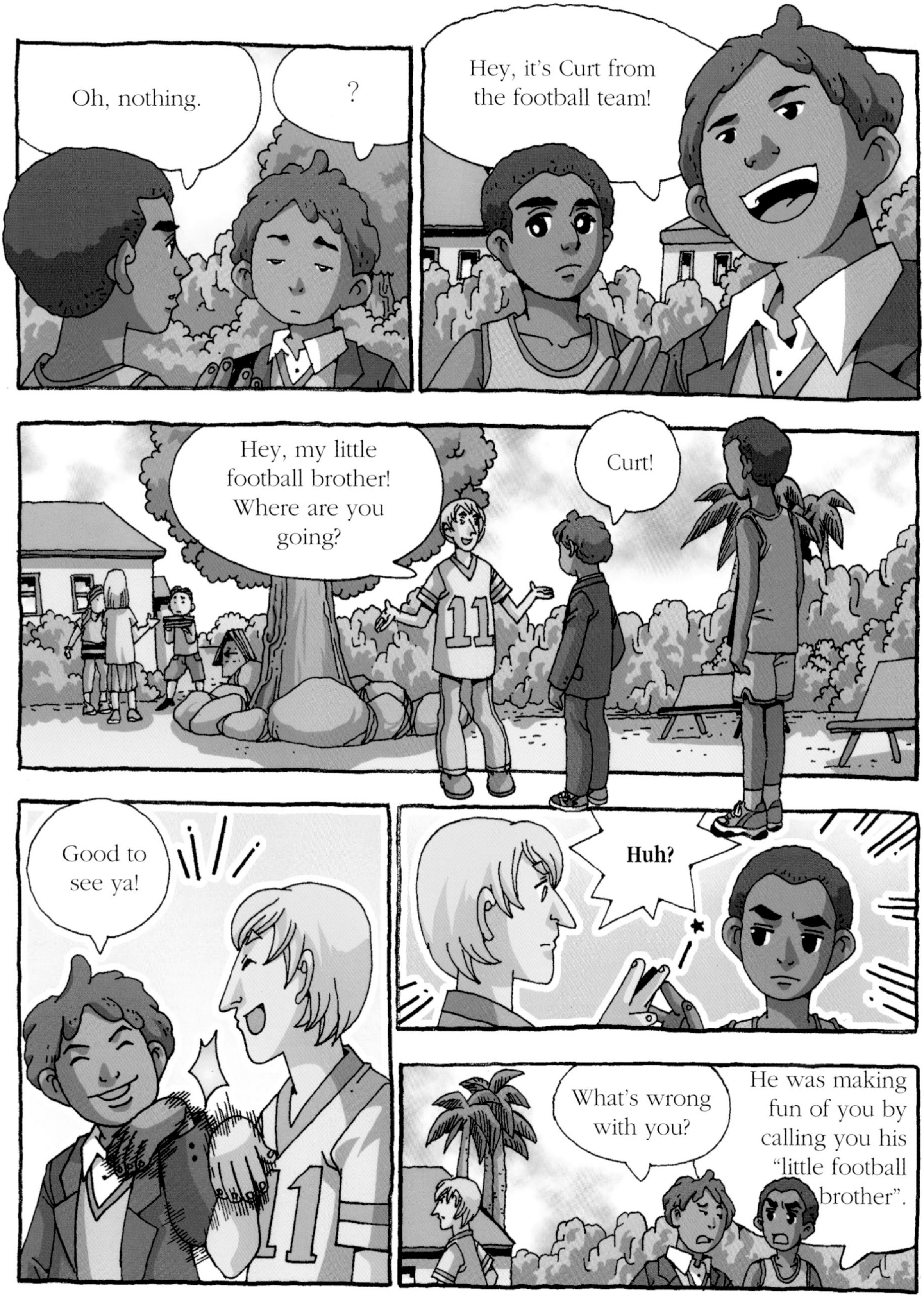
Oh, nothing.
?
Hey, it's Curt from the football team!
Hey, my little football brother! Where are you going?
Curt!
Good to see ya!
Huh?
What's wrong with you?
He was making fun of you by calling you his "little football brother".

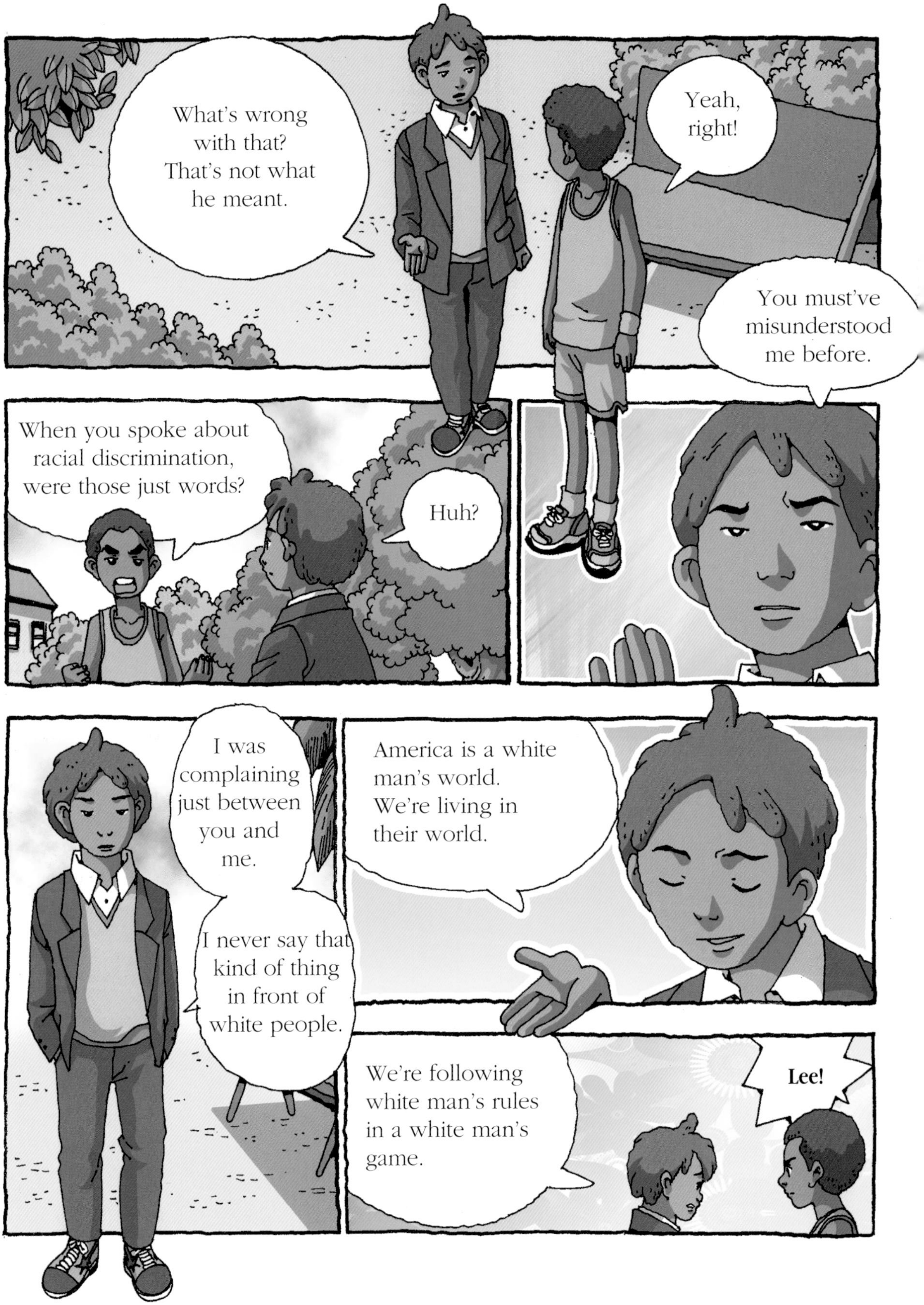
What's wrong with that? That's not what he meant.
Yeah, right!
You must've misunderstood me before.
When you spoke about racial discrimination, were those just words?
Huh?
I was complaining just between you and me.
I never say that kind of thing in front of white people.
America is a white man's world. We're living in their world.
We're following white man's rules in a white man's game.
Lee!

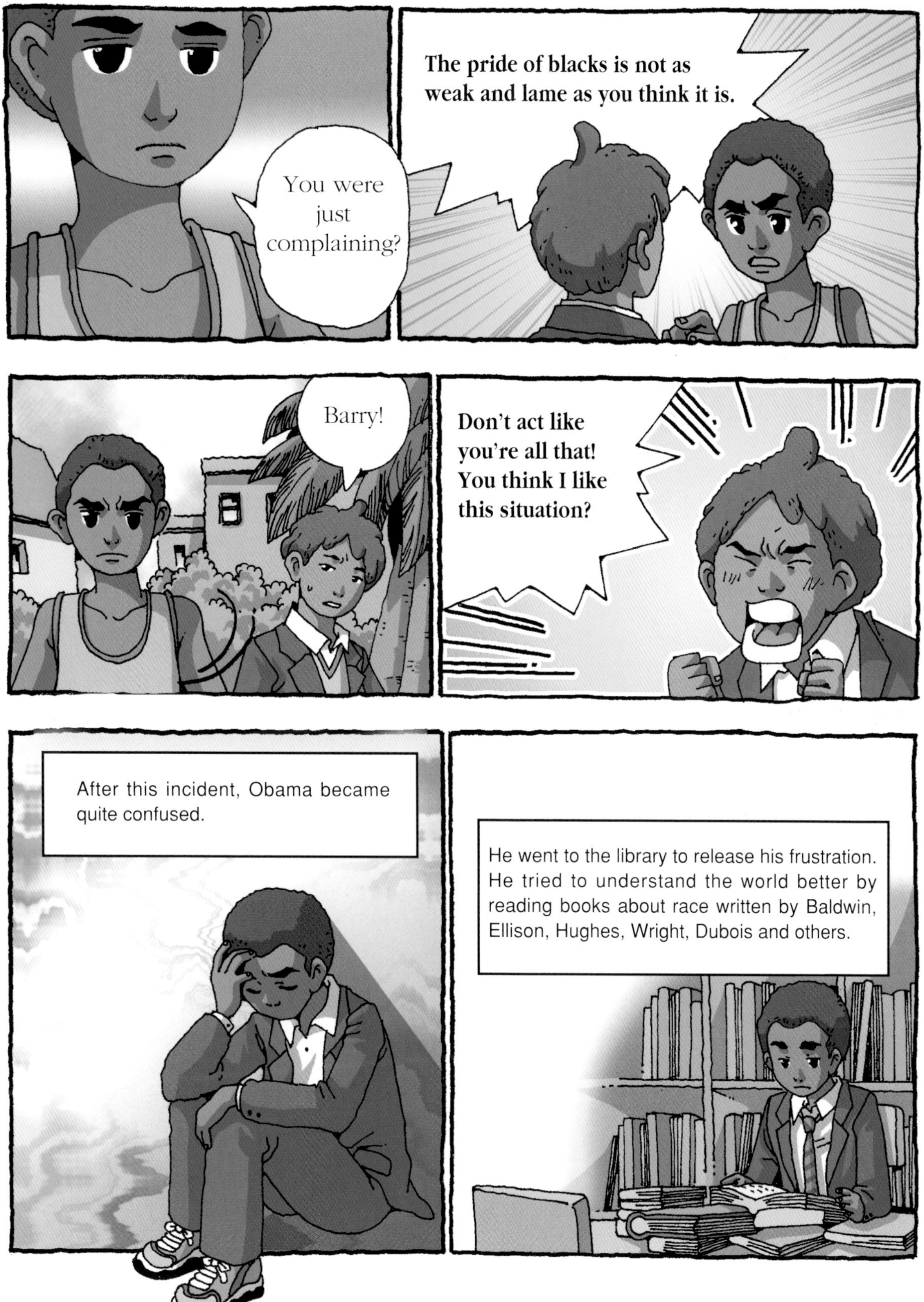
You were just complaining?
The pride of blacks is not as weak and lame as you think it is.
Barry!
Don't act like you're all that! You think I like this situation?
After this incident, Obama became quite confused.
He went to the library to release his frustration. He tried to understand the world better by reading books about race written by Baldwin, Ellison, Hughes, Wright, Dubois and others.

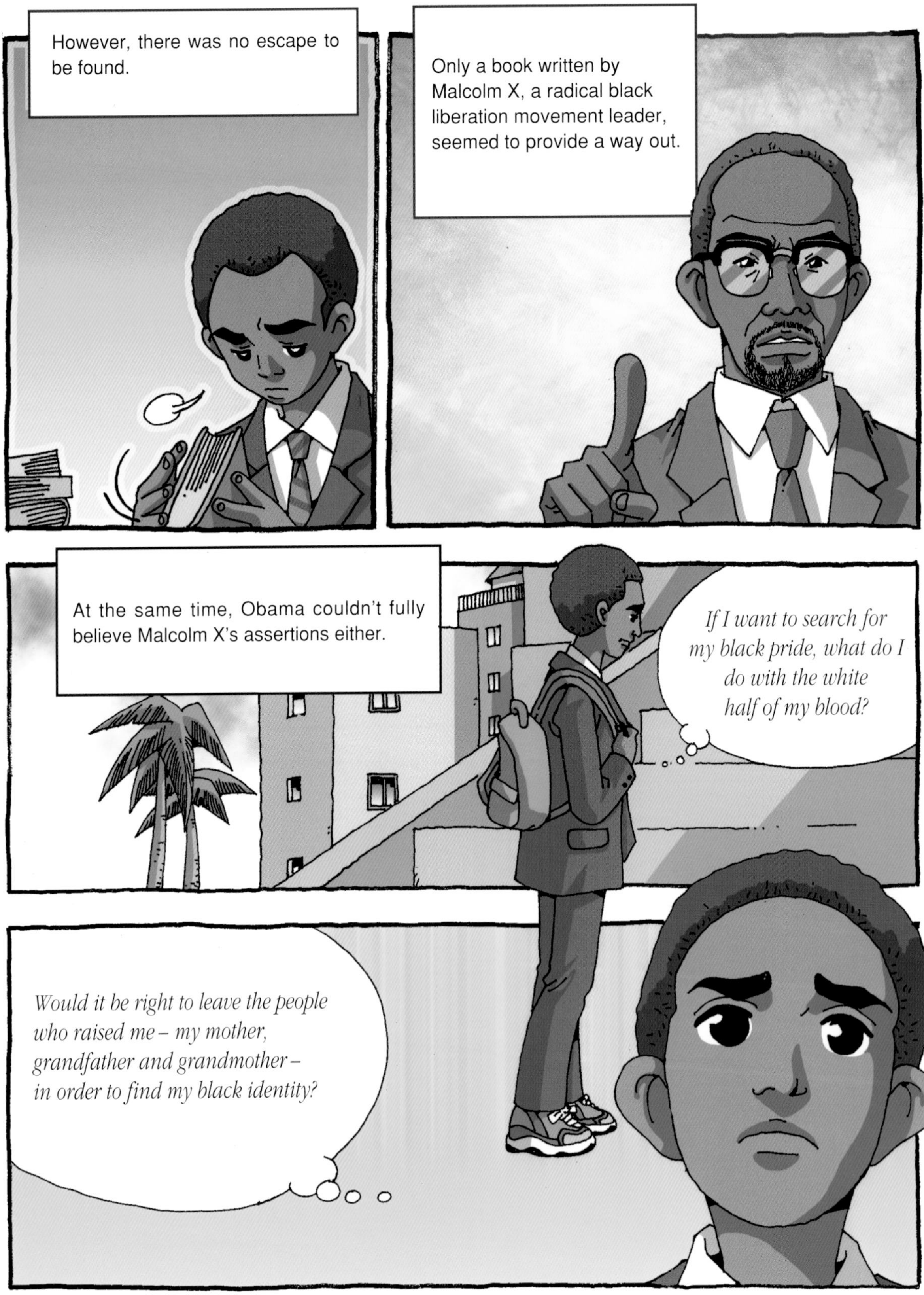
However, there was no escape to be found.
Only a book written by Malcolm X, a radical black liberation movement leader, seemed to provide a way out.
At the same time, Obama couldn't fully believe Malcolm X's assertions either.
If I want to search for my black pride, what do I do with the white half of my blood?
Would it be right to leave the people who raised me – my mother, grandfather and grandmother – in order to find my black identity?

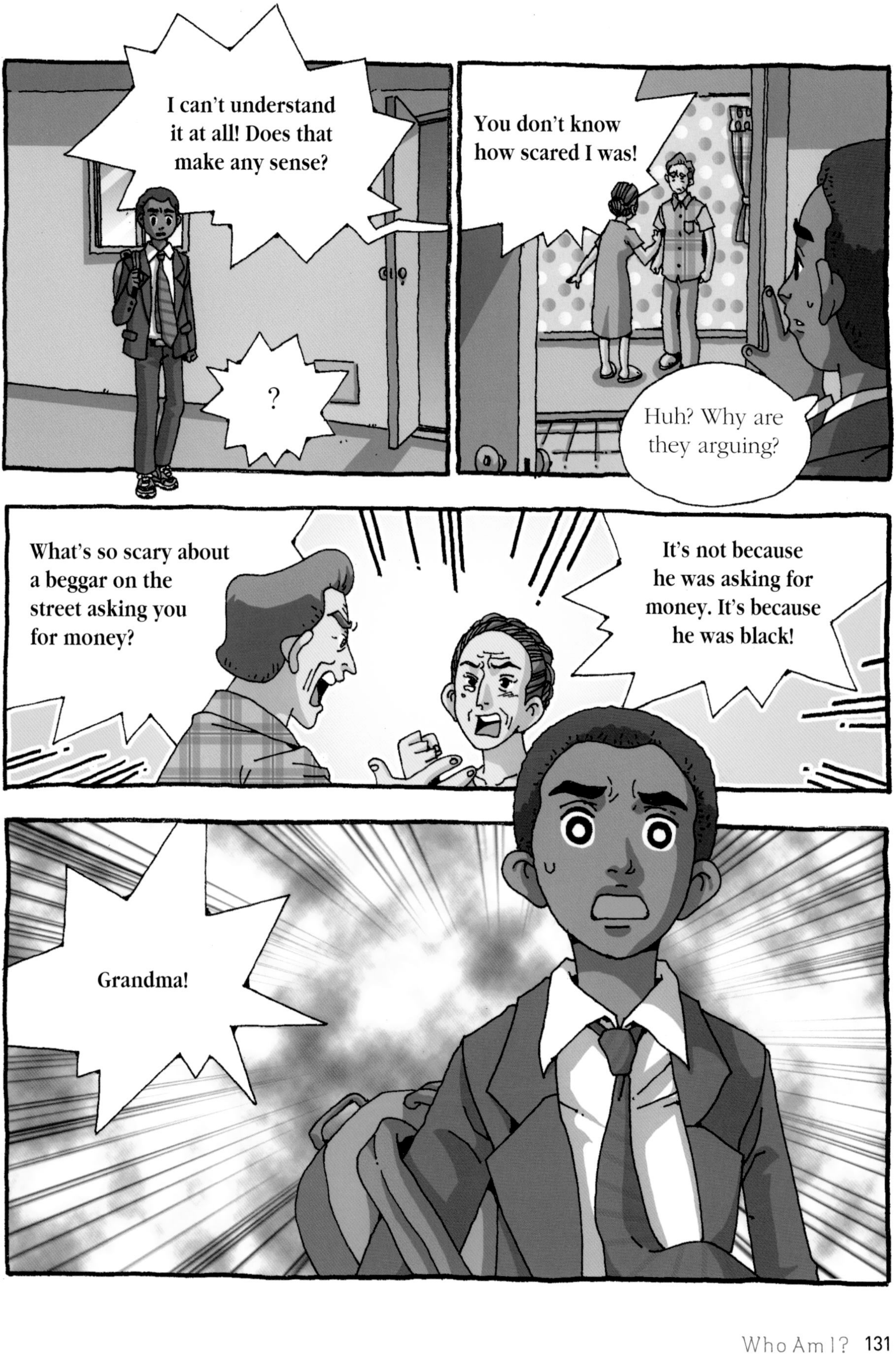
I can't understand it at all! Does that make any sense?
?
You don't know how scared I was!
Huh? Why are they arguing?
What's so scary about a beggar on the street asking you for money?
It's not because he was asking for money. It's because he was black!
Grandma!

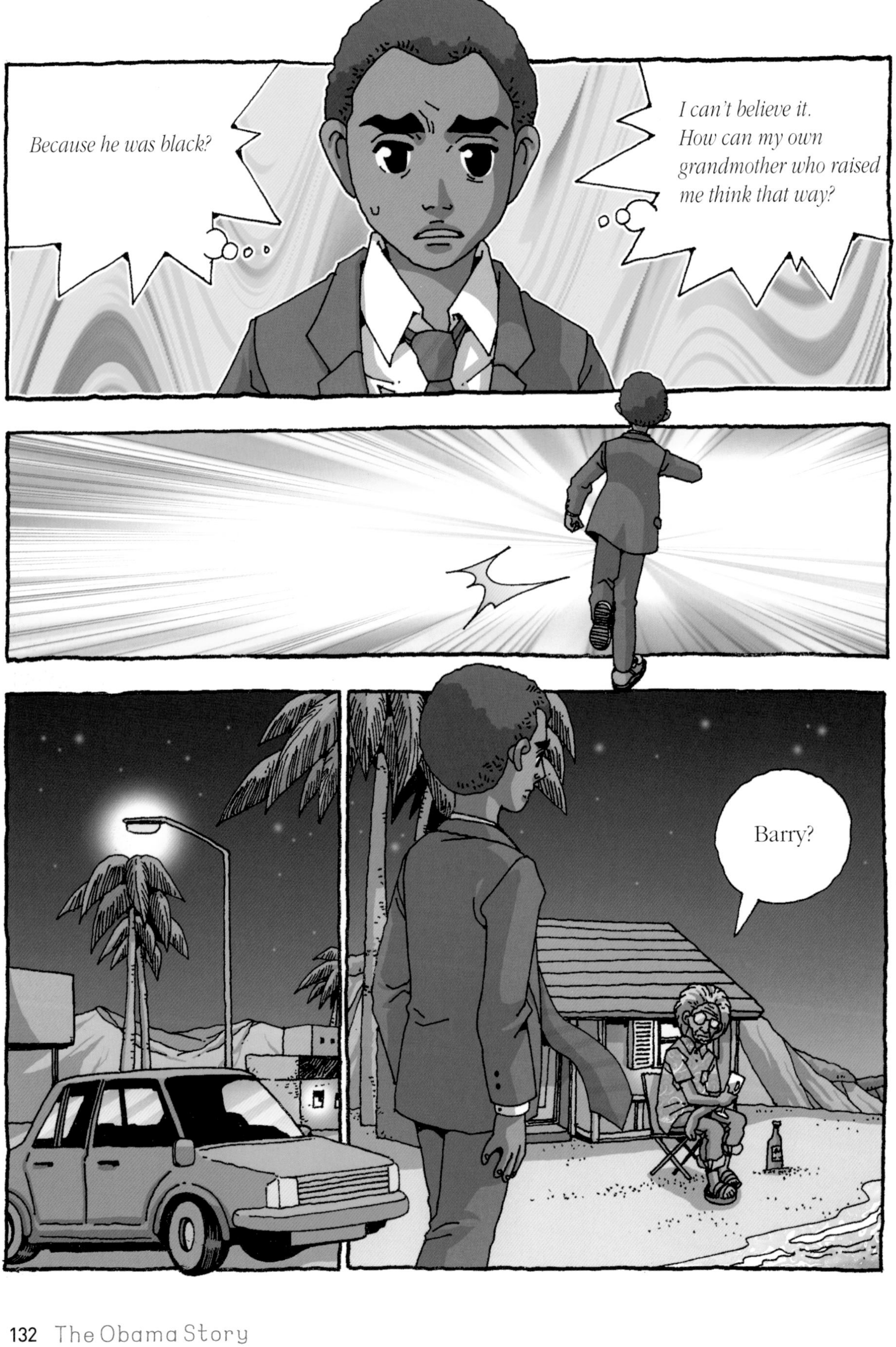
Because he was black?
I can't believe it. How can my own grandmother who raised me think that way?
Barry?

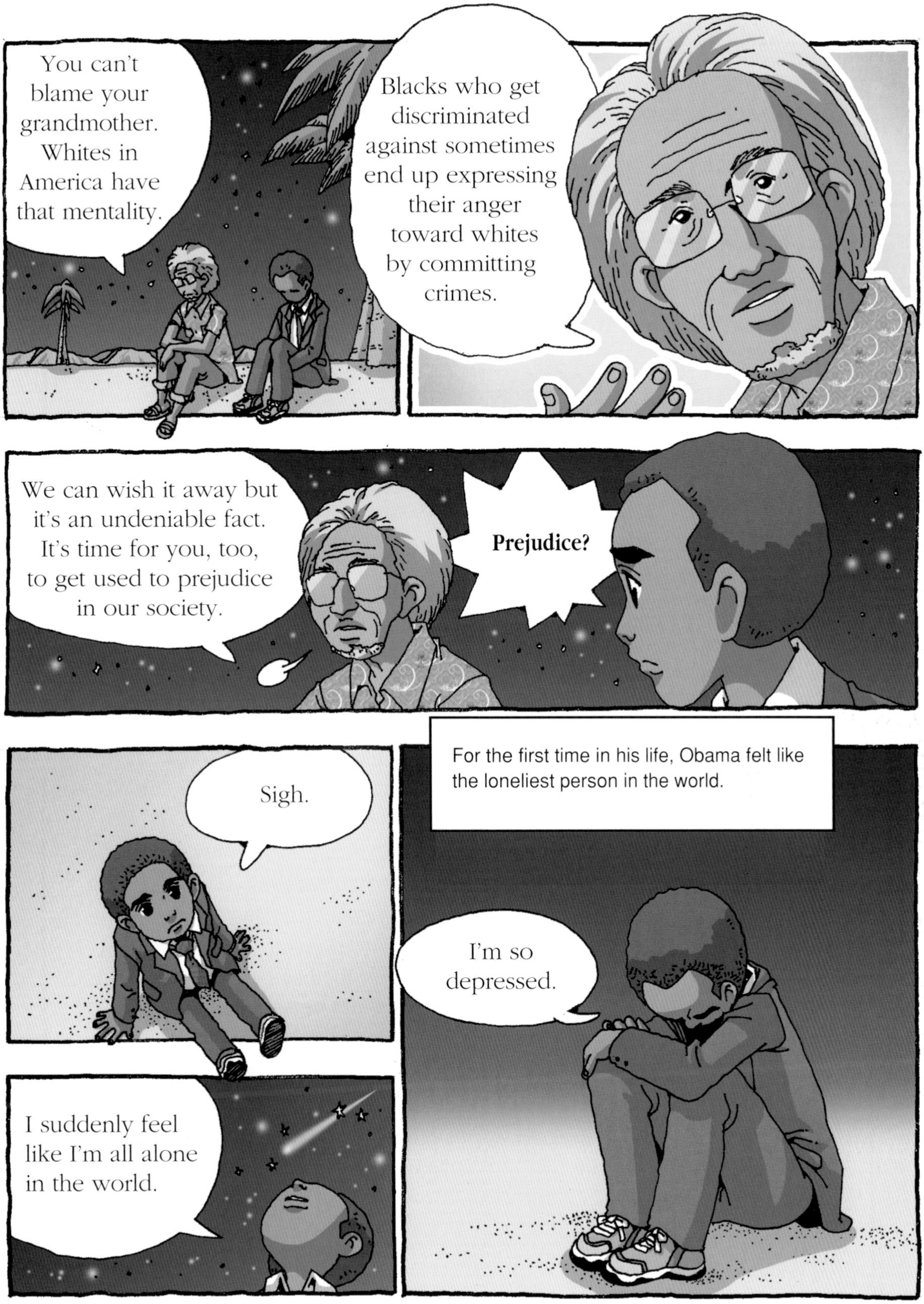
You can't blame your grandmother. Whites in America have that mentality.
Blacks who get discriminated against sometimes end up expressing their anger toward whites by committing crimes.
We can wish it away but it's an undeniable fact. It's time for you, too, to get used to prejudice in our society.
Prejudice?
For the first time in his life, Obama felt like the loneliest person in the world.
Sigh.
I suddenly feel like I'm all alone in the world.
I'm so depressed.

People who have influenced Obama 4

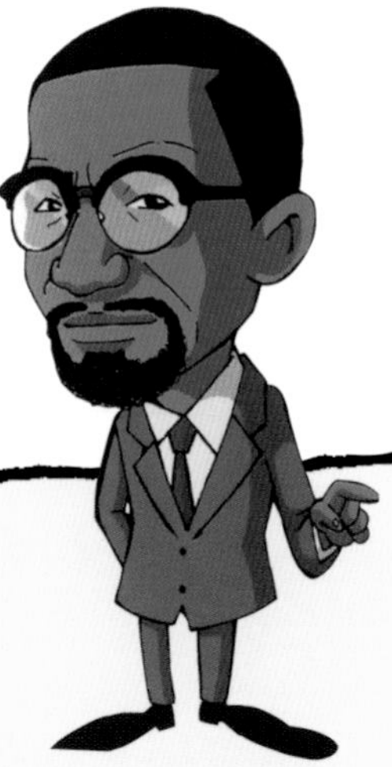

Malcolm X

Barack Obama was greatly influenced in his teenage years by both Martin Luther King Jr. and Malcolm X, who were both leaders in the black civil rights movement in America. Malcolm X, born on May 19, 1925 in Nebraska, was the fourth son of a family of six. His father was a pastor who preached that blacks needed to search for their roots. He received respect from the black community but was not well-considered among white supremacists. Malcolm's father ended up being murdered by white supremacists, and subsequently, Malcolm's mother, in an extreme state of shock, had to be committed to a mental hospital.

Meanwhile, Malcolm X, labeled a problem child, spent his youth wandering the streets until he was placed in a foster home. When he entered junior high school, he began to read a lot and study hard. However, one day before his graduation, his teacher made a racial remark, and Malcolm's heart hardened once more. When the students were presenting their future dreams, Malcolm stated that he wanted to study law and become a lawyer. In response, his teacher recommended he do something that was more suitable for blacks, such as carpentry or repairs.

After this incident, Malcolm X decided to become a civil rights activist. He wanted to urge blacks who had been passively opposing racial discrimination to stand up and fight more actively for their rights. Unlike his predecessors, Malcolm X spoke in a very simple and straightforward way, in order to persuade blacks who, at that time, generally had a low level of education. Malcolm X's challenging assertion that he would not compromise in the least with whites caused him to be at odds with many white people.

In the end, at the young age of 40, Malcolm X was shot and killed by a suspicious man in the audience as he was giving a speech. Thousands of African-Americans came to his funeral to grieve his death.

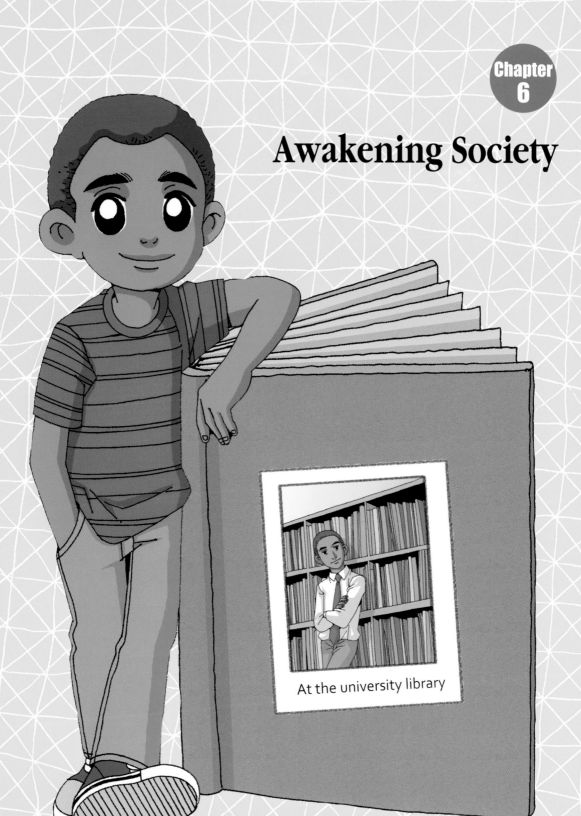

Awakening Society

At the university library

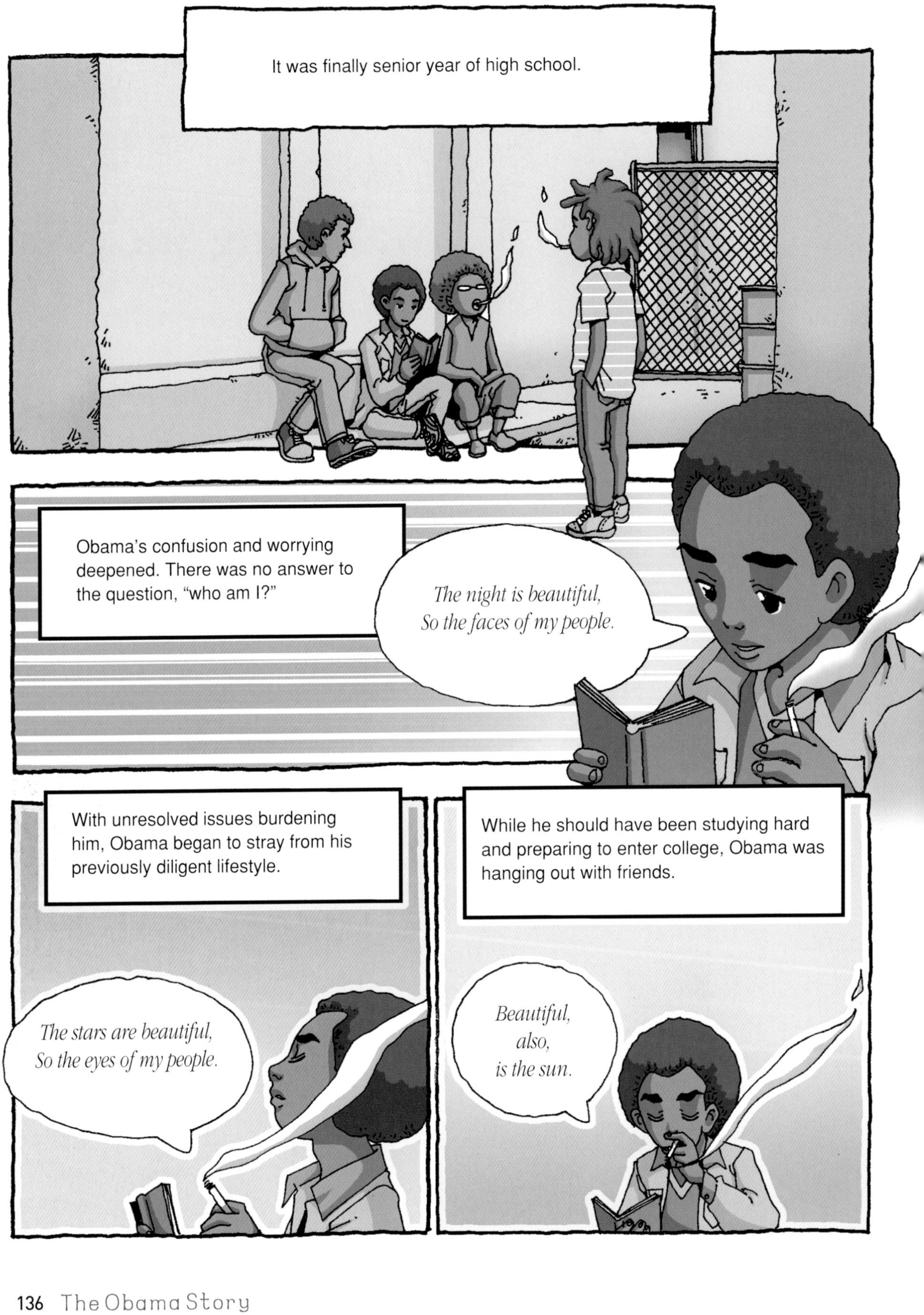
It was finally senior year of high school.
Obama's confusion and worrying deepened. There was no answer to the question, "who am I?"
The night is beautiful, So the faces of my people.
With unresolved issues burdening him, Obama began to stray from his previously diligent lifestyle.
The stars are beautiful, So the eyes of my people.
While he should have been studying hard and preparing to enter college, Obama was hanging out with friends.
Beautiful, also, is the sun.

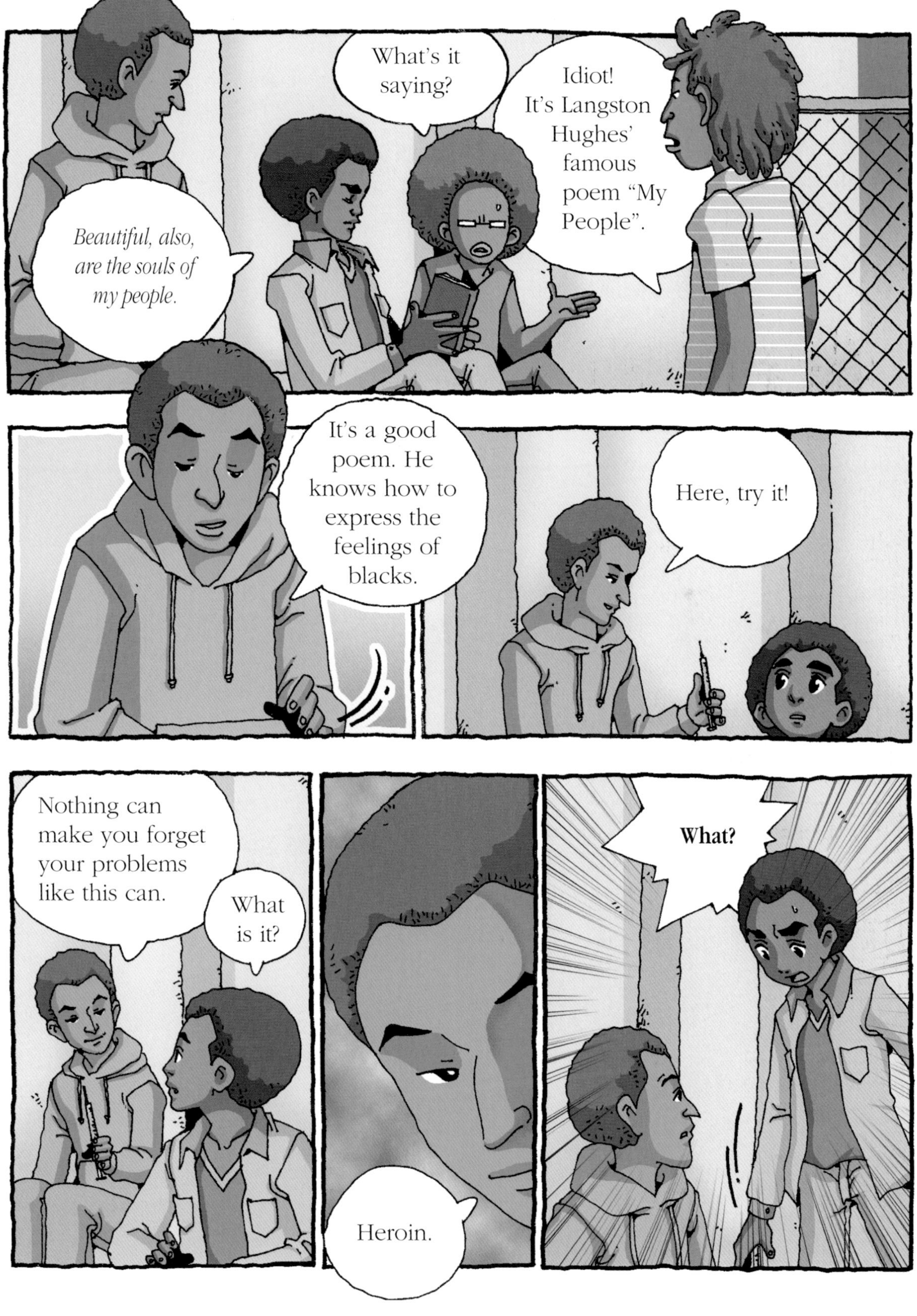
Beautiful, also, are the souls of my people.
What's it saying?
Idiot! It's Langston Hughes' famous poem "My People".
It's a good poem. He knows how to express the feelings of blacks.
Here, try it!
Nothing can make you forget your problems like this can.
What is it?
Heroin.
What?

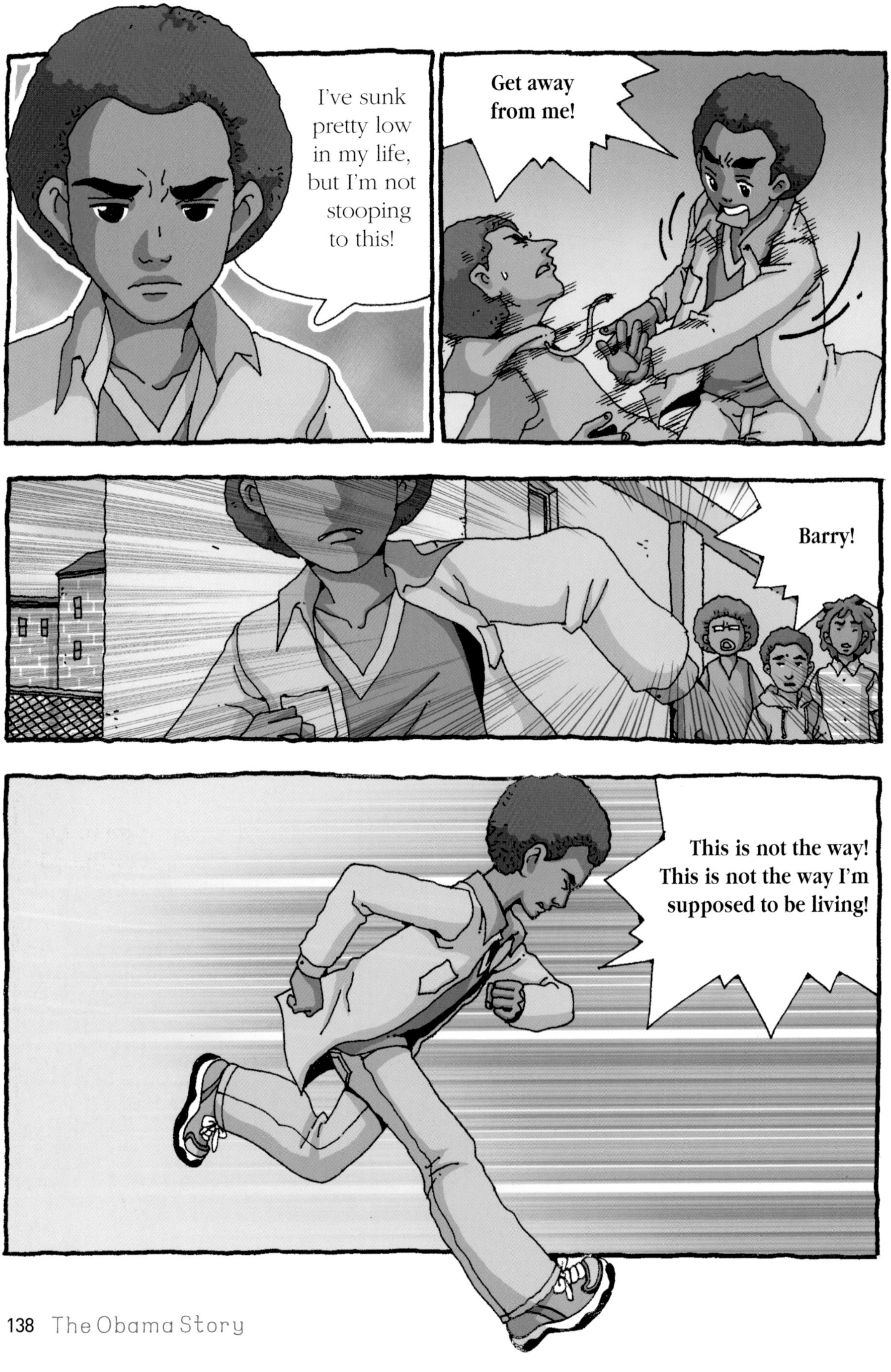
I've sunk pretty low in my life, but I'm not stooping to this!
Get away from me!
Barry!
This is not the way! This is not the way I'm supposed to be living!

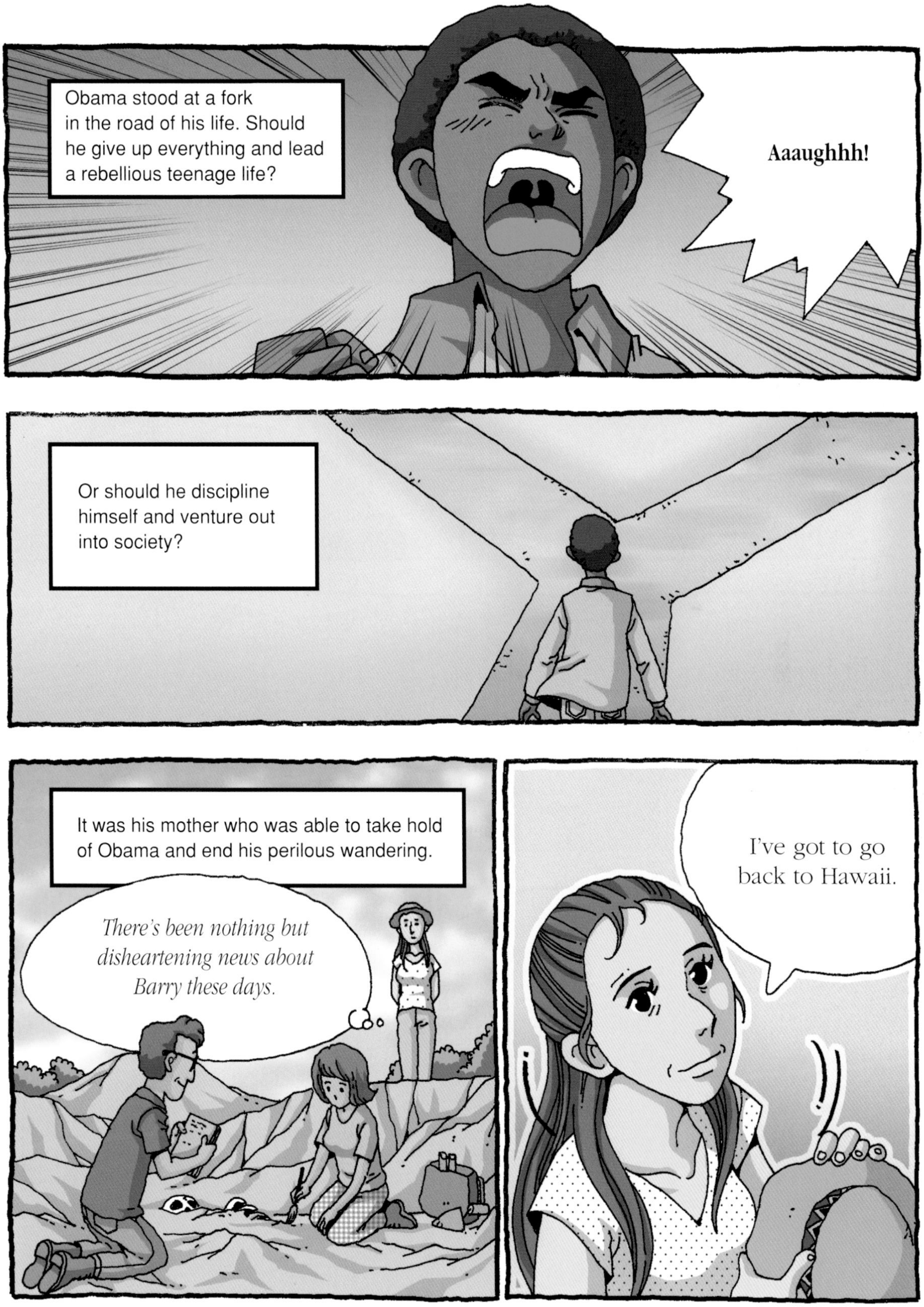

Obama stood at a fork in the road of his life. Should he give up everything and lead a rebellious teenage life?
Aaaughhh!
Or should he discipline himself and venture out into society?
It was his mother who was able to take hold of Obama and end his perilous wandering.
There's been nothing but disheartening news about Barry these days.
I've got to go back to Hawaii.

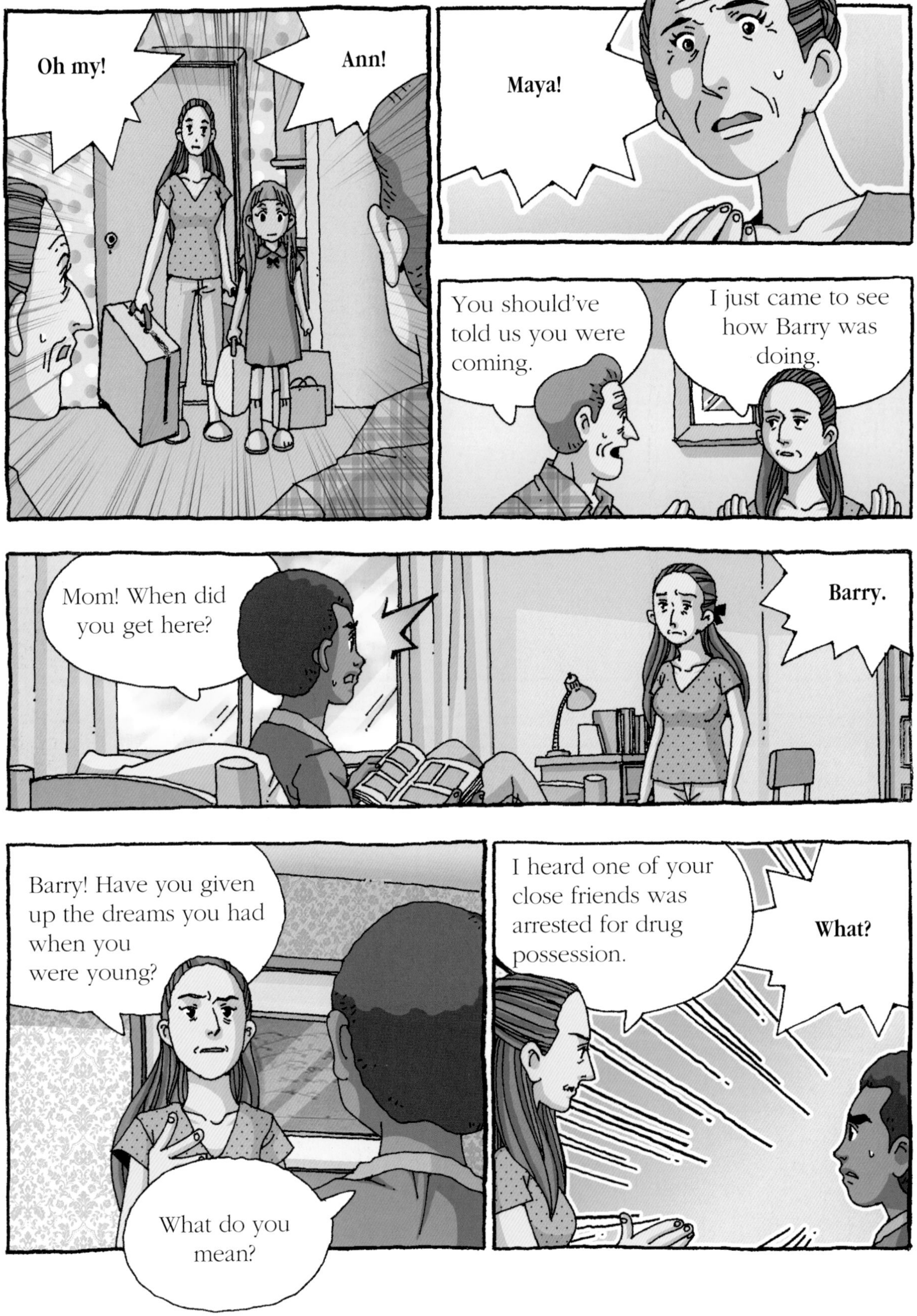

Oh my!
Ann!
Maya!
You should've told us you were coming.
I just came to see how Barry was doing.
Mom! When did you get here?
Barry.
Barry! Have you given up the dreams you had when you were young?
What do you mean?
I heard one of your close friends was arrested for drug possession.
What?

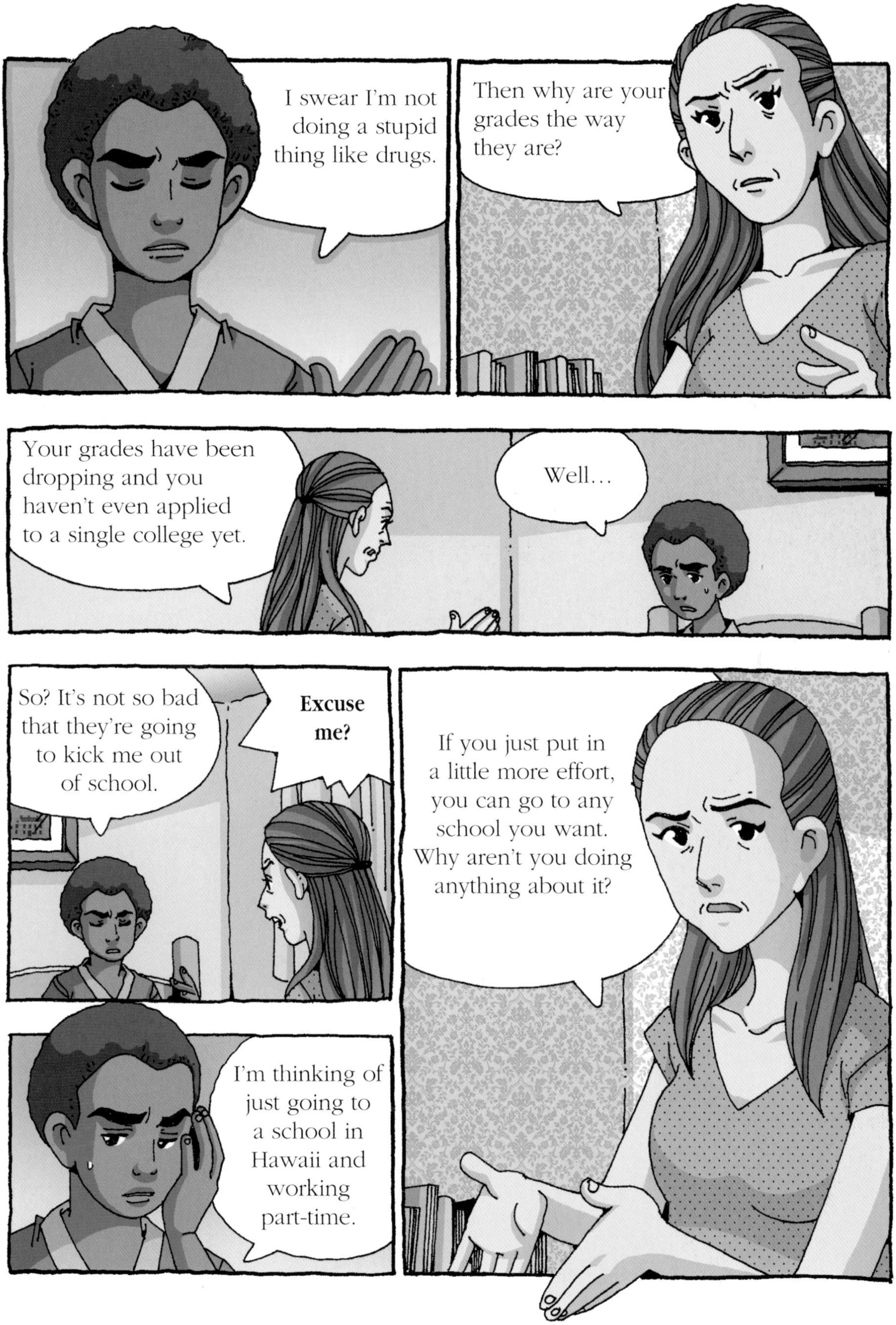
I swear I'm not doing a stupid thing like drugs.
Then why are your grades the way they are?
Your grades have been dropping and you haven't even applied to a single college yet.
Well…
So? It's not so bad that they're going to kick me out of school.
Excuse me?
If you just put in a little more effort, you can go to any school you want. Why aren't you doing anything about it?
I'm thinking of just going to a school in Hawaii and working part-time.

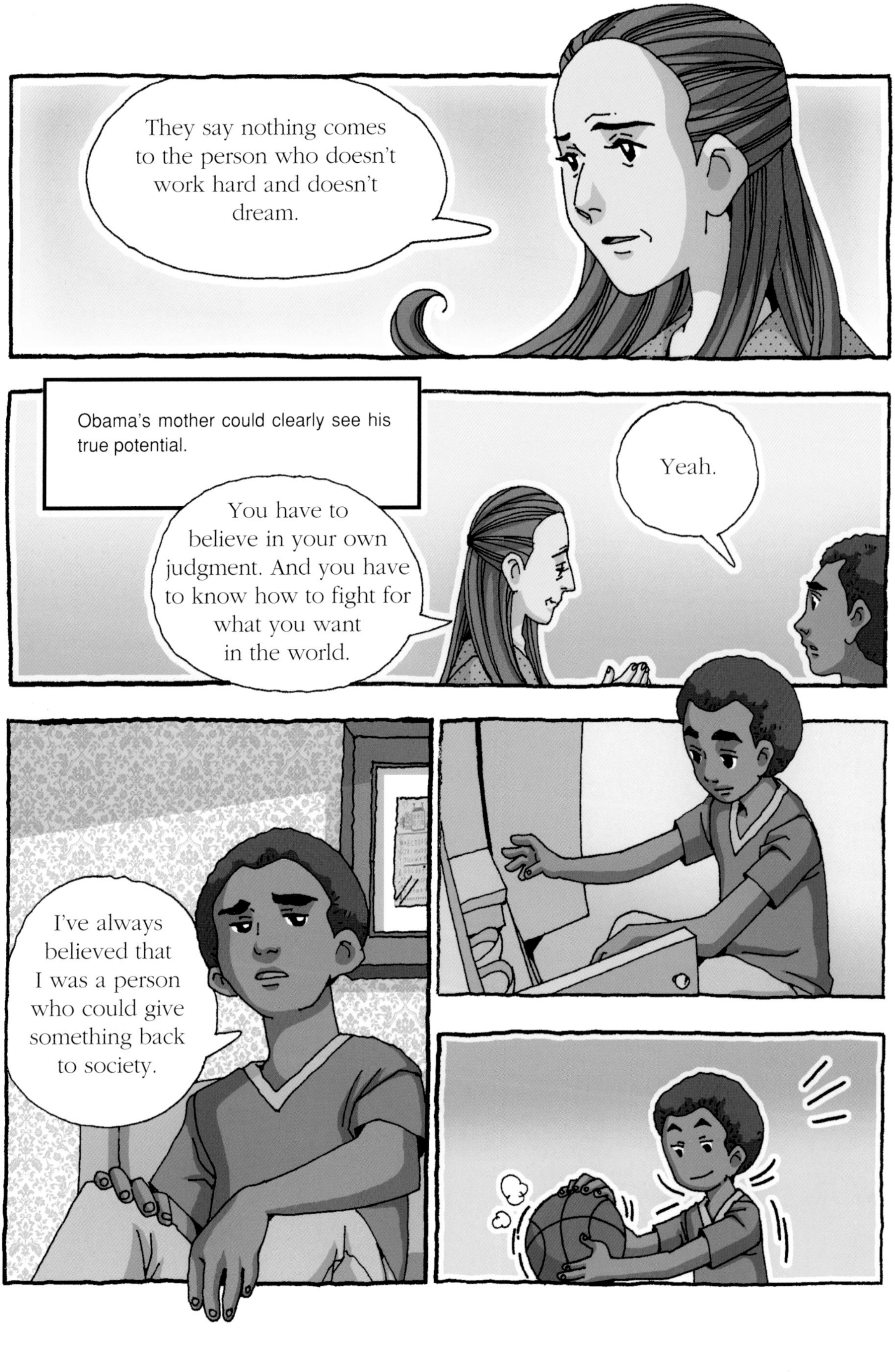
They say nothing comes to the person who doesn't work hard and doesn't dream.
Obama's mother could clearly see his true potential.
You have to believe in your own judgment. And you have to know how to fight for what you want in the world.
Yeah.
I've always believed that I was a person who could give something back to society.

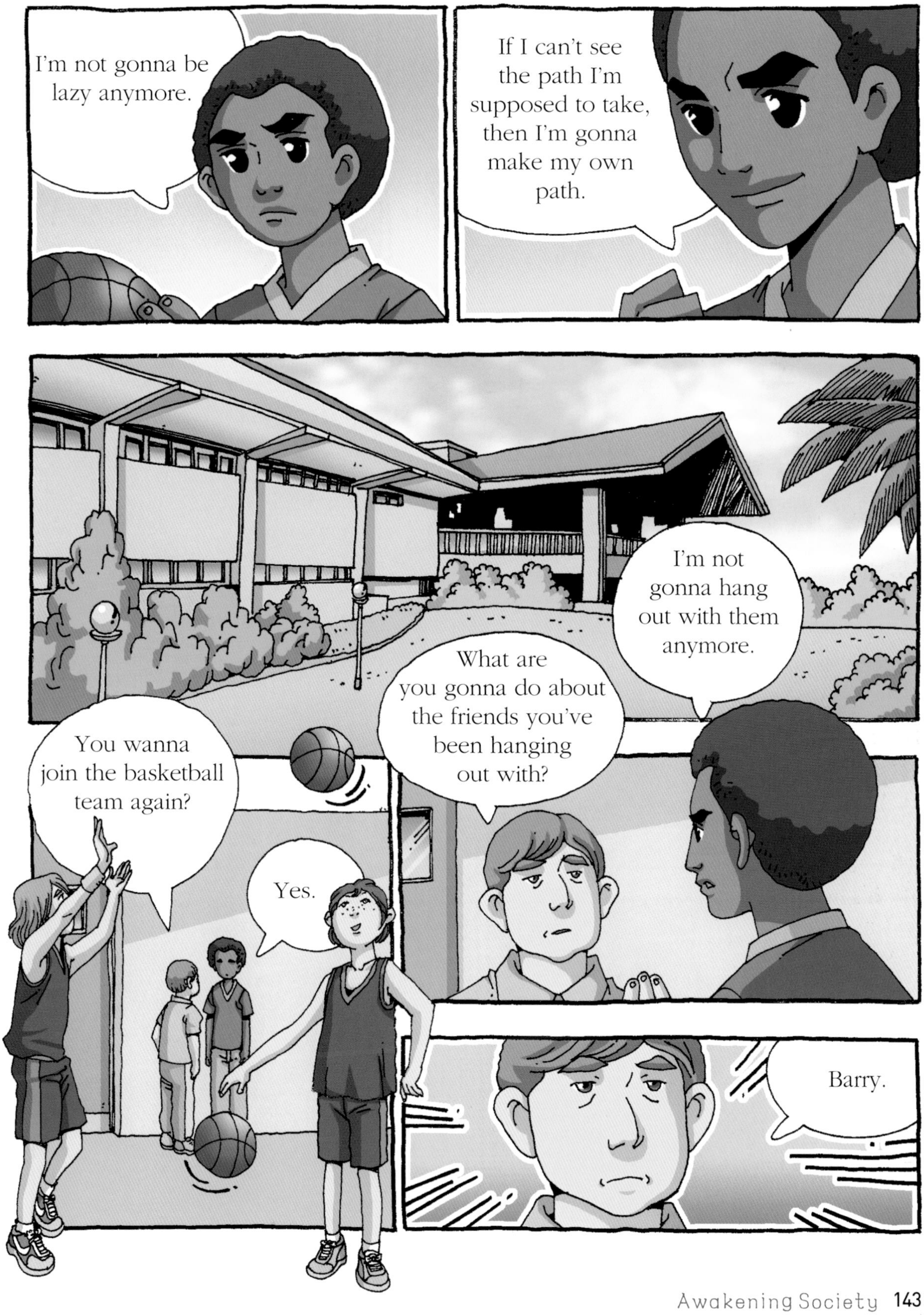
I'm not gonna be lazy anymore.
If I can't see the path I'm supposed to take, then I'm gonna make my own path.
I'm not gonna hang out with them anymore.
What are you gonna do about the friends you've been hanging out with?
You wanna join the basketball team again?
Yes.
Barry.

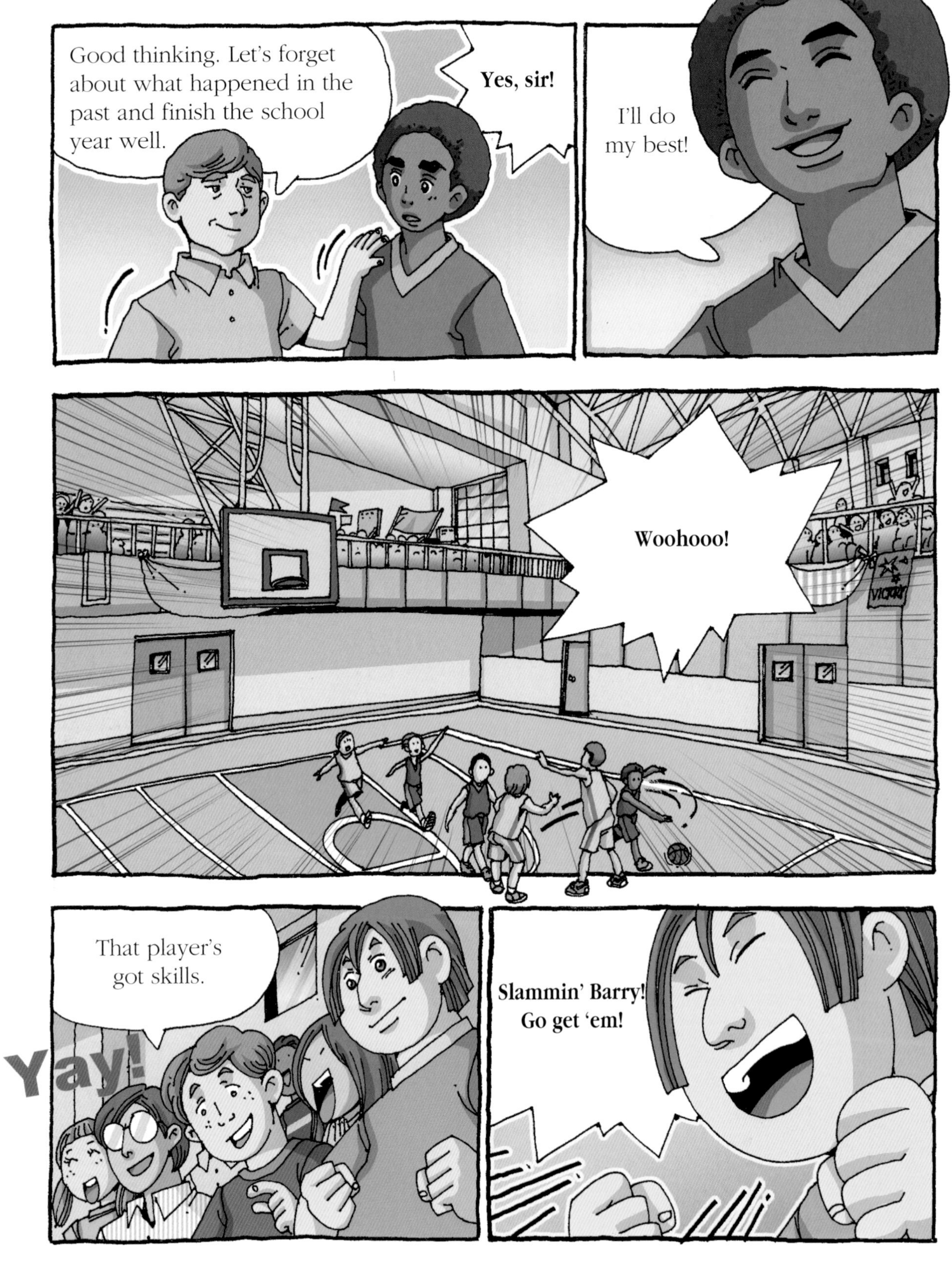
Good thinking. Let's forget about what happened in the past and finish the school year well.
Yes, sir!
I'll do my best!
Woohooo!
That player's got skills.
Yay!
Slammin' Barry! Go get 'em!

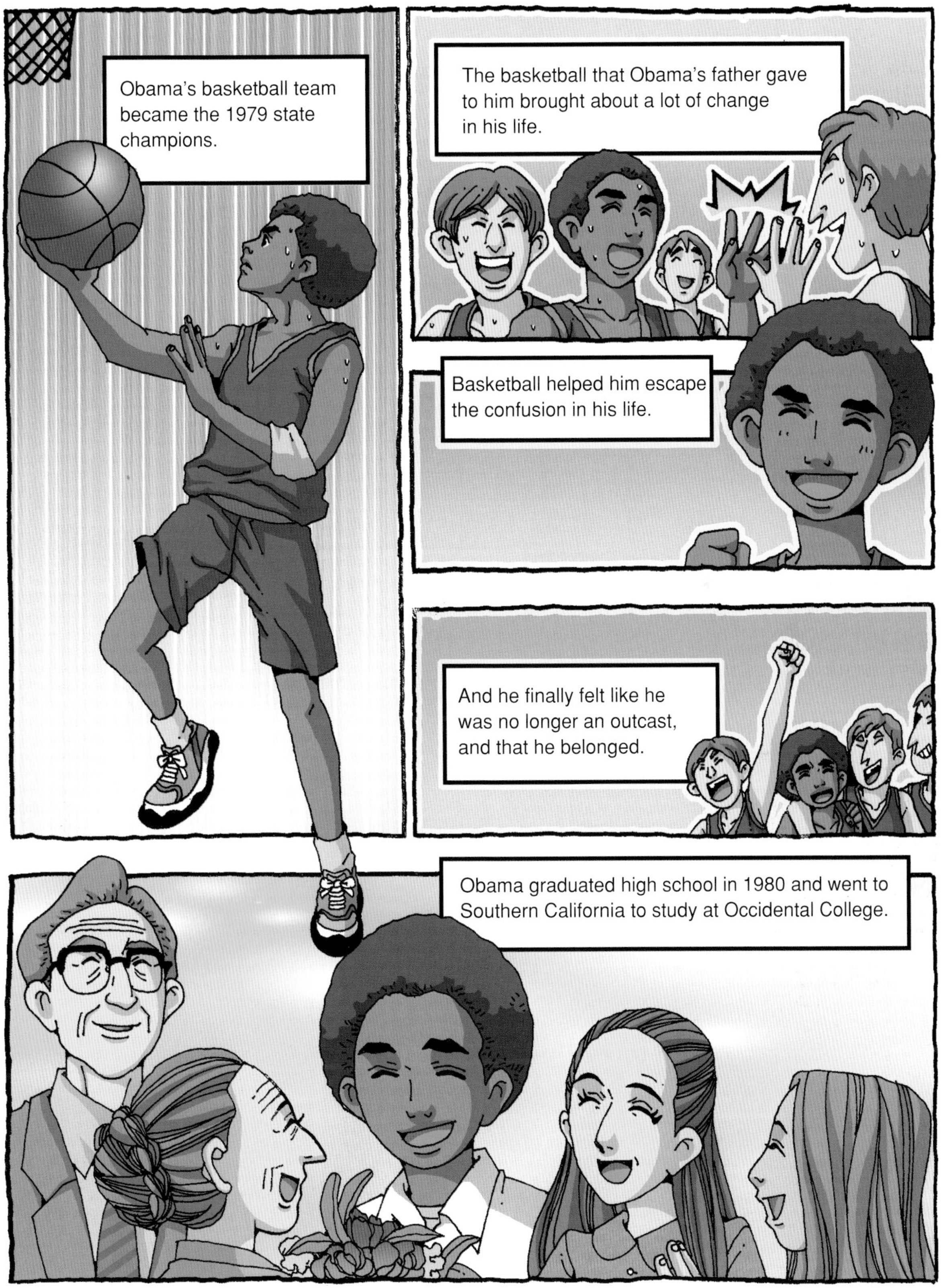
Obama's basketball team became the 1979 state champions.
The basketball that Obama's father gave to him brought about a lot of change in his life.
Basketball helped him escape the confusion in his life.
And he finally felt like he was no longer an outcast, and that he belonged.
Obama graduated high school in 1980 and went to Southern California to study at Occidental College.

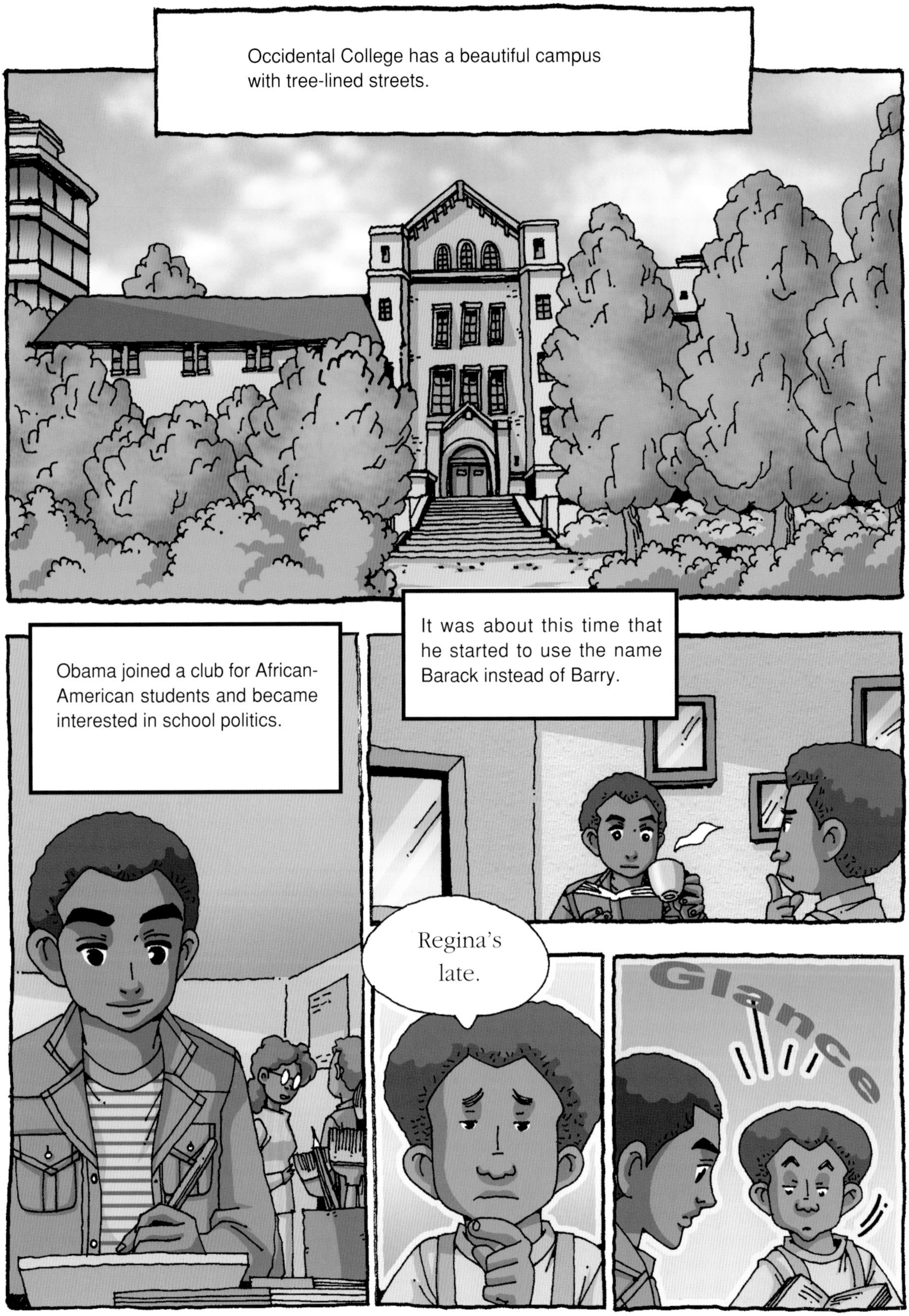
Occidental College has a beautiful campus with tree-lined streets.
Obama joined a club for African-American students and became interested in school politics.
It was about this time that he started to use the name Barack instead of Barry.
Regina's late.
Glance

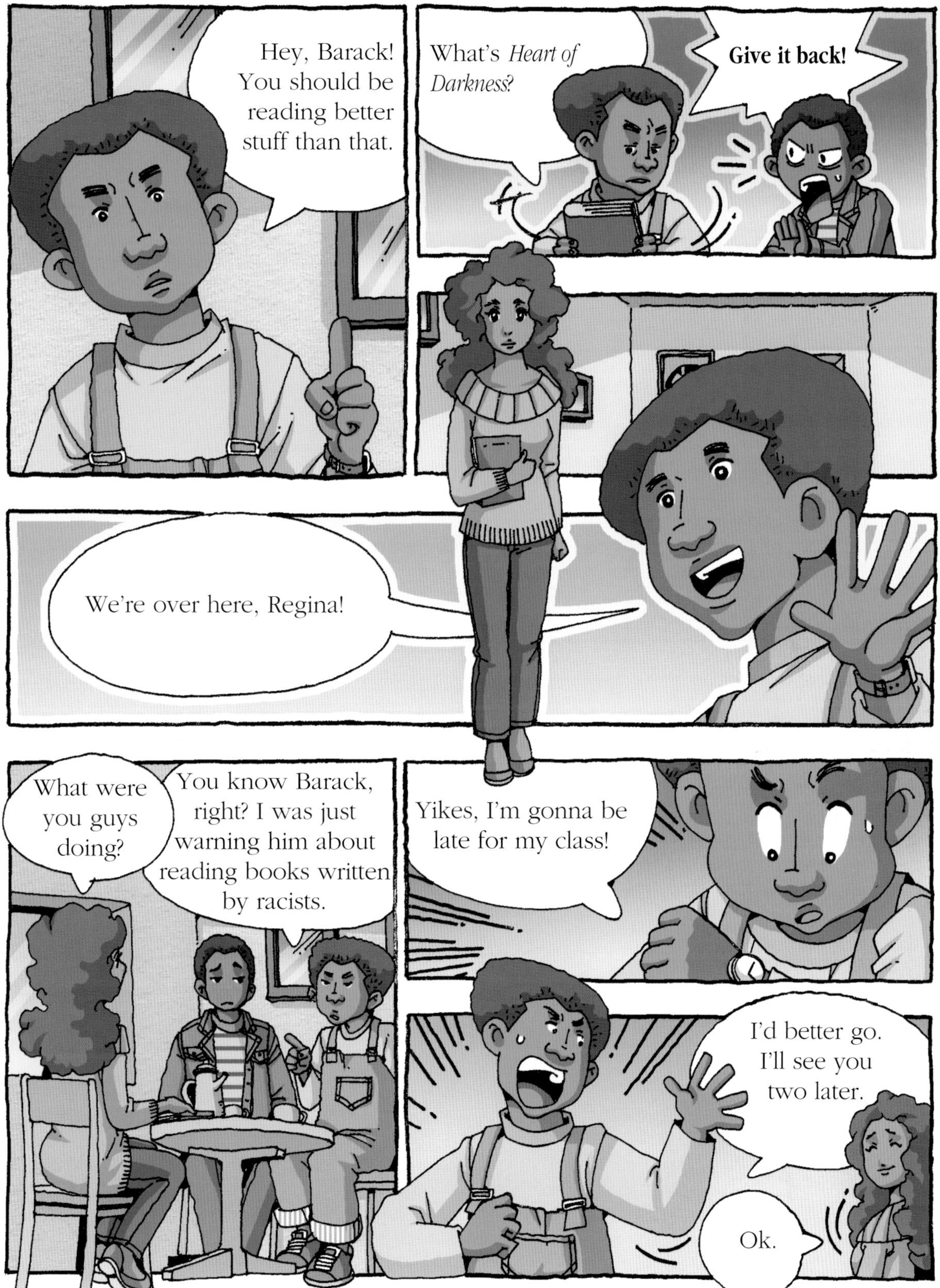
Hey, Barack! You should be reading better stuff than that.
What's *Heart of Darkness*?
Give it back!
We're over here, Regina!
What were you guys doing?
You know Barack, right? I was just warning him about reading books written by racists.
Yikes, I'm gonna be late for my class!
I'd better go. I'll see you two later.
Ok.

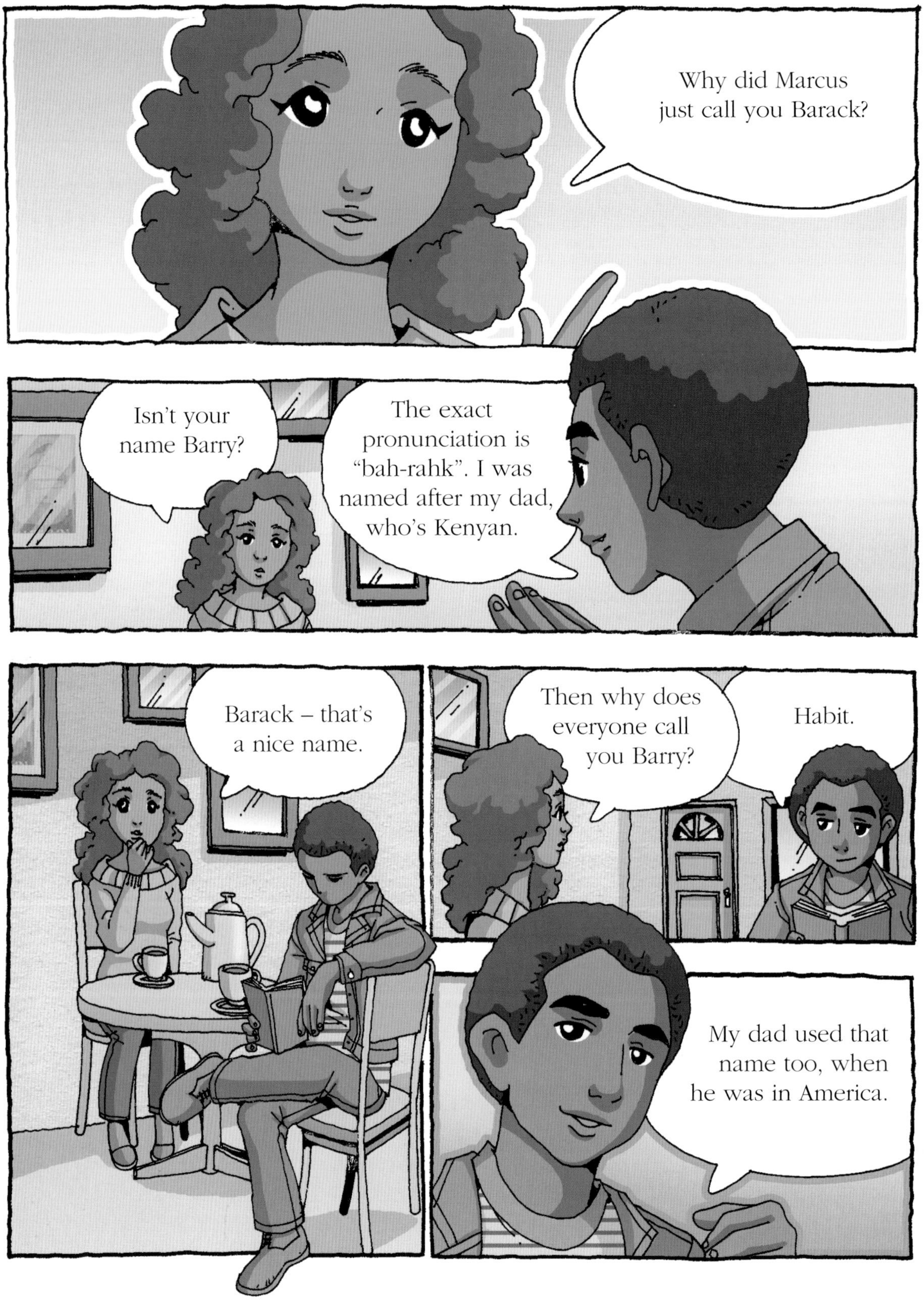

Why did Marcus just call you Barack?
Isn't your name Barry?
The exact pronunciation is "bah-rahk". I was named after my dad, who's Kenyan.
Barack – that's a nice name.
Then why does everyone call you Barry?
Habit.
My dad used that name too, when he was in America.

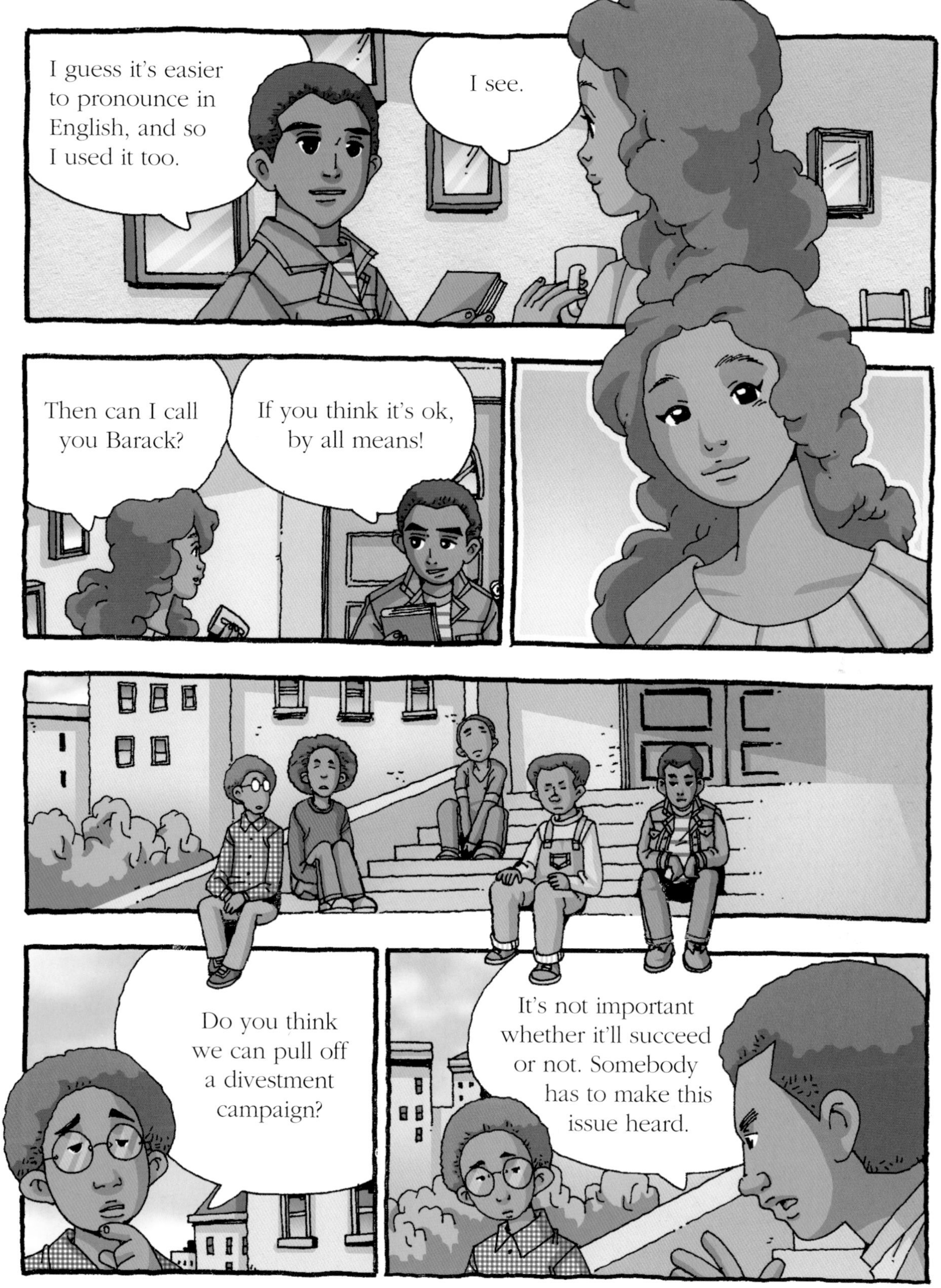
I guess it's easier to pronounce in English, and so I used it too.
I see.
Then can I call you Barack?
If you think it's ok, by all means!
Do you think we can pull off a divestment campaign?
It's not important whether it'll succeed or not. Somebody has to make this issue heard.

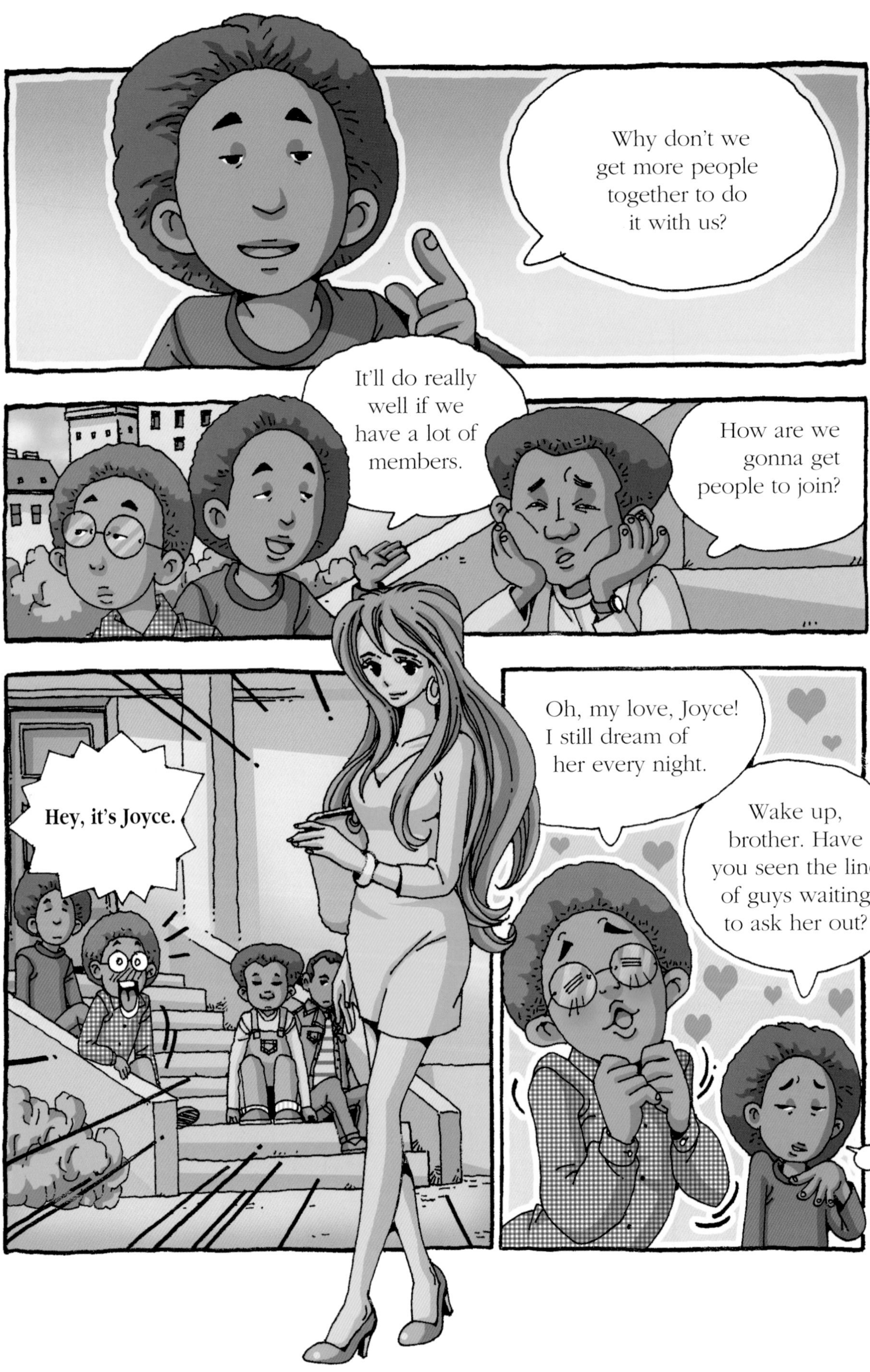
Why don't we get more people together to do it with us?
It'll do really well if we have a lot of members.
How are we gonna get people to join?
Hey, it's Joyce.
Oh, my love, Joyce! I still dream of her every night.
Wake up, brother. Have you seen the line of guys waiting to ask her out?

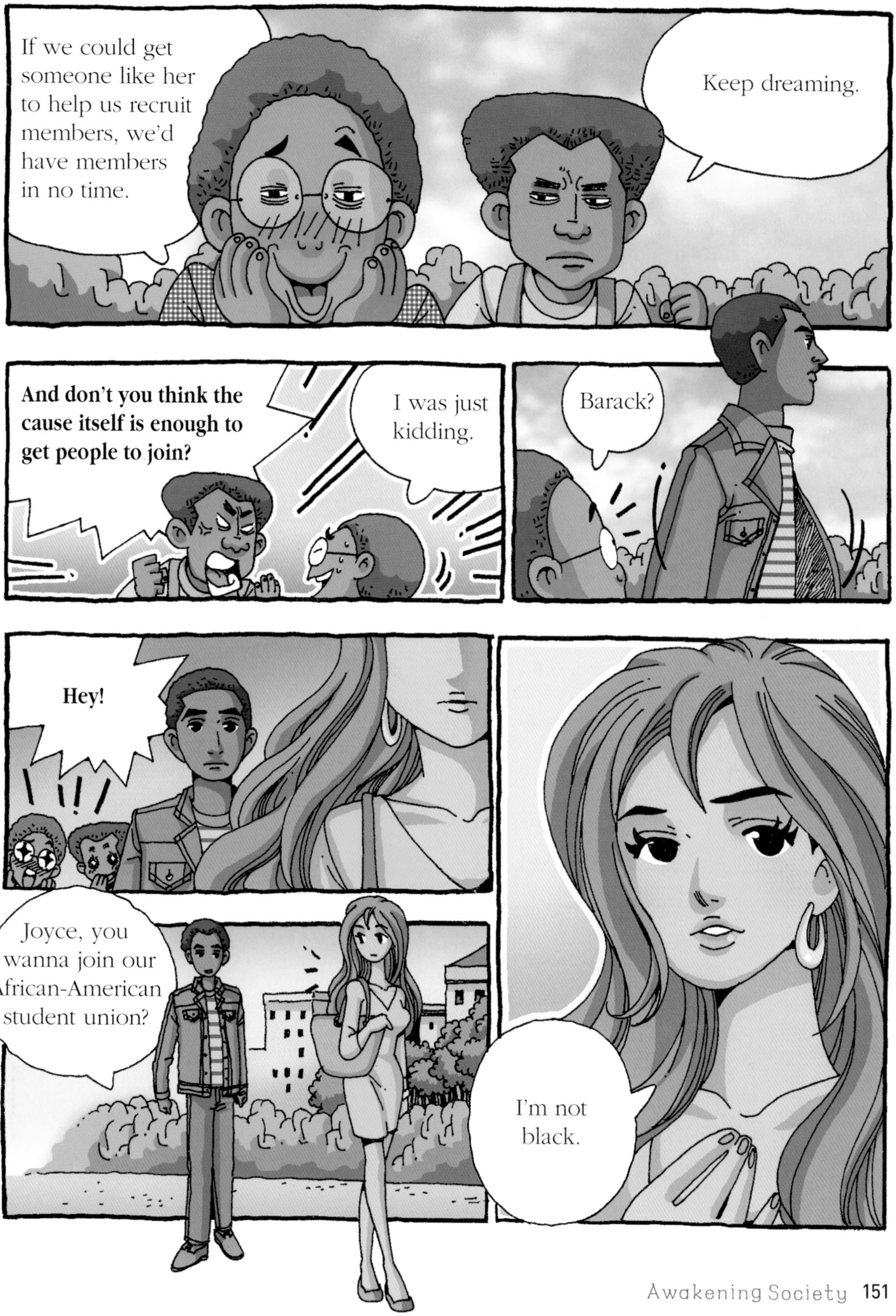
If we could get someone like her to help us recruit members, we'd have members in no time.
Keep dreaming.
And don't you think the cause itself is enough to get people to join?
I was just kidding.
Barack?
Hey!
Joyce, you wanna join our African-American student union?
I'm not black.

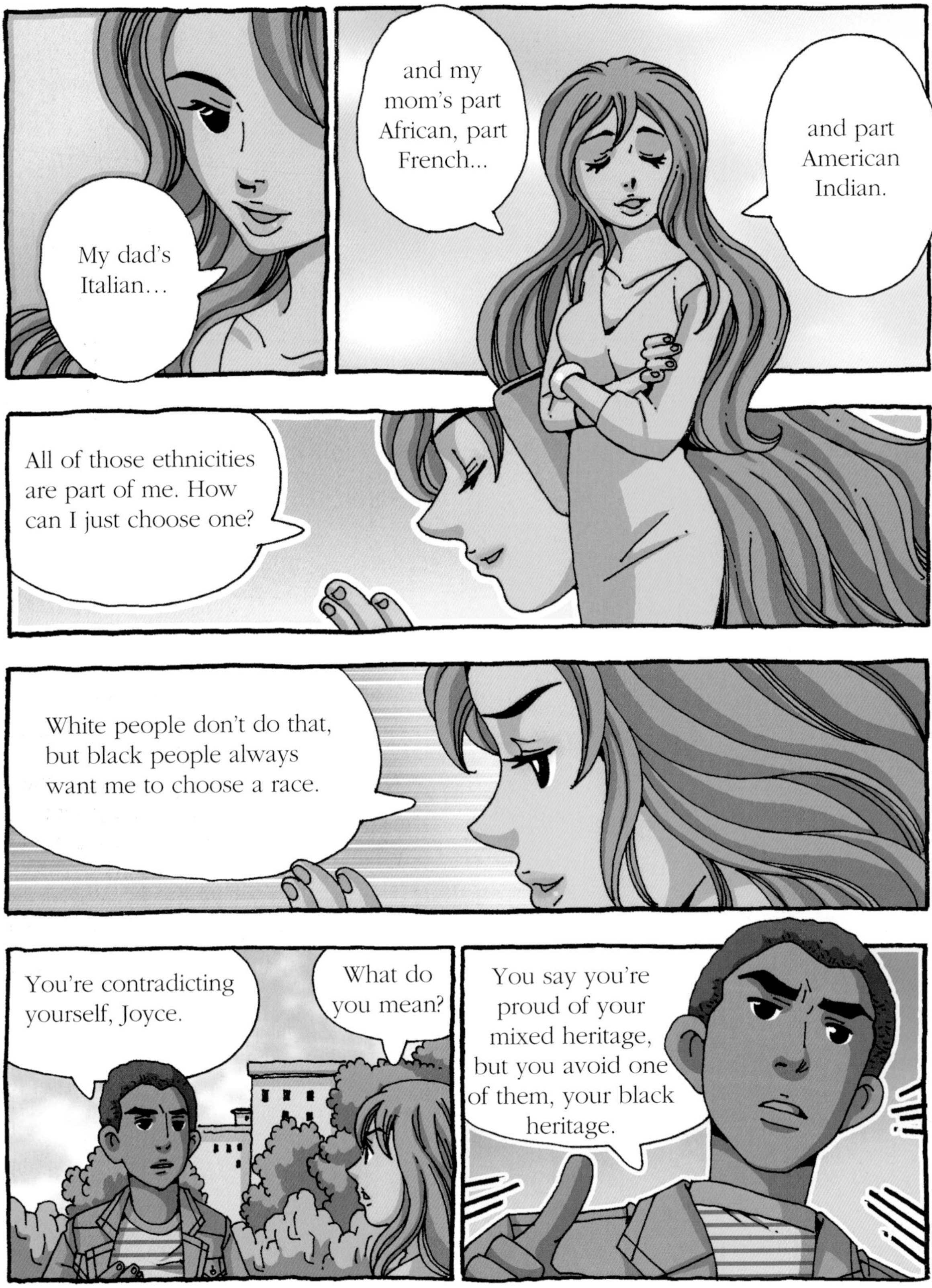
My dad's Italian...
and my mom's part African, part French...
and part American Indian.
All of those ethnicities are part of me. How can I just choose one?
White people don't do that, but black people always want me to choose a race.
You're contradicting yourself, Joyce.
What do you mean?
You say you're proud of your mixed heritage, but you avoid one of them, your black heritage.

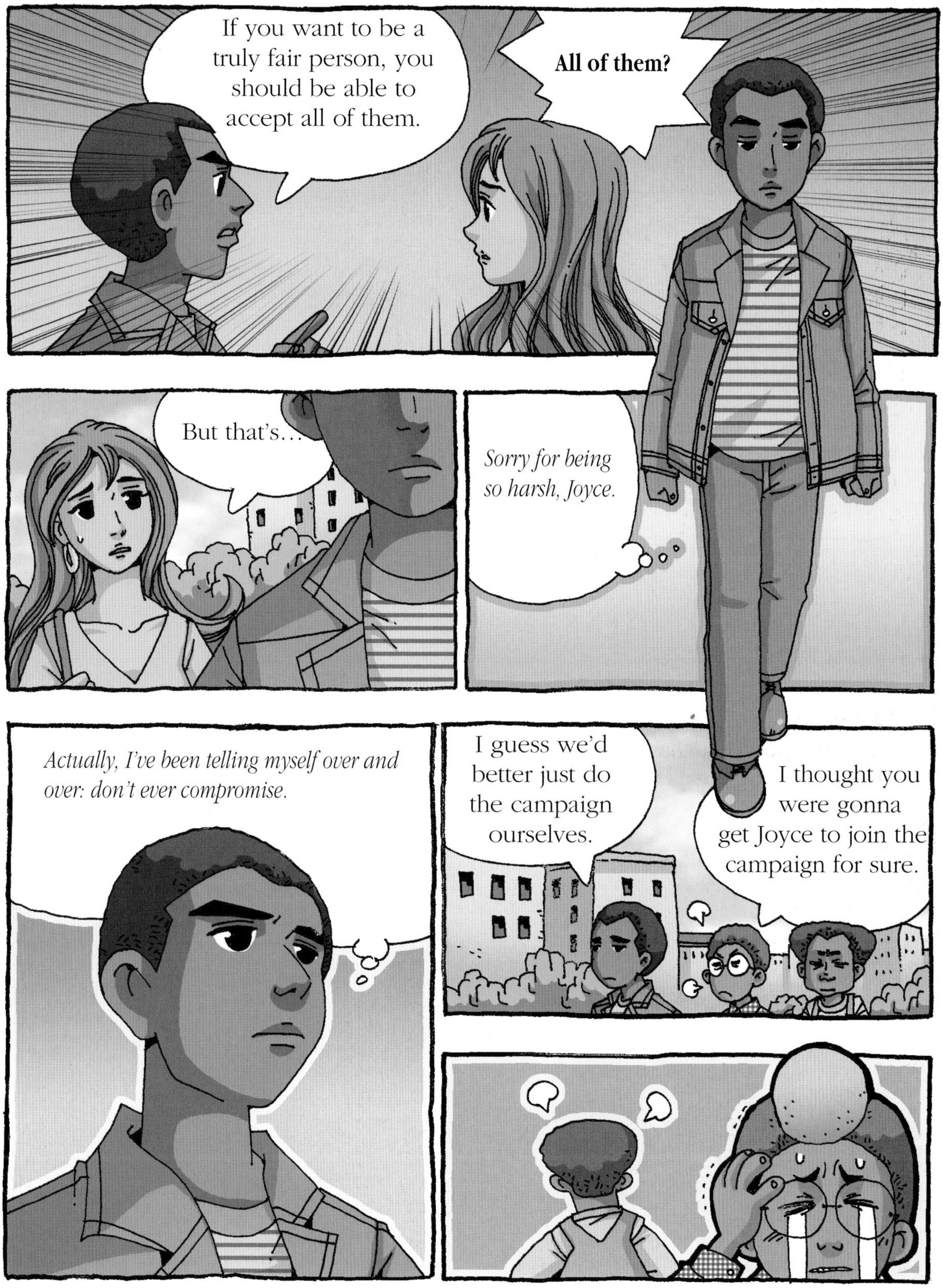
If you want to be a truly fair person, you should be able to accept all of them.
All of them?
But that's…
Sorry for being so harsh, Joyce.
Actually, I've been telling myself over and over: don't ever compromise.
I guess we'd better just do the campaign ourselves.
I thought you were gonna get Joyce to join the campaign for sure.

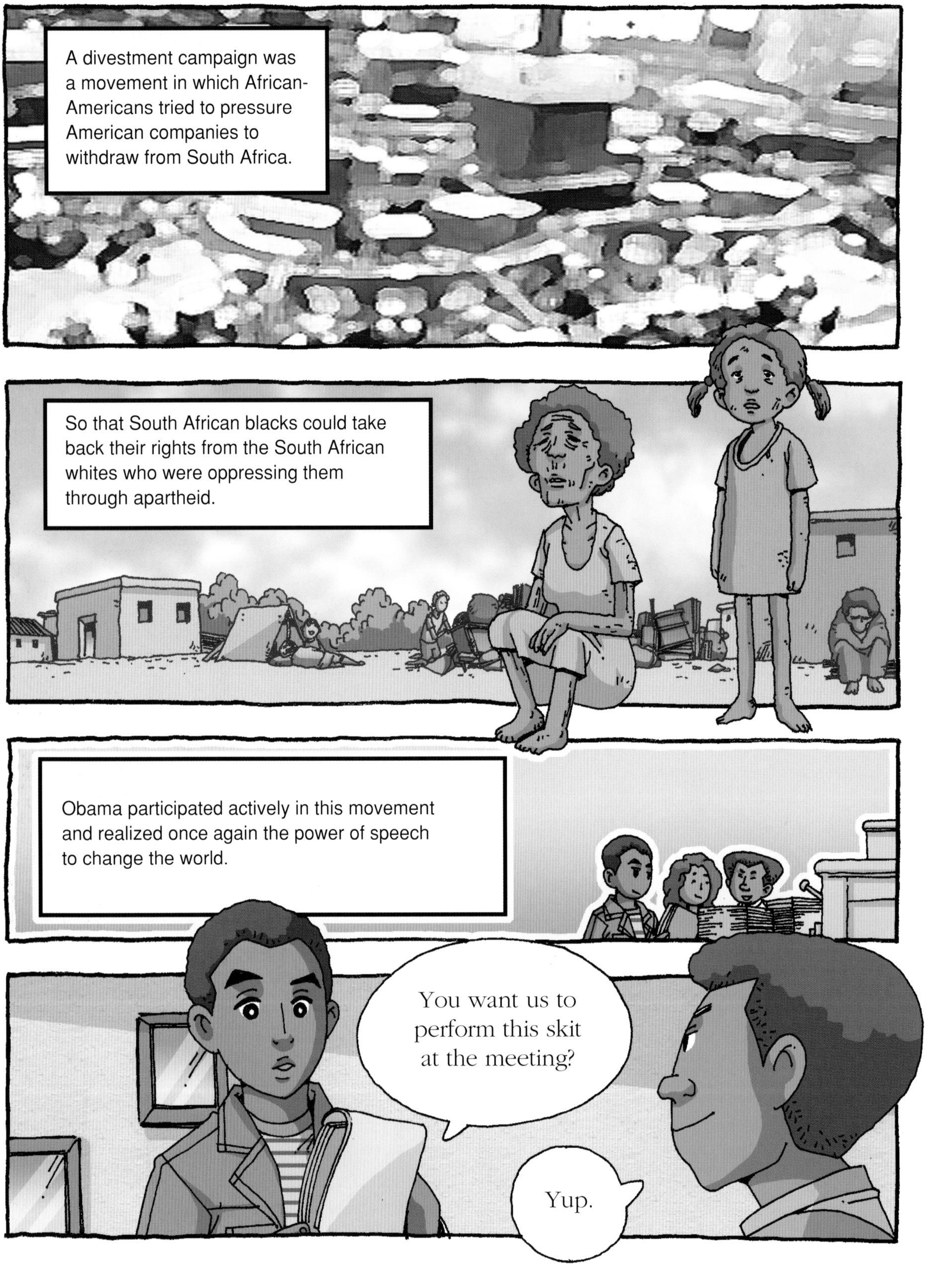
A divestment campaign was a movement in which African-Americans tried to pressure American companies to withdraw from South Africa.
So that South African blacks could take back their rights from the South African whites who were oppressing them through apartheid.
Obama participated actively in this movement and realized once again the power of speech to change the world.
You want us to perform this skit at the meeting?
Yup.

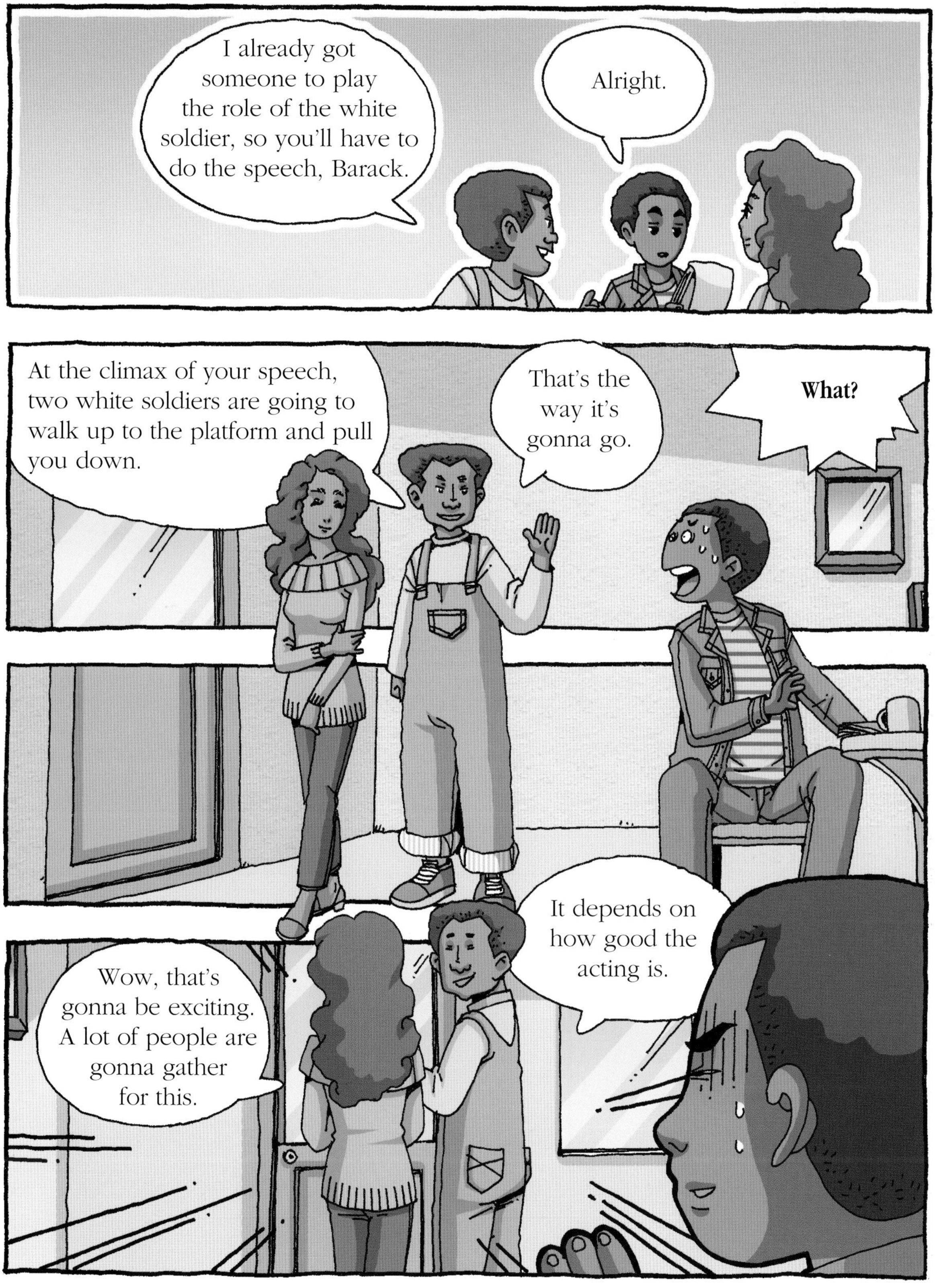
I already got someone to play the role of the white soldier, so you'll have to do the speech, Barack.
Alright.
At the climax of your speech, two white soldiers are going to walk up to the platform and pull you down.
That's the way it's gonna go.
What?
Wow, that's gonna be exciting. A lot of people are gonna gather for this.
It depends on how good the acting is.

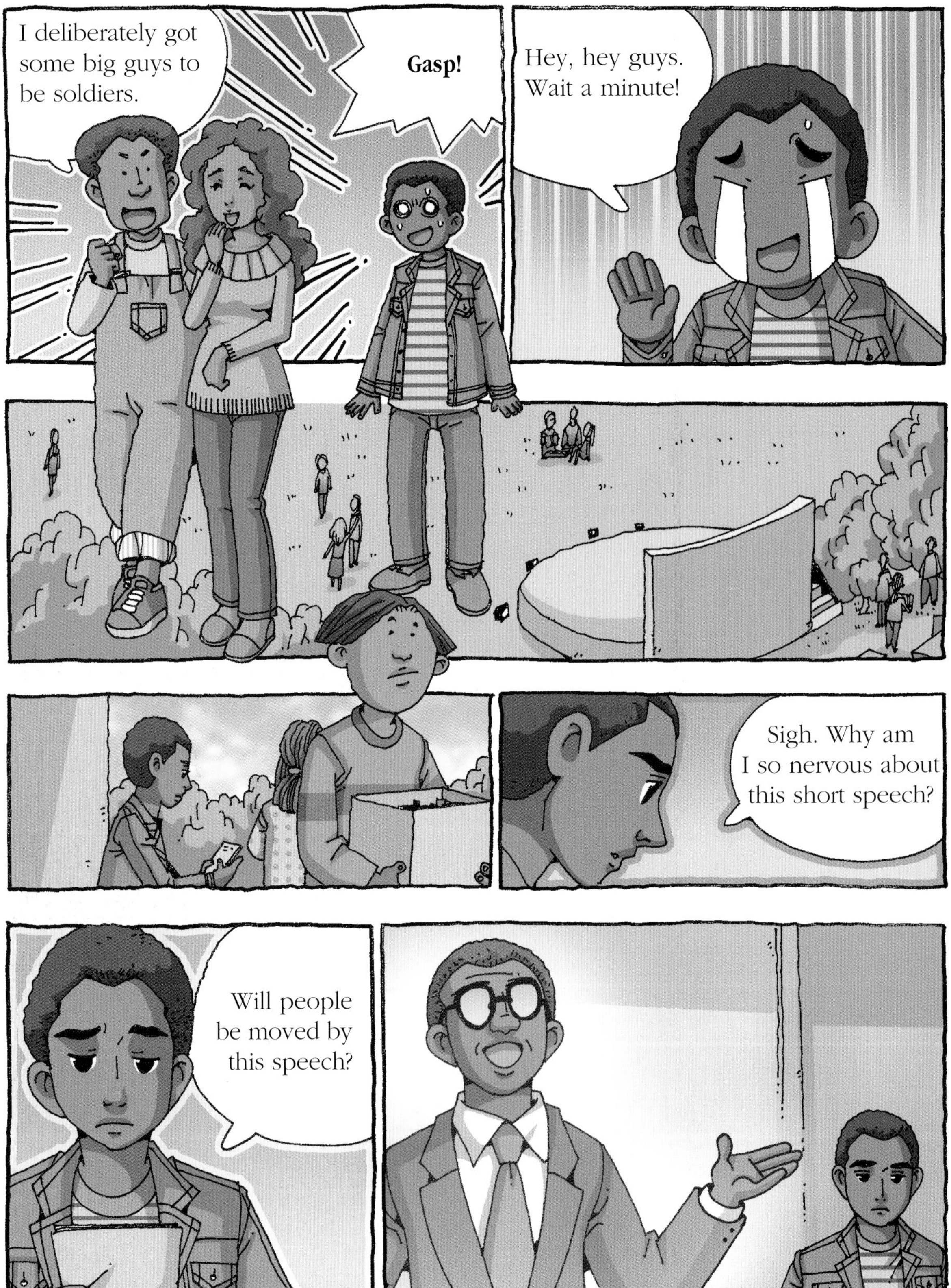
I deliberately got some big guys to be soldiers.
Gasp!
Hey, hey guys. Wait a minute!
Sigh. Why am I so nervous about this short speech?
Will people be moved by this speech?

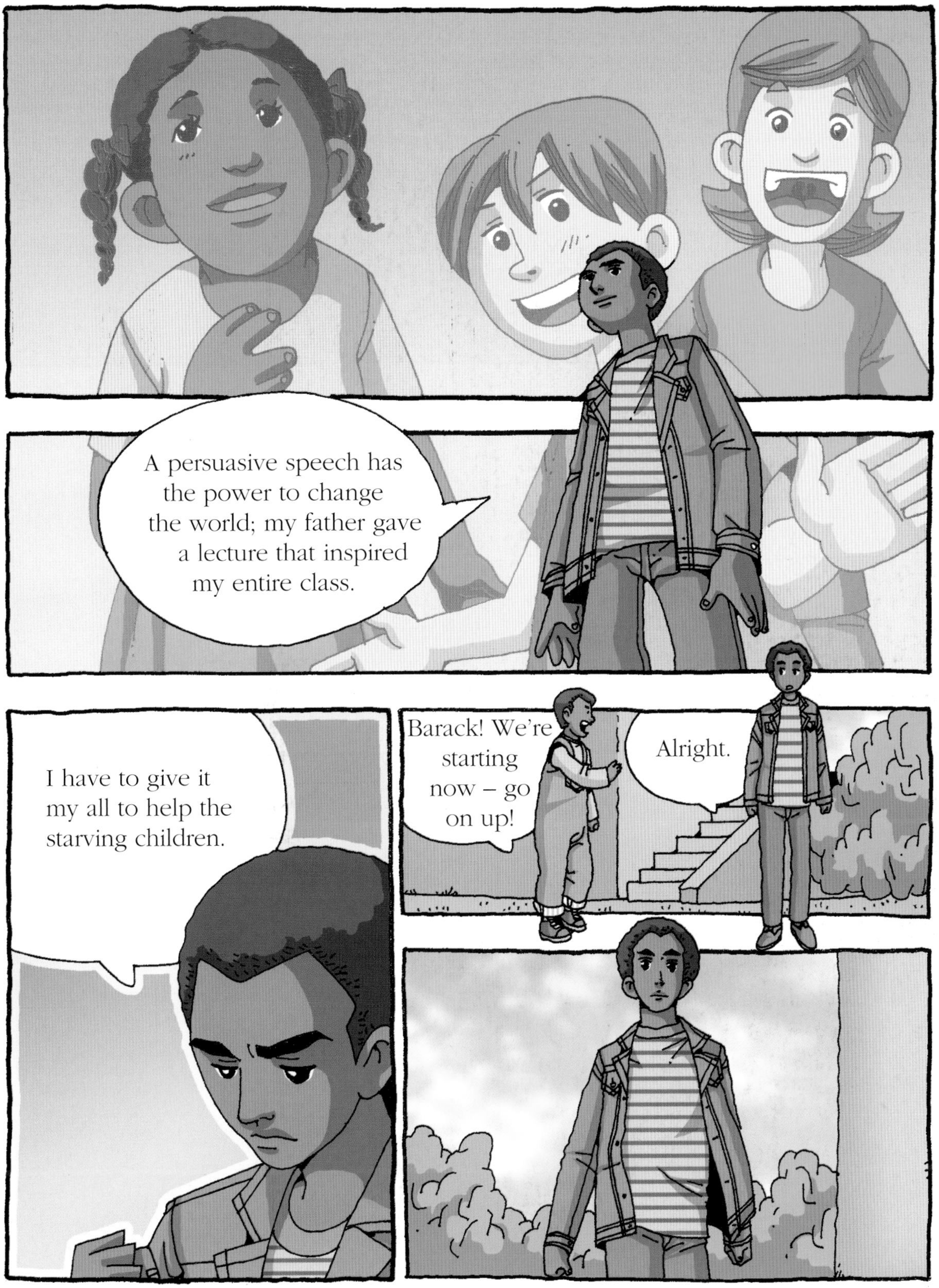
A persuasive speech has the power to change the world; my father gave a lecture that inspired my entire class.
I have to give it my all to help the starving children.
Barack! We're starting now – go on up!
Alright.

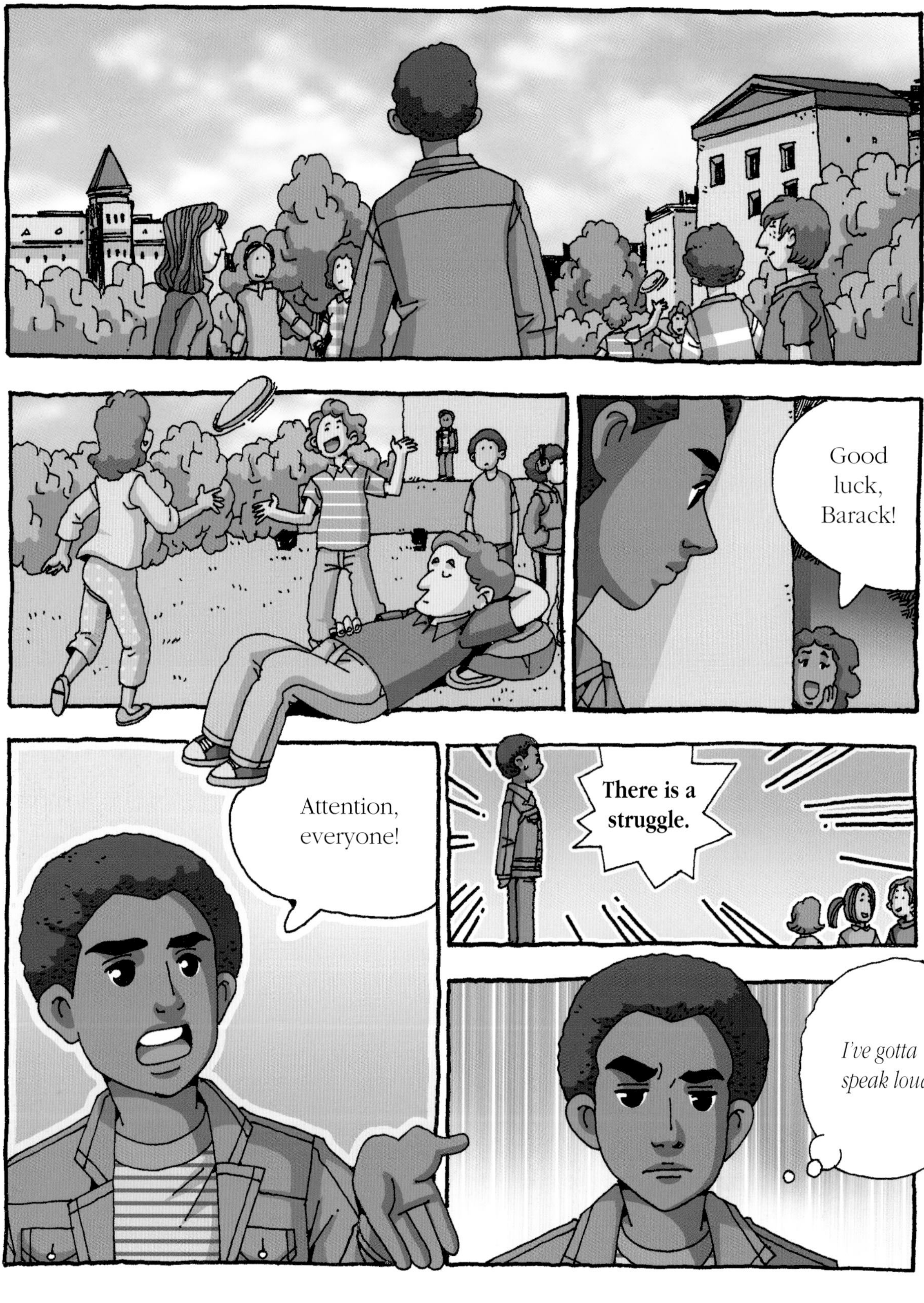
Good luck, Barack!
Attention, everyone!
There is a struggle.
I've gotta speak louder.

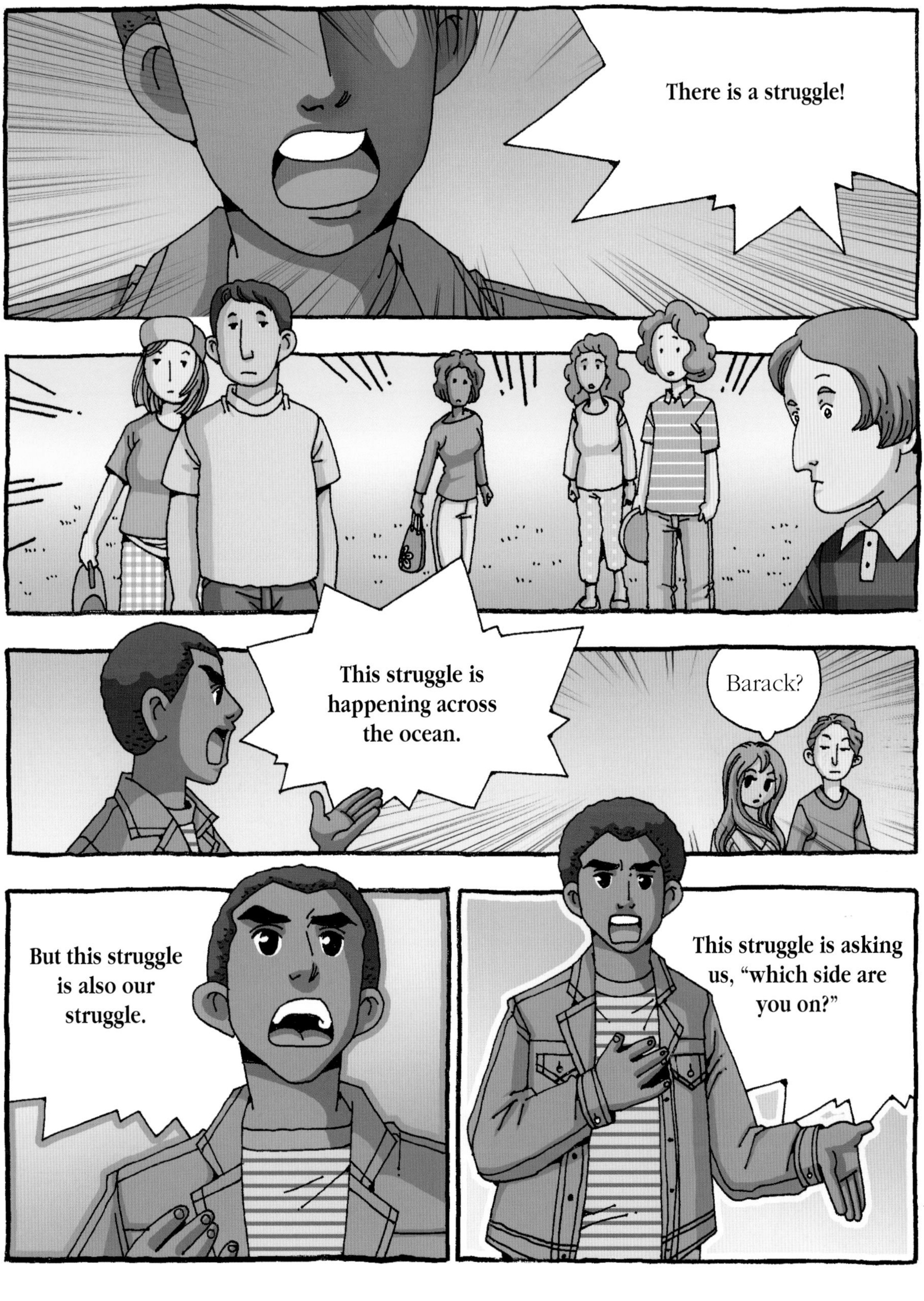
There is a struggle!
This struggle is happening across the ocean.
Barack?
But this struggle is also our struggle.
This struggle is asking us, "which side are you on?"

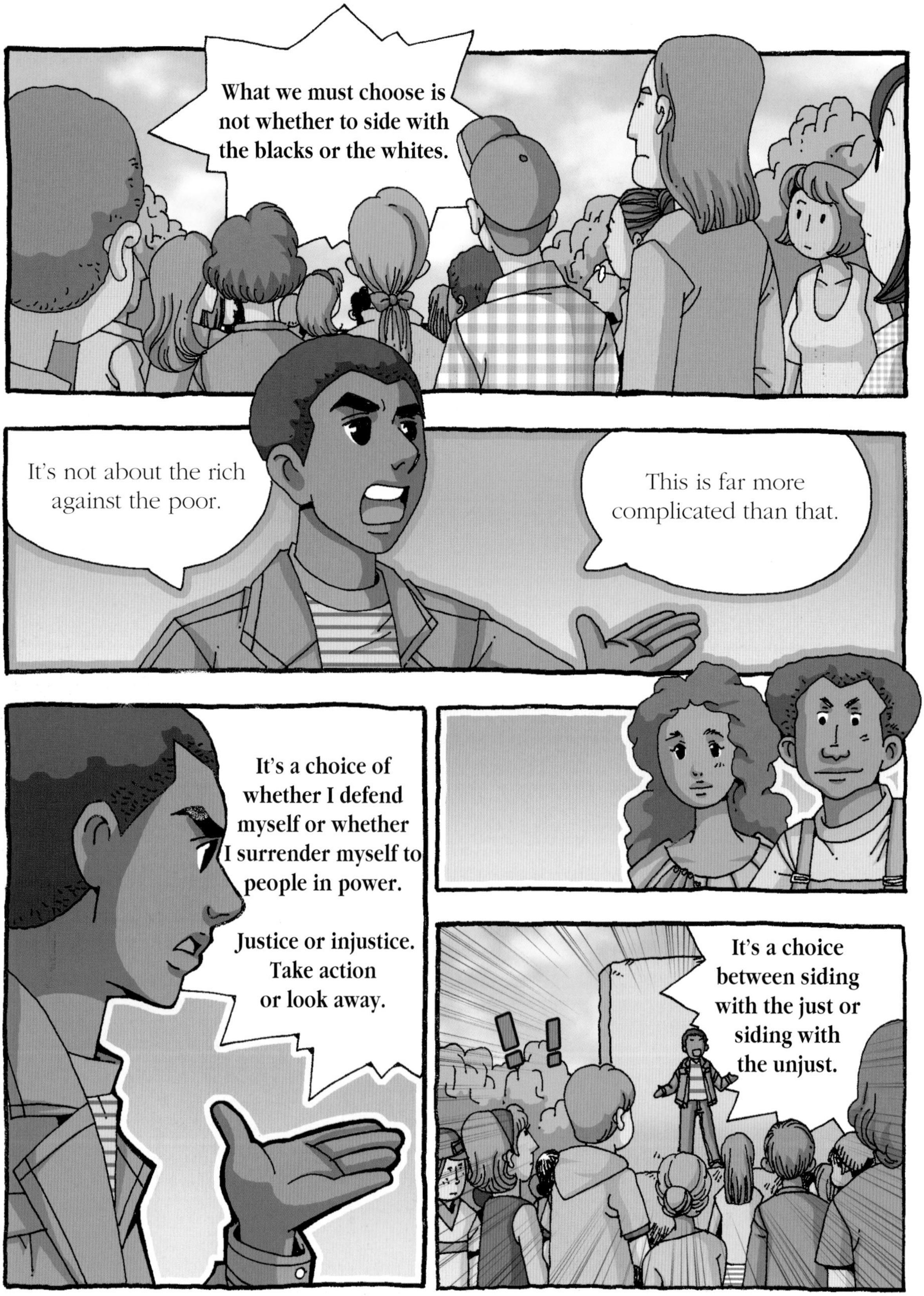
What we must choose is not whether to side with the blacks or the whites.
It's not about the rich against the poor.
This is far more complicated than that.
It's a choice of whether I defend myself or whether I surrender myself to people in power.
Justice or injustice. Take action or look away.
It's a choice between siding with the just or siding with the unjust.

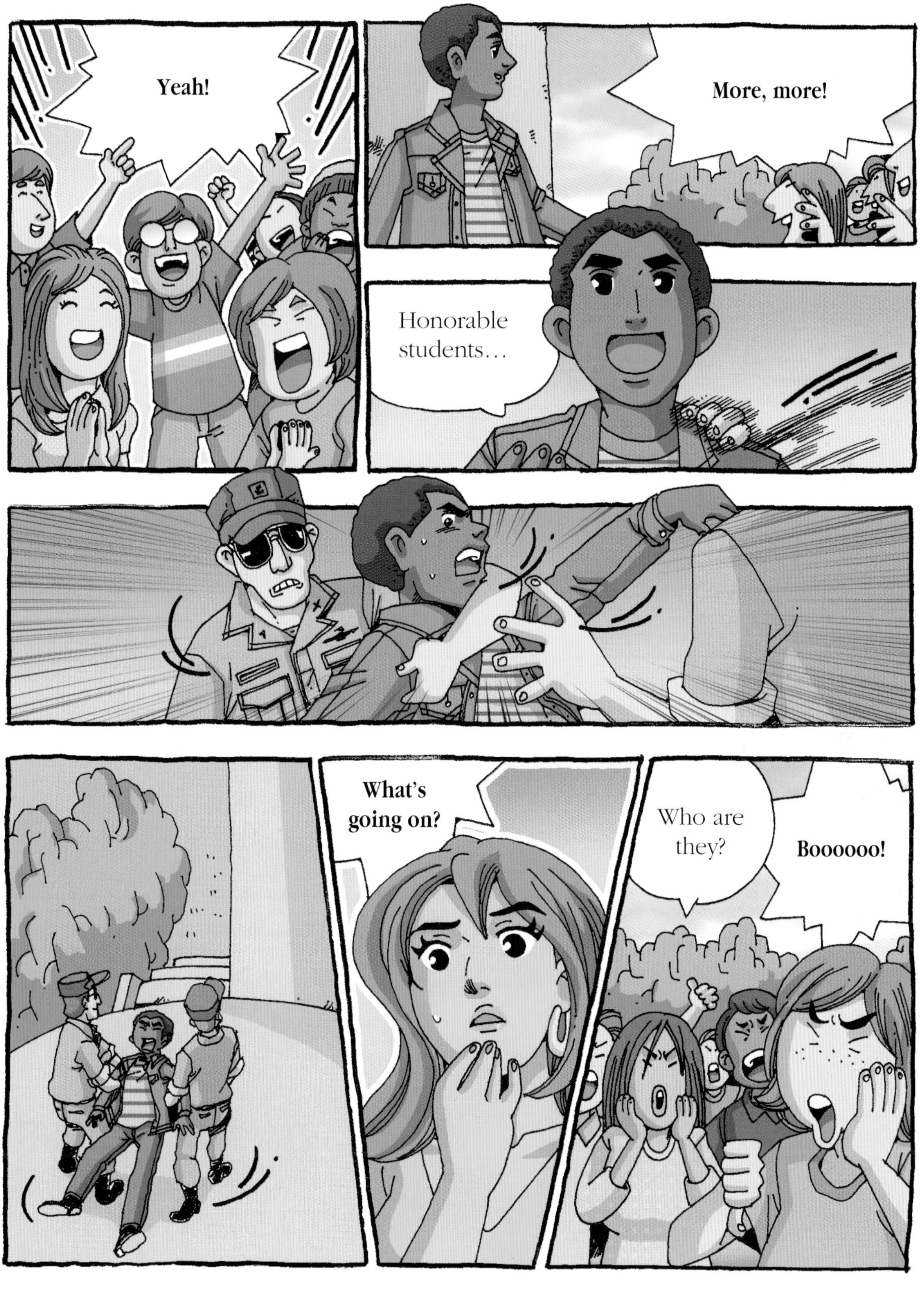
Yeah!
More, more!
Honorable students…
What's going on?
Who are they?
Boooooo!

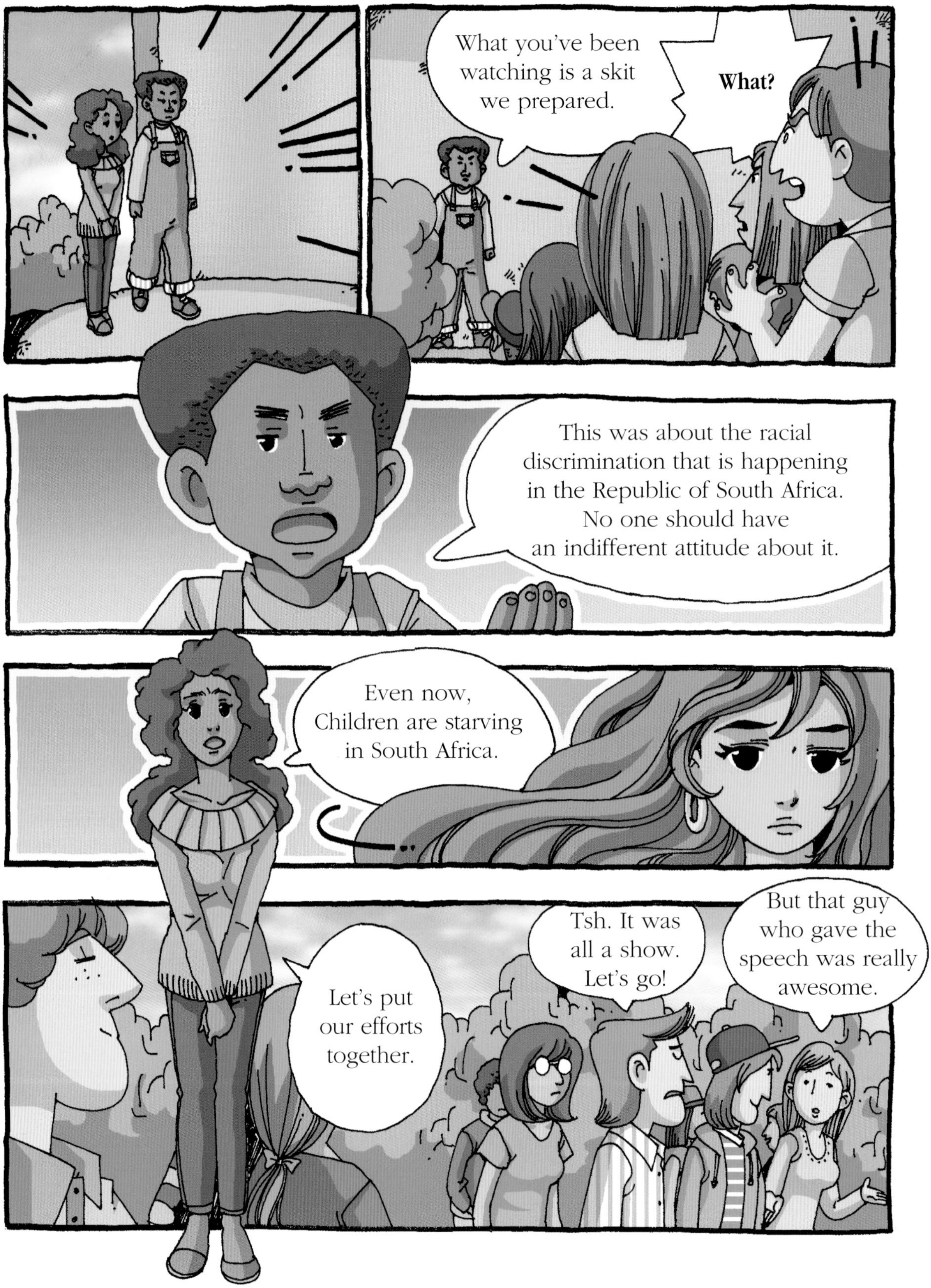
What you've been watching is a skit we prepared.
What?
This was about the racial discrimination that is happening in the Republic of South Africa. No one should have an indifferent attitude about it.
Even now, Children are starving in South Africa.
Let's put our efforts together.
Tsh. It was all a show. Let's go!
But that guy who gave the speech was really awesome.

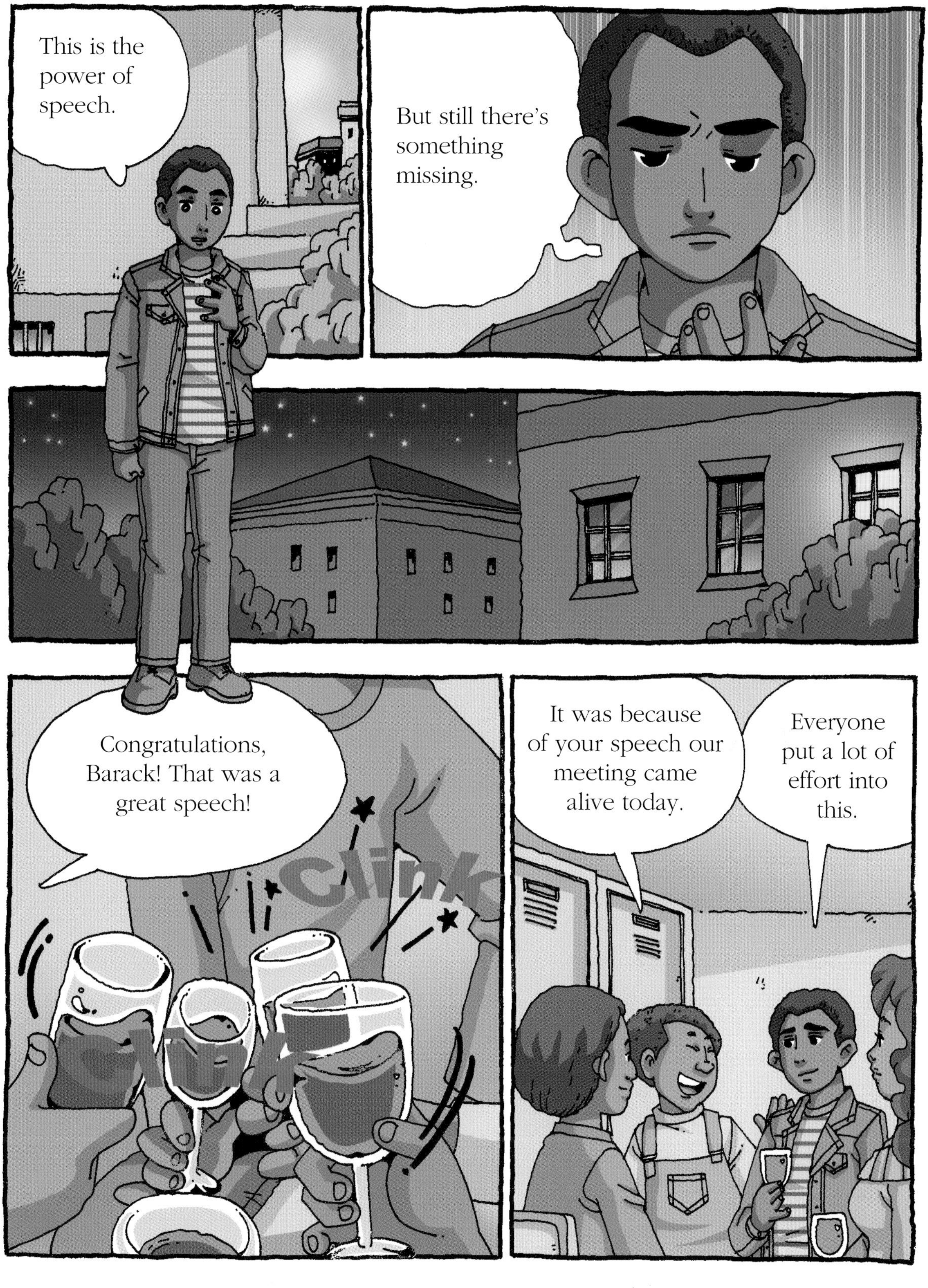
This is the power of speech.
But still there's something missing.
Congratulations, Barack! That was a great speech!
Clink
Clink
It was because of your speech our meeting came alive today.
Everyone put a lot of effort into this.

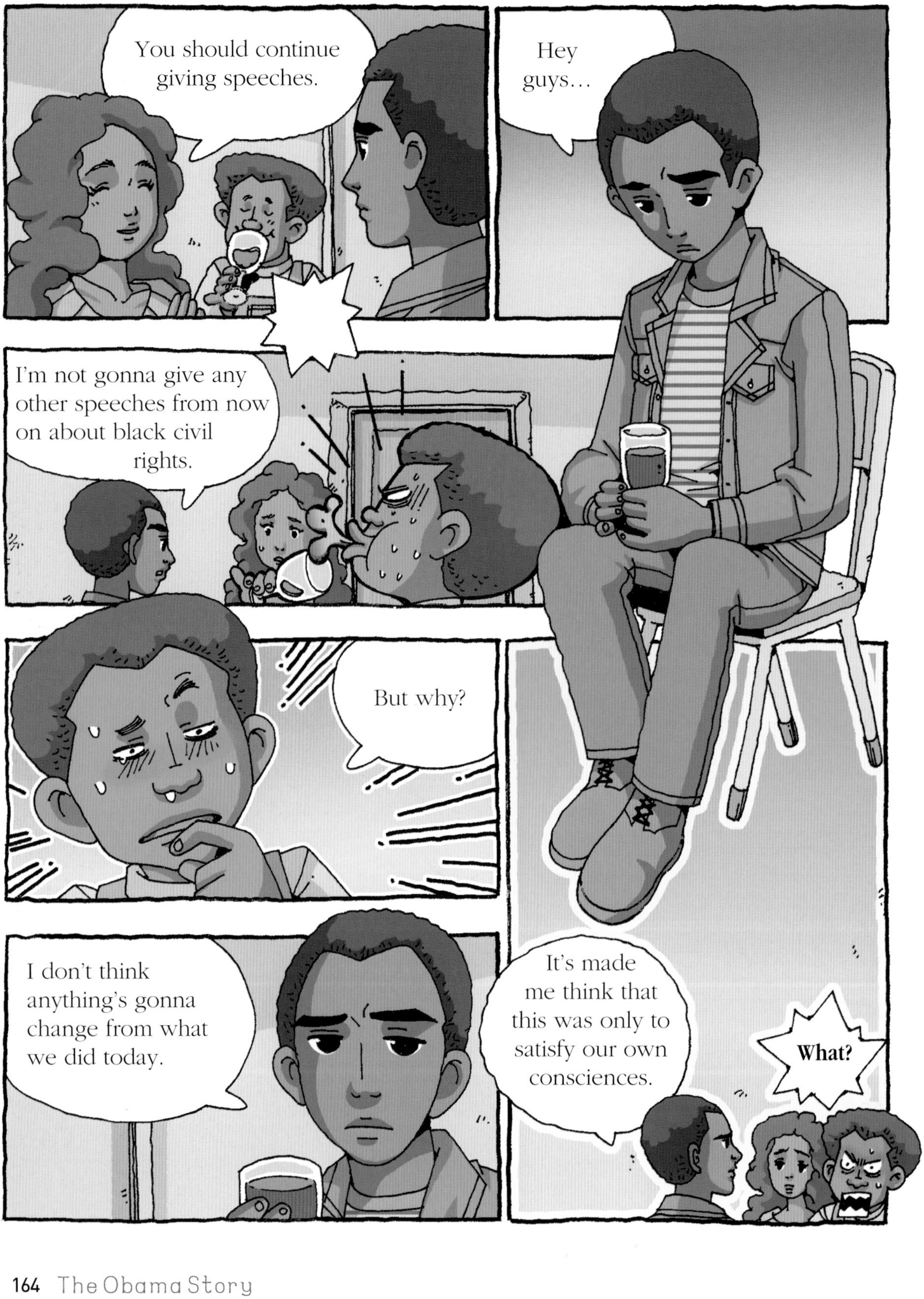

You should continue giving speeches.
Hey guys…
I'm not gonna give any other speeches from now on about black civil rights.
But why?
I don't think anything's gonna change from what we did today.
It's made me think that this was only to satisfy our own consciences.
What?

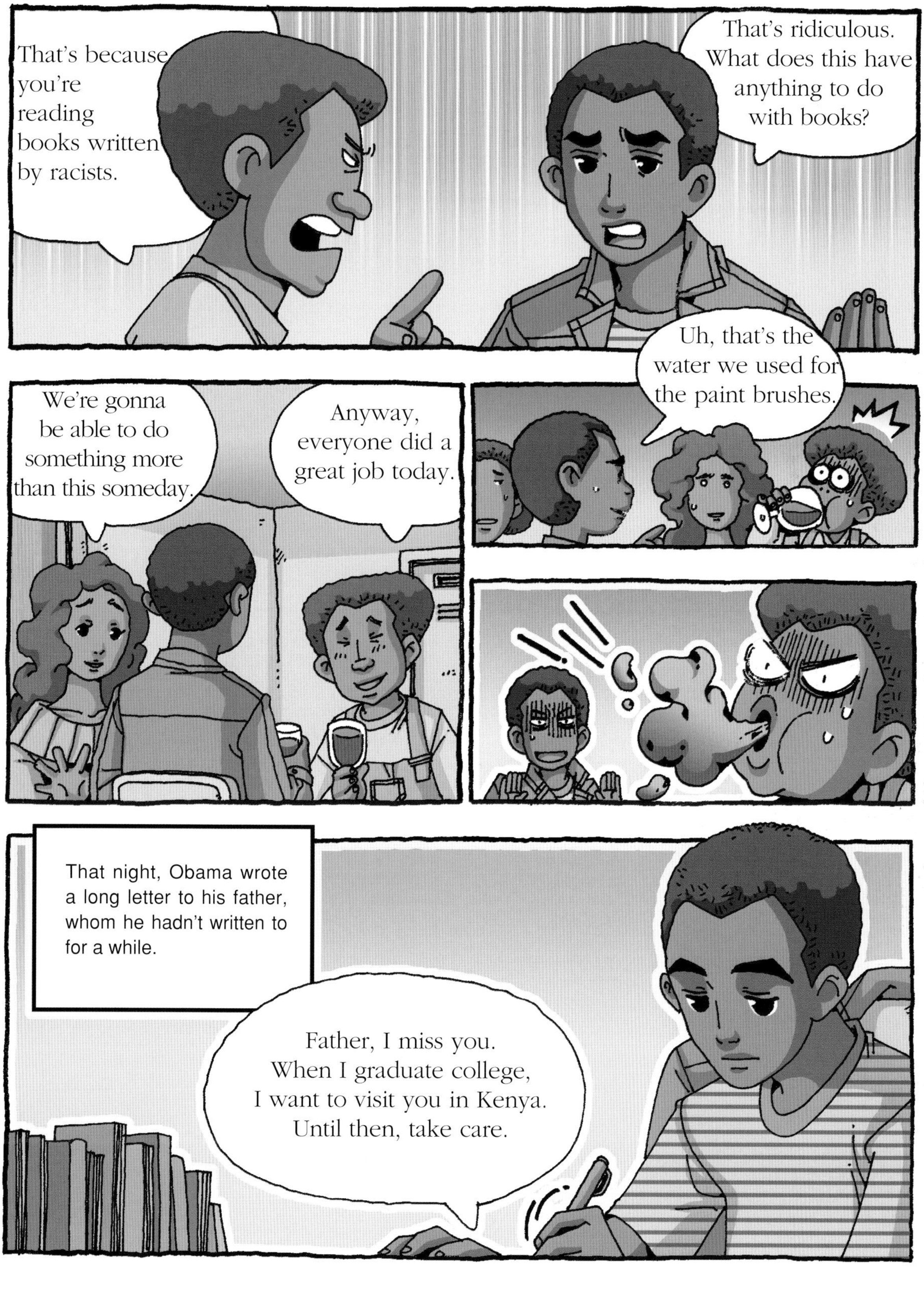
That's because you're reading books written by racists.
That's ridiculous. What does this have anything to do with books?
We're gonna be able to do something more than this someday.
Anyway, everyone did a great job today.
Uh, that's the water we used for the paint brushes.
That night, Obama wrote a long letter to his father, whom he hadn't written to for a while.
Father, I miss you. When I graduate college, I want to visit you in Kenya. Until then, take care.

Getting to know Obama 2

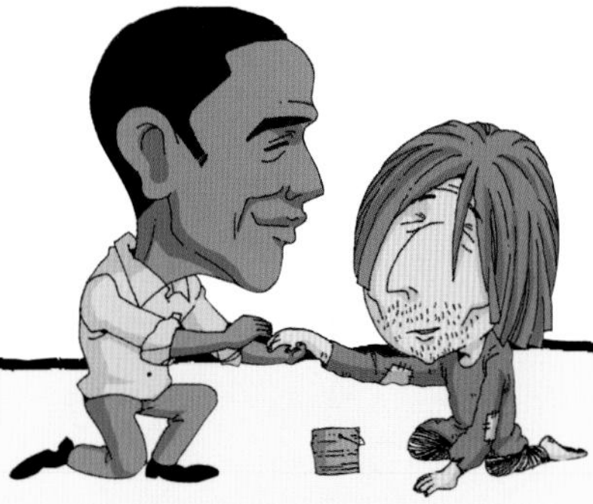

Obama as a Community Activist

Serving as a community activist meant learning the needs of those in society who've been hurt in one way or another, bringing them together, and making their voice heard by legislators who could help improve their situation. The work that Obama did as a community activist was to turn people's complaints into action to improve their living conditions.

The first town meeting Obama organized referred to "weapons and public peace". To Obama's chagrin, however, only 13 people attended the meeting. He realized later that the topic of gangs in the city was too broad to capture the community's interest.

Obama's first successful community project was the "Altgeld Gardens Public Housing Tenants' Organization." Altgeld Gardens was a community adjacent to a garbage landfill and a sewage facility. The environmental pollution was so bad that a constant foul odor filled the air and prevented trees from growing in the area. Obama gathered the residents of this community together and promised to request the government to improve their living conditions.

Obama was also concerned about the troubled youth who were aimless and lost, as he was in his teenage years. So he submitted a proposal for a program to draw active participation from parents of these youth. It was called "Youth Counseling Network," and drew a very positive response from the community.

Chapter 7

A Search for His Roots

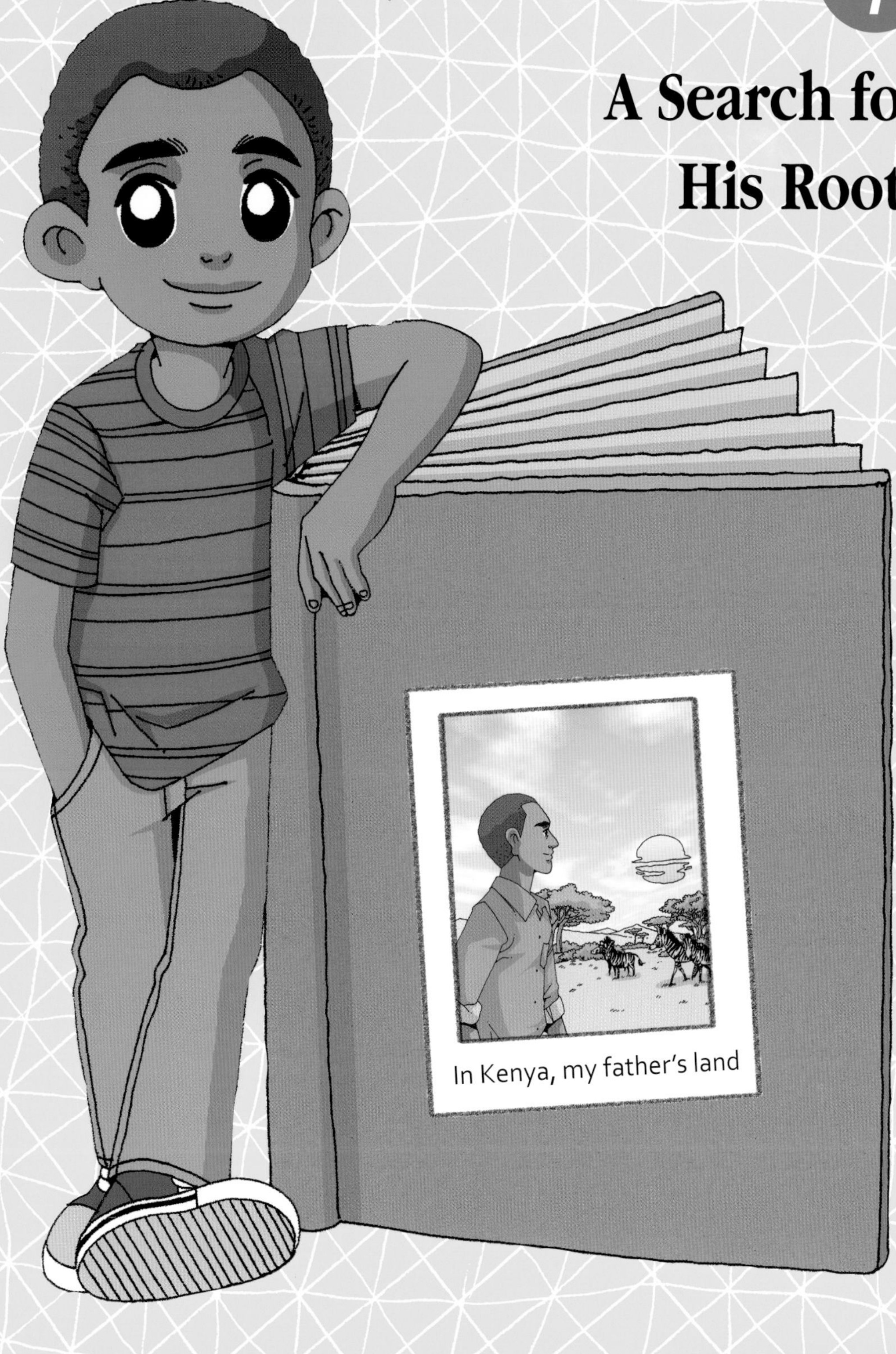
In Kenya, my father's land

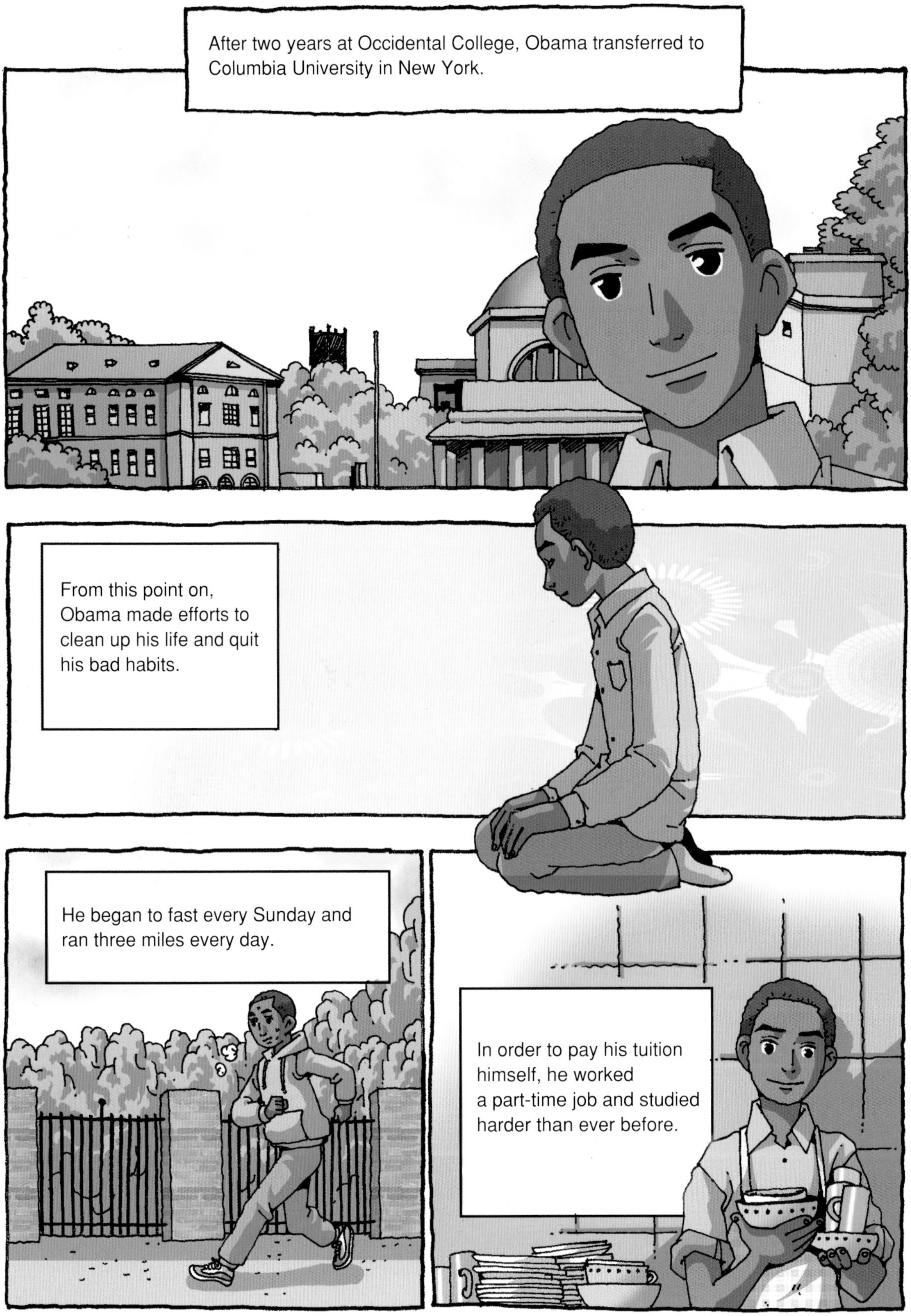
After two years at Occidental College, Obama transferred to Columbia University in New York.
From this point on, Obama made efforts to clean up his life and quit his bad habits.
He began to fast every Sunday and ran three miles every day.
In order to pay his tuition himself, he worked a part-time job and studied harder than ever before.

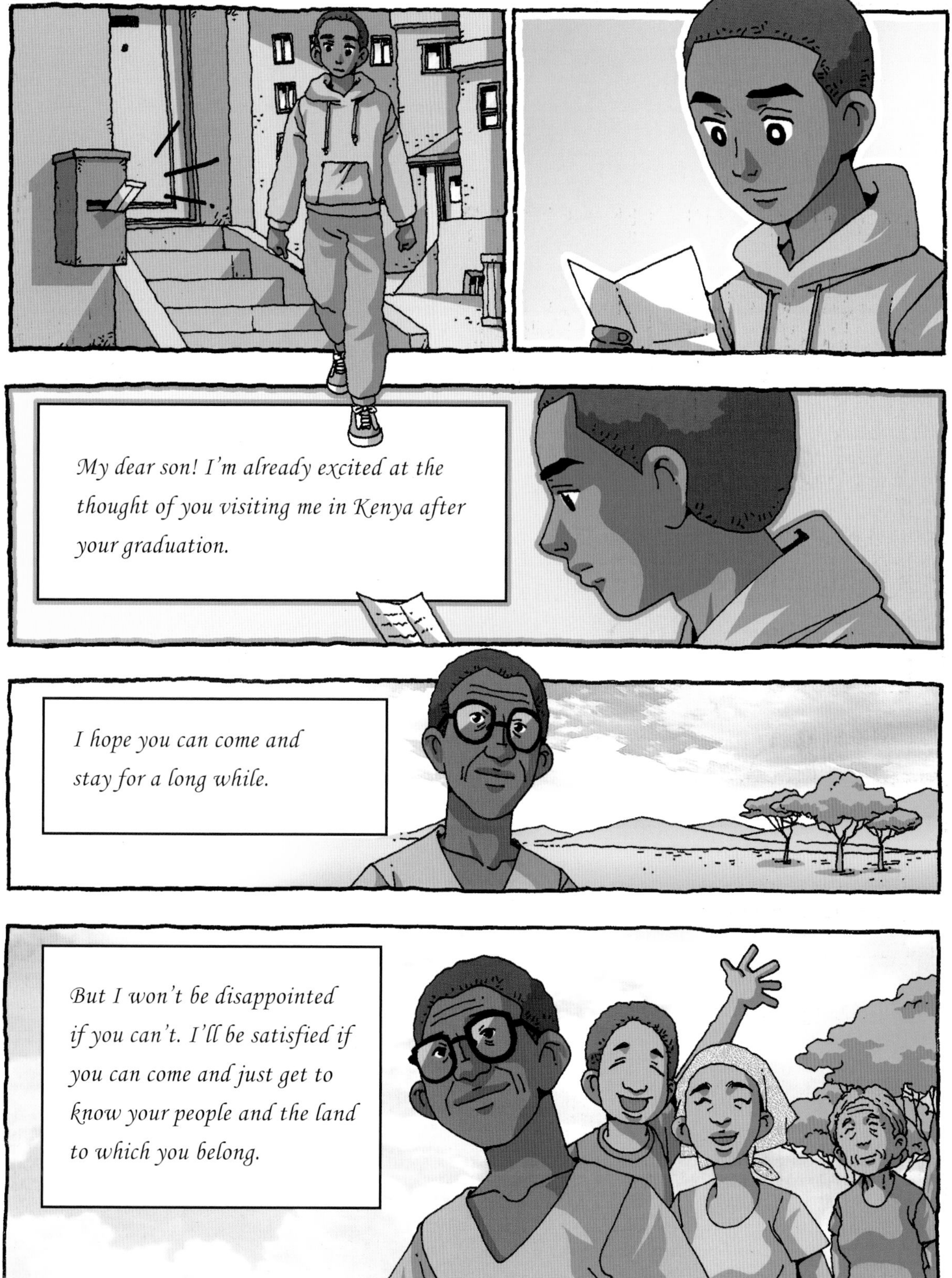
My dear son! I'm already excited at the thought of you visiting me in Kenya after your graduation.
I hope you can come and stay for a long while.
But I won't be disappointed if you can't. I'll be satisfied if you can come and just get to know your people and the land to which you belong.

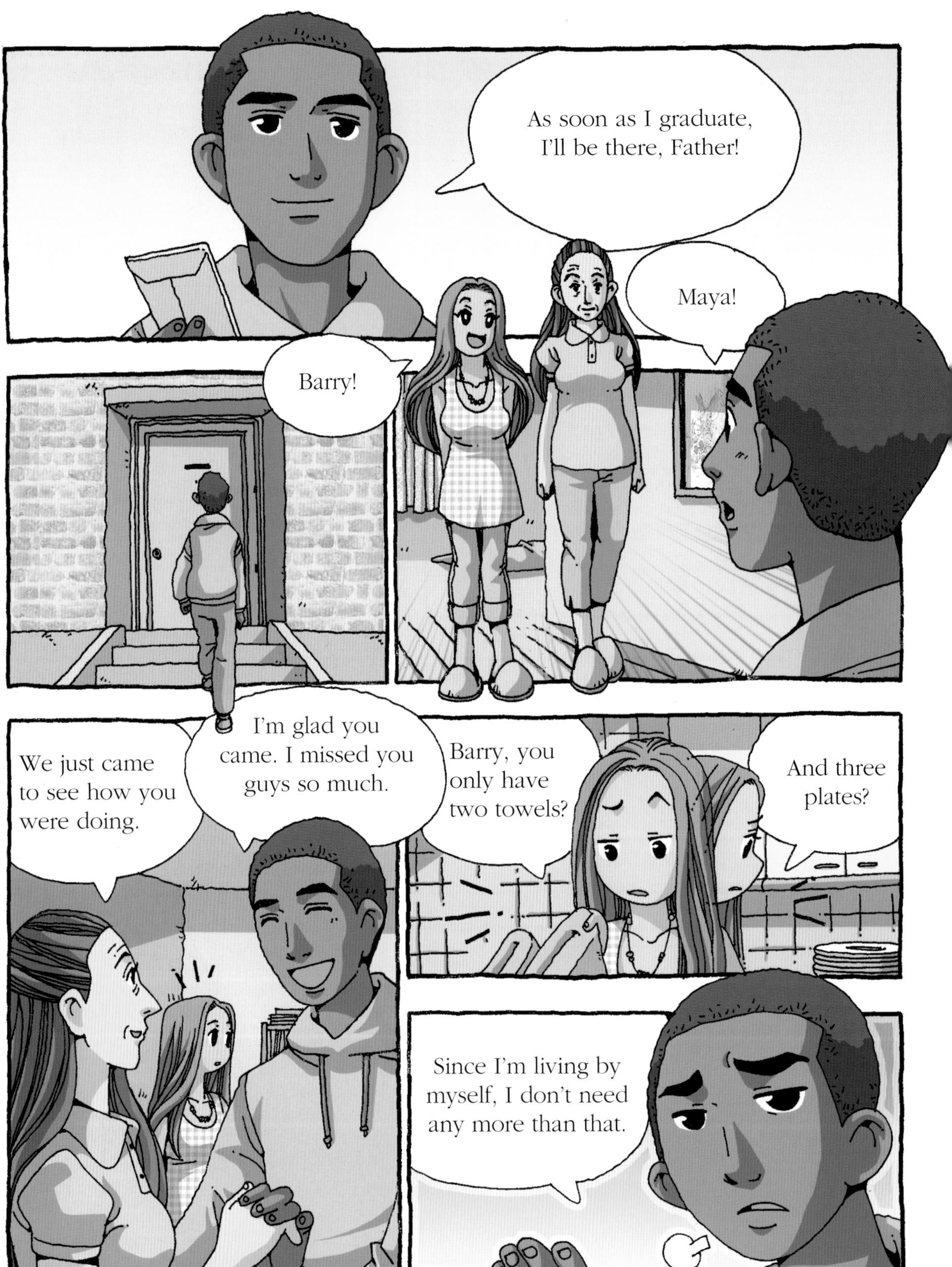
As soon as I graduate, I'll be there, Father!
Maya!
Barry!
We just came to see how you were doing.
I'm glad you came. I missed you guys so much.
Barry, you only have two towels?
And three plates?
Since I'm living by myself, I don't need any more than that.

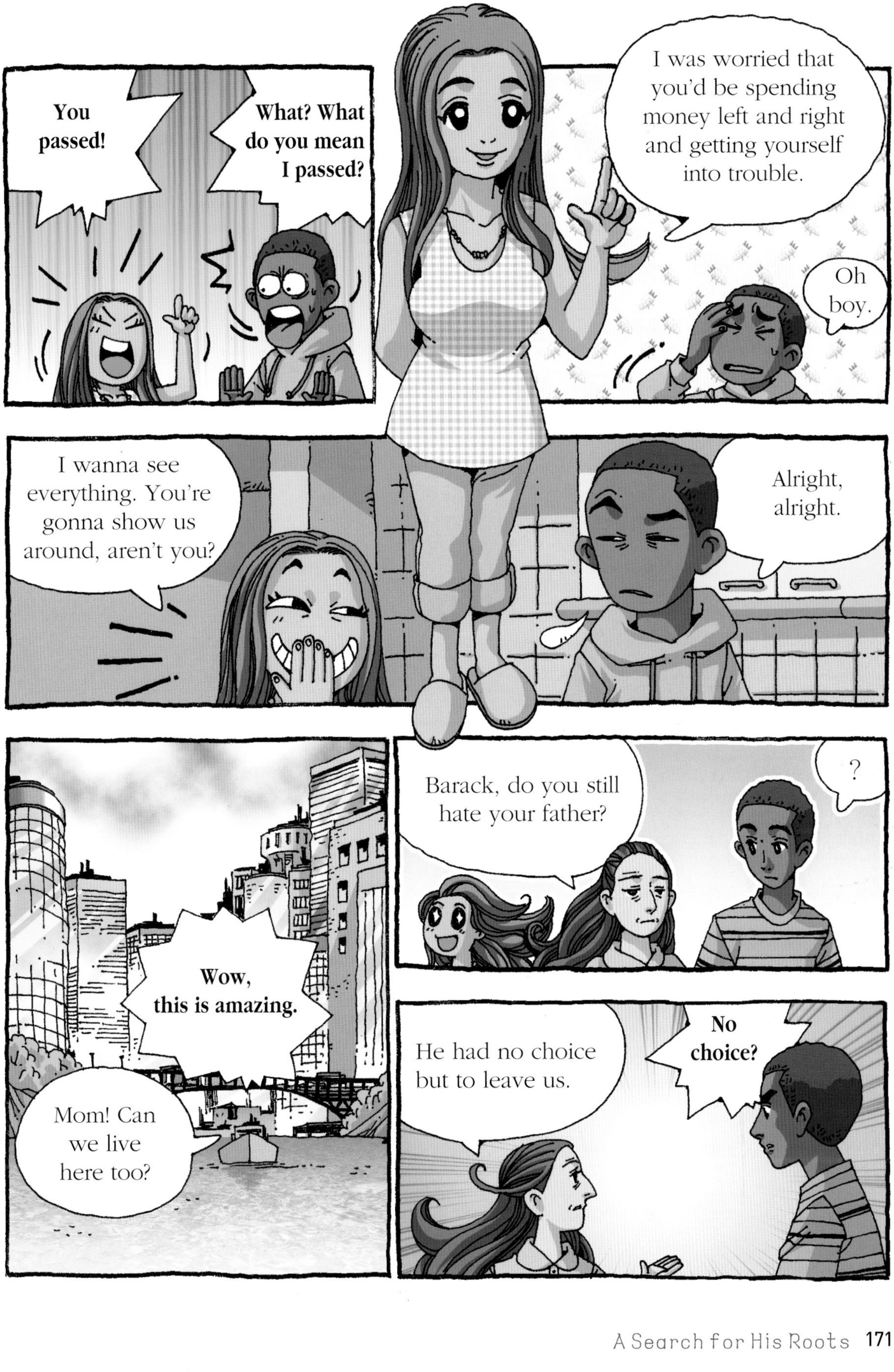
You passed!
What? What do you mean I passed?
I was worried that you'd be spending money left and right and getting yourself into trouble.
Oh boy.
I wanna see everything. You're gonna show us around, aren't you?
Alright, alright.
Wow, this is amazing.
Mom! Can we live here too?
Barack, do you still hate your father?
?
He had no choice but to leave us.
No choice?

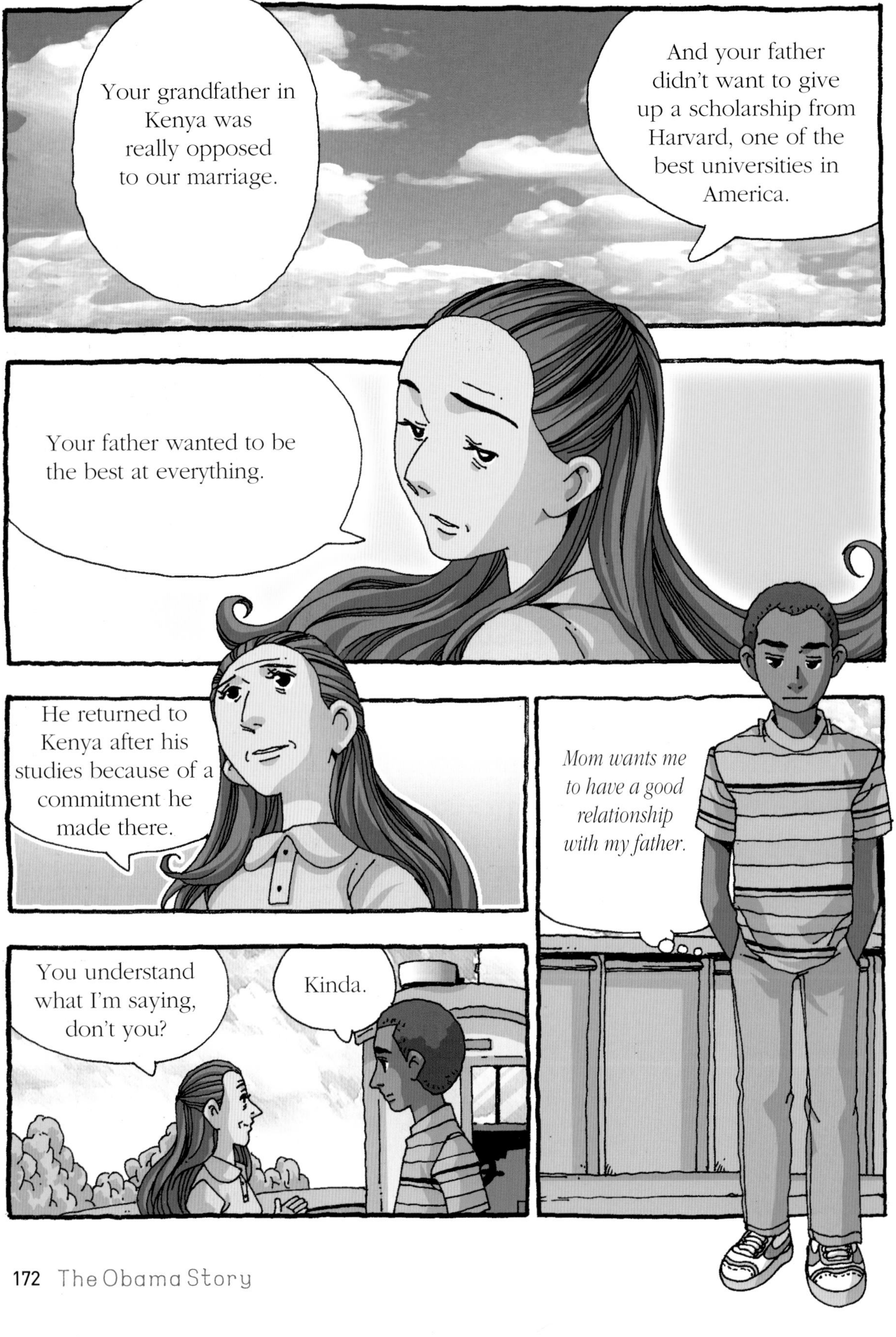
Your grandfather in Kenya was really opposed to our marriage.
And your father didn't want to give up a scholarship from Harvard, one of the best universities in America.
Your father wanted to be the best at everything.
He returned to Kenya after his studies because of a commitment he made there.
Mom wants me to have a good relationship with my father.
You understand what I'm saying, don't you?
Kinda.

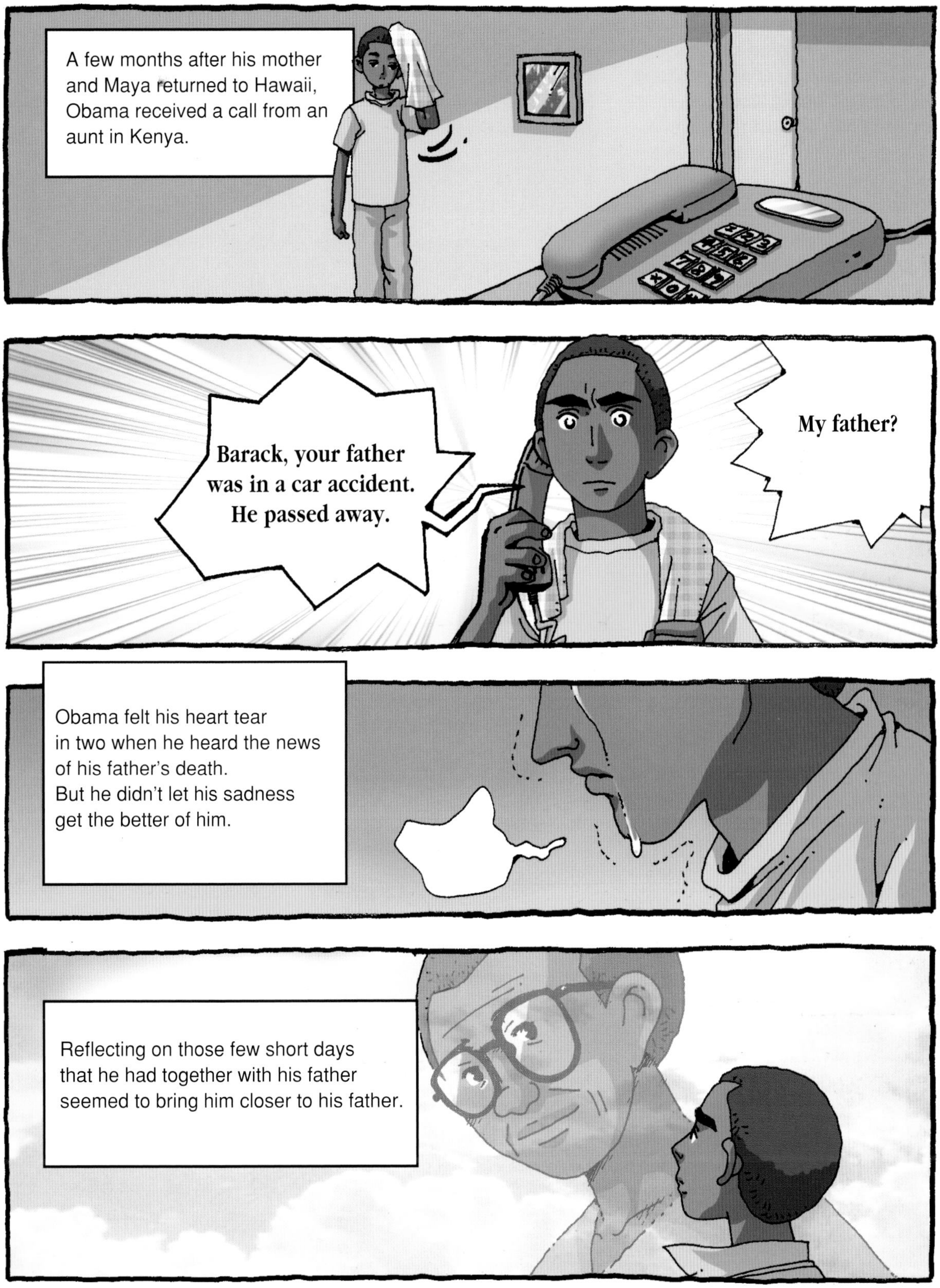
A few months after his mother and Maya returned to Hawaii, Obama received a call from an aunt in Kenya.
Barack, your father was in a car accident. He passed away.
My father?
Obama felt his heart tear in two when he heard the news of his father's death. But he didn't let his sadness get the better of him.
Reflecting on those few short days that he had together with his father seemed to bring him closer to his father.

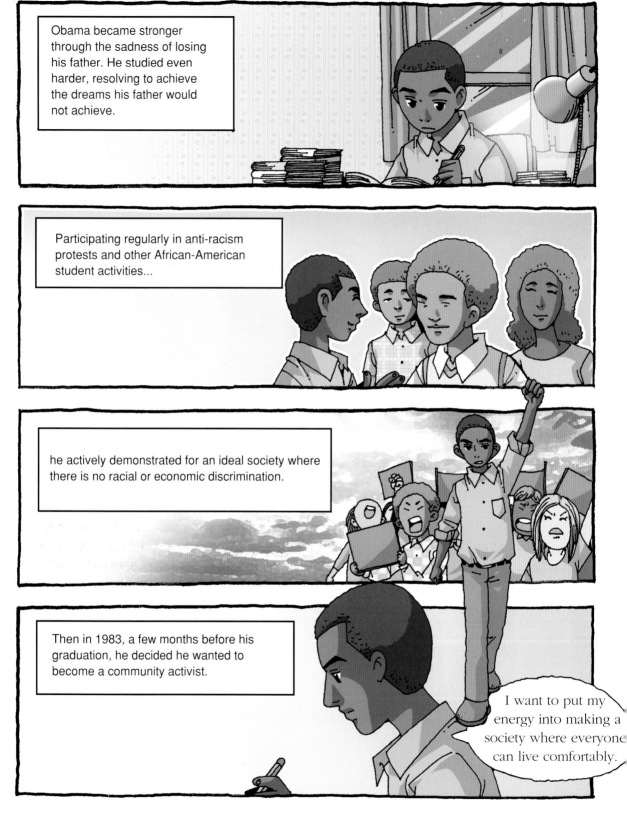

Obama became stronger through the sadness of losing his father. He studied even harder, resolving to achieve the dreams his father would not achieve.

Participating regularly in anti-racism protests and other African-American student activities...

he actively demonstrated for an ideal society where there is no racial or economic discrimination.

Then in 1983, a few months before his graduation, he decided he wanted to become a community activist.

I want to put my energy into making a society where everyone can live comfortably.

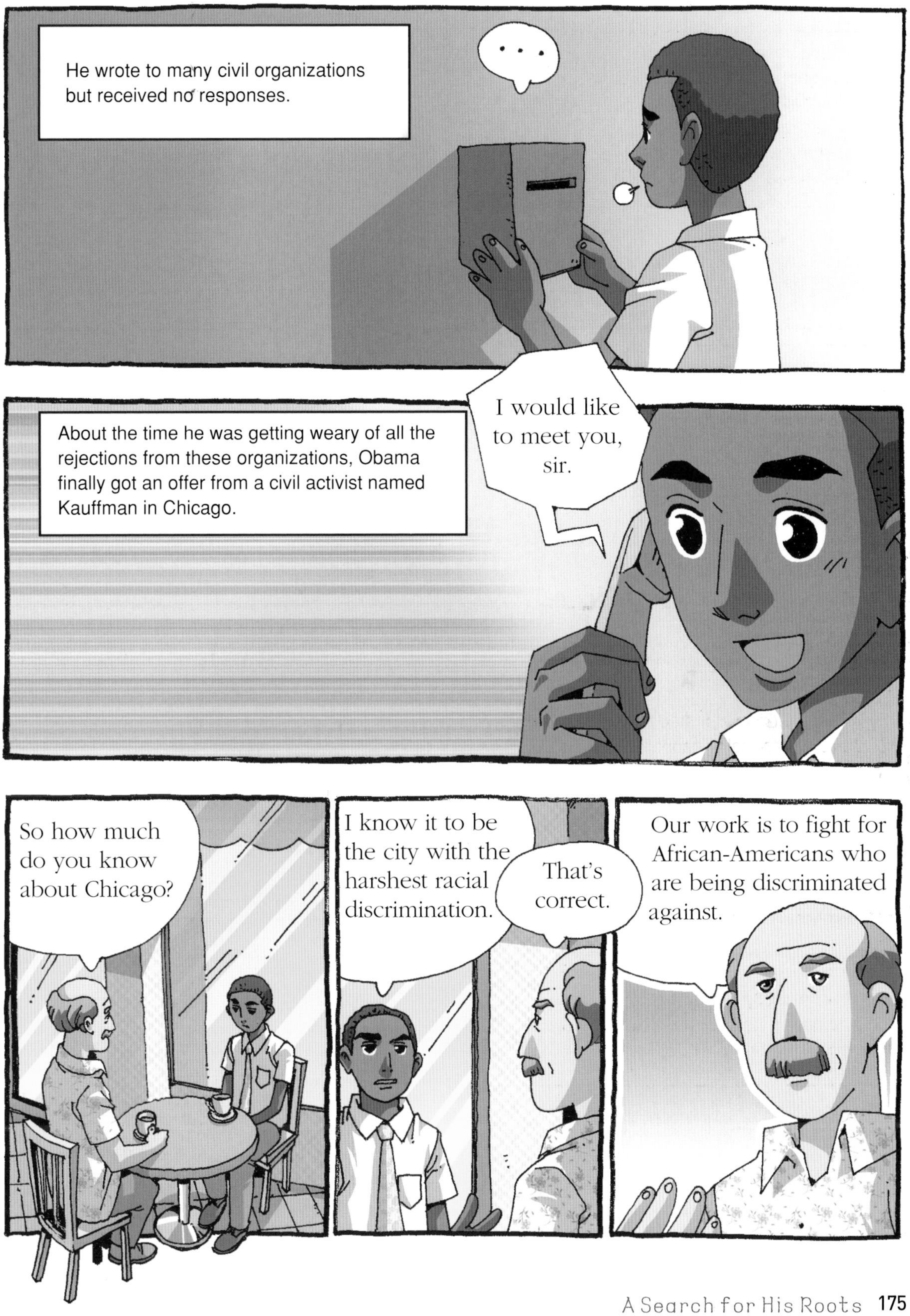
He wrote to many civil organizations but received no responses.
. . .
About the time he was getting weary of all the rejections from these organizations, Obama finally got an offer from a civil activist named Kauffman in Chicago.
I would like to meet you, sir.
So how much do you know about Chicago?
I know it to be the city with the harshest racial discrimination.
That's correct.
Our work is to fight for African-Americans who are being discriminated against.

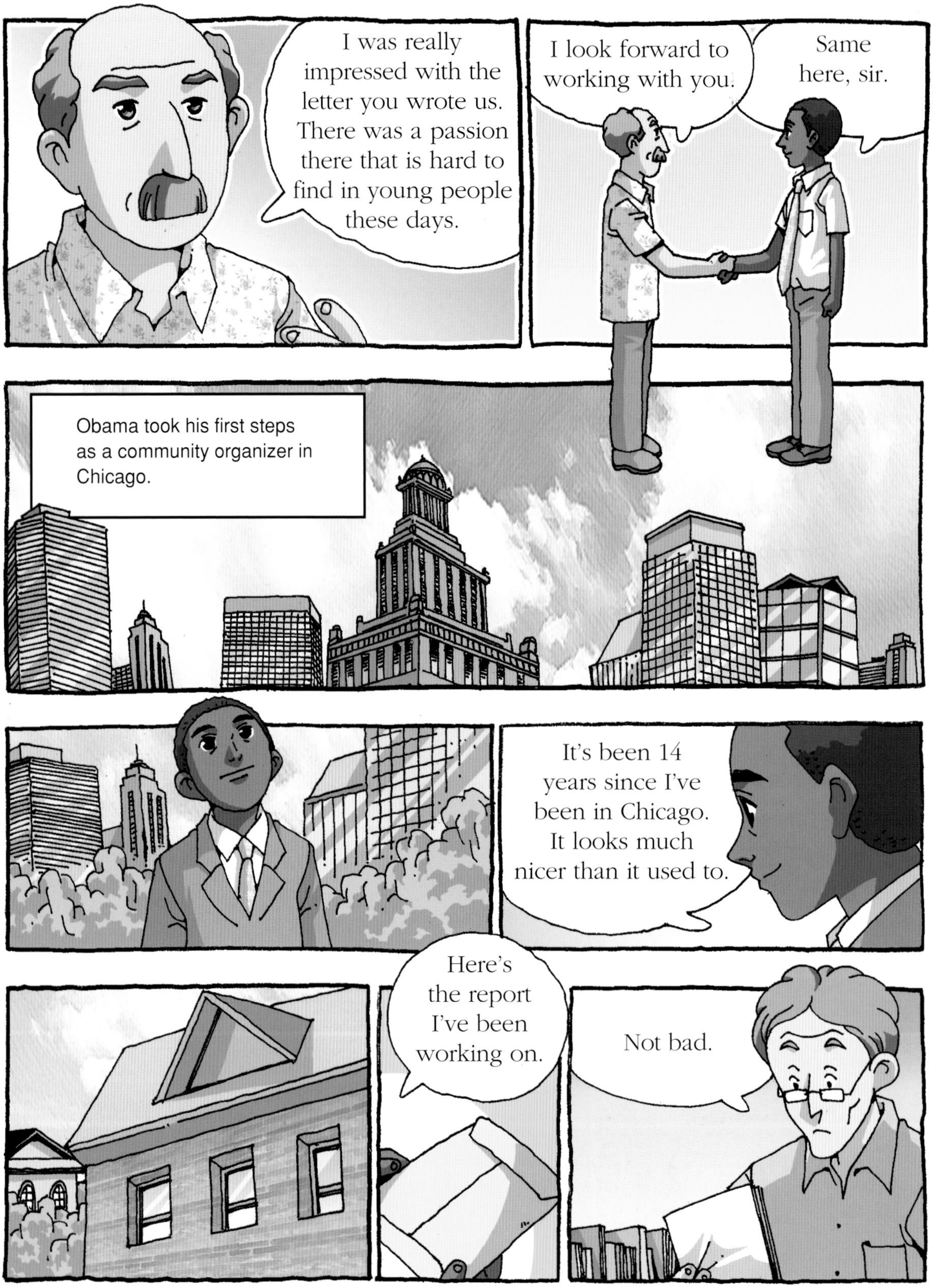
I was really impressed with the letter you wrote us. There was a passion there that is hard to find in young people these days.
I look forward to working with you.
Same here, sir.
Obama took his first steps as a community organizer in Chicago.
It's been 14 years since I've been in Chicago. It looks much nicer than it used to.
Here's the report I've been working on.
Not bad.

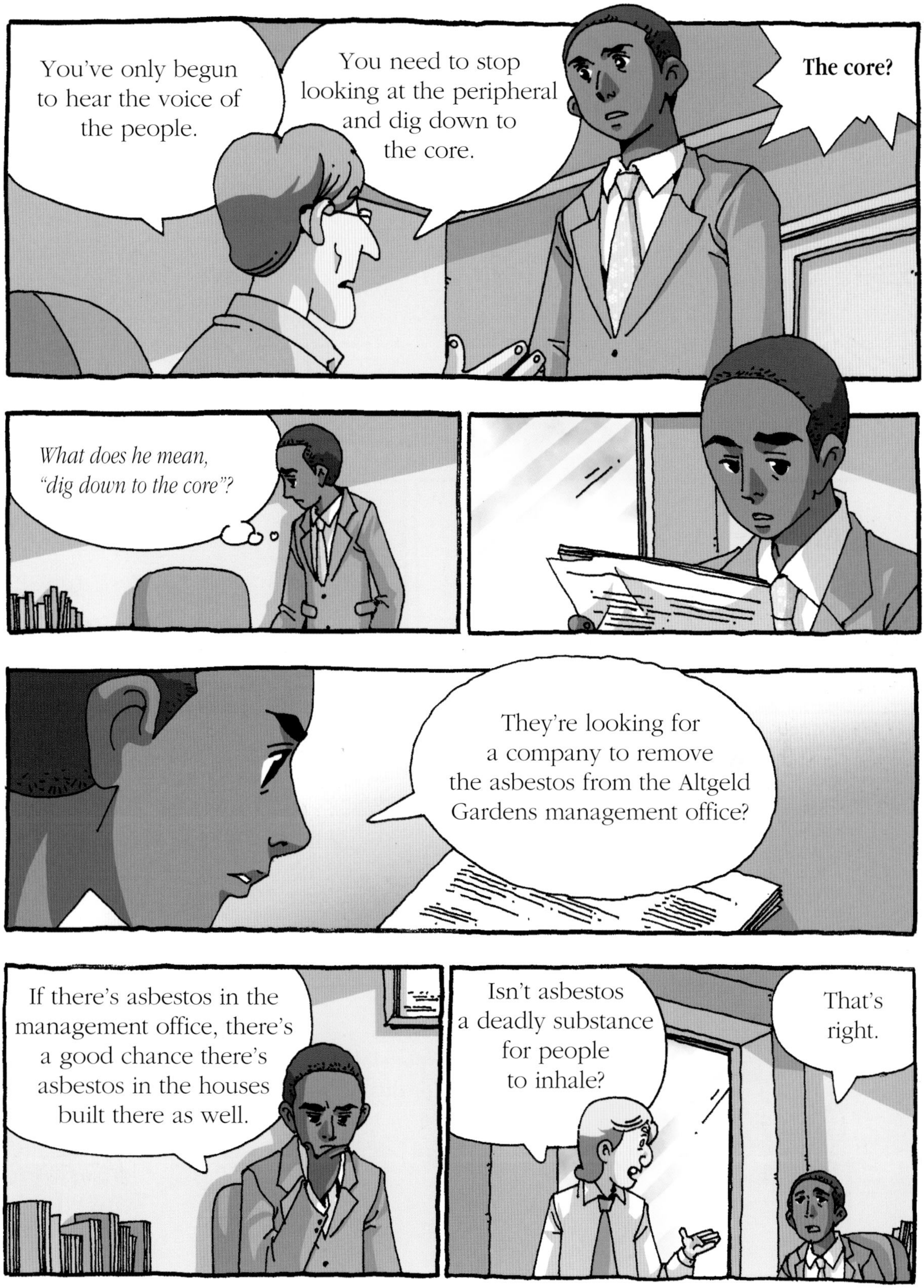
You've only begun to hear the voice of the people.
You need to stop looking at the peripheral and dig down to the core.
The core?
What does he mean, "dig down to the core"?
They're looking for a company to remove the asbestos from the Altgeld Gardens management office?
If there's asbestos in the management office, there's a good chance there's asbestos in the houses built there as well.
Isn't asbestos a deadly substance for people to inhale?
That's right.

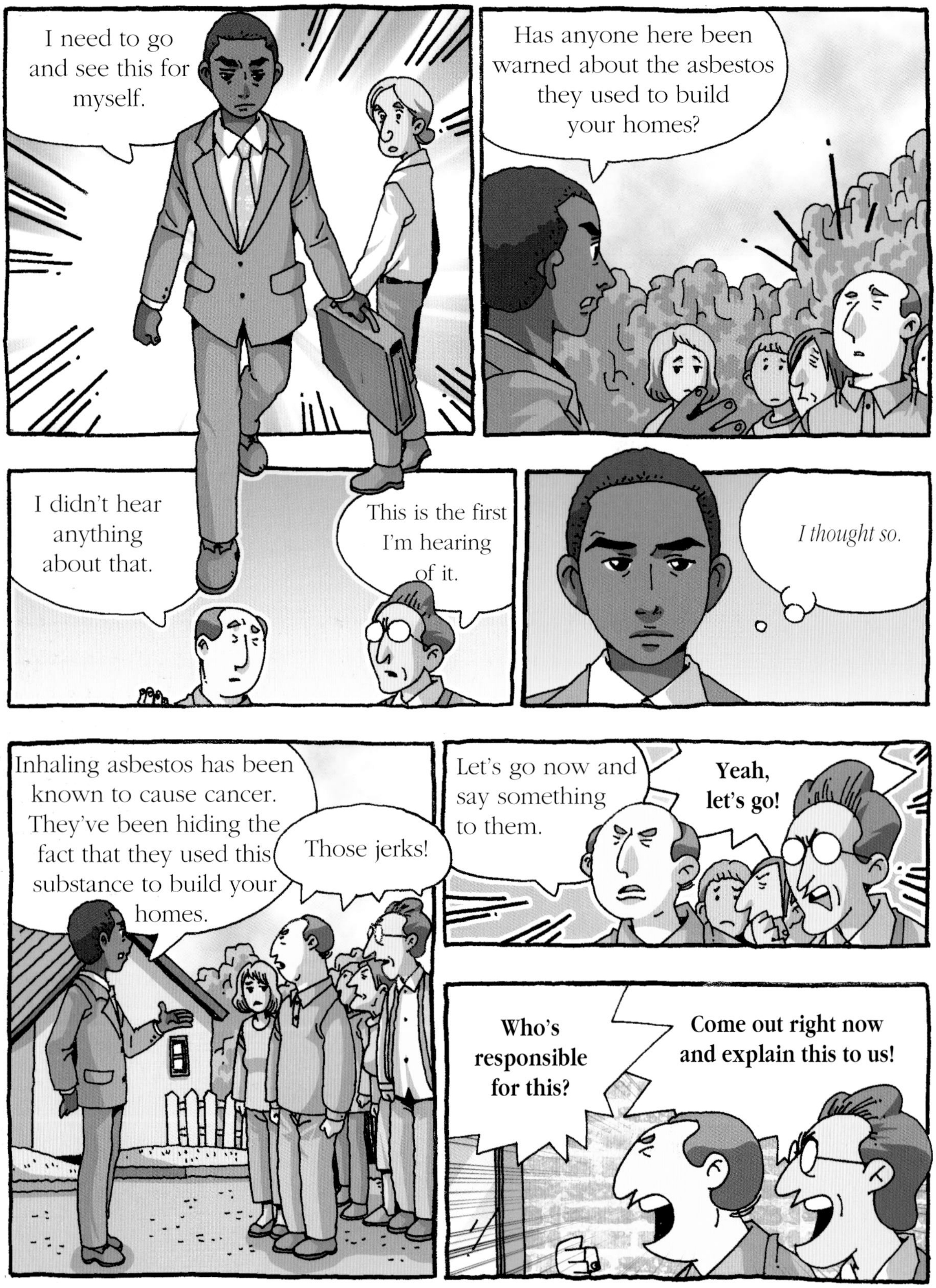
I need to go and see this for myself.
Has anyone here been warned about the asbestos they used to build your homes?
I didn't hear anything about that.
This is the first I'm hearing of it.
I thought so.
Inhaling asbestos has been known to cause cancer. They've been hiding the fact that they used this substance to build your homes.
Those jerks!
Let's go now and say something to them.
Yeah, let's go!
Who's responsible for this?
Come out right now and explain this to us!

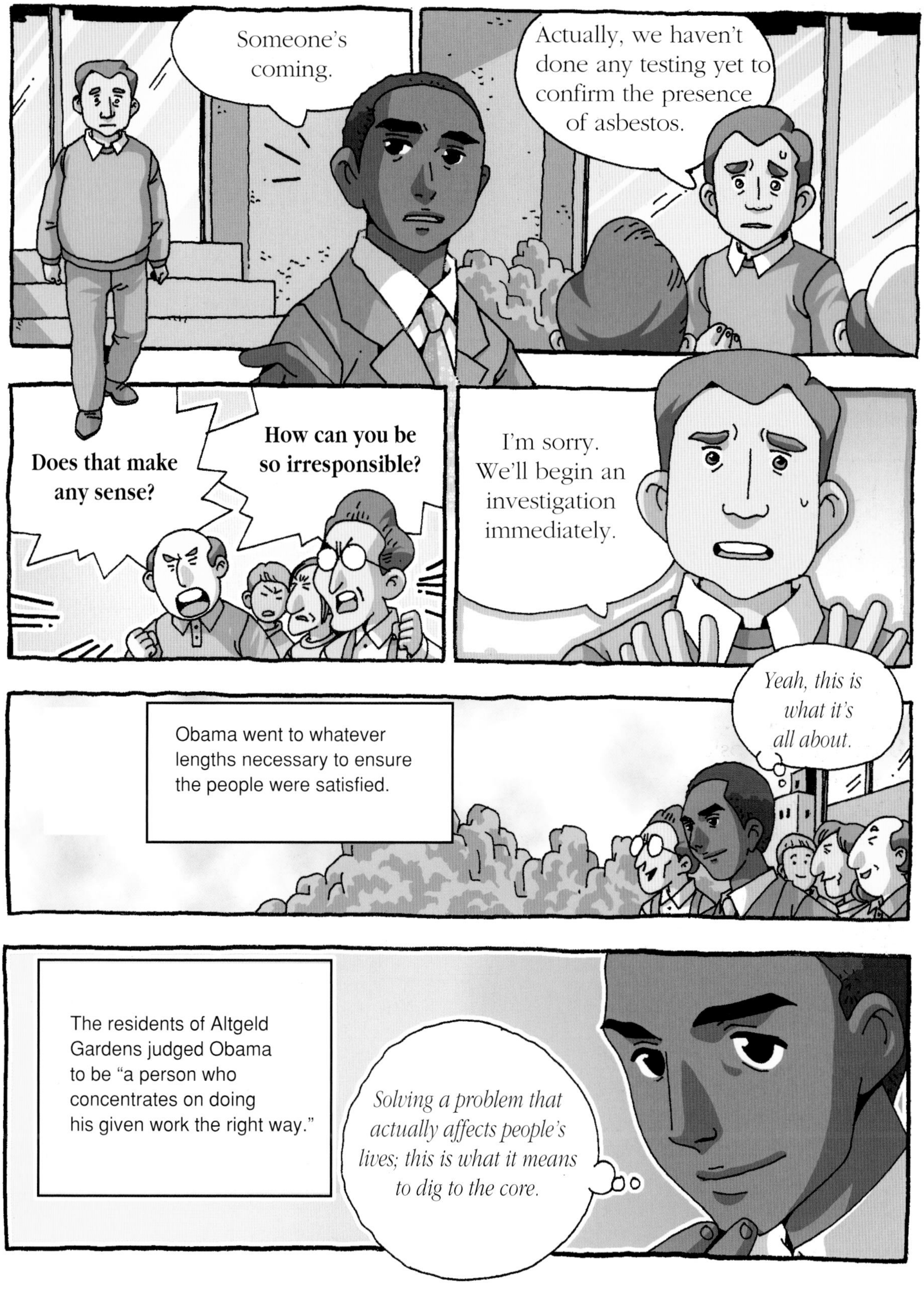

Someone's coming.
Actually, we haven't done any testing yet to confirm the presence of asbestos.
Does that make any sense?
How can you be so irresponsible?
I'm sorry. We'll begin an investigation immediately.
Obama went to whatever lengths necessary to ensure the people were satisfied.
Yeah, this is what it's all about.
The residents of Altgeld Gardens judged Obama to be "a person who concentrates on doing his given work the right way."
Solving a problem that actually affects people's lives; this is what it means to dig to the core.

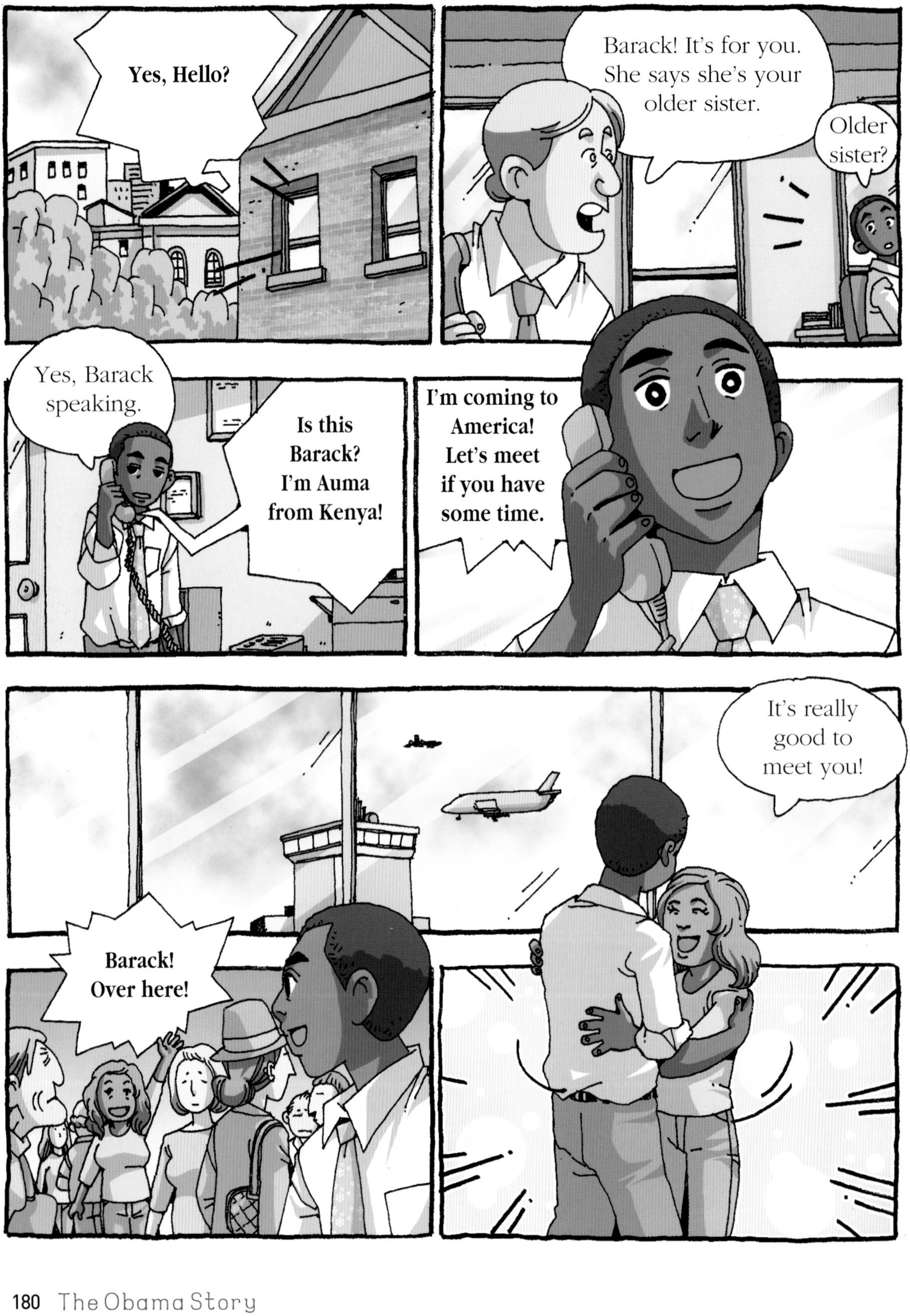
Yes, Hello?
Barack! It's for you. She says she's your older sister.
Older sister?
Yes, Barack speaking.
Is this Barack? I'm Auma from Kenya!
I'm coming to America! Let's meet if you have some time.
Barack! Over here!
It's really good to meet you!

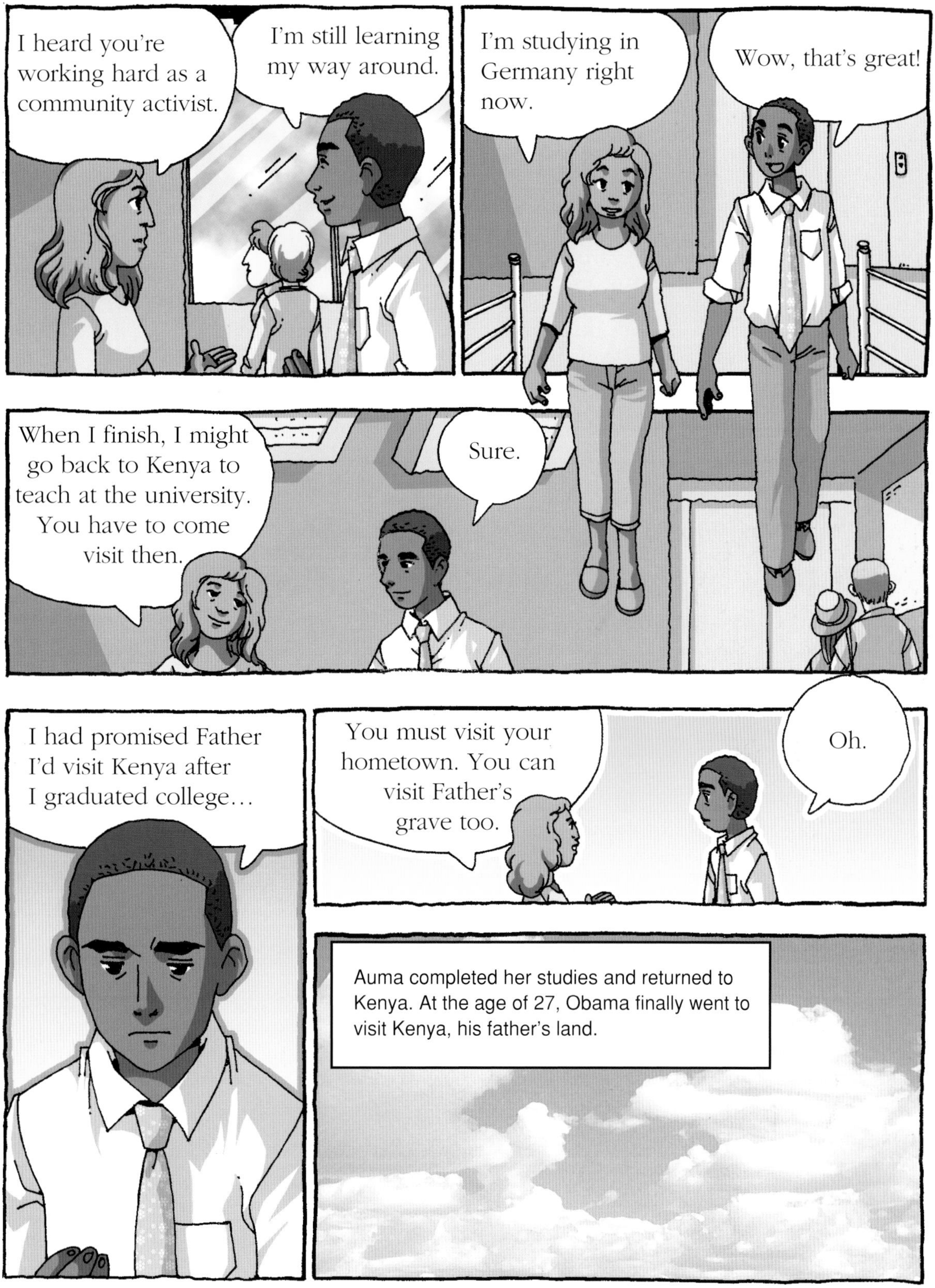
I heard you're working hard as a community activist.
I'm still learning my way around.
I'm studying in Germany right now.
Wow, that's great!
When I finish, I might go back to Kenya to teach at the university. You have to come visit then.
Sure.
I had promised Father I'd visit Kenya after I graduated college…
You must visit your hometown. You can visit Father's grave too.
Oh.
Auma completed her studies and returned to Kenya. At the age of 27, Obama finally went to visit Kenya, his father's land.

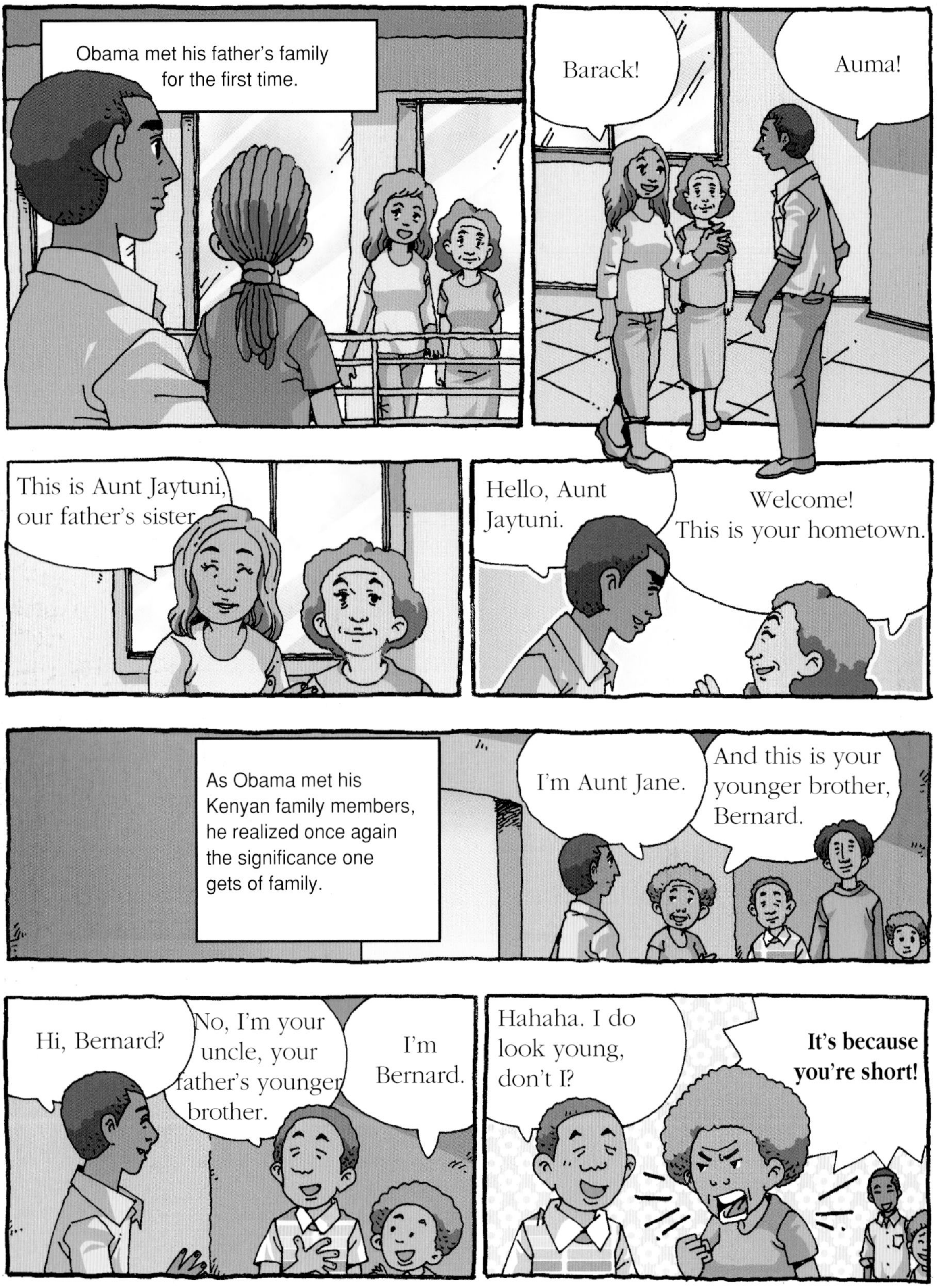

Obama met his father's family for the first time.
Barack!
Auma!
This is Aunt Jaytuni, our father's sister.
Hello, Aunt Jaytuni.
Welcome! This is your hometown.
As Obama met his Kenyan family members, he realized once again the significance one gets of family.
I'm Aunt Jane.
And this is your younger brother, Bernard.
Hi, Bernard?
No, I'm your uncle, your father's younger brother.
I'm Bernard.
Hahaha. I do look young, don't I?
It's because you're short!

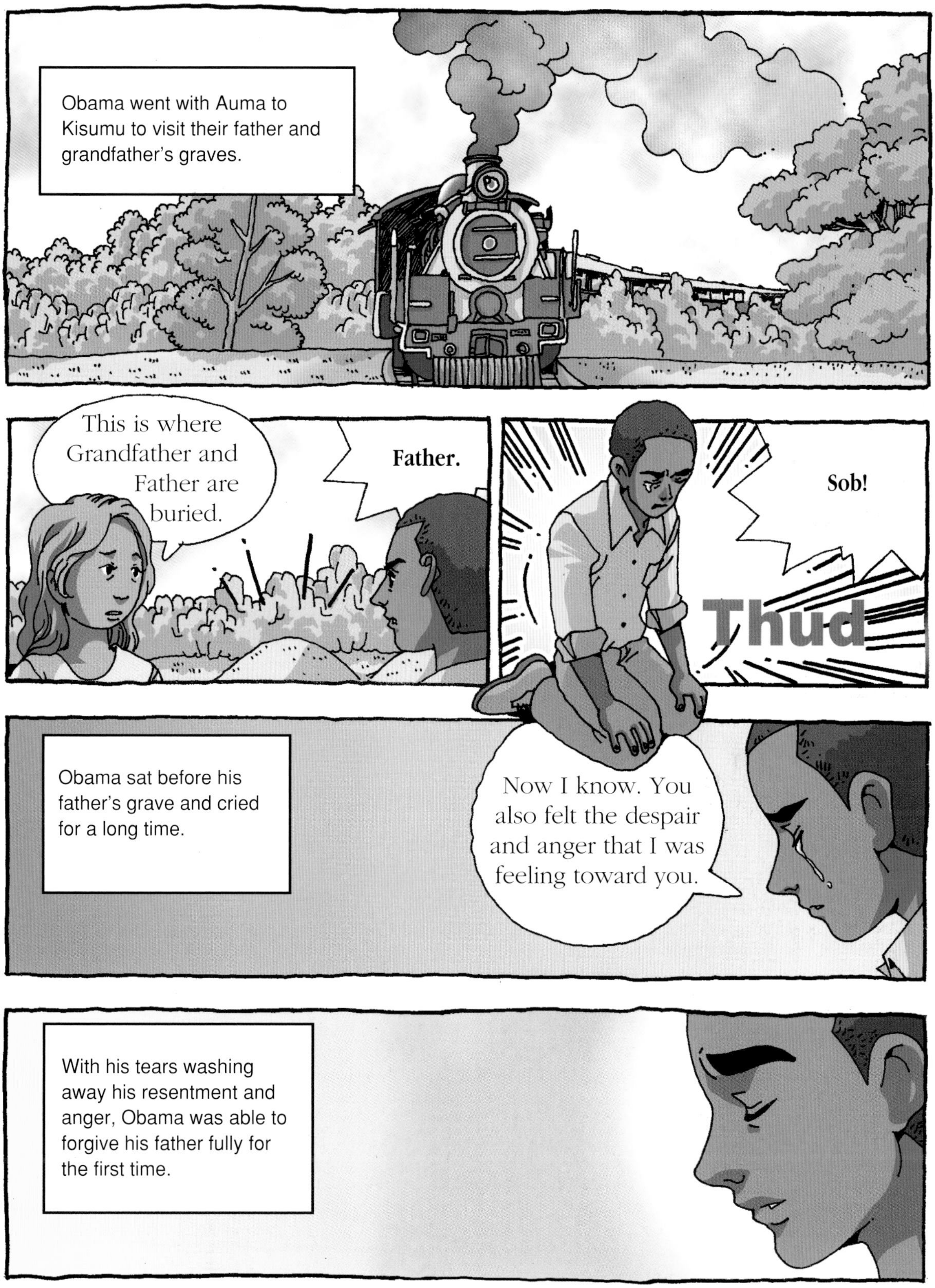
Obama went with Auma to Kisumu to visit their father and grandfather's graves.
This is where Grandfather and Father are buried.
Father.
Sob!
Thud
Obama sat before his father's grave and cried for a long time.
Now I know. You also felt the despair and anger that I was feeling toward you.
With his tears washing away his resentment and anger, Obama was able to forgive his father fully for the first time.

Getting to know Obama 3

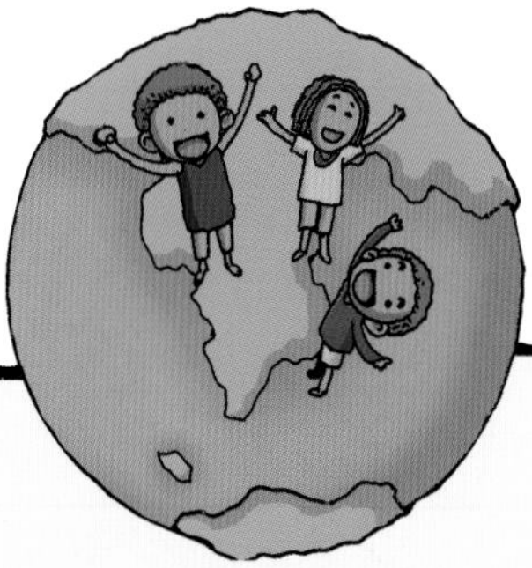

Kenya, Obama's Second Home

Kenya is located on the east side of the African continent. Nairobi is the capital city. Although Kenya is right at the equator, the climate is mild and pleasant because of its high elevation.

The name Kenya, which means 'white mountain,' is derived from the name of its highest peak, Mount Kenya. The highest mountain in all of Africa, Mount Kilimanjaro, is located on the border of Kenya and Tanzania. Kenya is well-known for it's incredibly beautiful land- the Nairobi National Park and 11 other national parks make it a paradise for wildlife.

The population is about 33 million, made up of 40 different ethnic groups. The ethnic group which Obama's father belonged to is the Luo tribe, which is made up of roughly 2,650,000 people. The well-known Masai tribe is also one of the ethnic groups in Kenya.

The two languages used widely in Kenya are English and Swahili. Their major religion is Christianity, which accounts for 80% of the population. Their main food staples are bread, fish, vegetables and fruit. They also enjoy 'ugali,' a sticky cornmeal bread, and 'chapati,' which is similar to pancakes. Kenya is also known for their fine coffee.

In addition, Kenya is famous for the marathon. In the marathon event in the Olympics or other international competitions, Kenyan competitors often break world records and go home with many medals.

Chapter 8

Courageous Dream, Great Fulfillment

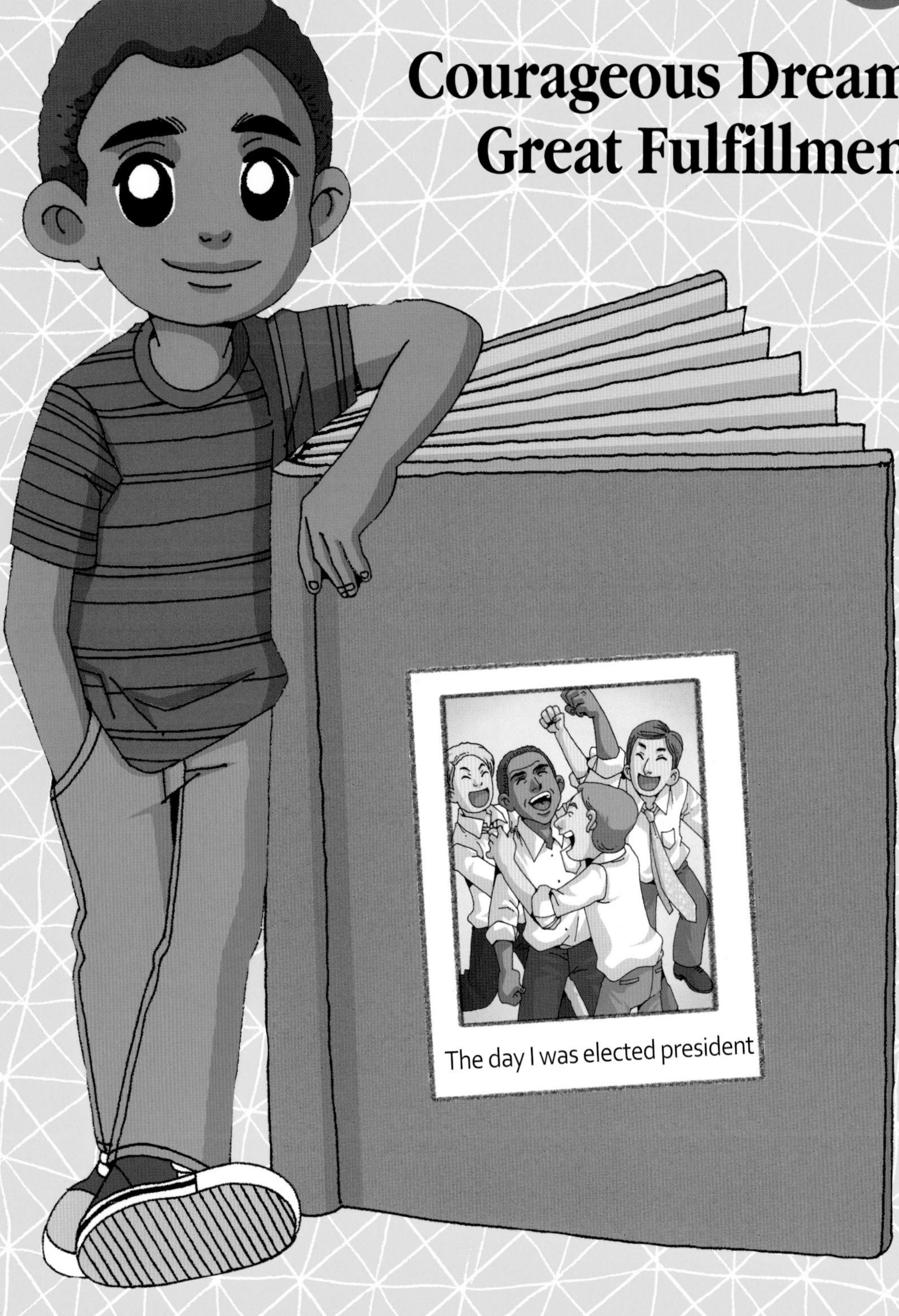
The day I was elected president

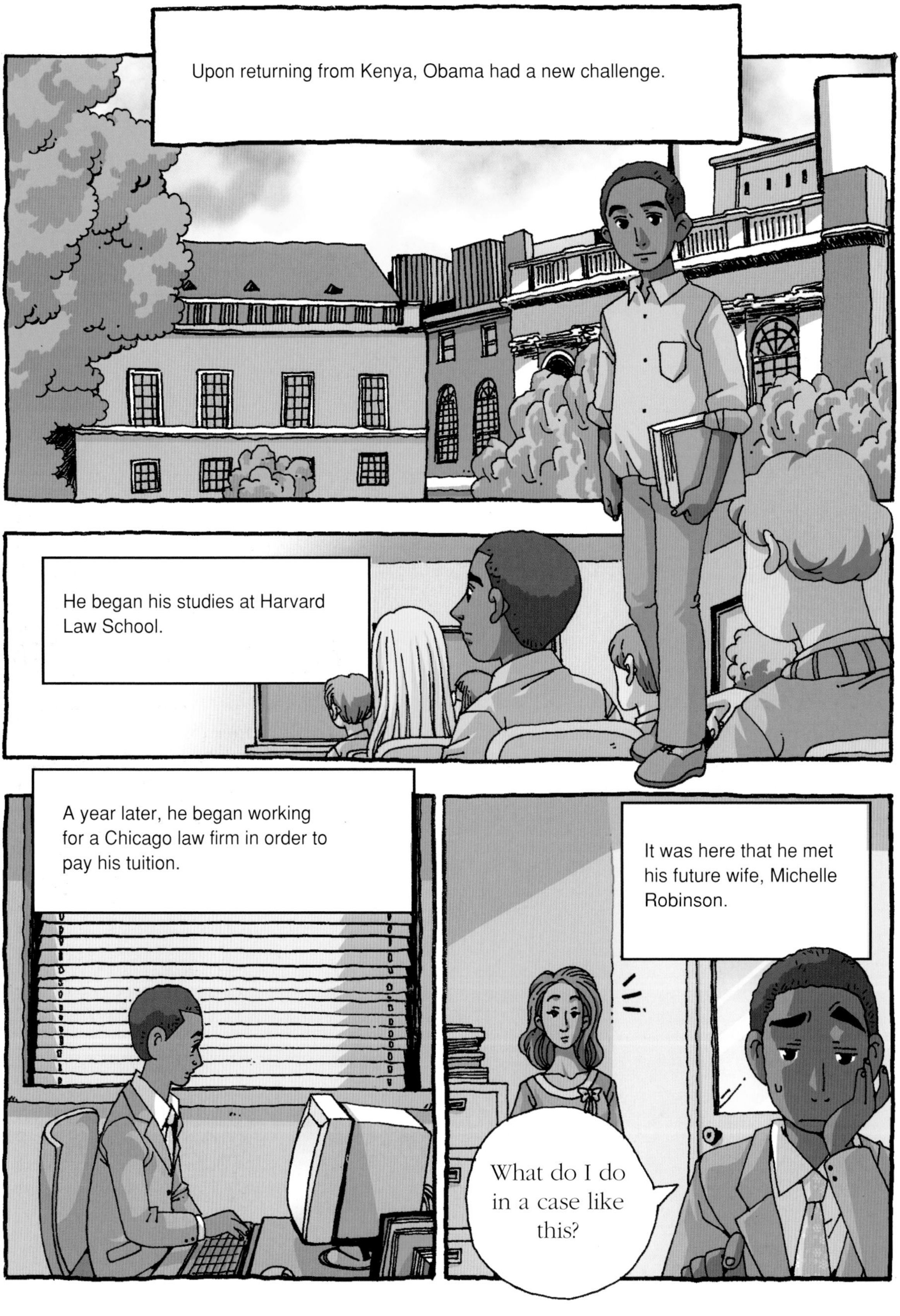

Upon returning from Kenya, Obama had a new challenge.
He began his studies at Harvard Law School.
A year later, he began working for a Chicago law firm in order to pay his tuition.
It was here that he met his future wife, Michelle Robinson.
What do I do in a case like this?

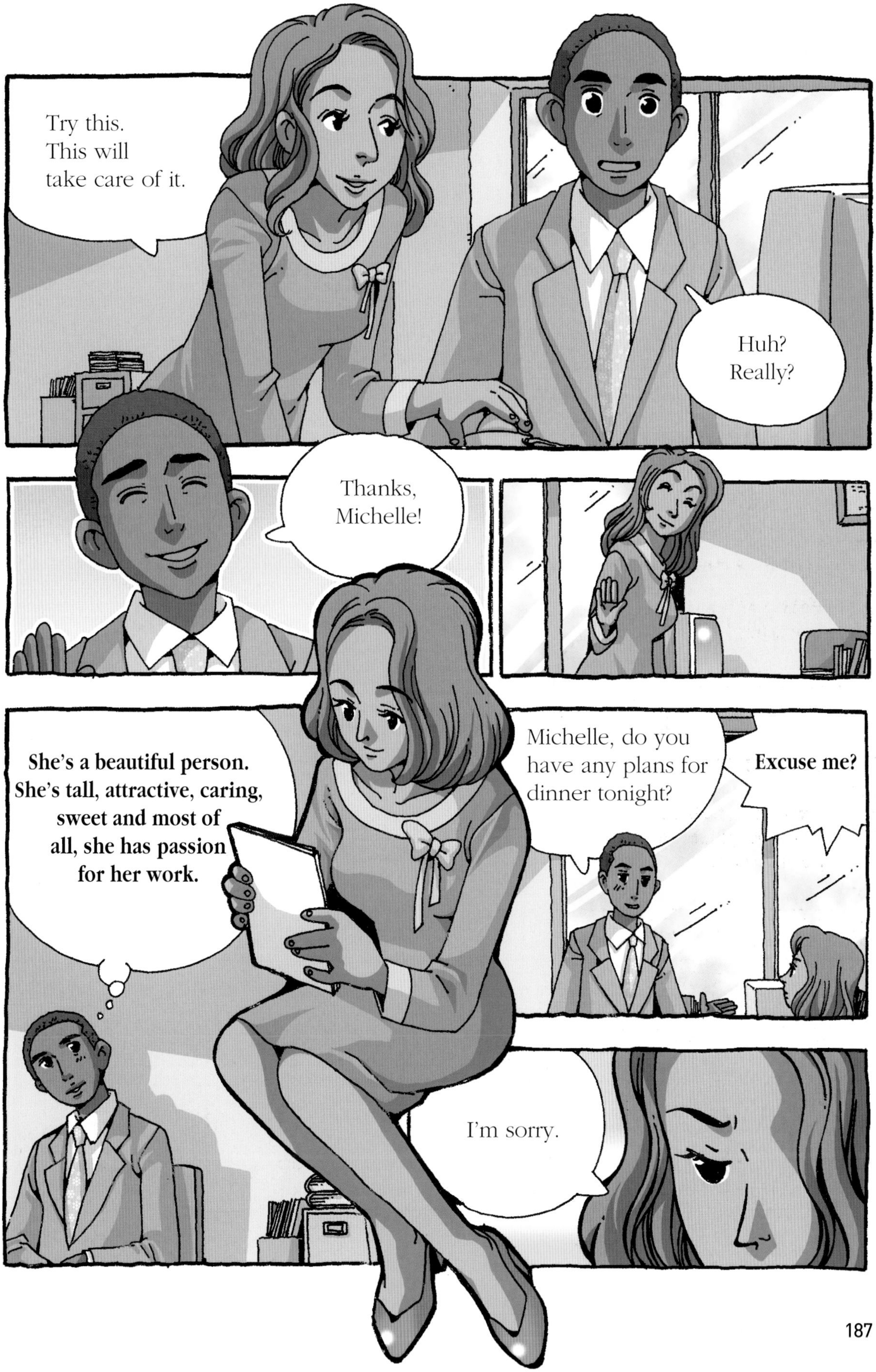
Try this.
This will
take care of it.
Huh?
Really?
Thanks,
Michelle!
She's a beautiful person.
She's tall, attractive, caring,
sweet and most of
all, she has passion
for her work.
Michelle, do you
have any plans for
dinner tonight?
Excuse me?
I'm sorry.

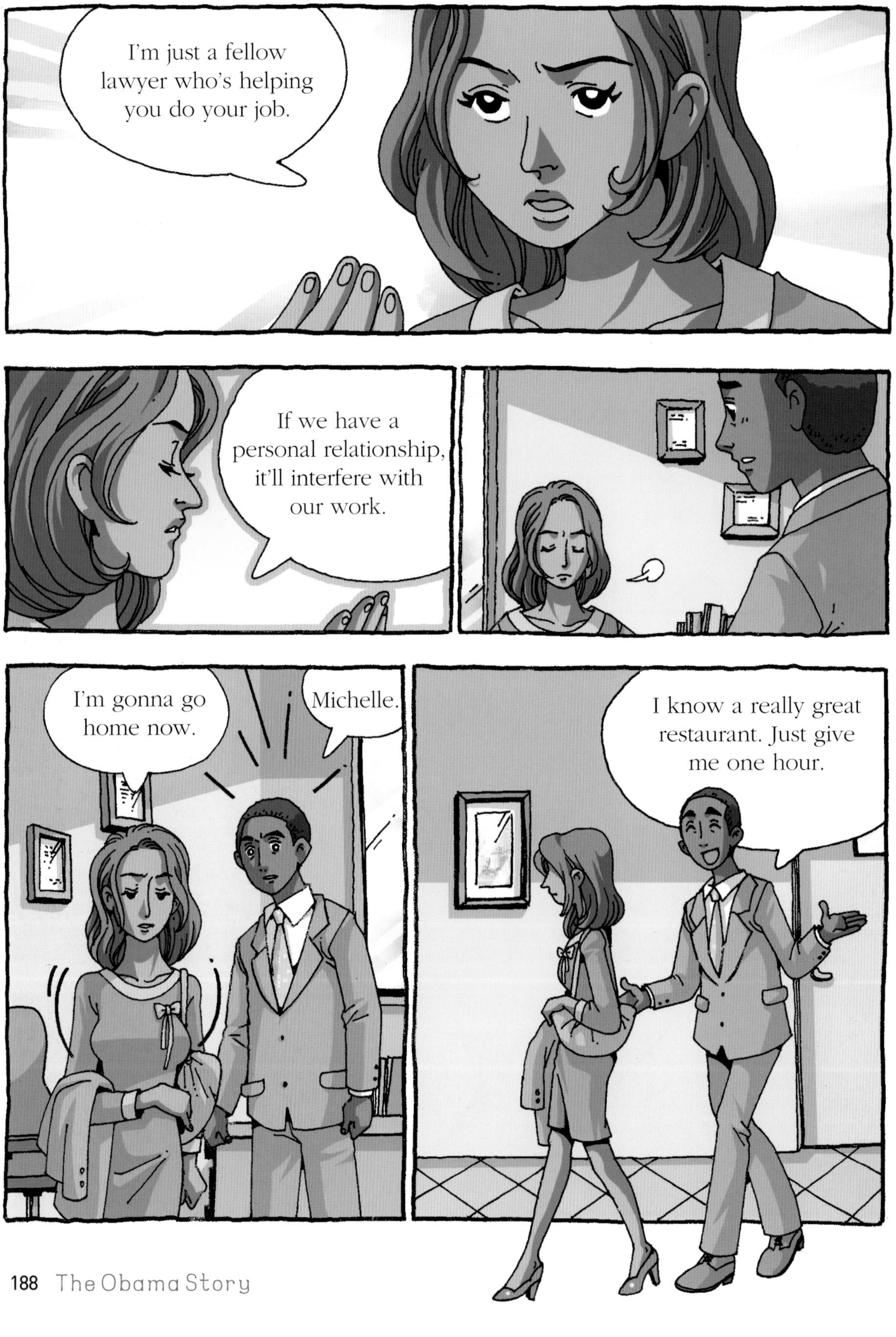
I'm just a fellow lawyer who's helping you do your job.
If we have a personal relationship, it'll interfere with our work.
I'm gonna go home now.
Michelle.
I know a really great restaurant. Just give me one hour.

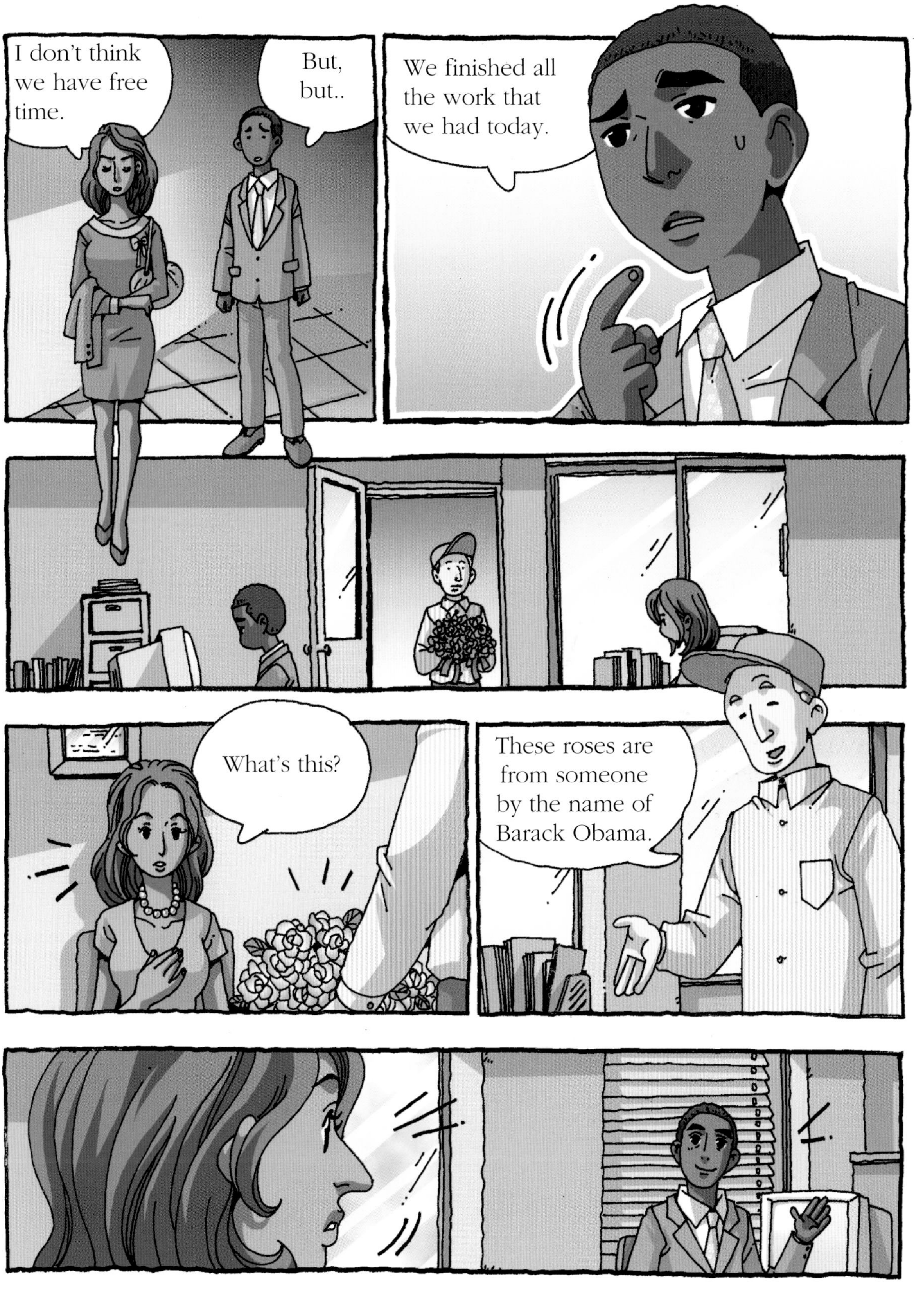
I don't think we have free time.
But, but..
We finished all the work that we had today.
What's this?
These roses are from someone by the name of Barack Obama.

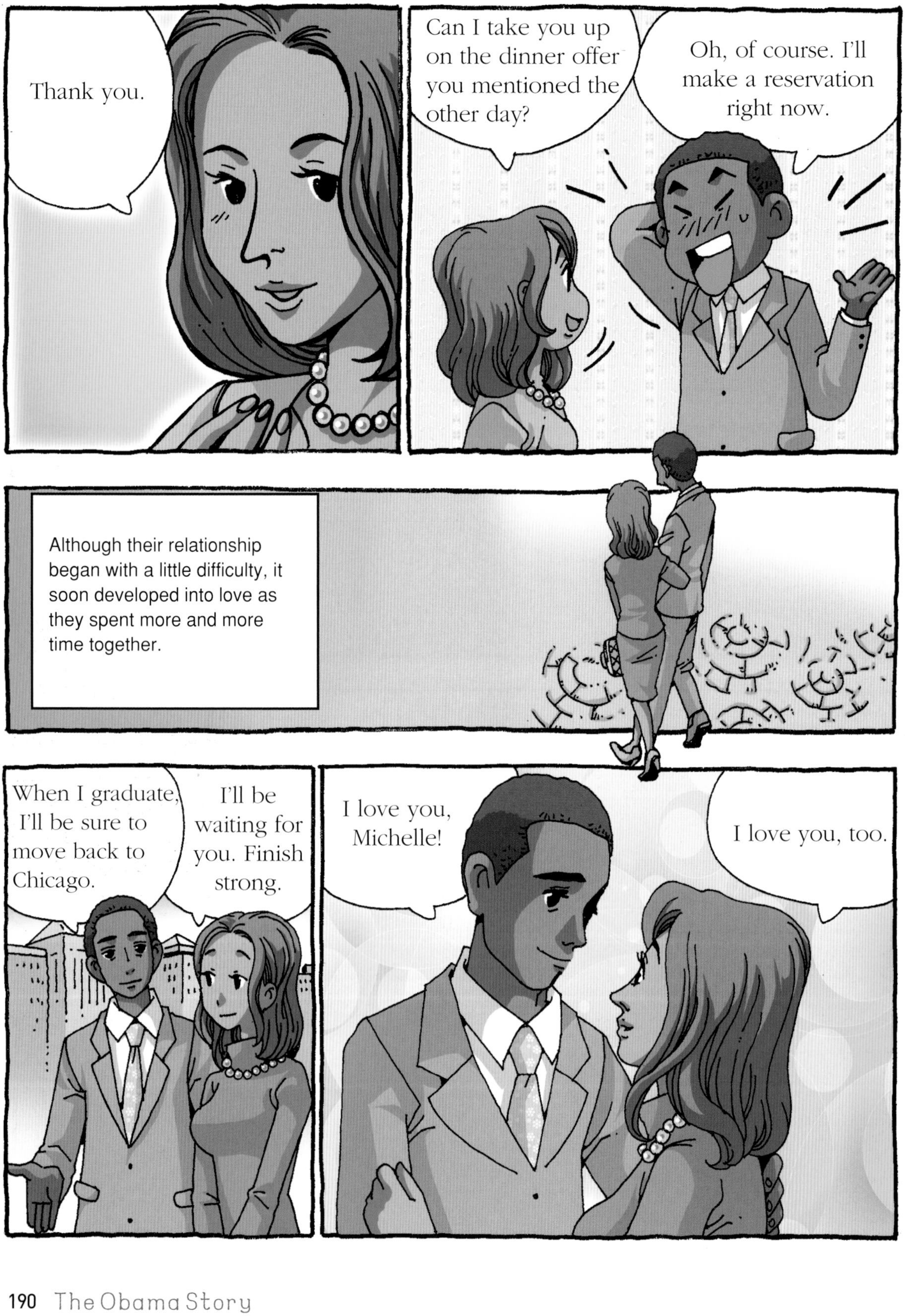
Thank you.
Can I take you up on the dinner offer you mentioned the other day?
Oh, of course. I'll make a reservation right now.
Although their relationship began with a little difficulty, it soon developed into love as they spent more and more time together.
When I graduate, I'll be sure to move back to Chicago.
I'll be waiting for you. Finish strong.
I love you, Michelle!
I love you, too.

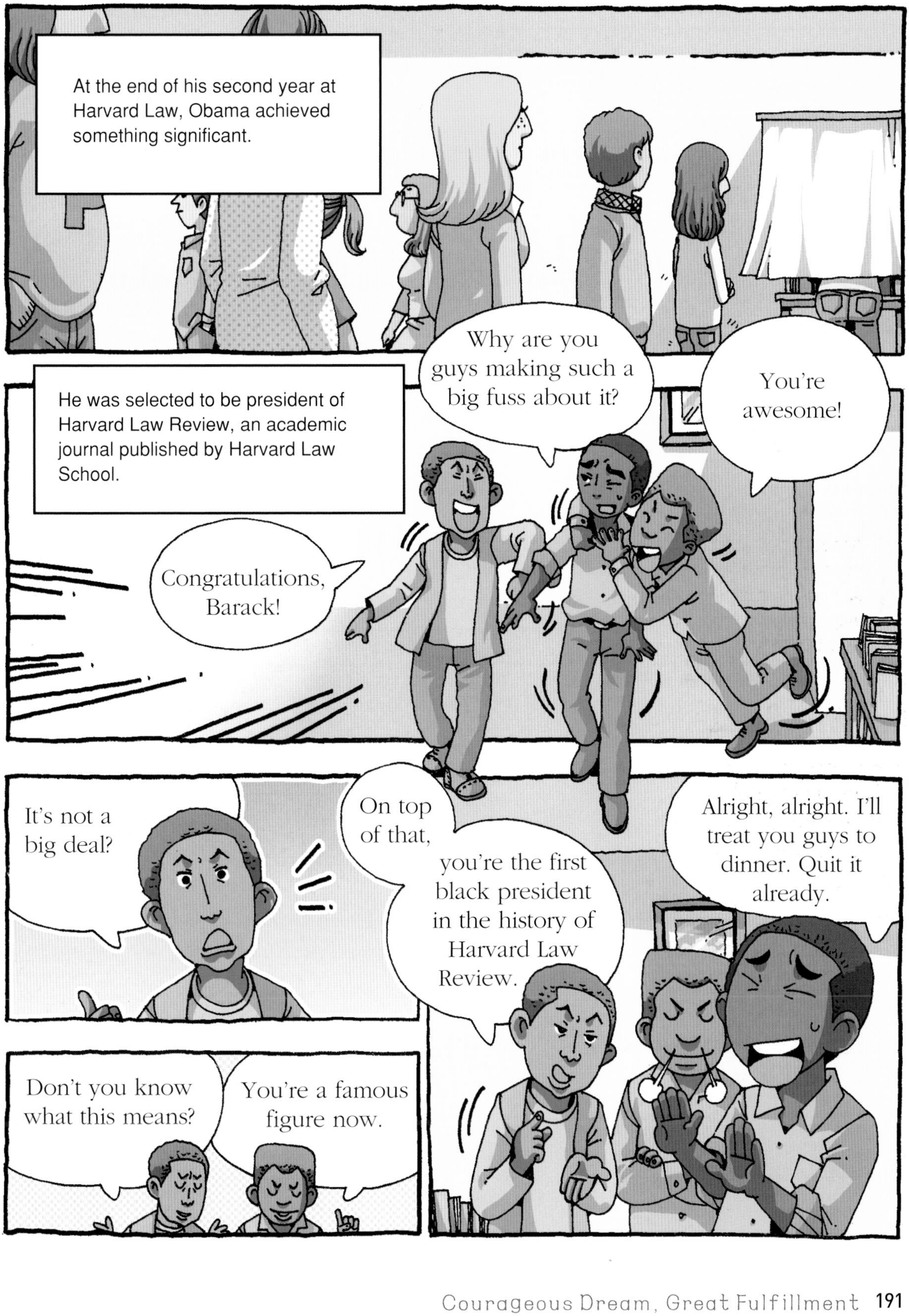
At the end of his second year at Harvard Law, Obama achieved something significant.
He was selected to be president of Harvard Law Review, an academic journal published by Harvard Law School.
Congratulations, Barack!
Why are you guys making such a big fuss about it?
You're awesome!
It's not a big deal?
Don't you know what this means?
You're a famous figure now.
On top of that,
you're the first black president in the history of Harvard Law Review.
Alright, alright. I'll treat you guys to dinner. Quit it already.

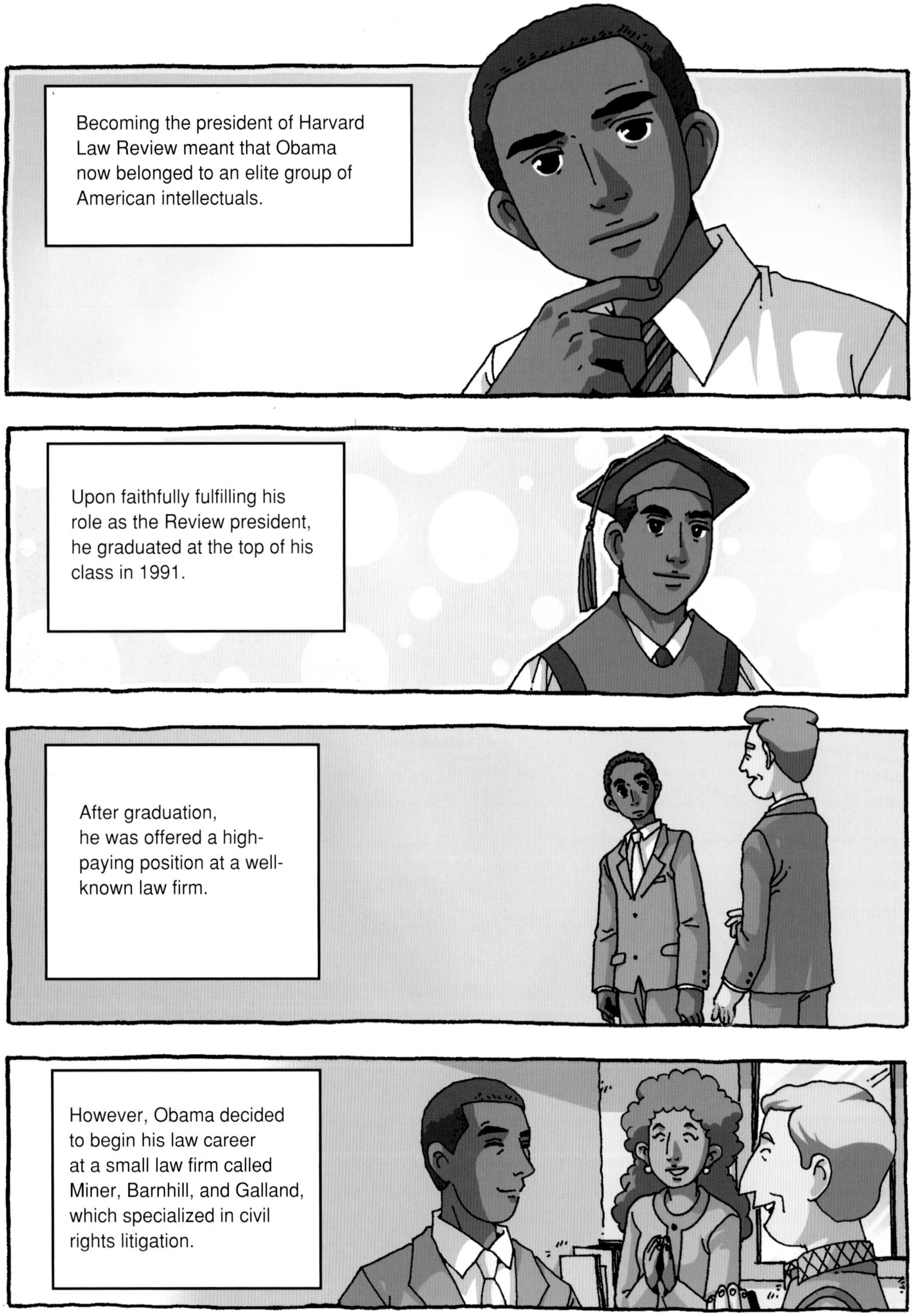
Becoming the president of Harvard Law Review meant that Obama now belonged to an elite group of American intellectuals.
Upon faithfully fulfilling his role as the Review president, he graduated at the top of his class in 1991.
After graduation, he was offered a high-paying position at a well-known law firm.
However, Obama decided to begin his law career at a small law firm called Miner, Barnhill, and Galland, which specialized in civil rights litigation.

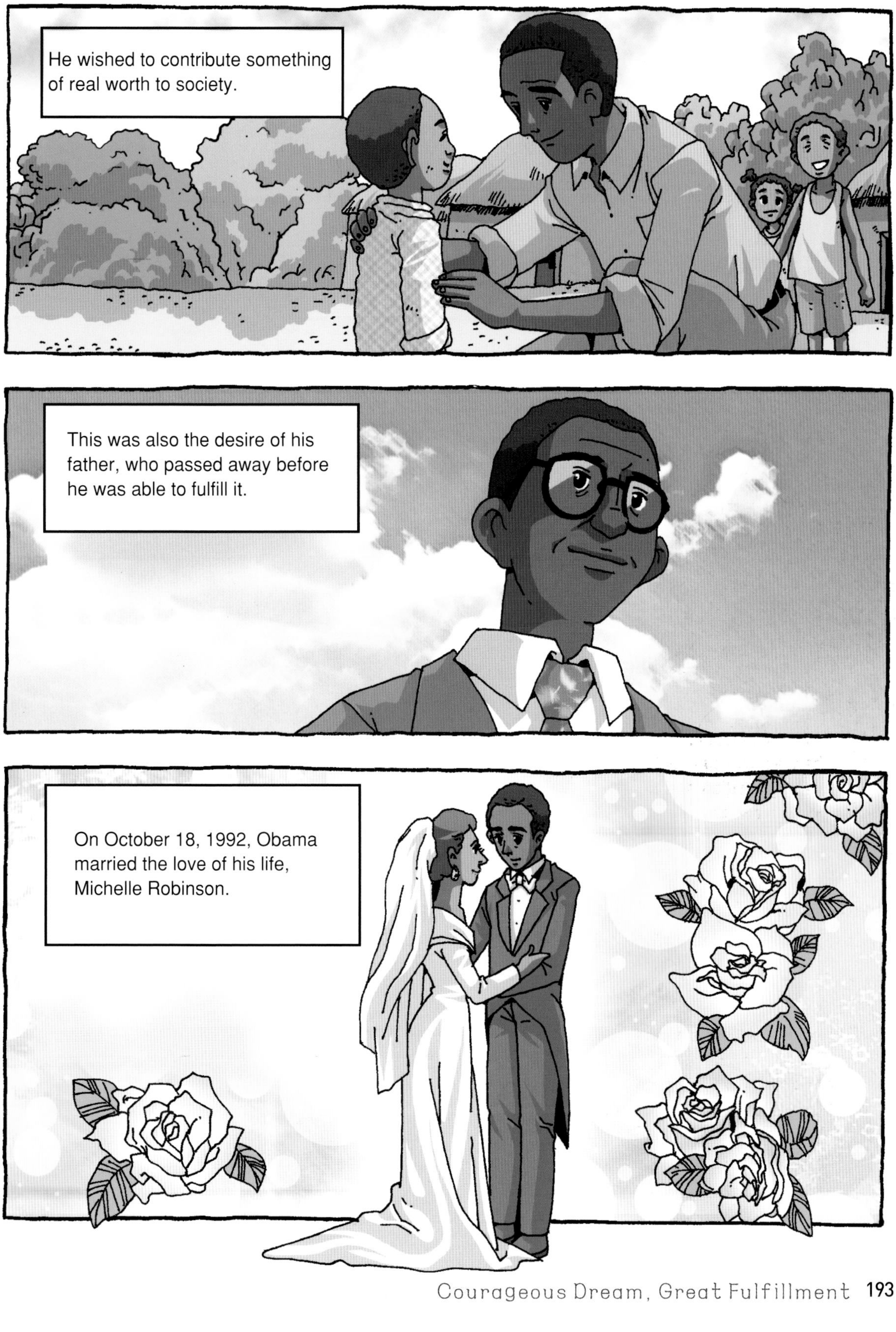
He wished to contribute something of real worth to society.
This was also the desire of his father, who passed away before he was able to fulfill it.
On October 18, 1992, Obama married the love of his life, Michelle Robinson.

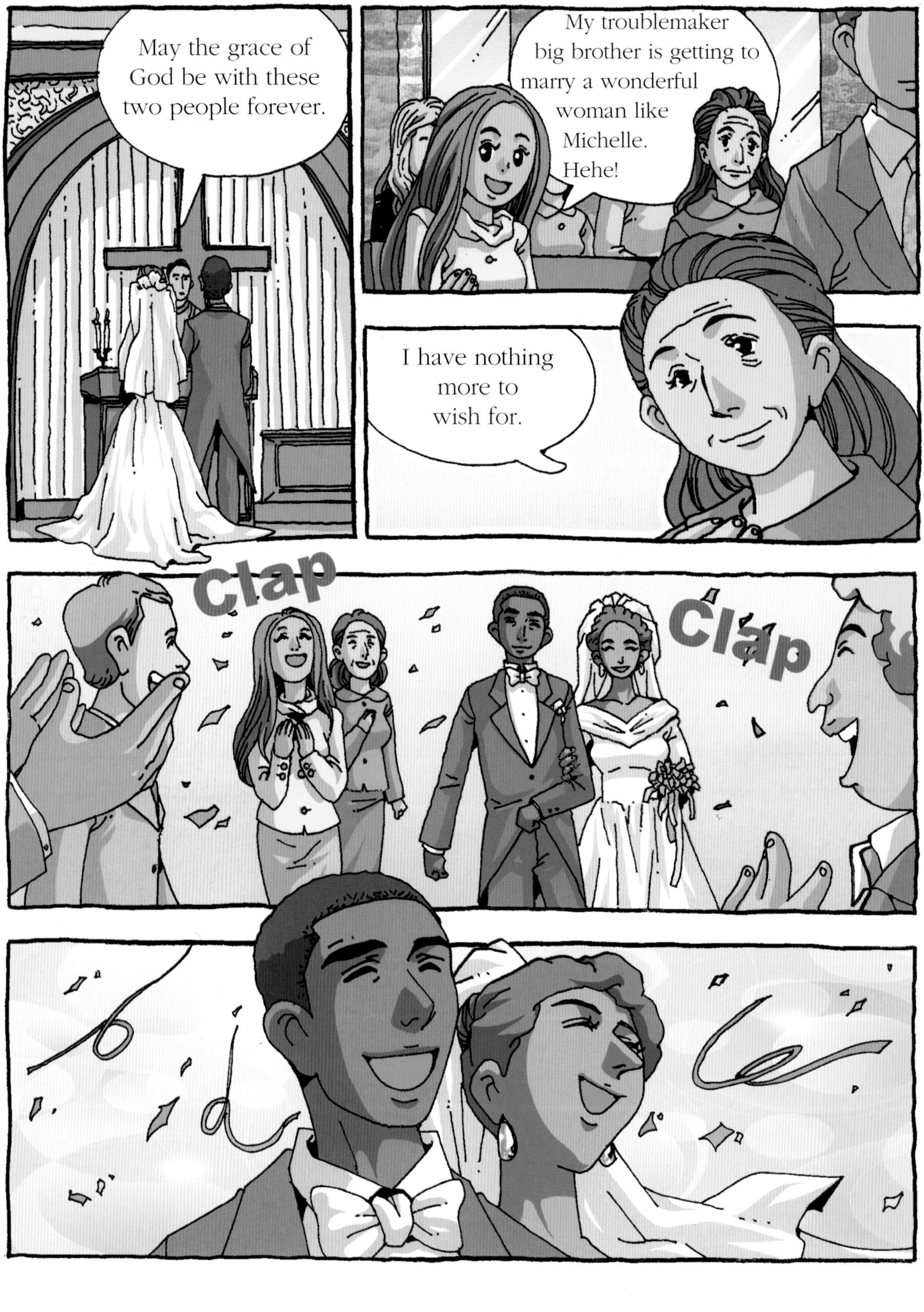

May the grace of God be with these two people forever.
My troublemaker big brother is getting to marry a wonderful woman like Michelle. Hehe!
I have nothing more to wish for.
Clap
Clap

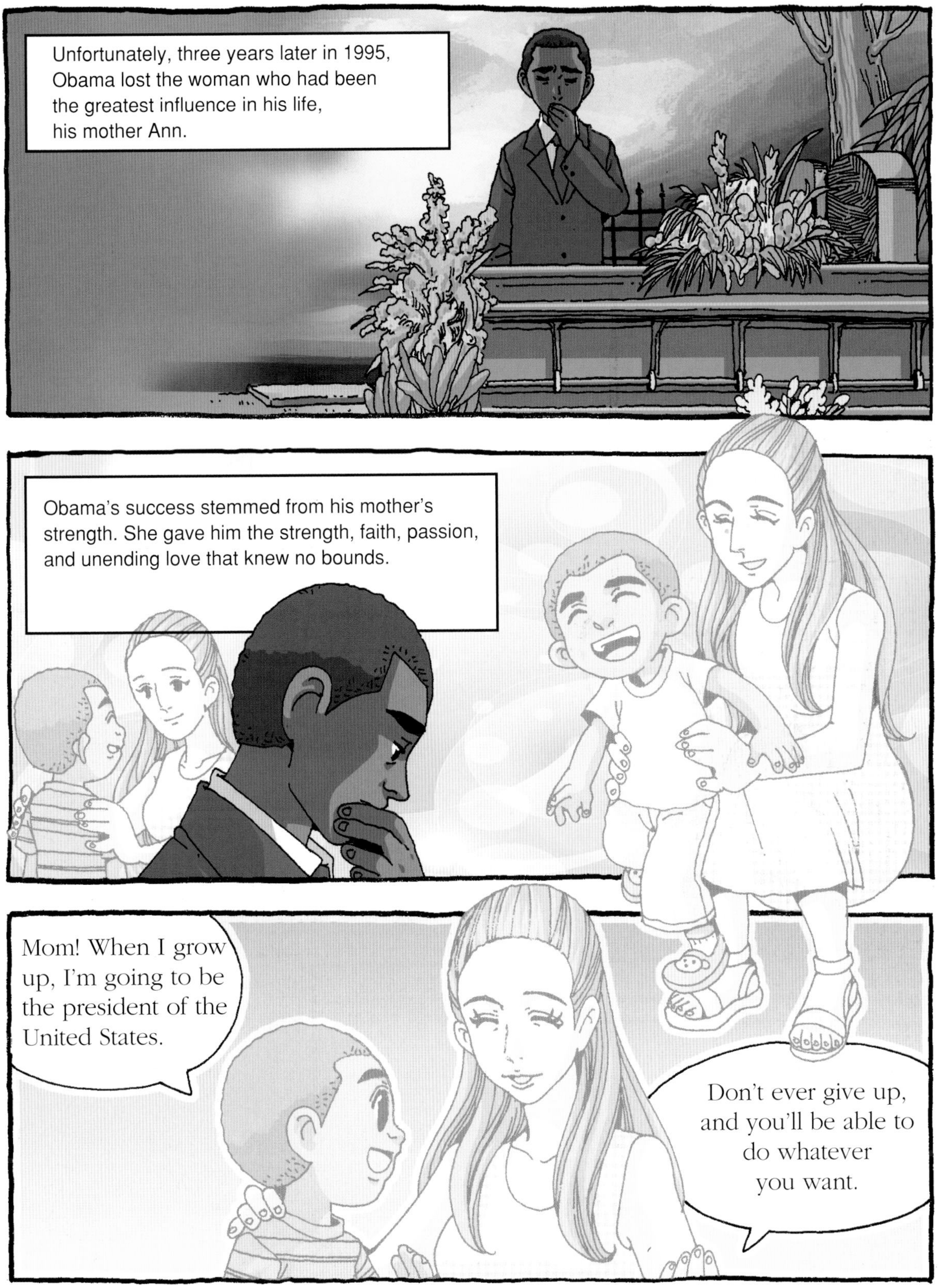
Unfortunately, three years later in 1995, Obama lost the woman who had been the greatest influence in his life, his mother Ann.
Obama's success stemmed from his mother's strength. She gave him the strength, faith, passion, and unending love that knew no bounds.
Mom! When I grow up, I'm going to be the president of the United States.
Don't ever give up, and you'll be able to do whatever you want.

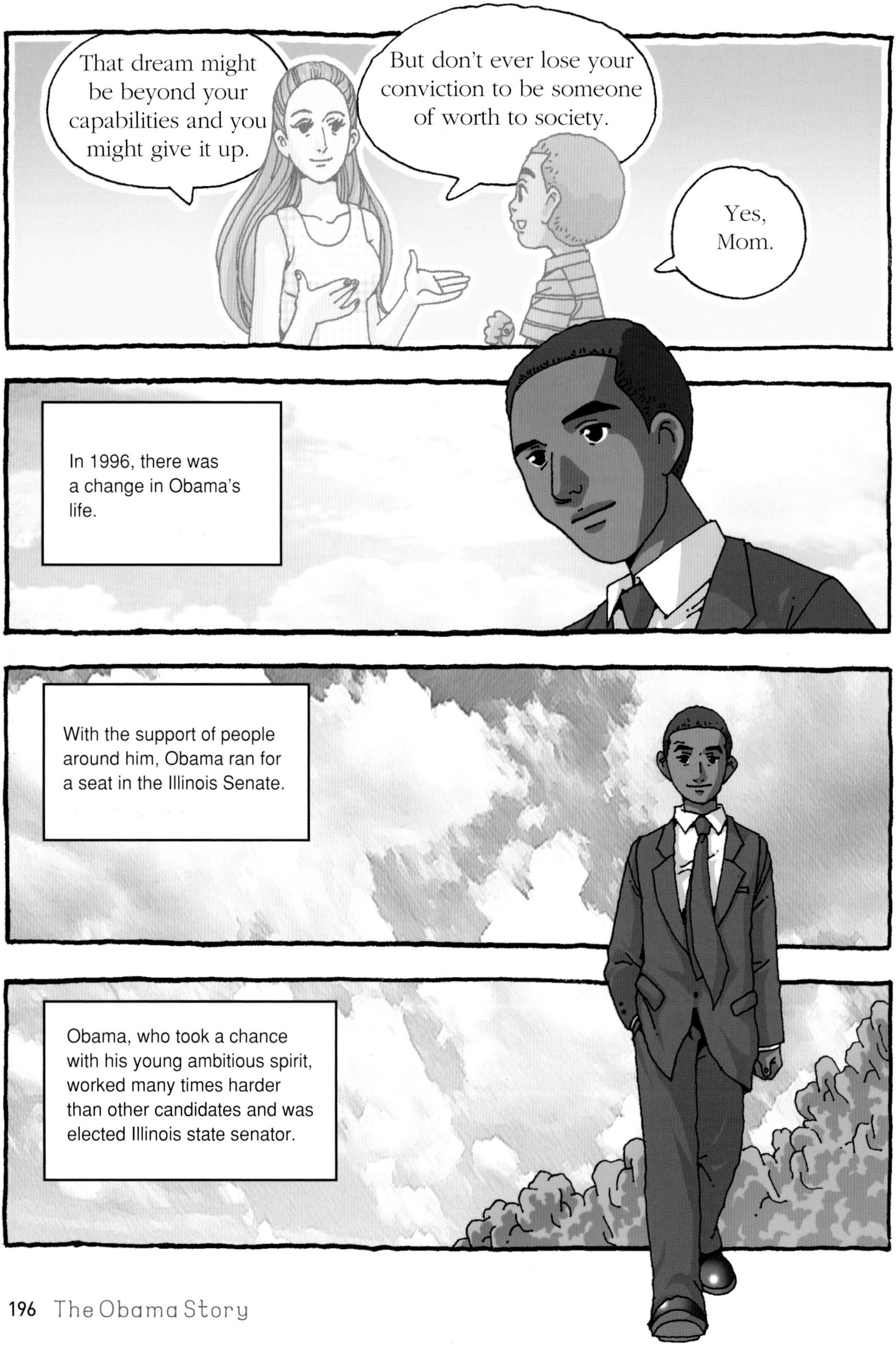
That dream might be beyond your capabilities and you might give it up.
But don't ever lose your conviction to be someone of worth to society.
Yes, Mom.
In 1996, there was a change in Obama's life.
With the support of people around him, Obama ran for a seat in the Illinois Senate.
Obama, who took a chance with his young ambitious spirit, worked many times harder than other candidates and was elected Illinois state senator.

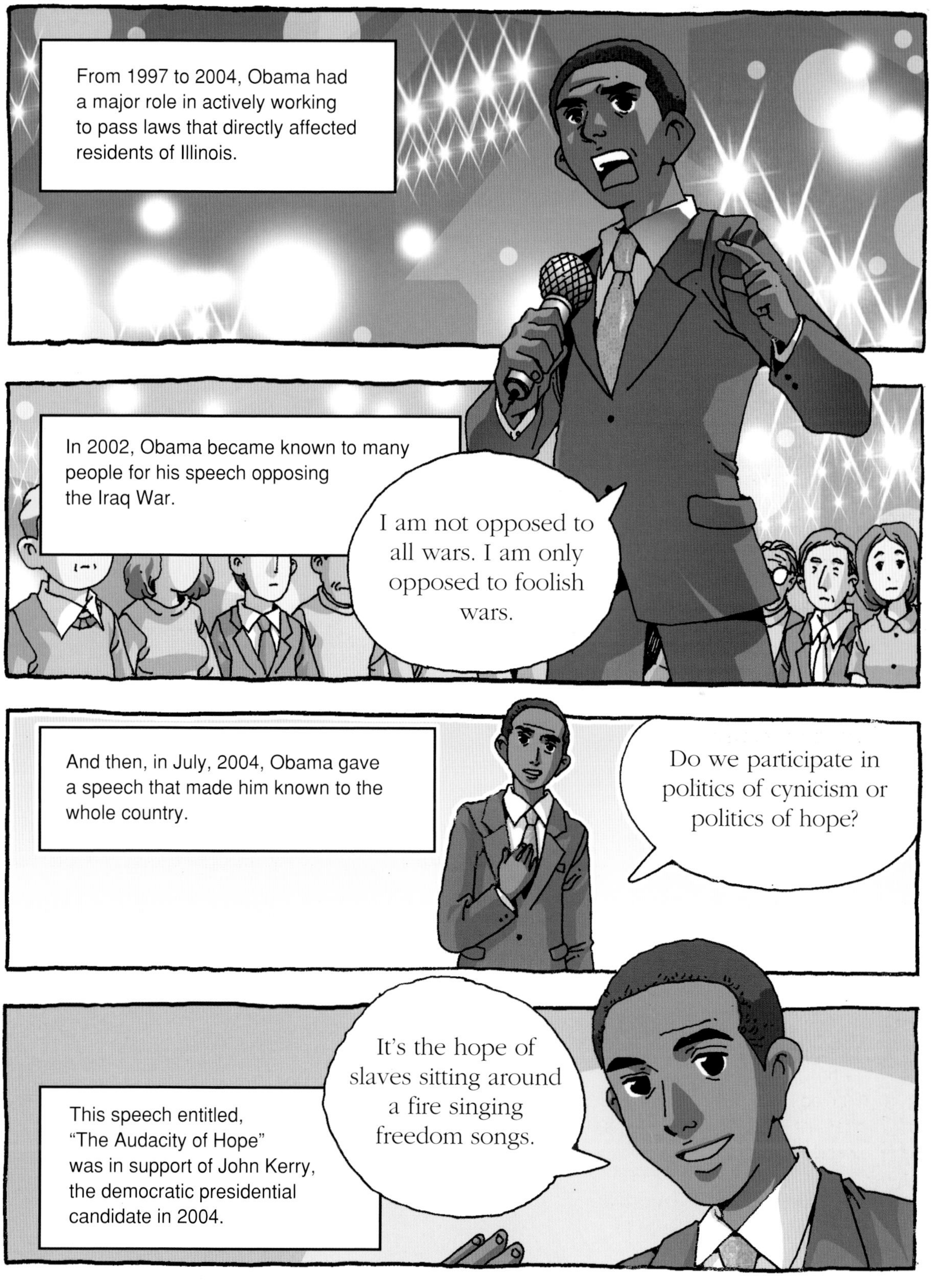
From 1997 to 2004, Obama had a major role in actively working to pass laws that directly affected residents of Illinois.
In 2002, Obama became known to many people for his speech opposing the Iraq War.
I am not opposed to all wars. I am only opposed to foolish wars.
And then, in July, 2004, Obama gave a speech that made him known to the whole country.
Do we participate in politics of cynicism or politics of hope?
It's the hope of slaves sitting around a fire singing freedom songs.
This speech entitled, "The Audacity of Hope" was in support of John Kerry, the democratic presidential candidate in 2004.

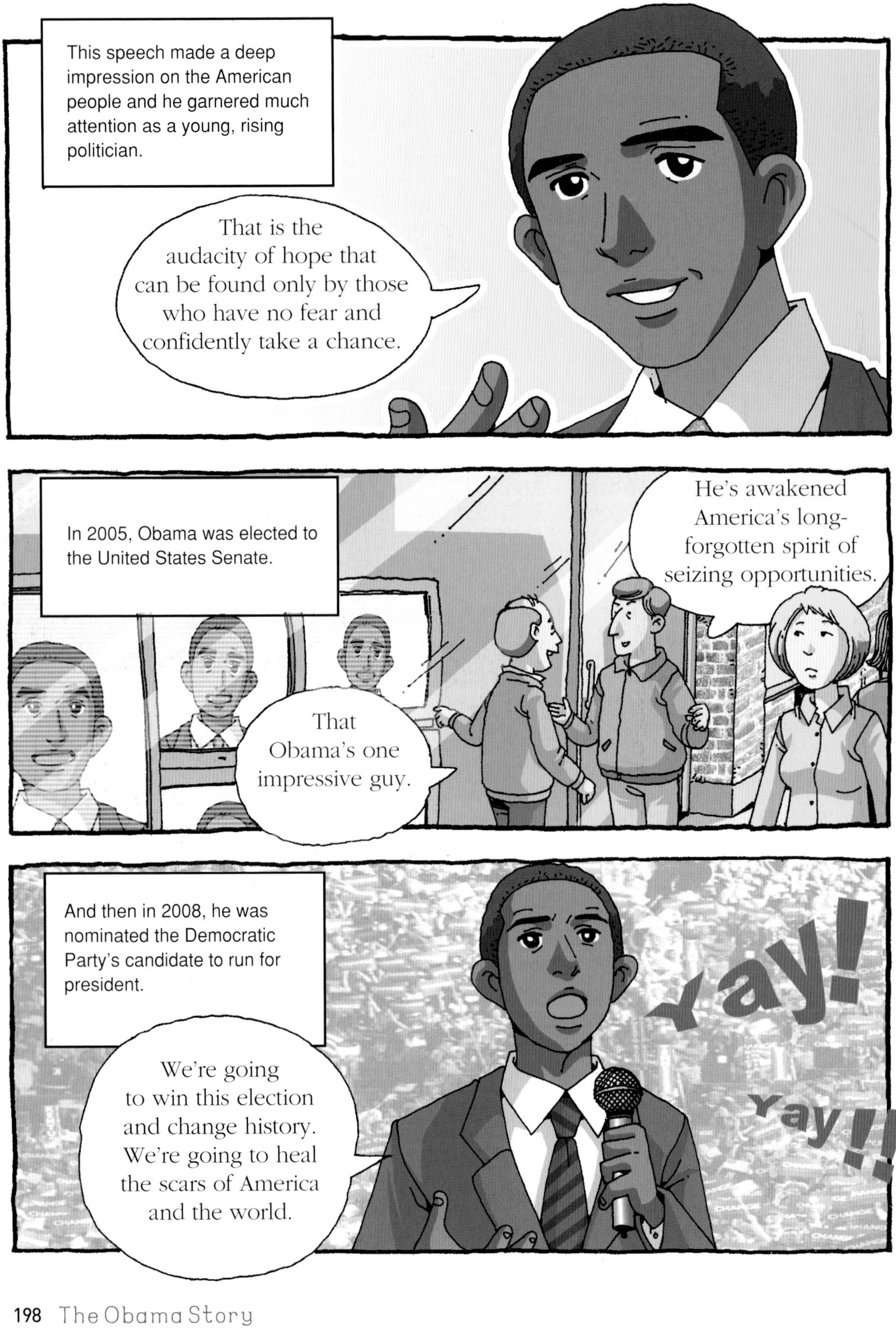
This speech made a deep impression on the American people and he garnered much attention as a young, rising politician.
That is the audacity of hope that can be found only by those who have no fear and confidently take a chance.
In 2005, Obama was elected to the United States Senate.
He's awakened America's long-forgotten spirit of seizing opportunities.
That Obama's one impressive guy.
And then in 2008, he was nominated the Democratic Party's candidate to run for president.
Yay!
We're going to win this election and change history. We're going to heal the scars of America and the world.
Yay!!!

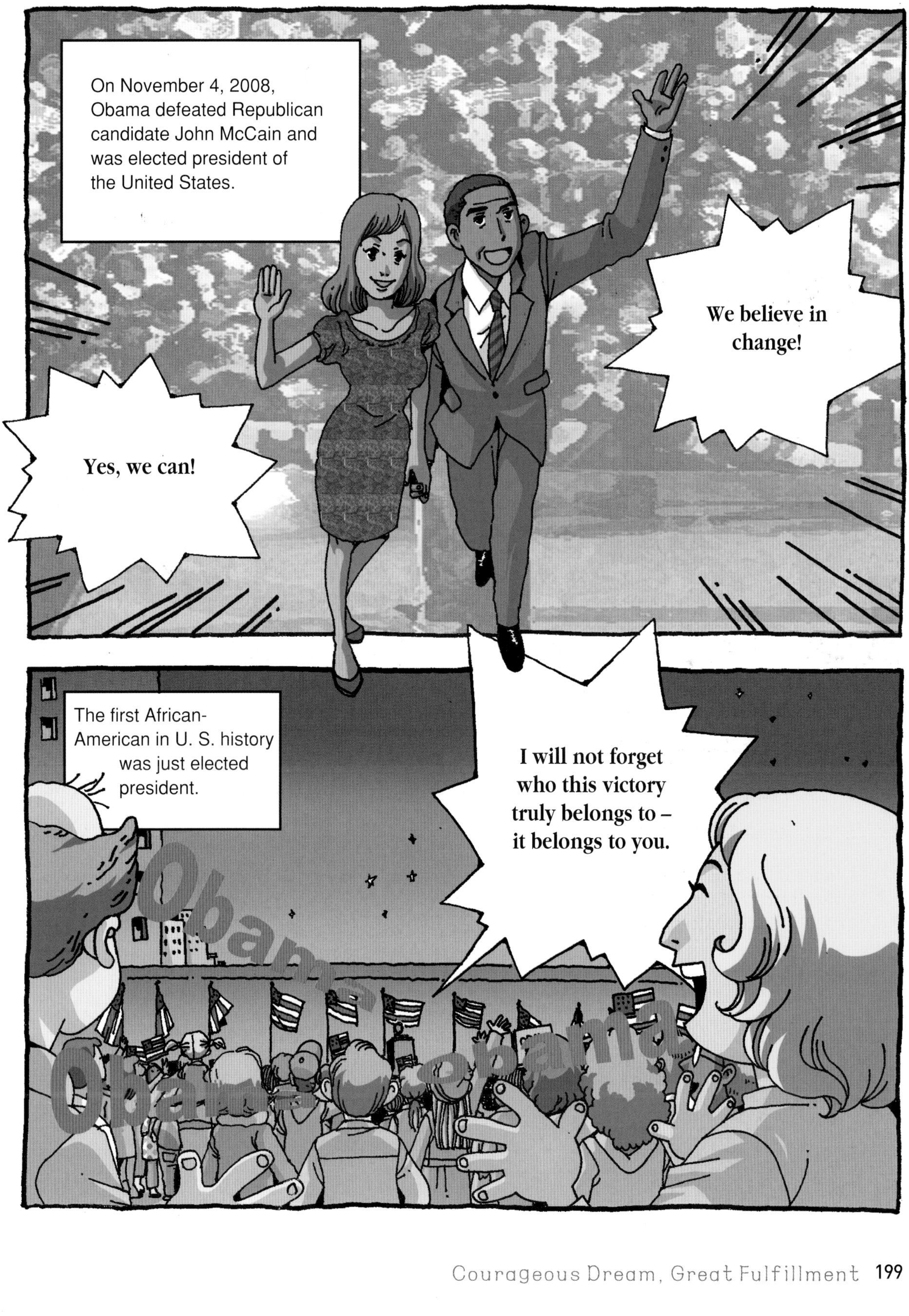
On November 4, 2008, Obama defeated Republican candidate John McCain and was elected president of the United States.
We believe in change!
Yes, we can!
The first African-American in U. S. history was just elected president.
I will not forget who this victory truly belongs to – it belongs to you.
Obama
Obama
Obama
Obama

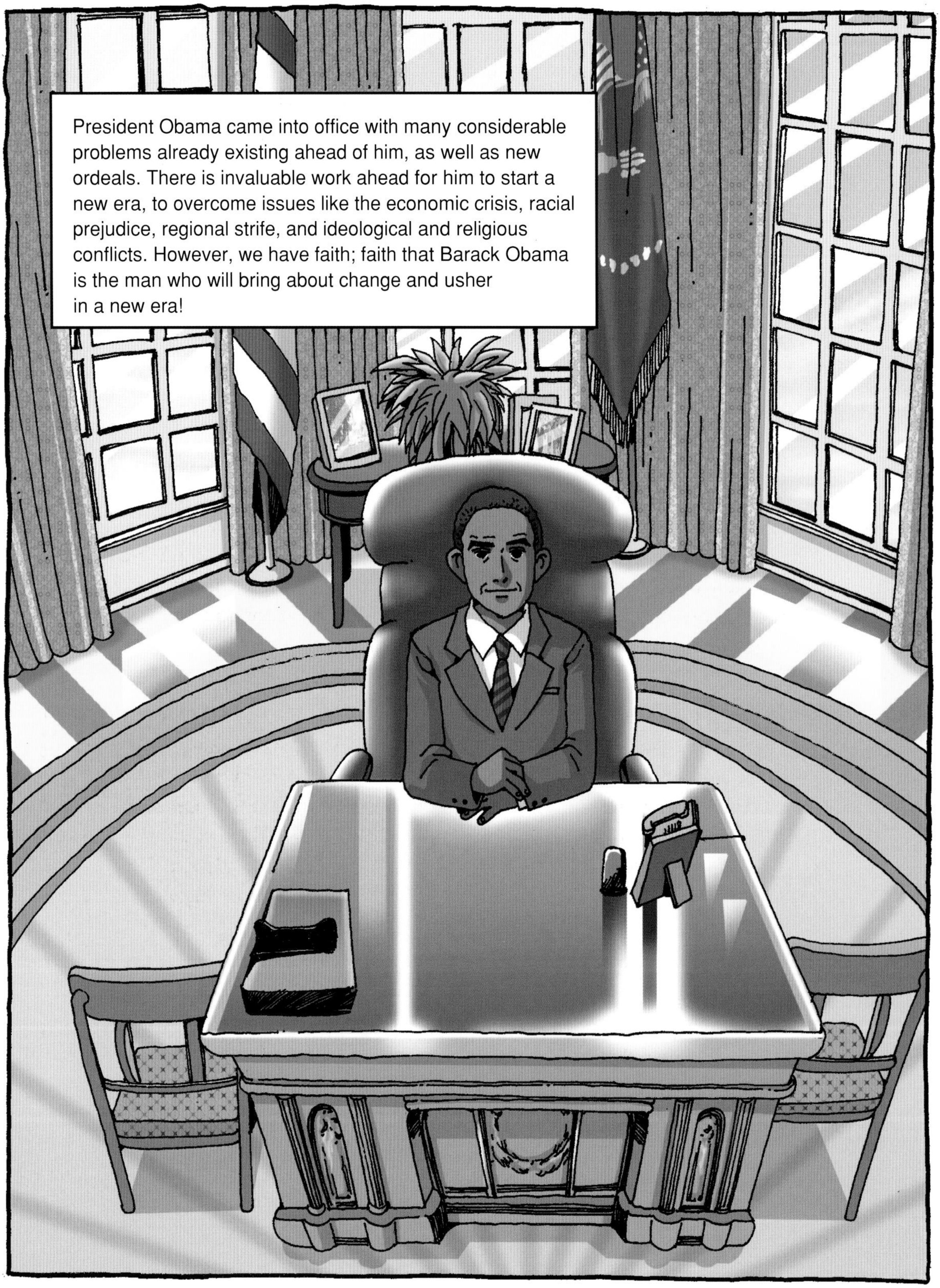
President Obama came into office with many considerable problems already existing ahead of him, as well as new ordeals. There is invaluable work ahead for him to start a new era, to overcome issues like the economic crisis, racial prejudice, regional strife, and ideological and religious conflicts. However, we have faith; faith that Barack Obama is the man who will bring about change and usher in a new era!

The Election of the 44th President of the United States

In 1996, Obama first set his foot in politics when he became a legislator in the Illinois state senate. In 2004, he was the only black legislator at the time in the U.S. Senate. Then on February 10, 2007, Obama announced his candidacy for the presidential race. At that time, many people supported Senator Hillary Clinton and didn't think that African-American Barack Obama would ultimately become the Democratic candidate for the presidential race. To the surprise of many, Obama was able to win over Senator Clinton to become the Democratic Party's presidential candidate.

Around that time, Senator John McCain was selected as the Republican Party's presidential candidate. As he competed with 13 other candidates in the Republican Party, he was able to steadily raise his approval rating. In addition, after Obama won the democratic nomination, many supporters of Hillary Clinton surprisingly switched their support to John McCain rather than to Obama. The results of the election were quite unpredictable at this point. In addition, in September, when McCain announced his vice presidential candidate Sarah Palin, McCain's approval ratings rose higher than Obama's.

However, in October, as America's economic crisis worsened, Obama once again began to rise considerably in the polls and in the end, led McCain by a significant six percent. Obama won support from ethnic minorities, women, the socially underprivileged, and people in the low income bracket. Many people have high expectations of the first African-American president to fulfill the important role of delivering America from racial and religious conflicts and economic difficulties.

A Summary of Barack Obama's Presidential Election Speech

If there is anyone out there who still doubts that America is a place where all things are possible; who still wonders if the dream of our founders is alive in our time; who still questions the power of our democracy, tonight is your answer.

It's the answer spoken by young and old, rich and poor, Democrat and Republican, black, white, Latino, Asian, Native American, gay, straight, disabled and not disabled. It's been a long time coming, but tonight, because of what we did on this day, in this election, at this defining moment, change has come to America.

I will never forget who this victory truly belongs to – it belongs to you.

It is for the millions of Americans who volunteered, and organized, and proved that more than two centuries later, a government of the people, by the people and for the people has not perished from this Earth. This is your victory.

The road ahead will be long. Our climb will be steep. We may not get there in one year or even one term, but America – I have never been more hopeful than I am tonight that we will get there. I promise you – we as a people will get there.

There will be setbacks and false starts. There are many who won't agree with every decision or policy I make as President, and we know that government can't solve every problem. But I will always be honest with you about the challenges we face. I will listen to you, especially when we disagree. And above all, I will ask you to join in the work of remaking this nation the only way it's been done in America for 221 years – block by block, brick by brick, calloused hand by calloused hand.

This victory alone is not the change we seek – it is only the chance for us to make that change. And that cannot happen if we go back to the way things were. It cannot happen without you.

So let us summon a new spirit of patriotism; of service and responsibility where each of us resolves to pitch in and work harder and look after not only ourselves, but each other.

This election had many firsts and many stories that will be told for generations. But one that's on my mind tonight is about a woman who cast her ballot in Atlanta. She's a lot like the millions of others who stood in line to make their voice heard in this election except for one thing – Ann Nixon Cooper is 106 years old.

She was born just a generation past slavery; a time when there were no cars on the road or planes in the sky; when someone like her couldn't vote for two reasons – because she is a woman and because of the color of her skin.

And tonight, I think about all that she's seen throughout her century in America – the heartache and the hope; the struggle and the progress; the times we were told that we can't, and the people who pressed on with that American creed: yes we can.

At a time when women's voices were silenced and their hopes dismissed, she lived to see them stand up and speak out and reach for the ballot. Yes we can.

When there was despair in the dust bowl and depression across the land, she saw a nation conquer fear itself with a New Deal, new jobs and a new sense of common purpose. Yes we can.

When the bombs fell on our harbor and tyranny threatened the world, she was there to witness a generation rise to greatness and a democracy was saved.
Yes we can.

She was there for the buses in Montgomery, the hoses in Birmingham, a bridge in Selma, and a preacher from Atlanta who told a people that "We Shall Overcome."
Yes we can.

A man touched down on the moon, a wall came down in Berlin, a world was connected by our own science and imagination. And this year, in this election, she touched her finger to a screen, and cast her vote, because after 106 years in America, through the best of times and the darkest of hours, she knows how America can change. Yes we can.

America, we have come so far. We have seen so much. But there is so much more to do. So tonight, let us ask ourselves – if our children should live to see the next century; if my daughters should be so lucky to live as long as Ann Nixon Cooper, what change will they see? What progress will we have made? This is our chance to answer that call. This is our moment. This is our time – to put our people back to work and open doors of opportunity for our kids; to restore prosperity and promote the cause of peace; to reclaim the American Dream and reaffirm that fundamental truth – that out of many, we are one; that while we breathe, we hope, and where we are met with cynicism, and doubt, and those who tell us that we can't, we will respond with that timeless creed that sums up the spirit of a people:

Yes We Can.

2008, Grant Park, Chicago, Illinois